W9-CXP-772

The American Destiny

Volume 20

Post-Vietnam America
& Index

The American Destiny

An Illustrated History of the United States

Editor in Chief
Henry Steele Commager

Editors
Marcus Cunliffe
Maldwyn A. Jones
Edward Horton

Orbis · London

EDITOR IN CHIEF: Henry Steele Commager, now Professor Emeritus at Amherst College, has taught at Columbia, Cambridge, Oxford and other universities. In a long and illustrious career he has written many books in his own right, including *Theodore Parker, The American Mind, Majority Rule and Minority Rights*, and *The Empire of Reason*. He is the co-author (with Samuel Eliot Morison) of *The Growth of the American Republic*, editor of *Documents of American History*, and (with Richard B. Morris) of the fifty-volume *New American Nation* series.

SENIOR EDITORS: Marcus Cunliffe, now University Professor at George Washington University, and formerly of Manchester and Sussex Universities, has also taught at Harvard and Michigan. His books include *The Literature of the United States, George Washington: Man and Monument, Soldier and Civilians, The American Presidency,* and *Chattel Slavery and Wage Slavery*. Maldwyn A. Jones is Commonwealth Fund Professor of American History at the University of London. He has been a visiting professor at Harvard and at the Universities of Chicago and Pennsylvania. He has written extensively on American ethnic groups. His books include *American Immigration,* a volume in the *Chicago History of American Civilization,* and *The Limits of Liberty: American History, 1607-1980*.

Designed, authored and produced by
Orbis Book Publishing Corporation Ltd.
3rd Floor Greater London House
Hampstead Road
London NW1 7QX
England
Publisher: Martin Heller
Editorial Director: Brian Innes
Managing Editor: Edward Horton
Deputy Editor: Lawson Nagel
Art Editor: Derek Copsey
Picture Editor: Lynda Poley

Contributors to this volume include:
Robert Beisner, The American University, Washington D.C.; Hugh Brogan, University of Essex; Alex Brummer, Washington correspondent of *The Guardian*; Marcus Cunliffe, George Washington University; James O. Horton, George Washington University, and Lois E. Horton, George Mason University

Published in the United Kingdom by
Orbis Book Publishing Corporation Ltd.
3rd Floor Greater London House
Hampstead Road
London NW1 7QX
England

Library of Congress Catalog Card No. 73-8423
© 1986 Grolier Enterprises Inc.
ISBN 0-7172-8191-4

Printed in Yugoslavia.

Contents

1 A DECADE OF TRANSITION 9
Politics Since Nixon *by H. Brogan* 10

2 FOREIGN POLICY AFTER VIETNAM 23
Diplomacy in Crisis *by R. Beisner* 24

3 THE ECONOMIC LANDSCAPE 43
Rust Bowl and Silicon Valley *by A. Brummer* 44

4 CHANGES IN SOCIETY 55
Pluralism and Fragmentation *by J. O. and L. E. Horton* 56

5 THE NATIONAL SPIRIT 67
Aspects of Americana *by M. Cunliffe* 68

THE CONSTITUTION 82

BIBLIOGRAPHY 86

GENERAL BIBLIOGRAPHY 86

INDEX 89

Introduction

The bicentennial year 1976 was planned in advance as a triumphant climax to mark the close of President Nixon's second term. When it arrived, he had resigned and was in seclusion. His nominated successor, Gerald R. Ford, was signifying his intention to campaign for office on the record established by the "accidental" Ford administration of the previous couple of years. Amid a mass of Democratic contenders, Jimmy Carter of Georgia emerged as his party's somewhat surprising nominee. Ford v. Carter, in the presidential campaign of 1976, was not exactly politics as usual. And the bicentennial celebrations likewise felt odd to those who were aware of how much Richard Nixon had anticipated the chance to associate himself with a key anniversary in the nation's history. The *New Yorker* magazine probably spoke for a good many Americans in saying that it could not offer more than two cheers out of three for all the patriotic hoopla.

Nevertheless the multitudinous bicentennial commemorations, large and small, contrived and spontaneous, did reveal a generally cheerful spirit. Perhaps part of the message was that America was strong not because of Washington D.C. but almost in spite of Congress and the White House. That, after all, was one reason why Carter's campaign won enough votes to make him president – a plain man from Plains, Georgia.

Perhaps, too, a resilient people with a short collective memory was ready to forget the traumas of the Johnson and Nixon years. In the process, Americans were therefore quick to complain that the Carter administration lacked excitement and inspiration. Magazines began to carry more and more articles with titles like "Where Have All the Heroes Gone?" There was a growing reaction, which the born-again, self-made businessman Jimmy Carter seemed both to typify and to resist, against permissive social mores and the burgeoning apparatus of the welfare state.

Ronald Reagan, former movie star and ex-Governor of California, came into the victor's limelight in the next presidential campaign of 1980 as the champion of traditional American values. Jolly, benign, unruffled, the "Great Communicator" projected with superb effect an aura of optimistic yet tough leadership. His personal popularity remained high, although much in his first administration met with criticism. He secured another remarkable personal victory over the Democratic candidate Walter F.

Mondale in the 1984 campaign. Beginning his second term in 1985, only a few days short of his seventy-fifth birthday, Reagan ebulliently overcame an operation for cancer, and laughed at the notion of himself as a lame duck president. The land was full of heroes, according to his upbeat rhetoric. Editorialists tended to agree with him, even if they were not entirely sure how many cheers to allot to cult-figures such as the singer Bruce Springsteen, or the pugilists and lone avengers portrayed in the movies of Sylvester Stallone. Patriotism seemed back in fashion along with a wave of economic and moral conservatism.

Some commentators were convinced that the new spirit was here to stay. The armed forces were strong again, the Dow-Jones average was on the up, bumper stickers carried slogans like

THE BEST WAY TO GET ON YOUR FEET
IS TO GET OFF YOUR ASS!!

Post-bicentennial America, then, could be seen to be "back", in the Republican terminology, to "walk tall" once more. Other commentators, however, were less sure. They questioned whether "Reaganomics" was any sort of success, given deficits and debts on an unprecedented scale. They were skeptical as to the results of the military build-up begun under Carter and accelerated under Reagan. Some even feared that the very structure of American government might be proving quite unable to cope with its weight of responsibilities, domestic and foreign. Kevin Phillips, author of a confidently positive 1969 book, *The Emerging Republican Majority*, confessed to considerable disenchantment in a subsequent analysis, whose enigmatic title, *Post-Conservative America*, bore a gloomy subtitle: *People, Politics, and Ideology in a Time of Crisis*. For Phillips the system was severely impaired, and the truth was bound to come out before long.

In balance, the decade after 1976 was undoubtedly more sanguine in mood than the previous one. The jeremiahs who had predicted a national collapse seemed to have guessed wrong. So did the dreamers who imagined a transformed America, purged of greed and bellicosity. Teachers, a little bewildered and occasionally exasperated, reported that their young charges often had never even heard of the people and issues that had bulked so large only a little while earlier. Recent history, for the exuberantly matter-of-fact rising generation, was pretty much ancient history.

Chapter 1

A DECADE OF TRANSITION

With the resignation of Richard Nixon in 1974 the reputation of the presidency reached an all-time low and to Gerald Ford fell the immediate task of restoring confidence in the office of the nation's chief executive. Although Jimmy Carter won votes through his status as a Washington outsider, he experienced grave difficulties in his relationship with Congress during his single term. And with the resounding triumph of Ronald Reagan in 1980, reaffirmed four years later, it appeared that traditional values had been reasserted in American political life.

White House

Politics Since Nixon

All eras are eras of transition. Every identifiable period has a character of its own. These truisms are beautifully illustrated by the years following the resignation of Richard Nixon from the Presidency of the United States. Time went fast; soon America was in the second decade after the end of the Watergate affair; new departures were proclaimed a dozen times by politicians; but the obstinately provisional nature of the epoch always reasserted itself. Nothing had been settled, even by the beginning of President Reagan's second term. Perhaps the provisional manifested itself most conclusively in 1980, when Reagan was first elected president. A former Governor of California, he was a man of 69, almost as old when he assumed office as General Eisenhower had been when he laid it down. He was re-elected in 1984, by an even larger majority than before (he received 489 electoral votes in 1980, 525 in 1984).

Clearly most Americans had been impressed by his performance. They approved of his economic stewardship, under which inflation and unemployment had fallen, while the gross national product had increased, though not by very much or very rapidly. They applauded his assertive nationalistic speeches and accepted his defense budgets, which grew enormously and very rapidly indeed. They were comforted by his cheery resilience, so unlike his predecessor's gray talk of a national malaise, and by his assurances that "America is back."

So they re-elected him. But they could hardly pretend that he was a man of the future. Indeed, the bright young Republicans, such as David Stockman and Congressman Jack Kemp, who had been tipped as the men about to take over the running of America, found themselves increasingly impotent as the Reagan years went on. Stockman retired from the directorship of the Office of Management and the Budget to make money on Wall Street; Kemp consoled himself with dreams of winning the presidency in 1988. Meanwhile, the Reagan administration went its way, full of contradictory impulses and arguments, but always in the end responding to its chief's blithe assurance, to his apparent belief that effective speeches were synonymous with effective policies, and that all would come right in the end, however little you did about it. He was a perfect president for an era in which the people were unready to make hard choices.

They had had enough hard choices in the too-recent past. Most Americans alive between 1963 and 1974 had been cruelly marked by the events of that bad time. It had begun with the assassination of a glamorous, much-admired president and been continued with other no less horrifying murders, including those of Martin Luther King and Robert Kennedy. The proud democracy had also seen its institutions first perverted and then betrayed by the very officials sworn to preserve, protect and defend them. Tens of thousands of young men had been killed, hundreds of thousands wounded, in a war which ended in defeat and besmirched America's international good name. The civil rights movement had promised great things for American blacks; but even so, most of them remained thrust down into an urban under-class of appalling hopelessness. The prodigal American economy, having for the first time become dependent on imported oil, was vulnerable to outside pressure, which came with the great oil shock of 1973 when the Organization of Petroleum Exporting Countries, a producers' cartel, raised prices by 261.5 per cent, with calamitously inflationary effect. A complicated cultural crisis, composed in part of feminism, in part of self-assertion by a youthful generation with vast spending power, and in part of a revolt, on the model of the civil rights movement, by all sorts of minority groups which felt themselves oppressed, confronted the old society of what came to be called "Middle America" with a challenge it was emotionally ill-equipped to meet.

Having lived through so many dramas, the voters naturally enough opted for a quietly prosperous life and a reassertion of ancient verities. But it is impossible also not to suspect that they got what they wanted by, as it were, borrowing a decade from time. The problems they dreaded were postponed, not solved.

It is important to remind ourselves that "the voters" were not synonymous with "the people." Turnout in the presidential election of 1976 was 54.3 per cent. It had been 60.6 per cent in 1968 and 64 per cent in 1960. By 1984 it was down to 53 per cent, as low as in 1948 – itself the worst performance since 1924. No president in this century has ever received the votes of a majority of the actual voting age population: even Franklin Roosevelt in 1936 only got 37 per cent. The story in state and congressional elections has been even more dismal. The right to full citizenship seems to be little valued by something perilously near half the American people. Voting has become more and more something which the well-off do and the disadvantaged do not. This inevitably affects the issues to which politicians feel they must address themselves. Thus during the seventies inflation (which averaged 9.6 per cent during the Carter presidency) replaced unemployment as the problem which most voters felt to be most important. The result was that the Democrats, the party which cared above all about unemployment, lost their way, and the main debate came to be that conducted between the right and left wings of the Republican party, the one which cared above all about inflation.

President Gerald Ford and Vice President Nelson Rockefeller (appointed by Ford) in the Oval Office. From the time of Nixon's resignation in August 1974 until the inauguration of Jimmy Carter in January 1977, political leadership was exercised by two men who had not been elected by popular ballot to the positions they held.

Robert Hunt Library

*Crowds attend a "Survival Rally" in New York in 1975.
President Ford stood firm in refusing to use federal
funds to solve the city's financial crisis.*

It was therefore commonly said that America was moving to the right. It might with equal justice have been said that all too many Americans were dropping out of the republic. And the right-wing tide seemed to have turned by the 1982 elections, when the Democrats picked up 7 governorships and 26 seats in the House of Representatives. True, in 1984 they lost 15 House seats and one governorship; but this was more than compensated by their net gain of two Senate seats. Even President Reagan's triumphant re-election did not seem to be quite so devastating as his original victory had been.

The Cost of Politics

If large-scale abstention was one of the two main constraints on American politics, the other was its ever-soaring cost. It was now clear that with the coming of television and the computer, political expenses had taken a quantum leap. The prolonged boom of the post-1945 years had generated huge amounts of personal wealth, some of

which certain persons were prepared to lavish on the politicians and the causes which they favored. They were encouraged by kindly tax laws and, after Congress had tried to restrict fund-raising, by ingenious tax lawyers with sharp eyes for loopholes. The impulse of the rich to amuse themselves by buying a piece of the political action, as they might otherwise have bought Impressionist paintings or paid for cancer research, stimulated politicians to think up ways of spending the funds thus provided.

Technology provided the means. The airwaves, thanks to America's private enterprise culture, had always been allotted to corporations, and these made candidates who wanted more than a bare minimum of television coverage pay lavishly for the privilege of broadcasting. Reagan's 1984 TV advertising cost about $30 million, and Mondale's $25 million. It was not a privilege the candidates could afford to do without. The size of the country, the size of the population, the skeptical, if not downright cynical attitude of most Americans to politicians, made the business of getting their favorable attention eternally difficult; radio and television were essential devices for overcoming the problem. (Indeed, without broadcasting, American democracy might long ago have collapsed.) Printed circulars and advertisements in the newspapers, the favored devices of an earlier day, were now obsolete. In the new day, public opinion polls were also essential tools of the trade, and they

too were infernally expensive. So was perpetual flight about the country, whether in specially chartered private planes or by normal passenger service. So was analysis of the poll results, for it required plenty of computer time.

Techniques for raising the necessary funds developed, but were expensive in themselves. It had never been easy for a really poor man to get far in American politics; now it was becoming impossible. A 1985 survey showed that even the House of Representatives was becoming a rich man's club. Worse still, politicians had to spend more and more of their time soliciting funds, a risky and degrading process which the honest among them disliked as much as did Hubert Humphrey when during the Watergate scandal he denounced campaign financing as a curse: "It's the most disgusting, demeaning, disenchanting, debilitating experience of a politician's life. It's stinky. It's lousy. I just can't tell you how much I hate it. [But] when you are desperate, there are things you just have to do." The quest for funds not only began to take up too much time and energy, and to entail too great a risk of falling foul of the law (as some of Humphrey's own aides did), it also began sharply to circumscribe even honest politicians' freedom of action. Sponsors liked to feel they were getting value for so much money.

Worst of all, a candidate's choice of sponsor might determine his chance of election, as Walter Mondale found in 1984 when, as the leading candidate for the Democratic presidential nomination, he went after the funds which organized labor could provide. His opponents successfully tagged him as the slave of special interests; and although he won the nomination, he lost the general election disastrously. The great political parties themselves suffered. Money now tended to be given to candidates, rather than to parties, in support of single issues rather than party platforms; so party cohesion and discipline continued to decline, at first most conspicuously among the Democrats but also, as time went on, among the Republicans.

The parties' loss was the voters' opportunity. The 1976 post-Watergate election law at any rate sought to weaken the influence of big spenders by allotting federal funds for major party candidates (though it placed third-party candidates at a disadvantage). This gave great opportunity to the public bodies most experienced in soliciting small contributions from ordinary citizens, the churches of America pre-eminent among them. Perhaps this was the secret of the influence of the so-called Moral Majority and other such groups in the late seventies and early eighties. Explosions of Protestant fundamentalism had occurred before and will no doubt occur again. They are less powerful than passionate; but even if they cannot swing enough votes to decide a presidential election they can supply vast sums of money and innumerable campaign workers. Hence the respect with which politicians treated them in the Carter and Reagan years. As always when the godly get the upper hand, the gaiety of nations was much increased. The 1980

election presented the entertaining sight of easygoing Ronald Reagan trying to bring some of his usual conviction to the statement (forced out of him in a TV interview) that he had been born again.

The reformed election law had another unforeseen consequence. Long, long ago the AFL-CIO discovered that if it set up a front organization for "political education" it could legally give money and workers to the candidates it supported. The Right was surprisingly slow to take up this invention, but in the late seventies it had no choice, so what were called "Political Action Committees" flourished. These bodies were usually fronts for the Republican party, but since they professed to be concerned with issues rather than parties or men they dodged the law, and the traditional fat cats were back in business, on the large scale that the new technologies required. By 1984 there were 3,525 registered PACs. Their influence by then began to seem less decisive than had been feared.

On the other hand, the 1976 Campaign Finance Act, and a 1979 amendment, enabled political parties to generate and spend prodigious sums on "voluntary" campaigning efforts. Moreover, a rich individual could still claim the liberty to put his money where his mouth was, especially if he were a candidate himself. Thus encouraged, several millionaires spent sackfuls of dollars trying to get themselves elected to the Senate. Except for the special case of Jay Rockefeller in West Virginia, who had already established a respectable record as that state's governor, they were however not strikingly successful. Yet the Republicans seemed to retain their financial edge over the Democrats. And skilled fundraisers such as Senator Jesse Helms of North Carolina proved able to amass large campaign "warchests" from PACs, lobbyists, constituents and others.

These were the uneasy waters through which three presidents had to steer the ship of state. It cannot be said that any of them did so with much distinction.

Ford in the White House

Gerald Ford was in the most difficult position. He came to the office in what it is to be hoped will remain unique circumstances. Vice President Spiro T. Agnew had resigned in disgrace in October 1973, and was soon afterwards fined and placed on probation for tax evasion while Governor of Maryland. (He was also strongly suspected of having accepted bribes.) On President Nixon's nomination Congress elected Gerald Ford to replace Agnew. In August 1974 he inherited the presidency itself when Nixon himself resigned.

Ford never forgot that the people had had no voice in his elevation. As he said in his first speech as president: "I am acutely aware that you have not elected me as your president by your ballots. So I ask you to confirm me as

your president with your prayers." His chief task, he thought, was to free his fellow-citizens from the obsessive nightmare of Watergate, and the best thing that can be said of him is that he succeeded. He did this in large part merely by being himself. He was a patently decent man, whose career, from his days as a star football player onwards, had been unmarked by any show of undue brilliance or political deviousness. He had no enemies, he was the devoted husband of a delightful wife, and the proud father of four attractive children. It was impossible to fear the corruption of the presidency while Ford held office; and his selection of Nelson Rockefeller as his vice president was a well-calculated gesture to all those respectable Americans who had reason to fear that they had been put onto Nixon's enemies' list.

But Ford's most important contribution to dissipating the nightmare was hotly debated. He pardoned Richard Nixon for all crimes that Nixon might have committed while in office, and did so only a month after he became president himself. This was a deeply unpopular action: it frustrated both the sense of justice and the desire for revenge, and probably cost Ford the 1976 election; but in retrospect there can be little doubt that it was the right thing to do. Ford knew that if Nixon was prosecuted the proceedings would drag on for at least a year and probably longer. He judged that the national interest would not be served by such an extension of an affair which had brought the government of the United States to a halt for a year and a half already; and he reasoned that if he was going to act,

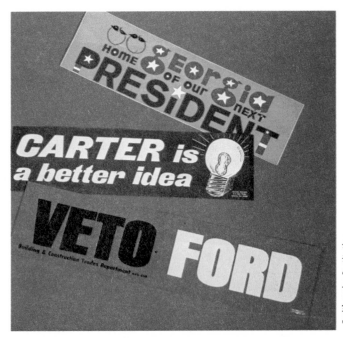

Smithsonian Institution

In the 1976 election Gerald Ford (below) campaigned hard to gain acceptance as president in his own right. He won approval for his honesty and decency but found it difficult to dispel the view that he was an "accidental" president. Above, and Below right: Pro-Carter and anti-Ford buttons and stickers from 1976. Right: Jimmy Carter, the Georgia peanut-farmer, was promoted as a Washington outsider who embodied simple, homely, traditional values.

Camera Press

he should do so as promptly as possible. Even the shameless subsequent behaviour of Richard Nixon does not weaken this logic, and as Ford pointed out at the time, it was worth something to have got Nixon to accept a pardon, for by doing so he in effect pleaded guilty to some at least of the charges against him. And the Watergate affair did at last recede into the past. It was a notable achievement.

Nothing else he did was nearly so impressive. Ford was essentially a Middle West Republican of the old school, decent, respectable, and unimaginative. Betty Ford, who had been a modern dancer in her youth, had divorced her first husband, supported the Equal Rights Amendment, and who had bouts with breast cancer and alcoholism, was much more in touch with the outlook and sorrows of modern America. By her gallantry and kindliness she not only saved herself but became something of a national heroine. Ford had nothing equivalent to offer. He could stand up against America's foreign foes, veto legislation (which he did frequently) and try cautiously to bring down inflation without plunging America into a recession. It was not an inspiring record, and the president, being apparently accident-prone, made it seem worse than it was. Jokes about his physical clumsiness became common, and easily modulated into sneers at his mental capacity. Various coarse remarks of Lyndon Johnson's were remembered and repeated. During a television debate with Democratic candidate Jimmy Carter in the presidential election of 1976, Ford inexplicably remarked that there was no Soviet domination of eastern Europe, and stuck to the assertion even when challenged. Probably he was suffering from stage fright, but it did him no good with voters of East European ancestry.

All in all, it is surprising that he lost the election so narrowly, by only 2 per cent of the popular vote. Such an outcome can only mean that, on the whole, Americans approved the character and record of their accidental, unelected president. But his campaign held out no vision of the future. It had no theme.

Carter's Road to Washington

Jimmy Carter was eventually destroyed by the opposite characteristic. In terms of the past, his entire presidential career was quite exceptional; it is not clear that it will look so unusual from, say, the vantage point of 2000. Carter may have been no more than the comet of a season; or he may have been a portent. Either way, he was a notably clear-cut phenomenon. There were no ambiguities about him, least of all of that useful sort which has enabled so many successful presidents, from Franklin Roosevelt to Ronald Reagan, keep ahead of the game by being all things to all men.

Carter's road to the White House was cleared by the civil rights revolution which made it possible for a white from

Camera Press

President Carter fields a question at a press conference.
These occasions were seldom comfortable for Carter,
who disliked having to explain policy in response to
impromptu questions.

the Deep South to aspire realistically to the presidency for the first time since the Civil War. Carter's hold on the South, where he carried every state except Virginia, was largely a function of the black vote, which was solidly Democratic; and that vote had only been made possible by the Voting Rights Act of 1965. But Carter could also depend on the South's intense regional pride to assist him with the white vote: in a sense his victory was the Confederacy's revenge. It was also helpful that Gerald Ford had no particular hold on conservative Southern affections, unlike Ronald Reagan in 1980.

It was also an asset that Carter, though liberal in Southern terms, was conservative in national ones. Indeed, some labelled him a "Republicrat," for his campaign, with its anti-inflationary emphasis and promises of a balanced budget and limited federal activism, was notably unlike the stance taken by every other Democratic candidate since the New Deal. In fact it resembled those of Dwight D. Eisenhower rather than anybody else's. Carter had sensed the voters' growing economic anxiety: prices were rising and share values, in real terms, were falling.

But Carter's special asset was that he and his associates were the first to see what the various changes in the organization of the Democratic party portended, and to act on the insight. Thanks to the new "McGovern" rules the presidential nomination was no longer something in which the party leaders, the senators, governors and mayors, had any say; it was to be secured by a patient cultivation of the grassroots, in season and out of season, for years in

advance of the election, by a small, dedicated team of workers, so that there might be a harvest when the caucuses met and the primary elections were held. Cool manipulation of journalistic compulsions would do the rest. For neither television nor the press could resist the idea of a bandwagon, and once it had started to roll they pushed. They stopped talking of "Jimmy Who?" (in January 1976 only 4 per cent of Democratic voters supported Carter for the nomination) and began to hail the inevitable winner. In Pennsylvania Carter won his seventh primary, having lost only in Massachusetts, and it was as good as over.

His campaign for the office, as opposed to the nomination, was considerably less successful. It was marked by several examples of the sort of gaffe which was to become familiar in the next few years – his statements in a *Playboy* interview that he had occasionally looked at women with lust in his heart did him no good either with the pious or with the ribald – but against Gerald Ford he could hardly lose; nor did he.

Political and Personal Difficulties

Carter went to Washington triumphant. But in retrospect it is clear that his ultimate failure was already largely determined. Its roots lay both in the new president's ideas about American politics and in his own character, of which his ideas were largely the expression. As to his ideas, they may be reduced to two main points: his misapprehension of the nature and function of the national Democratic party, and his total misunderstanding of the nature, function, and power, relative to the presidency, of Congress. In a phrase, his conception of American political leadership was profoundly faulty.

In the general election he had been running not so much against Ford as against Richard Nixon and Watergate, hence his promise to give the American people as good a government as they deserved. This went down well on the hustings; the trouble was that Carter in office soon showed that he thought his fine phrase meant something. He believed he owed his election to his special relationship with the American voters. He did not see that he owed it at least as much to the zeal and effective organization of the Democratic party. In a low turnout election he had won by only 2 per cent of the popular vote. He could hardly be said to have taken the country by storm.

Party loyalty must have had a lot to do with his victory – registered Democrats still vastly outnumbered registered Republicans. Carter never seems to have taken this fact on board. Even after his defeat in 1980 he could refer to the Democratic party as the albatross round his neck. If it was indeed a handicap to him in his bid for re-election, it was because he had made it so: he had done little or nothing to satisfy its traditional concerns and aspirations. He had

secured a temporary dip in unemployment, it was true, but at the price of continuing inflation. This allowed the Republicans to take the economic issue away from the Democrats for the first time since the Depression. It was a sorry record, and sufficiently explains why so many loyal Democrats stayed at home on election day in 1980, or voted for the independent Republican candidate, John Anderson.

It was just one manifestation of the problem of Carter's provincialism. Goergia was a one-party state where success in politics depended on a man's personal following and effectiveness on the stump. Carter simply did not realize that the national Democratic party was a different animal, operating in a different system. He made a similar but worse mistake about Washington. Truman, Eisenhower, Kennedy, Johnson, Nixon, Ford – all had had a long experience of national politics by the time they came to the presidency; all except Eisenhower had served in Congress. They were insiders. Jimmy Carter was more of an outsider than any of his predecessors since Woodrow Wilson, possibly since Zachary Taylor. He made a virtue of it. Watergate gave him ample warrant for thinking that a spring-cleaning was overdue, but he made the wrong inferences. He talked of reviving Cabinet government, but since he did not grasp that Cabinet government only works if it is an instrument of party authority and leadership, the experiment failed. It had been meant only as a corrective to the secrecy and compulsive centralization of the Nixon White House.

Much worse was Carter's attitude to Congress. That body did not need reform any more than usual, though members were, as usual, being sent to prison for corruption: had it not, in the most remarkable piece of self-assertion for over a hundred years, actually carried through the difficult and unpleasant business of driving Richard Nixon from office? Anyway, Congress was "reforming" itself. Spawning more and more sub-committees, and filling up with independent-minded senators and congressmen, it was becoming less and less amenable to control and leadership. If anything needed amendment it was the presidency itself, and Carter would have been forgiven had he simply taken for granted that his election had done all that was necessary in the way of uprooting and rearrangement.

There were other necessities besides spring-cleaning. In fact the United States faced a wide range of critical problems; to deal with them effectively required, as always, collaboration between both ends of Pennsylvania Avenue, and that in turn necessitated strong and skillful presidential leadership, for Congress was no longer capable of taking the lead itself, if it ever had been. Carter could not provide that leadership, for he did not really respect congressional politicians. He liked to call himself a Southern populist, but in reality his attitudes were at least as much those of a Southern Progressive, with the unfortunate Progressive dislike of party politics and professional politicians.

In this as in so much else he may have been misled by his Georgian experience. As governor he had been able to dominate the state legislature, and had employed himself usefully on reorganization of the state's executive branch. Congress is a much more intractable creature than any state legislature, and the president's obsession with executive reorganization won him no friends. He indicated to the Democratic leadership that he had a mandate from the people and he expected Congress to help him carry it out promptly and without arguing. Senators and congressmen, well aware that most of them had run ahead of Carter in their states and districts, replied that they had their own mandate from the voters. So there was a stalemate which lasted throughout Carter's presidency.

Failure to Cultivate Congress

Carter had some legislative successes, to be sure, such as the ratification of the Panama Canal treaties in 1979 and the adoption of an energy policy which eventually put the OPEC problem to rest, and laid the foundations of the prosperity of the Reagan years – though even in that case the president infuriated the public by allowing a shortage of gasoline to occur which led to endless lines of impatient motorists in the summer of 1979. As time went on he grudgingly adapted to the needs of his position and tried to cultivate Congress. But his heart was not in it. As he said himself, he never felt easy when horsetrading and compromising and generally trying to do business in the fashion of Capitol Hill. It was more natural for him to make sweeping pronouncements, hoping that they would generate enough popular support to force Congress into line. He also made the mistake of swamping Congress with legislative proposals without indicating which should have priority. It had worked in Georgia, where he had calculated that even if most of his bills were rejected, some would be accepted, and that would be success. Again the model was inapplicable, and Carter was warned that he should not launch so many new projects, but as he said in his diary, "it's almost impossible for me to delay something that I see needs to be done."

His temperament, in other words, drove him along his disastrous course. He was by instinct a problem-solver, a manager, a technician, happiest with concrete difficulties to which concrete solutions could be applied. He had a passion for detail, and tended to lose himself in paperwork which should have been delegated to others.

Carter nevertheless had merits as a president which were too little recognized at the time. He was hardworking and highly intelligent, and had the priceless quality of learning from at least some of his mistakes, as he demonstrated, for example, in his relations with the Soviet Union, where initial brashness was rather rapidly replaced by prudent and businesslike diplomacy (though it all went for nothing

Library of Congress

President Carter enjoyed meeting factory workers at a large plant (above), but he was never happier than when back home in Plains, Georgia (below).

Camera Press

when the Soviet Union invaded Afghanistan in December 1979). He also had an accurate sense that the world was less amenable to American power and desires than it had been, and that United States policy should take account of the fact. "Even our great Nation has its recognized limits," he remarked in his inaugural address. "We cannot afford to do everything, nor can we afford to lack boldness as we meet the future." Unfortunately his boldness usually failed, and as time went on the American electorate grew restive with the president's somewhat pessimistic attitude. It suggested that there were insuperable difficulties ahead, and that was not an acceptable message.

Carter's other suggestion, that there was a malaise on the national spirit, also went down badly, for so far as most people could see the only malaise was in the Carter administration, which was getting more and more unpopular. The president lost authority, and did not mend matters by his fatal gift for making himself ridiculous in public, as when he collapsed while running in a mass rally. No one who saw it could forget the photograph of a slight, draggled, anxious figure at the end of its tether. It was not the image of a man in command of events, as a president ought to be, or to look. It summed up all too vividly what Carter had come to seem to most of the voters. He appeared to have wasted the years of power they had given him. They turned him out.

New Leader, New Style

It can hardly be supposed that his successor spent much time studying Carter's mistakes. Ronald Reagan had a natural gift for politics which spontaneously saved him from the traps into which Carter so regularly fell; he also had a team of personal advisers who were much more attuned to the realities of national politics than Carter's Georgians had been (it is perhaps significant that California is a state with a vigorous two-party tradition). But it is instructive to compare the two men's records. For one thing, presidents seem to go in pairs, and between them these two symbolize an era just as, for example, Truman and Eisenhower symbolize the era of the cold war.

Both men exploited the outsider theme but Reagan's stance in the matter reflected much deeper political realities than Carter's. Carter's distrust of the corrupt capital city was little more than a variation on the old theme of "throw the rascals out." Reagan's ostentatious crusade against big government orchestrated a motif which had been dear to the Right ever since the election of Franklin Roosevelt, but which only captured majority support in the era of inflation. It appealed to those who knew or suspected that there was a great deal of waste and inefficiency in the numberless operations of the federal government – that incoherent accumulation of New Deal programs, of Fair

Deal programs, of New Frontier and Great Society ones. It appealed to the South and West, self-confident in their new wealth, power and numbers and as impatient as all earlier American frontiers with interfering, exploiting Eastern political notions. No wonder that Reagan took Carter's somewhat muted conservatism and played it full blast on the trombones, reaffirming, for example, Carter's pledges to balance the budget. Furthermore, there could be no doubt that Carter's real constituency had been at the liberal end of the spectrum, whatever the president's own uneasiness with liberalism.

Reagan's conservatism, by contrast, was firmly founded on a cluster of interlocking attitudes and interests. He could represent those who were indifferent to the problems of the black, the poor, and the city; those whose nationalism made them see world politics as permanently reducible to Soviet-American rivalry; and those who longed, as many citizens have always longed, for an imagined past when America was wholly pure and Protestant. He could appeal to those who made money out of defense and lost it (through taxation) in expenditure on welfare. He could represent the perceptible reaction against the enthusiastic conservation politics of the seventies. All in all, his was a much more formidable coalition than the one led by poor Jimmy Carter or his equally unlucky follower, Walter Mondale. It was so formidable, in fact, that it had already deflected Carter from his chosen course and would probably have won a presidential election, if not in 1980 then in 1984, even if Ronald Reagan had not been available to lend his own qualities to the ticket.

Reagan, then, was lucky in his following and lucky in his opponent, a discredited president, whose impotence to rescue the American diplomats held hostage in Tehran by Iranian revolutionaries reinforced the dismal impression he had made. But Reagan's followers were lucky in him. His training as an actor made it easy for him to project himself as a friendly, easygoing fellow, who nevertheless had deep convictions on certain points and who could promise radical changes in American government with complete sincerity. A new defense policy would restore American strength, which he said had been dangerously eroded, and bring the Russians to heel; cutbacks in federal expenditure would permit substantial tax reductions which in turn would generate new prosperity. In vain it was pointed out that the sums did not add up. Neither then nor at any later date were opponents able to make charges of incompetence, ignorance or dishonesty stick to Ronald Reagan in the public mind. In despair, his critics talked of the "Teflon" factor.

Like other presidents – like Jimmy Carter – Reagan could often be forced by public outcry to change course or dismiss unpopular subordinates, such as his Secretary of the Interior, James Watt. Like other presidents he could suffer downturns in the opinion polls. What was so baffling was that he always managed to glide away from such

Throughout the 1980 campaign, Ronald Reagan coupled confidence in the nation's future with a rousing appeal for a new sense of national pride.

setbacks. Not only did he suffer no permanent damage, rather his reputation for invulnerability was increased by every crisis. Journalists tended to give up in despair. To begin with they eagerly reported the numberless occasions when Reagan, as the euphemism had it, "misspoke" himself. When they found that few cared, except insofar as Reagan's gaffes made good jokes, they gradually stopped mentioning them.

No one could doubt Reagan's good humor, or his polish as a political performer, or his courage, displayed notably on the occasion in 1981 when he was shot by a deranged adolescent, and in 1985, when he was operated on for cancer. It all made a good contrast to Jimmy Carter's tendency to disappear behind the furniture. But Reagan's authority as president rested on more than charm. He knew that a successful political program should be kept simple, that not too much should be attempted at any one time, and that all the arts of arm-twisting, back-slapping and compromise were necessary to get measures through Congress. Again the contrast with Carter is patent. The biggest triumph of the Reagan years was the sweeping tax cut he signed into law on August 13, 1981. The fact that he had

19

Camera Press

In 1981 President Reagan narrowly escaped death in an assassination attempt, and impressed Americans with the speed of his recovery.

only been in office for eight months is not the least astonishing aspect of the achievement.

But what, in the end, did it all amount to? The word "revolution" is the most debased in the political lexicon, and the "Reagan Revolution" was as vacuous as any other such slogan. America in 1984 had changed in no essentials from America in 1980, and in few details. Even the tax cut had merely shifted the burden from income to payroll taxes, from federal to state taxation. Cuts in welfare expenditure had badly hurt the poorest of society; the richest members had wallowed in increased affluence; but neither phenomenon points to a particularly new departure. The middle class gained very little from Reagan's policies, but lost nothing. The hugely increased outlays on defense, and the fanatic enthusiasm with which they were defended, could not hide the fact that much of the expenditure was wasted and did little or nothing to make the world a safer place; indeed, at times it seemed as if America's security had been entrusted to an alliance of crooks and lunatics.

Above all, the gigantic federal deficit began to threaten not just Reagan's modest economic achievements, but the possibility of any creative policy, whether liberal or conservative, for the foreseeable future. If it remained

inconceivable that the United States, of all countries, might go bankrupt, it was nevertheless mathematically certain that before long her leaders would have to spend most of their time struggling with the monstrous national debt and its consequences. It was not in the least what the bold men of the Right had expected when they sent Ronald Reagan riding into Washington.

1984 and Beyond

Any other president, in any other era, would have paid a stiff price for letting this state of affairs come about; but not Ronald Reagan in 1984, although the issues were already clear to any who cared to face facts. Charm carried the day, assisted by the continuing confusion of the Democratic party. Unable to find a convincing vision to answer Reaganism, it tore itself apart in the attempt to find a presidential candidate who could answer Reagan; and the attempt failed. The last Kennedy brother was damaged goods, the squalor of his private life having been public knowledge since the Chappaquiddick accident; even if that could be forgotten, which was unlikely, Edward Kennedy's political stance boiled down to the New Deal revivalism which pleased only the converted, who did not form a voting majority. Senator Gary Hart of Colorado, being a

man of the new West, was more than willing to try to blend a modified Reaganism with the traditions of the Democratic party, but the trick proved to be beyond his strength.

Walter Mondale, who eventually carried off the nomination, was in many ways the best potential president available. A decent man from the decent, liberal state of Minnesota, he had had a long training in public affairs, first as one of Hubert Humphrey's assistants, then as a US senator, finally as Jimmy Carter's vice president. But he was a hopeless candidate against the Great Communicator, who went into the campaign as a president who had kept his promises and might be expected to do so again (hence the slogan, "You ain't seen nothing yet") – except that, this time round, he was too shrewd to promise anything.

Mondale did his best, in the honest Carter tradition, to talk sense to the people, not least by saying that he would deal with the deficit by raising taxes if he were elected. This did not go down well. The farmers of America were beginning to feel the pinch, but otherwise the ill effects of Reagan finance were not yet perceived. The strong dollar, buoyed up by high interest rates, was a matter of national pride. And even the farmers voted for Reagan. The time for hard choices had not yet come round again. Mondale was defeated and retired from politics.

"Grow old along with me, the best is yet to be." It would be easy to dismiss the years after Nixon as those of a prolonged escapist picnic, for which presumably a high price would be paid in the end. But to do so would not be altogether fair. If national politics seemed at times as vacuous as during the nineteen-twenties, at other times issues emerged which showed, both by their character and their resolution, that passions could still be effectively aroused. For instance, it was palpable in 1981 that one of the main desires of the Reagan men was to weaken the conservation laws and their administration so that the great heritage of land and water administered by the Department of the Interior and its various agencies could be more easily exploited by private interests. The Republican victory of the previous year, especially the capture of the Senate, seemed to promise that the great raid would be successful. Members of the environmentalist Sierra Club rent their garments. Yet by the end of 1983 James Watt, the anti-conservationist Secretary of the Interior, and the Reagan-appointed senior officials in the Environmental Protection Agency had been driven from office (and one of them went to prison), victims in large part of their own arrogance and stupidity, but losers also to a well-sustained and intelligent campaign against them and their policies.

Within the administration, which, as someone remarked, was more like a coalition government than a single-minded one-party operation, there was a constant battle over policy, whether defense, foreign or economic – a battle fought all the more intensely because the president was invariably the least reflective and the least well-informed of the combatants. The education of Ronald Reagan became

Walter Mondale and Geraldine Ferraro, the Democratic team in 1984, could make no headway against the surge of support for the incumbent Republicans.

Camera Press

one of the main tasks of his advisers, and one of the most difficult. Yet Reagan had his own shrewdness as a politician, and since he was protected, by whatever means, from the consequences of his mistakes, the administration usually ended up lurching along in the direction that the president felt was most comfortable, with some unforeseen results.

It was natural enough that the policy of a man determined to cut back the functions and size of the federal government should strengthen the prominence and importance of state governments; natural, too, that the partisan successes of the Congressional Republicans in 1980 should provoke a more disciplined, partisan attitude among the Democrats than they had found it necessary to adopt for nearly 20 years; but who expected Reagan to convert the Democrats to protectionism? Yet so it was. The president's fiscal and economic policies brought a flood of foreign capital and, much less welcome, of foreign produce into the country. American producers, whether lumbermen, farmers or manufacturers, began to protest furiously; and the Democrats, anxious to protect themselves and, if possible, to damage the Republicans, agitated for tariff measures against foreign competition. In this way they reversed a party doctrine going back 150 years, while Reagan stood fairly fast by the free trade convictions of his youth (only, prudent man, he began to talk of "fair trade").

Battle was joined seriously in 1985, and was perhaps the

*Mondale courted the support of organized labor in 1984
but his crushing defeat left the Democrats demoralized
and in search of new approaches to the issues of the age.*

first sign that the era of transition, of borrowed time, was coming to an end. If so, the era was going to end with the parties having transformed themselves. For the first time since 1932 the Democrats will have adopted the posture of the party of opposition, which does not have to consider what would happen if it were called on to carry out its policies, while the Republicans will have been thrust, willy-nilly, into the posture of the party of government, which dares not make too many reckless commitments. If so, it would be a supremely ironical comment on the presidency of a man who, from first to last, has stood for the repudiation of just that prudent, worldly-wise, Washingtonian consensus which has on the whole commanded the government of the United States since the end of the Second World War. There is a further aspect, too. It might also signify that the habit of winning or losing elections is more important in determining a party's character and creed than any other consideration.

A Time of Adjustment

Obviously the post-Nixon decade cannot accurately be interpreted until something of its long-term consequences is known. But it is nevertheless striking that none of the great questions posed by the various calamities of the early seventies seem to have been settled. In foreign policy the United States floundered from crisis to crisis, expedient to expedient, without any effective guiding plan (except for Jimmy Carter's insistence on making respect for human rights the foundation of his administration's diplomacy) other than the obstinate belief that what was good for the United States must be good for the world, and that what was good for the United States was an ever-accelerating arms build-up. The closely-meshed social and economic

problems, some aspect of which touched the life of every American, were tackled with almost equal ineffectiveness by all three administrations. Ford and Carter were not given long enough to see if their policies could be made to work, and although Reagan's tax-cut generated enough demand to stimulate a surprising long-lived recovery, on the whole his domestic record was one of inch-by-inch retreat, imposed on a reluctant but pragmatic president by an increasingly restive Congress. His proposals for a tax reform seemed doomed to end in nothing, like Jimmy Carter's before him.

The institutional problems which looked so urgent in 1974 also persisted. A steady rise in litigation threatened to swamp the judicial system and provoked regular sharp complaints from Chief Justice Warren Burger, yet nothing was done. The deterioration of city government continued. The period's only achievement in that area was the rescue of New York from bankruptcy.

The Democratic party, having scrapped old rules, had yet to find a new system which would not make it difficult for a candidate to win the presidential nomination in any way that gave him a hope of winning the election afterwards (the effect of the incessant primaries in this respect being much like that of the incessant balloting that went on at the presidential convention in the bad old days of the two-thirds rule). By 1985 Congress seemed little less wayward than it had been in 1975. Under President Reagan war between the departments and bureaux was as bad as ever; in some respects – notably the conflict between the Department of Defense and the State Department – it was perhaps worse. And at the centre of all storms lay the White House, itself a battlefield, and which continued to reflect the attitudes and personality of the incumbent president more than any institution of government. If that was the case, then a new Nixon might find it as easy to erect an "imperial presidency" as the old one had.

It would be easy to interpret all this as institutional decay leading inexorably to a crisis. Yet the outstanding fact of the Ford-Carter-Reagan years is that the crisis did not come. It can hardly be said that the course of events was satisfactory, but it could have been very much worse. It is even possible to point to signs of renewal. Thus Massachusetts, which lies at the heart of the so-called Frost Belt and which had seemed to be set inexorably to decline along with that region, again became one of the fastest growing states of the Union, partly thanks to the energetic and enlightened policy of its government, and partly to the availability of its unique concentration of scientific, technological and intellectual capital. New leaders began to emerge in Congress. Perhaps in the end it will prove that the decade of transition was the one in which America slowly, painfully, and only half-consciously made the adjustment from a heroic time of high hopes to the more humdrum but ultimately less disappointing climate of accepted limitations, as once prophesied by Jimmy Carter.

Chapter 2

FOREIGN POLICY AFTER VIETNAM

The trauma of America's involvement in the Vietnam War exerted a profound influence on US diplomacy from the mid-1970s. There was a widespread desire to resist military entanglements, yet Henry Kissinger's policies of détente and arms control came under attack and were soon in tatters. Jimmy Carter's attempts to chart a new course met with little success, and strained relations with America's allies. Ronald Reagan came into office determined to boost US military strength and restore national pride, although bold slogans were not always capable of being easily fulfilled.

Diplomacy in Crisis

Once more the helicopter blades, a haunting symbol of the Vietnam War, flap-flap-flapped on television screens as Americans stared at the fiasco of their countrymen and desperate Vietnamese fleeing from the roof of the US embassy. It was late April, 1975. Saigon had fallen to the Communists of North Vietnam. Fearing such an outcome, President Gerald R. Ford had implored Congress for another billion dollars for the beleaguered government of South Vietnam. But Democrats and Republicans alike had no more stomach for the war and refused another cent. Humiliated, Ford and Secretary of State Henry Kissinger accused Congress of betraying an ally and tarnishing Washington's honor. The president, however, moved to cut his losses. No sooner had Saigon been rechristened Ho Chi Minh City than Ford declared to tumultuous applause in a New Orleans speech that the war in Vietnam was "finished as far as America is concerned."

The debacle ended a creative interlude in American diplomatic history. The policy built by Richard Nixon and Henry Kissinger was crumbling in 1975. Americans thought that détente with the Soviet Union favored the Russians; China chafed at the pause in *its* détente with the United States; the Middle East was again stalemated after the

The end of America's entanglement in Vietnam: weary soldiers oversee the evacuation of personnel from the US embassy in Saigon, April 1975.

fading of Kissinger's triumphs following the Yom Kippur War of October 1973; Washington wrangled with NATO allies; and Congress regularly stuck spokes into the wheels of policy.

The effects of the "Vietnam Syndrome," the reaction to the disaster in Indochina, where over 56,000 Americans had died, marked Washington's response in the years ahead wherever an alert American public spotted the potential of a bloody third-world intervention. "No more Vietnams" was the slogan of the decade; the very idea of using military force in behalf of national policy was now rejected by many. Combined with the Watergate scandal, Vietnam had discredited the White House: neither Congress nor the public any longer conceded superior presidential wisdom in policy making. The American consensus on the cold war dissolved into a medley of opinions and impulses, all challenging executive dominance of American foreign policy.

Other nations watched for cues as the United States searched for a new diplomatic order. Even though most had applauded the American withdrawal from the war, South Vietnam's collapse and the domestic attack on executive authority raised questions about Washington's role as a world leader, a sign of the loss of "credibility" Kissinger and his predecessors had feared. Moscow took new liberties. The Chinese harbored doubts about the inconstant Americans. Old allies, whether Israel, Britain or West Germany, began charting more self-reliant and self-interested courses. However sensible America's withdrawal from Vietnam might have been, the ragged rout of 1975 left behind a crisis of confidence.

Changes in the international order compounded the diplomatic problems. Soviet military power grew more rapidly than Washington's. America's ability to influence its allies diminished. The escalation of oil prices provoked a string of economic shocks, producing inflation and industrial stagnation in the West. Once weak nations flexed new muscles, growing more resistant to superpower pressures (including those of the Soviet Union). Yet, even as the diffusion of international power allowed weaker states to assert their independence, the concentration of nuclear power in American-Soviet rivalry remained the key threat to world peace.

The rise of other states, the higher costs of fielding armies and navies, and the fragmentation of domestic opinion, imposed a new awareness of America's limited power. Washington helmsmen trimmed their sails to meet this new breeze. Nixon and Kissinger tried circumventing the problem with sleight of hand abroad and secrecy at home, hoping to find a safe port by taming the Soviets and devolving military responsibilities on to America's client states. When détente fell apart after 1973, however, their whole policy began disintegrating with it.

Reassembling a coherent foreign policy after Nixon's decline involved overcoming more numerous conflicts within the executive branch itself. Presidents retained the power to set a steady course but only by choosing between key advisers, a politically costly process. Conflict flourished as the White House staff, the head of the National Security Council, the secretary of state, the secretary of defense, and various underlings wrestled for control of the presidents who were supposed to be governing. As policy makers lurched from one decision to another, they delayed talks with foreign diplomats until they could first negotiate accords among themselves.

With the breakdown of policy coherence, new spokesmen leaped forward to volunteer their ideas. Most such schemes for putting Humpty Dumpty together again suffered from typical liberal and conservative illusions. Liberal pragmatists placed too much stock in reason, the conservative ideologues in the efficacy of force and toughness. Liberals often implied that foreign conflicts could be resolved without losers, conservatives that all compromises represented losses for the United States. Both exaggerated the capacity of the United States to dictate events abroad and underestimated the capacities of other nations.

End of the Kissinger Era

When Gerald Ford became president in August 1974, he reaffirmed Kissinger's mandate in foreign policy. But others challenged him, especially in Congress, where they attacked his personal integrity, his past use of the Central Intelligence Agency, and – by tying most-favored-nation

Widespread protests showed the strength of US opposition to the Vietnam War. "No More Vietnams" was a potent slogan against military interventionism.

trade status for the Soviet Union to the freer emigration of Jews from that country – his policy of détente. Offstage, Ronald Reagan contested Ford's hold on office with a hard-line assault on arms control and détente with both Russia and China. Sandwiched between the right and left, Kissinger experienced two years of unbroken frustration. The complex of policies contrived with Nixon fell apart as a result of this domestic rebellion – and of a singularly undomesticated Soviet Union. As détente became a faded dream, a gloomy Kissinger called for strong responses to Soviet expansionism, but neither Congress nor the public would approve anything suggestive of "another Vietnam."

Only weeks after the fall of Saigon, Ford and Kissinger seized a chance to display the American eagle's claws. In mid-May 1975, Communist Cambodian naval units seized the US merchant ship *Mayaguez* in international waters. Washington responded almost at once with force. Americans suffered 40 fatalities (most in an accident) while sinking Cambodian vessels, bombing and strafing the mainland, and assuring the release of the *Mayaguez* and her crew. Conservatives applauded, but anti-war groups predictably discounted the need for armed action.

Nixon had made arms control the centerpiece of American-Soviet relations, and Kissinger hoped to follow up the 1972 SALT I treaty on strategic arms limitation with an early completion of SALT II. In Vladivostok in November 1974, American and Soviet negotiators agreed temporarily to cap the number of intercontinental-range missiles either party could deploy at 2400, no more than 1320 to be armed with multiple, independently-targeted ("MIRVed") warheads. But hawkish critics lambasted the adminstration for

US marines land on Koh Tang island in operations that led to the rescue of the Mayaguez *and her crew, seized by Cambodia in international waters in 1975.*

not gaining a cut in the aggregate explosive power of Russian missiles, which were much larger (if less accurate) than the Americans'. Kissinger aimed in SALT II for actual reductions of strategic missiles, rather than mere ceilings, and talks wore on, but his magic had vanished. The 1976 American presidential campaign and disputes at the conference table ended the chance for a new treaty during Gerald Ford's administration.

In the meantime, the vaunted "structure of peace" cracked under Moscow's pressure. Weaving a network of political and economic inducements, Kissinger had hoped to bring Leonid Brezhnev around to the advantages of status quo policies. The Soviet Union, however, had never promised such docility; nor had Kissinger managed to reconcile "détente" with the punishments required when Moscow departed from his script. These problems first became obvious when Brezhnev blatantly supported enemies of Israeli and American interests during the Yom Kippur War in October 1973. Russian "violations" of détente accelerated after Nixon fell to Watergate. What kind of "structure of peace," critics angrily asked, permitted the Soviets to promote communism in Portugal, smile on Hanoi's overwhelming of Saigon, put Angola under Marxist control with the use of Fidel Castro's troops, persecute dissenters and balk Jewish emigrants in the Soviet Union, and the whole time pile armaments on armaments? And what kind of government in the midst of this behaviour would agree to the 1975 "Helsinki Accords," thus tacitly approving the Soviet domination of eastern Europe?

Moscow named Washington as the villain of détente, citing Kissinger's exploitation of the Yom Kippur War to

detach Egypt from the Soviets' orbit and exclude it from any role in settling the Arab-Israeli conflict. The United States had also rewarded Romania's maverick behavior and, worst of all, taken China's side in the Sino-Soviet dispute. Americans of course saw the matter differently; in 1975 Kissinger described the management of "the emergence of the Soviet Union as a superpower" as "the problem of our age."

Events in sub-Sahara Africa, long ignored in Washington, reflected the ruins of détente, the strength of anti-interventionist feeling in post-Vietnam America, and Kissinger's belated effort to attend to regional problems. The Angola issue illustrates the first and second, American efforts in Rhodesia and South Africa the third.

After Angola achieved independence from Portugal in 1974, competing black revolutionaries vied for power. The Russians backed the eventual winners, the Popular Liberation Movement (MPLA), while China and the United States aided two other groups. Scorning his African experts' advice, Kissinger defined the struggle as nothing less than a test of the Soviet Union's commitment to détente and he had the CIA begin covert aid to opponents of the MPLA. Believing that American acquiescence would invite more Soviet expansionism later, he acted secretly in fear that the rambunctious post-Watergate Congress would never approve funding if asked. When the first of 19,000 Cuban troops surfaced in Angola during the summer of 1975, the administration stepped up CIA aid. Only after the CIA's role was publicly revealed did the government ask Congress to vote money for the anti-Soviet groups. A November 1975 poll, however, reported that 72 per cent were opposed to involvement in "liberation" wars that might result in American military intervention. The Senate killed the administration's bill 54-22 in December 1975, the House by 323-99 a month later. An exasperated Ford complained that Congress had "lost its guts." Though China had discreetly cut its losses earlier, Kissinger obstinately defined the outcome as a catastrophe for the West. Washington refused to consider recognizing the MPLA government until all Cuban troops had left. Not surprisingly, Angola cuddled even closer to Cuba and the Soviet Union.

A sign that the United States had learned a lesson in Angola appeared when Kissinger dramatically reversed American policy in southern Africa later in 1976. In the summer he traveled to Africa, courting leaders of black governments with promises that Washington would insist on "majority rule" in the continent. Far from ignoring the cold war, he hoped to immunize the region from Soviet influence by encouraging moves for a peaceful transition to black rule in Rhodesia (Zimbabwe) and Namibian independence from South Africa. He also wished to protect economic interests in the region, from which the United States imported large portions of its cobalt, platinum, vanadium, and ferro-chromium. South Africa itself contained over $1.25 billion in American investments and had grown in

strategic significance since the development of a new US base in the Indian Ocean.

To improve relations between South Africa and black-ruled states in the region, and so stabalize the area as a whole, Kissinger began what the Reagan administration would call "constructive engagement," an effort to use friendship for South Africa to produce reforms in apartheid. Potentially useful in giving Washington leverage in Pretoria, the policy also handicapped its relations with all black Africa.

Modest as it was, Kissinger's African initiative was his last success. Other policy goals eluded his reach. In the Middle East, he helped establish a secure demilitarized zone between Israel and Egypt in the Sinai desert, but his gradualist approach to the region had otherwise run dry. Congress refused to restore military aid to Turkey, cut off after its invasion of Cyprus. Centrifugal forces grew within NATO. Europeans not only no longer believed in an imminent Soviet threat, they were not about to abandon a détente that both created handsome profits and lessened tensions with the East. Thus, the alliance unwound a little bit more.

By the election autumn of 1976, few still thought of Henry Kissinger as a brilliant policy maker. Détente with Russia was a wreck, with China it was stalled. Arms control, too, was at a standstill. Names like Panama and Angola stood for frustration. Kissinger's undoubted skills had run up against the destruction of a president, attacks on defense spending, exposure of the CIA, and fear of armed intervention. Most Americans now believed that he had concentrated too much on the Russians and Chinese while ignoring America's neighbors and allies. Left, right, and center, critics deplored the lack of principle or morality in American policy. Voters looked for a new approach and found Jimmy Carter of Georgia.

Carter's New Course

Had he not been followed by a movie actor, the onetime naval officer and born-again Christian peanut farmer Jimmy Carter might rank as America's most unlikely president. He entered the White House with no experience beyond his home state and none whatever in world affairs. But for voters disenchanted with Watergate and Vietnam, a short resumé was an advantage. The 1976 campaign revealed little about how this intelligent, earnest, plain-speaking and – toothy smile notwithstanding – almost humorless man would approach the knotty world problems facing him.

Since Carter had cultivated an anti-establishment reputation, pundits took notice when he selected Cyrus Vance, a Washington insider and old hand in Democratic governments, as secretary of state. Vance stood to conduct a

sedate, patient diplomacy aimed at restoring better relations with the Soviet Union. Carter's national security adviser was Zbigniew Brzezinski, a prominent foreign affairs scholar from Columbia University who had tutored Carter on the Trilateral Commission, which Carter had joined to find diplomatic viewpoints and connections. Sponsored by David Rockefeller, the commission's unexceptionable aim was peace through cooperation and closer ties among the United States, western Europe and Japan. Named secretary of defense was Harold H. Brown, another experienced establishment figure. Finally, Carter responded to unorthodoxy by choosing the Reverend Andrew Young, onetime compatriot of Martin Luther King, Jr, as ambassador to the United Nations, where he was counted on to forge better ties with third-world nations.

Carter's efforts to chart new paths would occur in the now familiar setting of decaying détente, squabbling bureaucrats, lack of a popular foreign policy consensus (except for anti-interventionism), and skepticism abroad about Washington's reliability. In his memoirs Cyrus Vance stated that Carter's diplomatic team came to Washington determined to achieve a stronger NATO, a new strategic arms control pact with the Soviets, better relations with China *and* the USSR, a stable settlement of the crisis in southern Africa, peace in the Middle East, a Panama Canal treaty and "a principled yet pragmatic defense of basic human rights."

What this understates is President Carter's moral zeal. After the shame of Vietnam, he planned nothing less than putting his country back on the side of the angels. The

President Carter confers with two members of his foreign affairs team, Secretary of State Cyrus Vance (left) and UN Ambassador Andrew Young.

Camera Press

Carter's call for greater human rights in Russia was strongly supported by this New York group, shown campaigning against Soviet oppression of Jews.

Robert Hunt Library

United States, he declared in May 1977, had permitted an "inordinate fear of communism" to betray the best in itself. America faced a "new world," and its foreign policy would now stress "decency," "optimism" and principle. Washington would take the lead in defending "human rights" in all nations. It would do everything in its power to end arms sales, nuclear proliferation and the nuclear arms race itself. Adopting a "global" outlook, America would emphasize trilateral allied relations and an open mind to the grievances of poorer nations. Policy by superpower fiat was outmoded, Carter implied, as was the reliance on military force.

Carter wanted to end hostilities with past and current enemies, pursuing détente with China and the Soviet Union

and normalizing relations with Vietnam, Cuba and Angola. Hard-liners worried about the likely defense policy of such a president, as Carter the campaigner had urged withdrawal of the 50,000 American troops from South Korea and cancelling "superfluous" strategic weapons systems.

A Catalog of Blunders

Carter's sense of timing proved terrible, and his rush in 1977 to accomplish everything at once provoked criticism and resistance both at home and abroad. Promising an "absolute" commitment to human rights in his inaugural speech, he quickly discovered that while one could apply pressure more easily on friends than foes, both bridled at American meddling. Argentina and the Soviet Union were among the first to feel the pressure of Carter's humanitarianism. Argentina rebuffed his entreaties and in 1980 undermined the American grain embargo with massive wheat sales to Moscow. The Soviet Union, aghast at a president pontificating against its treatment of dissidents while declaring his devotion to détente, reacted with a new campaign of harrassment against dissenters.

Gestures toward solving armaments issues met setbacks, too. When Washington cut back sales of conventional weapons, its allies gleefully absorbed the old American markets. When Carter – hoping to discourage nuclear proliferation – attacked the trade in nuclear technology, he achieved little but anger Brazil, West Germany, France and Japan – all allies. Yet he later gave way entirely in a deal with neutralist India that drew far more comment than any victories against nuclear proliferation. In 1977 the president backed a comprehensive nuclear test ban only to reverse himself later, effectively killing negotiations on the subject. Talks on cutting conventional arms transfers collapsed in 1978, as did others on demilitarizing the Indian Ocean when Washington realized it didn't *want* the area demilitarized.

Though a majority of Americans polled now favored *more* defense spending, Carter began jettisoning weapons systems. He might have overcome criticisms of his June 1977 cancellation of the B-1 bomber project had he not handled the neutron bomb issue so clumsily. Designed to kill Warsaw Pact invaders with massive radiation while damping blast and fire damage, the "enhanced radiation weapon" was no more inhumane than other nuclear arms. Yet it aroused a wave of revulsion, especially among European peace activists. After tentatively deciding to cancel the weapon, Carter backtracked, now suggesting that he would restore the neutron bomb if NATO allies volunteered to

Camera Press

Recruits to the Somali army are instructed in arms maintenance. When Somalia attacked Marxist Ethiopia in 1977, the US gave moral support – but no weapons.

share the onus of deployment. Bonn's Chancellor Helmut Schmidt dutifully climbed out on a shaky political limb in the spring of 1978 to do exactly that, whereupon Carter, defying his advisers, sawed off the limb by cancelling the troublesome bomb. This fiasco left an indelible Carter trademark of amateurishness and inconstancy.

Strategic arms talks with the Soviet Union began no more auspiciously. Carter could have tried for a quick if unspectacular accord by crossing the t's of the near-agreement negotiated by the Ford administration. The Senate would probably have ratified such a treaty in 1977, allowing time for Carter then to develop more ambitious measures in a SALT III pact. Instead, against the advice of Vance and others, he dispatched his secretary of state to Moscow in March 1977 with a hurriedly assembled proposal that sharply departed from past talks. Encompassing, among other measures, deep cuts in heavy, land-based missile forces, the plan would slash Moscow's arsenal of heavy ICBMs. The Kremlin, already raw from Carter's human rights demands, found both the proposal and Washington's break from continuity disturbing. Soviet Foreign Minister Andrei Gromyko publicly rebuffed Vance, and the administration had to start from scratch.

Initiatives in the third world fared little better. Hopes for normal ties with Vietnam vanished amid Hanoi's demands for "reparations," conclusion of a treaty with Moscow, and invasion of Cambodia. Though Ambassador Young's efforts to encourage a pacific passage to majority rule in Rhodesia (Zimbabwe) met some success, they angered conservatives at home.

Intrigues in the Horn of Africa led to another blunder. Alarmed when a Marxist regime took power in Ethiopia, Washington soon received pleas for aid against the Ethiopians from neighboring Somalia, for several years also a client of the Soviet Union. Eager to displace the Russians,

The Panama Canal had long been a source of contention between the USA and Central American countries, and in 1977 two treaties were signed that would end US control of the waterway in the year 2000. The treaties eventually received Senate approval – but only just, and after two years of bitter debate that soured relations with Panama itself.

the administration responded incautiously, and in July 1977 Somalia invaded Ethiopia's Ogadan province in the expectation of early American arms shipments. Embarrassed by this aggression, Carter tacked again, denying arms to the invaders. Outmatched by a foe now backed by Cuban troops, the Somalis retreated to their borders.

Carter thoroughly prepared himself for an effort to finesse Kissinger's step-by-step diplomacy in favor of a general Arab-Israeli settlement, poring over diplomatic records and talking with a stream of Middle East dignitaries. The climax of these preliminaries came in an American-Soviet announcement on October 1, 1977 calling for multiparty talks in Geneva under the co-chairmanship of Washington and Moscow. With one startling stroke Carter had negated Henry Kissinger's agile removal of the Russians from Middle East negotiations. The charismatic Anwar Sadat of Egypt rescued him with a dramatic flight to Jerusalem that set the stage for bilateral Egyptian-Israeli talks. Relieved, Carter unceremoniously dumped the Geneva conference, again to the annoyance of the Russians.

Carter's bid for a Panama Canal treaty seemed his most impressive early achievement. Reversing campaign promises to retain control of the canal, the president decided on a new settlement to protect the waterway from revolutionary violence and to remove the taint of American "colonialism." Two Panama treaties were signed in August 1977, but events quickly revealed that Carter would pay dearly for his victory. Prominent opponents attacked the pacts; polls

showed that 78 per cent of Americans who had opinions on the matter were against surrendering control of the canal. Nor was public sentiment shifting in Carter's favor, for he had neither consulted key congressmen during the talks nor, during the months of negotiation, sought to educate the public. The freshly-signed treaties faced an uncertain fate.

Confusion and Contradiction

By late 1977, American and foreign critics were speaking of a "Carterized" foreign policy marked by confusion, zigzags and general ineptness. United Nations Ambassador Andrew Young's flamboyant utterances hurt the administration's image, as did wrangling between Secretary Vance and National Security Advisor Brzezinski. The president reacted to their polarized advice by first adopting Vance's view, then Brzezinski's – and sometimes by melding improbable alloys of the two. Critics and the media also accused the administration of "weakness' and of forfeiting military force or the threat of its use as a tool of diplomacy. Defense Secretary Harold Brown later remarked that Vance resisted any action "that involved the risk of force," and Carter, Young and others (including Brown) often gave the same impression.

Carter never put this reputation for confusion and weakness behind him. By the end of 1978, what Washington viewed as a surge of Soviet belligerence, joined by a rightward swing of public opinion, overwhelmed Carter's original hopes for a new diplomacy. Still forced to act in a bipolar world, Washington policy makers said a reluctant farewell to détente and reembraced containment.

In the middle years of his term, Carter's human rights policy helped gain the release of political prisoners in Indonesia, Chile and several African nations, and reinforced halting steps toward democratic rights in Brazil, Peru and Ecuador. While these and other victories restored glitter to the tarnished American image, an active human rights policy proved devilishly difficult to execute. Attacks on Soviet practices arguably caused a new crackdown on dissidents in Moscow, jeopardized talks on other issues, and upset NATO allies anxious to preserve détente. Badgering such friends and allies as Iran and Turkey increased doubts about America's steadiness and loyalty. And overlooking the transgressions of South Korea, the Philippines and China called forth charges of hyprocrisy. Carter escaped none of these dilemmas.

US-Soviet relations gradually recaptured the foreground. Carter took office with no definite policy toward the Soviet Union except to pursue arms control, and that for mixed reasons, Vance wanting to strengthen détente and Brzezinski to inhibit the Russian military buildup. As time passed Carter's policy grew more ambivalent. He dealt with the Soviets almost as reliable partners in SALT discussions and, after the United States abandoned its March 1977 proposals, talks advanced enough to inspire forecasts of a signed treaty by the end of 1978. But on other issues Carter officials viewed the Soviet Union as a dangerous foe bent on menacing American security. With Vance and Brzezinski wrestling for control of Russian policy, Carter steered an erratic course, especially along "the arc of crisis" in the Middle East and Southwestern Asia. From their base in Ethiopia, the Soviets entrenched themselves in South Yemen, posing a threat to pro-western North Yemen. An April 1979 coup placed a pro-Soviet regime in power in Afghanistan.

The Soviets had complaints, too, especially about Carter's courtship of the Chinese. Growing American-Soviet friction had spurred Washington to move faster than planned on regularizing ties with China. Washington's goals shifted, too. Instead of using China and the Soviet Union as counterweights to the other, Carter now grasped the former as a virtual ally against the latter. This became apparent during Brzezinski's trip to China in May 1978, when he passed on American intelligence on Soviet activities and smiled benignly at his hosts' anti-Soviet remarks. (Touring the Great Wall with his new friends, he cried out, "Last one to the top fights the Russians in Ethiopia!")

Thereafter, discussions sped toward American recognition of the People's Republic of China and abandonment of official American ties with Taiwan. Carter triumphantly announced the agreement on December 15, 1978, only a week before scheduled Vance-Gromyko talks aimed at wrapping up the SALT II treaty. Moscow took umbrage and began dragging its heels on SALT issues. The China accord, which called for the end of US defense obligations to Taiwan a year later, particularly disturbed American conservatives. Criticism grew after the visit to the United States of China's leader, Deng Ziaoping, early in 1979. Carter and his advisers uttered only the mildest of protests when Deng informed them of his plans to teach the Vietnamese "a lesson" for their invasion of Cambodia. When Chinese forces invaded Vietnam in February, and the Americans' forewarning became public knowledge, Washington inevitably risked indictment as an accomplice in aggression.

The struggle to gain Senate ratification of the Panama Canal treaties occupied much of 1977 and 1978. The two pacts provided for the surrender of American control over the canal and adjoining area by January 1, 2000, while setting terms for Americans to use and help protect the canal after that date. The treaties produced a lengthy, corrosive debate in Washington and also strained relations with Panama. When the treaties were finally approved in the spring of 1979 with one vote to spare only after the Senate had attached reservations galling to both Carter and to Panama, the president must have been tempted to doubt whether the result justified the political costs.

Agreement at Camp David

Carter hoped for better results in the Middle East. After Sadat's journey to Jerusalem, Washington aimed at encouraging Isreal and Egypt first to settle problems between themselves, then at creating a means by which other Arab states would join in creating a "homeland" for the Palestinians on the West Bank and Gaza Strip while making peace with Israel. When Israeli-Egyptian talks flagged, Carter laid his own prestige on the line in September 1978 by summoning Sadat and Israel's Prime Minister Menachem Begin to Camp David in the Maryland mountains. There they were to hammer out a settlement under Carter's watchful eye. Most observers predicted failure, but after thirteen days of secret and contentious talks, in which Carter played the leading role, the three statesmen stunned the world by announcing two major agreements. The first, "A Framework for Peace in the Middle East," outlined the process for Israel, Jordan, the Palestinians and others to follow in settling problems of general concern. The second promised an Israeli-Egyptian peace treaty within three months, including terms for establishing formal diplomatic relations and transferring Israeli-held territory in the Sinai to Egypt within three years.

Carter's achievement boosted him in the eyes of Americans, but other Arab states saw Camp David as an Egyptian sell-out. Nor did Sadat and Begin behave according to the president's plan – especially Begin, who approved new Israeli settlements on the West Bank. Nonetheless, in March 1979 Carter secured the promised Israeli-Egyptian peace treaty with a daring diplomatic shuttle to the Middle East. Thereafter the "Camp David process" fizzled, victim of Egypt's isolation from other Arab states, Israel's obduracy on Palestinian issues, and continuing violence by the Palestinians themselves. American inattention may also have hurt, for other events had swept Camp David from the headlines.

One set of new headlines originated in Iran. In Tehran as 1977 ended, Carter toasted Iran as "an island of stability." Suddenly, however, the Shah's regime reeled from insurrection and disorder. In November 1978 he imposed martial rule but otherwise seemed paralyzed, constantly phoning Washington for suggestions. American officials were divided among themselves. Brzezinski favored a military crackdown and stout American support but Vance wanted an attempt to counter protest with liberalization. Carter thus faced a terrible choice not of his own making but the product of policies going back to President Truman. Shortly after the Shah abdicated in January 1979, the civilian regime he left behind was swept aside by the Ayatollah Khomeini's Islamic revolution. The outcome was a disaster for Washington: the "source of stability" in the "arc of crisis" had become the center of the crisis itself.

The Camp David accords between Menachem Begin (top left) and Anwar Sadat (top right) were a high point in Carter's diplomacy, but the coming to power of the Ayatollah Khomeini in Iran (above) was disastrous.

Generally, 1979 brought one disappointment after another to Carter. For a while, relations with China seemed an exception. While Vance was urging caution, Brzenzinski fought to "play the China card" against Moscow and gradually won over Carter. Trade with China rose briskly, as did the numbers of high officials trekking to the Middle Kingdom. By the end of the year, American instruments were collecting data on the Soviet Union from Chinese soil, and in 1980 the two powers cooperated in supplying arms

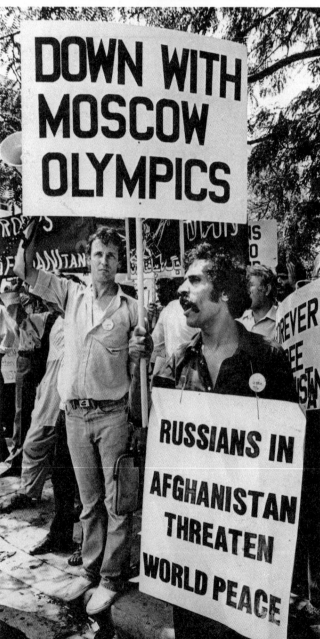

to Afghan guerrillas. Yet just as Washington pressed its case for other anti-Soviet actions or gestures, the Chinese drew back, content to have forestalled creation of a Soviet-American "condominium." Ironically, it had been Beijing's leaders who had played the "American card."

Despite unease about the developing Chinese-American relationship, Brezhnev joined Carter in signing the SALT II treaty at a Vienna summit meeting in June 1979. Due to expire in December 1985, the agreement reduced to 2250 the total number of strategic nuclear launchers either power could deploy by 1981, of which no more than 1320 could be MIRVed. Another "subceiling" placed a limit of 820 on land-based, MIRVed ICBMs. Mobile land-based launchers and sea- or ground-launched cruise missiles were banned until the end of 1981. Carter offered a sop to right-wing opponents by announcing a substantial defense buildup, including a decision to develop the multi-warhead MX missile. He also defended the treaty soberly: it would "not end the arms competition" but would "make that competition safer ... with clear rules and verifiable limits, where otherwise there would be no rules and there would be no limits."

The next six months could be called "The Killing of SALT II." Hawks attacked the agreement as a sell-out to the Russians, while liberals categorized it as a green light for ever more nuclear stockpiling. The public, confused by the pact's complexities and bored after the seven years of talk needed to move from SALT I to SALT II, applied no pressure for approval. Most hurtful to the treaty's chances were world events that stimulated a growing resurgence of anti-Sovietism in the United States. The Russians and Cubans continued their armed safaris in Ethiopia and Angola. A maladroitly handled controversy in the late summer over whether a new Soviet combat brigade had suddenly appeared in Cuba further damaged the treaty's prospects. A month later, militants in Tehran stormed the American embassy, seizing its staff as hostages and paralyzing the Carter administration for the next fifteen months. Then, during the Christmas holidays of 1979, the Soviet Union applied the *coup de grâce* by invading Afghanistan to install a regime that could protect past Kremlin investments. Before long, 100,000 Soviet troops were confronting fierce guerrilla resistance.

Horrified, Carteer described the invasion as the world's most dangerous moment since the Second World War. Seeing Afghanistan as a fresh instance of Soviet expansionism, the American government responded sharply. With Secretary Vance's influence fading, Carter adopted the harsher views of Zbigniew Brzezinski. He not only cancelled

Top left: A White House briefing on Afghanistan. It was feared that the Soviet invasion would boost Russian influence in the Persian Gulf. Left: Crowds protest against the invasion, which prompted a US boycott of the 1980 Moscow Olympics.

scheduled Soviet-American exchanges and embargoed credits and grain sales, but also banned Russian fishing fleets from American waters and declared a boycott of the 1980 Moscow Olympics. Finally, he withdrew the moribund SALT II treaty from the Senate and in his State of the Union message on January 23, 1980, announced in the "Carter Doctrine" that efforts by "any outside force to gain control of the Persian Gulf region will be regarded as an assault on the vital interests of the United States of America, and such an assault will be repelled by any means necessary, including military force."

Return to Containment

By January 1980 Carter had given up on détente and adopted the classic containment policy of the pre-Vietnam years, ushering the way for the Reagan administration a year later. Carter had actually been drifting toward a renewal of containment for some time. In the year and a half before the invasion of Afghanistan, he had secured promises from NATO allies to boost defense spending by 3 per cent annually, asked Congress to approve development and deployment of the MX missile, quietly changed his mind on pulling American troops out of South Korea, and agreed to counter Soviet deployments of intermediate-range missiles targeted on western Europe by sending 572 Pershing II and ground-launched cruise missiles to Europe (unless the Russians could be induced in negotiations to cut back their new missiles).

The militarization of Carter's policy continued after Afghanistan. He announced a 5 per cent defense spending increase and plans for a Rapid Deployment Force, sought bases near the Persian Gulf area, instituted draft registration, stepped up arms sales to friendly governments, and adopted a secret paper (Presidential Directive 59) outlining ways to fight a "long" nuclear war for concrete aims.

No consultations with NATO allies had preceded Carter's sanctions against the Soviet Union. US-NATO relations now worsened as a large gap appeared between American and European versions of détente. Despite nervousness about Russian missiles, West Europeans no longer feared an imminent Russian attack. They were reaping profits from better relations. Loath to accept responsibility for events outside Europe, the NATO allies would do little more than condemn the Afghan invasion verbally – and only West Germany joined the Olympic boycott. Secretary of Defense Harold Brown remarked bitterly that the message from Washington's allies was, "Yes, there should be a division of tasks – we'll sell stuff to the Russians and you defend us."

Everywhere Carter turned, including at home, where Edward Kennedy challenged his reelection, he found himself in trouble. The high hopes of Camp David dwindled as Lebanon once again fell into disorder. Palestinian Liberation Organization (PLO) raids stiffened Israeli opinion against concessions. Other Arab states further distanced themselves from Egypt and the United States. Nor did American gaffes help. First, UN Ambassador Andrew Young was forced from office after talking to PLO representatives in violation of American policy; then his successor in March 1980 voted for a resolution that condemned Israeli settlements on the West Bank and ordered that they should be dismantled, only to retract the vote the next day, pleading an error by the State Department. Both Arabs and Israelis were furious.

The return of the cold war to Central America and the Caribbean confounded Carter's hopes for improved relations with third world areas. When left-wing revolutionaries in 1979 seized control of tiny Grenada in the Caribbean, Washington responded with doses of disapproval that foreshadowed President Reagan's 1983 invasion. At the time, Carter was more worried about Nicaragua, where a decades-old, American-backed dictatorship was coming to an end. As the "Sandinista" rebellion grew, Carter first tried helping the tottering regime while pressing it for reforms. On the eve of the revolution early in 1979, he appealed for intervention by an Organization of American States military force that would preserve the peace and install an acceptable (non-Sandinista) government. The OAS rebuffed him, and the Sandinistas took power. Washington then tried accommodation, granting $100 million in aid, along with sermons about good behavior. As Carter's term ended, his government was accusing Nicaragua of playing godfather to left-wing rebels in neighboring El Salvador.

A rebellion had been underway in El Salvador, one of the harshest regimes in the hemisphere, since the mid-1970s. Though paying little attention, Washington at first backed the government. It continued aid when a reformist military junta seized power, despite the junta's failure to prevent assassination squads from murdering thousands of civilians. By 1980 Carter saw the problem as preventing "another Nicaragua" and continued the search for moderates worthy of sponsorship. After the brutal killing of four American churchwomen, he cancelled aid to the Salvadoran regime but soon restored it when rebels launched an offensive designed to gain victory before Reagan took office. Carter bequeathed Reagan a policy of supporting almost anyone who would fight leftist rebels.

Carter's administration died amid the agonies of the Iranian hostage crisis. The seizure of the hostages in November 1979 came shortly after he decided to admit the exiled Shah into the United States for medical treatment. This enraged Iranian militants, who had been demanding that the Shah return home to stand trail, and sparked the demonstrations that led to the capture of the embassy in Tehran. Pulled in different directions by advisers, Carter alternated between patient negotiation and acts of toughness, including freezing Iranian assets in the United States and other economic sanctions. Finally Carter broke dip-

Pressure to free the US hostages in Iran grew in 1980 (above). Although a few had been released in 1979 (below), the bulk did not go free until the day President Carter quit office in January 1981.

lomatic relations with Iran and expelled all its nationals from the United States, among them thousands of students.

When none of these measures produced results, nor any of the puny efforts of allies and international bodies, Carter in March 1980 ordered a military mission to try rescuing the hostages. The mission ended disastrously, with numerous American casualties, ruined and abandoned equipment, and the hostages even more securely under guard. Secretary Vance, who had opposed the rescue mission, resigned. Washington returned to quiet negotiations, aware now that events within Iran itself would probably dictate the timing of the hostages' release. With the help of able Algerian intermediaries, diplomacy finally succeeded in the last hours of Jimmy Carter's presidency, but not until Ronald Reagan had taken the oath of office.

Carter was undoubtedly sincere in his skepticism about the use of military force, his eagerness to break the mold of the cold war, his desire to accommodate the aspirations of third world nations, and his commitment to human rights. Although none of these ideas survived his four years in office, they spawned some of his most creditable efforts, including the Panama Canal treaty, Camp David, diplomatic relations with China, progress toward majority rule in Africa, and SALT II, which, though never ratified, the superpowers continued to observe.

Carter's defeats and the tarnishing of his victories resulted from lapses of mind and method. It was not only that he knew little history of the events he tried to direct. He also lacked any sense of the "ecology" of foreign policy, dealing separately with issues and oblivious to their relationships to one another. Thus, he asked the Soviets to accept his deep-cuts armaments proposal while haranguing them on human rights, and urged them to hurry along SALT II while he was opening formal ties with China. Often he and his advisers seemed unaware of the significance of what they were doing, failing for example to grasp the importance of reopening Middle East negotiations to Moscow in 1977, or of pushing the American-Soviet-Chinese relationship into unprecedented directions. Nor did Carter's team ever escape their reputation for clumsiness and policy zigzags, leaving in their wake a new term in the American political lexicon – "Carterization."

Finally, although Moscow also bears heavy responsibility, Carter helped produce the chilly US-Soviet relationship of the 1980s. Partly from ill luck, but also because of his own errors, Carter spurred the resurgence of the right wing in America. Failures with SALT and such fiascos as the one on the neutron bomb discredited arms control and the effort to forge a discriminating defense policy. The failure to arrive at a viable policy toward weaker nations paved the way for the Reagan administration's tougher line toward the third world. Carter unwittingly prepared the ground for President Reagan's nostalgia for American supremacy and the return to containment in an age when such old certainties would not suffice.

Reagan's Tough Stance

President Reagan entered office with strong convictions about American foreign policy. He intended not only to reverse the "decline" of American power, but, declaring the Vietnam War a "noble cause," to efface shame from government councils and have America "stand tall" again. Talk of limits would end. Reagan would task only Communist nations for human rights violations, while again embracing such old "friends" as Argentina and Guatemala. A rearmed United States would challenge the Russians and their minions wherever their mischief disturbed the world. Not interested in détente, the president sought the recapture of American supremacy.

Reagan also took office unburdened by previous study of foreign and military affairs. His repeated errors in press conferences kept the White House staff busy issuing "clarifications." After a 1982 trip to Latin America, he remarked, "Well, I learned a lot. . . . You'd be surprised. They're all individual countries." His ignorance most notoriously concerned nuclear issues, such as his apparent belief that submarine-launched nuclear missiles could be recalled once fired. Reigning but not governing, he little understood what arms control advisers were deciding and negotiating in his behalf. Almost three years into his term, he offhandedly noted his recent discovery that 70 per cent of the Soviets' strategic missiles were land-based (the very force his officials insisted the Russians must radically reduce). Because of his own failure to master basic information and his olympian approach to the presidency, major policies actually took shape below him, but only after bureaucratic infighting of which he remained unaware.

Reagan's ignorance would have mattered less had he surrounded himself with seasoned advisers. Among the least experienced to gain senior places were former California judge William Clark, for a time Reagan's national security adviser; his successor, marine officer Robert McFarlane; Secretary of Defense Caspar Weinberger, a Washington veteran but not in defense or foreign policy; political scientist Jeane Kirkpatrick, ambassador to the United Nations; two young hard-line assistant secretaries, Richard Perle in Defense and Richard Burt at State; and Reagan's second secretary of state, George Shultz, an academic economist known for skill in labor talks and for bureaucratic subtlety during earlier, non-diplomatic, service in Washington.

Some of the heftiest credentials were held by Reagan's first secretary of state, General Alexander Haig, a former assistant to Kissinger, chief of the White House staff, and NATO commander. Observers counted on Haig to steady the administration, but in office he repeatedly shot himself in the foot. The press ridiculed his swagger and butchered English: the United States, he said, was entering the "vortex of cruciality," and legislators investigating the CIA were "castrating our eyes and ears around the globe." Worse, his combative struggle to monopolize foreign policy decisions offended both Reagan and the "team players" around him, and Haig was fired in June 1982. The one thing this group of advisers never delivered on was Reagan's promise of a "coherent" foreign policy speaking with "one voice."

The Reagan administration quickly displayed a tough face, as though the normally genial president had adopted the slogan, "No more Mr Nice Guy." If economies of the southern hemisphere were ailing, Washington would offer capitalist gospel as medicine and reject whining about the duties of the industrialized nations. If a third world state chose to taunt Uncle Sam, Reagan intended to retaliate, not apologize for imagined sins. Carter had supported the lengthy international Law of the Seas negotiations that would require rich nations to share the wealth from future seabed mining. Reagan, on the other hand, refused in 1982,

General Alexander Haig (below left, with the president) was accused of lacking diplomatic flair and lasted less than 18 months as Secretary of State. He was succeeded by George Shultz (below) in 1982.

White House

Camera Press

FIGHT FOR THE FALKLANDS

The Falklands War of 1982 is proof that surprise never lies far below the surface in world affairs. The Falklands Islands, called the Malvinas by Latin Americans, lie southeast of Argentina, within reach of the chill winds of Antarctica. As early as the 1830s, lowly American diplomats had found themselves tangled in disputes of ownership over the Falklands, claimed by both London and Buenos Aires. The dispute never ended. Britain and Argentina were still parleying on the matter through the 1970s, but Washington paid little notice, the issue seeming to have little relevance to US relations with Latin America. It had none at all to the East-West conflict that defined reality for the Reagan administration.

Unaware of the Falklands tinderbox, the new administration in 1981 began paying respectful court to Argentina, reversing Jimmy Carter's disapproval of the generals, admirals and policemen who had created one of the hemisphere's worst human rights records. Reagan's advisers banked on Argentina for support of their anti-Communist initiatives in Central America. United Nations Ambassador Jeane Kirkpatrick enjoyed close ties with Argentine leaders. Secretary of State Alexander Haig also seemed friendly. Thus, at the time Argentina suddenly invaded the Falklands in April 1982, its military rulers believed not only that Britain lacked the will to defend its possession, but that the United States would remain neutral at worst.

They were mistaken on both counts. Ten thousand miles from the Falklands, economic troubles had put Margaret Thatcher's Conservative government on the political ropes. Mrs Thatcher saw a way to revive her popularity while restoring the Union Jack to its rightful place. Denuding NATO naval defenses, units of the British fleet immediately set off on the long voyage to rid the Falklands of their impudent captors. In Washington, there was no question of supporting Buenos Aires, though neither did the Reagan administration immediately take sides with Britain.

As the British navy headed south, Secretary Haig launched a diplomatic shuttle, hoping to arrive at a formula that would hold the combatants apart without blows being struck. But the beribboned officers in Argentina would not agree to anything less than sovereignty over the Malvinas, while London resisted any device that resembled a promise to consider surrendering the islands later (although earlier negotiations had moved in this direction).

On May 30, 1982 Haig announced the failure of his mediation. Washington joined the Common Market nations in imposing sanctions on Argentina, offered London intelligence data and logistical help, and vainly asked other states in the hemisphere to unite against the invasion. Argentina was left to its own devices. They were woefully insufficient, and Britain recaptured the islands in June after both sides had suffered quite heavy naval losses.

Haig was soon out of office, in small part because he had so exposed himself to failure on the Falklands. Argentina's regime, broken, would fall soon. Thatcher's government, though soon facing hard questions about acting with excessive bloodiness against the invaders, experienced a renewed popularity. And, if only a little, some Americans and Britons enjoyed recollections of "the special relationship."

HMS Invincible *returns to England after the Falklands War. The USA supported Britain after Haig's attempt at mediation failed.*

Rex Features

The decision by Reagan to give military and economic aid to help the government of El Salvador defeat left-wing revolutionaries provoked demonstrations (left) and concern in Congress lest El Salvador become "another Vietnam." Many of those who supported the US commitment blamed Fidel Castro, the Cuban leader, for allegedly fanning the flames of revolt (above).

with only three other nations, to sign the completed pact.

All through 1981, Washington bristled with belligerence, its new leaders apparently yearning for an opportunity to "stand tall." Colonel Muammar el-Qaddafi's Libya offered a likely target, and Washington provoked an incident in August by ordering the Mediterranean fleet to show the flag in the Gulf of Sidra. Though the ships were in international waters, Qaddafi rose to the bait. Two Libyan jets attacked and were shot down sixty miles off the Libyan coast.

Closer to home, El Salvador struck Secretry Haig as another good spot for an American "win." Despite continued Salvadoran bloodletting (about 40,000 civilians were murdered from 1979 to 1984), Reagan's officials rushed to quash the left-wing rebellion, armed with UN Ambassador Jeane Kirkpatrick's case for the superior, if latent, virtues of "authoritarian" states such as El Salvador (and Chile and Argentina) compared to the ineradicable evils of Soviet or Cuban "totalitarianism." Ignoring local conditions, Haig threatened to "go to the source" against what the State Department called "a textbook case of Communist aggression." The president dismissed the inadequately zealous US ambassador and sent fifty-five army advisers to help the Salvadoran military.

But Reagan's popularity notwithstanding, the Vietnam Syndrome was alive and well. Americans feared "another Vietnam" and protest mounted. European allies also criticized United States policy. In the summer of 1981 Congress

capped at fifty-five the number of advisers Reagan could send to El Salvador and tied financial aid to improvements in human rights. Officials toned down their rhetoric, got the story off the evening news, and began pressing for democratic elections and a crackdown on the death squads. Washington's favored leader, José Napoleon Duarte, lost the 1982 elections to the far right wing but recouped to win the presidency in 1984. By the end of 1984, Duarte's government and an improving military had stalemated the rebels, who showed signs of falling out among themselves. By 1985 Reagan had apparently delivered on his pledge to stop the "Communists" in El Salvador without using American troops.

The prime target of Reagan's anti-radical passion were the Marxists of neighboring Nicaragua. Washington cut off aid to its government, ominously charging Managua with exporting revolution to El Salvador. The administration paid only lip service to negotiating bids from Nicaragua itself and from the "Contadora" group of Venezuela, Colombia, Panama and Mexico. Washington spurned compromise, demanding the democratization and deradicalization of the Nicaraguan regime. Though public statements remained ambiguous, what American policy makers wanted was clear: to topple the Sandinista regime, using CIA-financed, Nicaraguan counter-revolutionaries based in Honduras. When Congress climaxed efforts to restrict Reagan's unofficial war in 1984 and 1985 by banning

Camera Press

The US funded opponents of Nicaragua's Marxist rulers,
Daniel Ortega and Thomas Borge (above), and US
troops invaded Grenada (below) in 1983 to overthrow its
Marxist government.

The Research House

militry aid to the Contras, private funding from right-wing
sources in the United States and informal guidance from
the National Security Council filled the gap. The Contras
staged more aggressive campaigns in the summer and fall
of 1985. All the while, US fleets steamed just beyond the
horizons of Nicaragua's coastlines.

Nicaragua seemed certain that American forces themselves would attack, particularly after they suddenly
invaded Grenada in October 1983. In 1979 and 1980 the
Carter administration had already ostracized this pro-
Soviet regime, demanding an end to ties with Cuba,
refusing to receive its ambassador, and criticizing its
internal policies. Reagan kept up the pressure, and when an
even more radical regime came to power, Washington
decided to act. Though no model of military efficiency, the
successful use of force to rid the hemisphere of a Marxist
government sufficed for Washington's purposes. Defended
first as a mission to rescue American medical students on
the island, then as a response to pleas for action from other
states in the Caribbean, the invasion's primary purpose
was to show all interested parties – notably the Soviet
Union, Cuba and Nicaragua – that Reagan meant business.
Condemned elsewhere as an elephant-against-a-gnat operation, the invasion aroused great alarm in Havana and
Managua, if not Moscow.

Cold War with the Russians

President Reagan claimed that the Soviet Union was a
mortal enemy, but his cautious behavior irritated hard-line
supporters. They relished his harsh, cold war rhetoric,
especially in 1983 when he called the Soviet Union an "evil
empire," the "focus of evil in the modern world." Given his
rhetoric, however, some of Reagan's actions were puzzling.
Thus, in March 1981, while throwing verbal bombs at the
Kremlin, he lifted Carter's grain embargo against the
Russian economy (a "basket case," according to advisers
who hoped to bankrupt it in the arms race). After Warsaw
cracked down on the popular Solidarity movement in late
1981, Reagan's tepid sanctions (relaxed in 1984) harmed the
Polish people more than either their military government or
its Russian overseers. A tough anti-Soviet administration
allowed wheat sales to the Russians but not the Poles. In
1982, still trying to target the Kremlin for punishment,
Reagan's sanctions misfired again. This time he strong-
armed America's NATO allies to cut off loans and equipment sales for a giant gas pipeline being built into western
European energy markets from the far reaches of the Soviet
Union. Haig's resistance to these sanctions helped get him
dismissed, leaving his successor. George Shultz, to iron out
a formula that finally allowed Reagan to relent.

In the late summer of 1983, Shultz and Reagan faced
another "opportunity" to confront the Soviet Union when its

airmen shot down a Korean airliner after it had violated Russian airspace. Why the plane strayed from its course is still uncertain, but the president and his secretary of state did not pause to sift evidence before condemning the Soviets as brutal murderers. A ban on landing rights in the USA for Aeroflot, the Soviet airline, was the only substantive punishment, but the Russians angrily reacted to Washington's denunciations, increasing the harassment of dissidents and boycotting the 1984 Los Angeles Olympics. American conservatives had wanted stronger action. As one of them, Midge Decter, had written in 1982: "I think if Reagan were not in office now, he'd be leading the opposition."

Those who wanted Reagan to make a greater effort to negotiate with the Russians outnumbered his conservative critics. The president pleaded that talk was not easy with a government that had four leaders in five years: Brezhnev died in November 1982, Andropov in February 1984, and Chernenko in March 1985. Once a young, healthy Mikhail Gorbachev took power, a summit conference was quickly scheduled for November 1985. Meanwhile, for whatever reasons, a great deal of time passed before Reagan, anticipating the 1984 election, began edging toward a US-Soviet dialogue. By then it was difficult to see what the years of anti-Soviet vitriol had accomplished. To paraphase Theodore Roosevelt, Reagan never spoke softly, he built an ever-bigger stick, but he never seemed eager to hit anyone with it.

Though cautious in dealing directly with the Soviet Union, the Reagan administration usually acted elsewhere as though Moscow deserved blame for virtually all world problems. Africa was no exception. Viewing the continent through a cold war prism, American officials saw strategic advantage in good relations with Somalia, Kenya, the Sudan and Zaire. They kept pressing Angola to send the troublesome Cuban troops home but also tried wooing the Angolans from Moscow by nudging South Africa to free neighboring Namibia.

The most explosive African issue was the fate of South Africa itself. Washington adopted the policy of "constructive engagement," an effort to protect its strategic and economic interests by amicably persuading South Africa to make peace with its neighbors, free Namibia when circumstances (the Cubans leaving Angola) warranted, and begin dismantling apartheid, its system of separating the races. A target of moral criticism, "constructive engagement" had nonetheless pushed a Namibian settlement closer to reality and facilitated better relations between South Africa and neighboring black states when crisis struck in 1985. Unprecedented acts of dissent in South Africa led to hundreds of blacks being killed by security forces. The readiness of Congress to issue sanctions against Pretoria forced Reagan to issue his own, milder ones, in September 1985.

After some hesitation, Reagan's anti-Sovietism also dic-

tated policy toward China. Having denounced Carter's "abandonment" of Taiwan, Reagan at first hinted at a reversal of the 1978-79 accords with China, producing a crisis in American-Chinese relations. When his experts convinced him that good ties with China meant bad news for Moscow, Reagan in 1982 started courting China so eagerly than an alarmed Beijing held him off, deciding to exploit America-Soviet hostility by repairing its own relations with Moscow. Still eager to increase the Kremlin's misery, Reagan in an April 1984 visit to China approved the sale of equipment of potentially military use to the Chinese and allowed American firms to build nuclear energy plants in China. When his speeches veered into anti-Soviet diatribes, however, his hosts censored them from public consumption. After the visit China turned sharply against United States policy in Central America, Africa and other third world areas.

In the Middle East the Reagan administration tried to cobble a "strategic consensus" uniting Israel, Egypt, Saudi Arabia and others against Russian expansionism. Neglecting local issues and the Camp David process, especially after the assassination of Sadat in 1981 and Israel's pullout from the Sinai in 1982, Washington seemed sleepily unaware of the need for new initiatives. Through most of 1981, American officials were fighting to carry out a huge sale of military hardware to Saudi Arabia, succeeding only after alienating Israel and irritating Congress.

US marines go ashore at Beirut in August 1982 as part of a peace-keeping force. In October that year, 239 Americans were killed by Moslem bombs in the city.

US Navy

While this struggle unfolded; while Reagan focused on his economic program; and while Secretaries Haig, promoting anti-Soviet strategic ties with Israel, and Weinberger, pushing Israel for more concessions, fought for control of policy, the Middle East drifted once again into war. Tel Aviv staged raids deep into Lebanon in reprisal for Palestinian attacks on the Israeli population. In late 1981 when Israel annexed the Golan Heights, dominating the plain to Damascus, an angry and reawakened Reagan administration imposed sanctions and aborted a new agreement for strategic cooperation against the Soviet Union. Yet when Israel invaded Lebanon in the summer of 1982, Begin and Israeli Defense Minister Ariel Sharon thought they had Haig's blessing. At first hesitant, Washington fell in with Israel's decision to march north to Beirut and throw the PLO out of Lebanon for good. After US marines had temporarily entered Beirut to help evacuate the embattled PLO, Reagan on September 2, 1982, put the Israelis back on the defensive by proposing a general Middle East settlement featuring negotiation of a Palestinian "homeland" on the West Bank and Gaza Strip, to be federated with Jordan.

Events quickly overtook Reagan's peace plan. In mid-September, Lebanon's Christian president, allied with Israeli interests, was assassinated, prompting Sharon's forces to occupy Moslem West Beirut. Israeli units then admitted allies of the late president to refugee camps in search of the assassins, leading to a massacre of several hundred Palestinians. As indignation thundered over Sharon and Israel, US marines came ashore in another multinational force to keep the peace. The Americans repeatedly took sniper fire in their vulnerable bivouac near the airport. They found themselves defending an unviable, Christian-dominated government against a growing wave of Moslem hostility. Their mission climaxed tragically when a Moslem suicide raid in October 1983 bombed the barracks, killing 239 marines. The American public clamored for vengeance but also for withdrawal. Reagan abruptly took the marines out early in 1984, no longer defining Lebanon as a "vital" interest.

The marines' slaughter, along with other terrorist acts against Americans, especially in the Middle East, provoked visions of retaliation in Washington, followed shortly by frustration at the dilemmas of reprisal. That Reagan often equated any armed rebellion with terrorism made the discovery of solutions no easier. He swallowed his chagrin in June 1985 when – denying throughout that Washington would ever parley with terrorists – American officials talked for two weeks to gain the release of thirty-nine Americans taken to Beirut by Shiite Moslems from a hijacked TWA airliner. Reagan was lucky in gaining the hostages' release so soon but could take credit, however reluctantly, for refusing to order acts of indiscriminate retaliation.

According to officials, Washington should not have met such difficulty in Beirut once the United States had rebuilt its military forces. Reagan brought to the White House an unclear military strategy but a determination to launch such a buildup and an expectation of immediate diplomatic dividends. Congress granted enough of his five-year $1.6 trillion program to make impressive gains in the US arsenal, restoring the B-1 bomber and neutron bomb programs, speeding work on the "stealth" bomber and cruise missiles, and laying the keels for dozens of new naval vessels. But Congress persistently spurned or cut back requests for the MX missile, viewing it as a provocative weapon unless based invulnerably.

The Nuclear Arms Debate

On nuclear issues generally, Reagan and his advisers often disturbed both domestic and foreign observers. Early in Reagan's first term, loose talk about abandoning mutual deterrence strategy, and preparing for a "protracted" nuclear war in which the United States would "prevail," aroused nervous tremors in NATO and reinvigorated the large peace movement in western Europe.

Arms control had fallen into disfavor among conservatives, including Reagan. However, when Carter had agreed in December 1979 to deploy 572 "theatre" weapons in Europe to respond to the buildup of Soviet SS-20 missiles targeted on western Europe, he also pledged to try negotiating a settlement of the issue with Moscow. Reagan appeared in no hurry to resume these talks, first held in October-November 1980. As the date of American deployment neared, vast protest demonstrations broke out in Germany, Britain and Italy. NATO governments, which had first demanded the missiles, now shook in indecision while Washington, initially cool to the whole project, insisted on deployment as a test of NATO unity. "We don't care if the goddamn things work or not," an American official would tell his staff in 1983. "After all, that doesn't matter unless there's a war. What we care about is getting them in." When the president finally felt compelled to act, he showed more interest in seizing the propaganda initiative than achieving a settlement. In a November 11, 1981 speech he proposed the "zero-option": no new American missiles in return for dismantling the nearly 600 Soviet intermediate missiles installed over the years. A public relations triumph, the speech got talks going again, but Reagan's unclear instructions and bureaucratic combat in Washington handicapped Paul Nitze's delegation in Geneva.

This pattern was repeated on the strategic missile issue. Quietly agreeing to observe the unratified SALT II accord so long as the Russians reciprocated, Reagan, in the words of Raymond Garthoff, was "flagrantly uninterested" in negotiating a new treaty. Talks might derail his rearmament program. Again, however, he found himself pushed in directions he opposed. Advocates of a "freeze" on building,

testing or deploying nuclear missiles gained wide following in the public, 57 per cent of which favored the freeze in a March 1982 poll. Moreover, Congress refused funds for the MX missile without negotiations that might eliminate the need for the weapon. Reagan again sought public relations gains, on May 9, 1982, proposing a new round of discussions, which would be called START for strategic arms reduction. Damning past accords for not moving toward disarmament, he proposed massive cuts in land-based missiles, feared for their accuracy and "first-strike" capability. Discussions were underway by mid-year, but again with United States officials still wrestling to produce a clear negotiating position.

Neither set of talks went well. Soviet negotiators offered major concessions on the intermediate-range missile issues, but the United States would not bite. In July 1982 when Nitze and his counterpart assembled a compromise settlement during an unofficial "walk in the woods," both Washington and Moscow repudiated it. As the talks entered their second year in mid-1983, Washington still believed the prospect of actual deployment would cause the Russians to submit to American demands. Bureaucratic warfare and Reagan's lax leadership left the United States virtually without a position at the START conference. A blue-ribbon advisory commission hardly helped the interagency contest over policy, but did puzzlingly endorse putting MXs in old silos on the theory that the much-bruited "window of vulnerability" had been closed.

Further complicating START was Reagan's sudden insistence in March 1983 on producing a gargantuan defense system against Russian missiles, quickly dubbed "Star Wars." With one stroke, he seemed to jettison the doctrine of deterrence and abrogate the 1972 United States-Soviet treaty banning large missile-defense systems. The Soviets reacted angrily, not mollified by the president's casual

promise to share the necessary technology. However skeptical that such a system could be built, Moscow feared even the possibility of a hostile America hurling first-strike weapons from behind a shield against retaliation.

START floundered in any case because American terms were flatly unacceptable to the Soviets. A Soviet general remarked in 1983, "You want to solve *your* vulnerability problem by making *our* forces vulnerable," an accurate view of Washington's demand that Moscow eliminate two-thirds of its land-based ICBMs, the heart of its nuclear force, while leaving the United States free to develop the MX, the B-1 bomber, the new Trident submarine missile, and a wide array of cruise missiles.

In November 1983 the United States deployed its first NATO intermediate missiles. As they had threatened to do, the Russian delegations walked out of both arms control conferences. The United States had made the 1979 NATO decision stick against heavy pressure from the Russians, who also suffered a propaganda defeat by leaving the negotiating table. Washington, however, had won only

"Armaments kill daily" is the message of a rally in Bonn (right). Peace movements grew in the 1980s as a result of nuclear rivalry and NATO's deployment of missiles such as Pershing (below).

public relations victories in return, and those of temporary duration. By the end of 1984, over a hundred of the new NATO missiles were in place, along with more Soviet SS-20s. Public pressure to try again was building, and after Reagan's reelection Secretary Shultz and Foreign Minister Gromyko organized new "umbrella" talks in Geneva, covering both intermediate and strategic forces.

By mid-1985 Reagan had fulfilled his promises to restore US military strength and stir the embers of American pride. Neither the defense buildup nor neo-nationalism, however, could translate into major foreign policy achievements. Nor were they without severe costs. Americans paid for the defense program with lacerated social programs and staggering budget deficits. Their "new patriotism" often ignored both logic and history. Reagan's greatest "victories" were the deployment of NATO's theatre missiles, which shook the alliance without alerting the chances of war, and the invasion of Grenada, which, though popular on the island itself, ignored the miseries that would spawn a Marxist revolution in the first place.

In Central America, Reagan could claim by 1985 that he had turned the tide in El Salvador and set Nicaragua in its place. But what directions Central America would take, and what role the United States would play later, remained unclear. The weakness of poor nations in the 1980s made them less troublesome to the United States than before, but their problems remained. Even the military spending campaign had outworn its welcome with the American public by 1985. Nor had the new insistence on American virtue and Soviet evil produced coherent policy. Thus, as Reagan continued opposition to restoring the military draft, he gladly sold grain to the "evil empire."

At the 1985 Geneva summit, President Reagan and the new Soviet leader, Mikhail Gorbachev, established a friendly personal relationship – but the political differences remained profound.

A Lack of Coherence

A decade of foreign policy since Vietnam had produced few dramatic changes. United States-Soviet relations in 1985 were difficult, sometimes hostile – as in 1975. Reagan's administration jockeyed for advantage in relations with the Chinese, if with less subtlety than Kissinger. Neither Kissinger and Ford, Carter nor Reagan had been able to do anything that actually promised an end to the nuclear arms race, Reagan least of all. All three administrations experienced frustration as allies asserted both their autonomy and their need for protection under the United States' nuclear umbrella. All three sought to resolve the historic conflicts of the Middle East, the late-20th century graveyard of reason. None could find the formula for "moderate" solutions to third world crises. Nor could they overwhelm the vagaries of public opinion and assertive Congresses, or discipline their bureaucracies. American foreign policy seldom achieved the coherence required for a dangerous world increasingly resistant to Washington's will.

True, foreign policy problems were often created by other nations. In the Middle East, for example, issues were ancient, desperate and intractable. The rest of the world, resenting America's omnipresence, sometimes inconsistently worried that Uncle Sam was less than omnipotent. The Ford, Carter and Reagan administrations inherited from their predecessors basic ideological postures and appalling involvement in superpower armaments rivalry.

The justified complaint of sensible Americans, and reasonable allies, was not that the White House had failed to solve every crisis round the globe. It was that the policy makers too often appeared to act without continuity, foresight or insight. The situation of the world in the late 20th century called for world leadership of the utmost skill and sagacity. Anything less might well be fatal.

Chapter 3

THE ECONOMIC LANDSCAPE

In the mid-1970s the world economy experienced its most serious crisis since the Depression of the 1930s. The impact on the United States was considerable. Steel and automobile plants went into varying degrees of decline and unemployment levels rose. But the rapid growth of cities such as Houston testified to the new importance of energy, high technology and service industries, while women entered the workforce in ever-increasing numbers. Whole sectors of the economy were deregulated by the government. The new economic climate forced major changes and had far-reaching consequences that affected every citizen.

Rust Bowl and Silicon Valley

The decade 1975-85 witnessed far reaching changes in the landscape and management of the American economy. The belching smokestacks of steel mills from Lackawanna, New York, to Youngstown, Ohio, – symbols of America's old industrial might – became eerily silent relics of a past industrial age. Many high wage, heavily unionized, out-dated American steel mills were forced out of business by the thrusting competition of more modern plant in Europe, Japan and newly industrialized countries from Brazil to Taiwan.

The once all conquering American automobile industry, a colossus which strode the globe, was forced into retrenchment by the foreign challenge. Detroit became a pale shadow of its former self. The Chrysler Corporation brushed with bankruptcy and was brought back from the dead with US government assistance in 1980-81. Satellite car towns like Flint, Michigan, that once boomed to the sound of the assembly lines, became industrial wastelands – testimony to the movement of car jobs away from the industrial North-East and Mid-West to the thrusting right-to-work, lower-tax Sunbelt states of Oklahoma and Tennessee in addition to the automobile-hungry market of California.

General Motors, that ultimate symbol of thriving American business, was driven into partnership with the upstart Japanese firm Toyota to make its cars more saleable and competitive. In its anxiety to maintain a technological edge the company under the guiding hand of its chairman of the early 1980s, Roger E. Smith, plunged headlong into the new worlds of data processing and aerospace. It devoted vast cash reserves to buy companies such as Hughes Aircraft in the hope it could marry Hughes's advanced production techniques to the industrial archeology of the internal combustion engine.

While industrial cities like Gary, Indiana, on the banks of Lake Michigan, watched their industrial greatness drain away other boom towns like Houston, Texas, prospered on the back of the surge in growth in energy, high tech and service industries. From the crowded banks of Route 128 in Massachusetts to the high tech Mecca of Silicon Valley, Americans flocked to new jobs in computer and information industries. Tall chimneys, blue overalls and satanic mills gave way to tinted glass and steel, white coats and the well manicured bright green grass verges which surround the new wave factories.

The nation's highways have become monuments to the service chains where millions of Americans now work. Women entering the workforce in ever greater numbers over the last decade may be photographed working in the coalmines but have, more often than not, found jobs serving

UPI-Bettmann Newsphotos/BBC Hulton Picture Library

Texaco

behind the counter in McDonalds or assembling microchips at Hewlett Packard. The freeways have become homes to accounting chains and medical centers, computer software firms and lawyers as well as the gas stations and restaurants that always formed part of their scenery.

Economic Turbulence

The changes in America's industrial base over the last decade have not occurred in isolation. They reflect the deep seated shifts which have taken place in the structure of the international economic environment and the United States'

The hefty increase in oil prices sent the economy into steep decline. When supplies became short, long lines at gasoline stations were common (below). The recession struck at the heart of the motor industry. Opposite: A worker laid off from Ford in Detroit applies for unemployment benefit.

financial structure. The American and international economies went on a roller coaster ride in the aftermath of the 1973 oil price shock. The 1970s were a decade of economic turbulence unprecedented in modern times. Oil prices surged as supplies became uncertain for the West as a result of firstly the Yom Kippur War of October 1973 and later the fall of the Shah of Iran in January 1979. Inflation in the United States surged, the prime interest rate – the key rate on which many commercial banks base their charges – moved into uncharted territory at 21.5 per cent in 1980. The US dollar first collapsed in value in late 1979 and then rose to new record heights against the currencies of the United States' trading partners in early 1985.

Against this tumultuous background many of the concepts used to guide American economic policy in earlier decades were discarded. The demand-management policies of John Maynard Keynes which had guided the United States through the smooth years of prosperity in the 1950s and 1960s became discredited. Politicians looked for new ideas and new gurus. Among those economists to capture the national mood was Milton Friedman, who made a

simple connection between the quantity of money circulating in the economy and inflation.

"Inflation is primarily a monetary phenomenon, produced by more rapid increase in the quantity of money than output. The behavior of the quantity of money is the senior partner; output, the junior partner," wrote Professor Friedman and his wife Rose Friedman in their bestselling volume *Free to Choose* in 1980. The Friedmanite theories of "monetarism" reached their peak of acceptance in 1979 when Paul Volcker, chairman of the American central bank, the Federal Reserve Board, publicly embraced them. By the end of the 1970s virtually every Western government and the world's central banker, the International Monetary Fund, had in large part come to accept Friedmanite principles. Wall Street and other financial communities treated the weekly money supply statistics, then published every Friday by the Federal Reserve, as holy writ.

But while the monetarism of the late 1970s provided a way of dealing with the menace of inflation and the threat of hyperinflation, it was seen by optimists such as Ronald Reagan as the economics of frugality and despair rather than hope. In the thoughts of the "supply-side" economists thrust into the limelight by Reagan during his 1980 campaign, and during his first term, America rediscovered

Passengers holding Air Florida tickets await further news after hearing that the airline had filed for bankruptcy, a casualty of deregulation.

UPI-Bettmann Newsphotos/BBC Hulton Picture Library

the economics of hope. While Reagan's administration would include disciples of Professor Friedman, notably Dr Beryl Sprinkel who served in the Treasury and as chairman of the Council of Economic Advisers at the White House, monetarism was pushed aside by a new school of incentive economics. With supply-side economics Americans could have it all, Reagan successfully argued during his victorious 1980 campaign: lower taxes, greater growth and large dollops of funding to rebuild what was perceived as America's declining military might.

Supply-side economics was very much the creature of California. It received its first public expression on June 6, 1978 when the voters of the state gave their approval to Proposition 13 – a populist measure proposed by tax reformer Howard Jarvis to reduce property taxes in the state. The revolution promoted by Jarvis spread rapidly across the country and found intellectual expression in the ideas of Arthur Laffer, an economist at the University of Southern California, whose famous "Laffer Curve" was said to prove that it was possible to cut taxes and increase revenues at one and the same time because of the growth which would be generated through the incentive effect of tax cuts.

Laffer's ideas were given popular expression in the work of George Gilder, whose 1981 book *Wealth and Poverty* was to prove a blueprint for reform of economic policy and the welfare system in the early 1980s. Gilder argued that "Welfare now erodes work and family and thus keeps poor people poor." His ideas gained political support during the tenure of David Stockman at the Office of Management and Budget between 1981 and 1985. Laffer's supply-side ideas found legislative expression in the Kemp-Roth Bill, written by Representative Jack Kemp of New York and Senator William Roth of Delaware, which formed the basis for the Reagan administration's epoch-making 1981 tax cut – the single most important event of the early 1980s.

Deregulating the Economy

Also in the campaign against big government embraced by presidents Jimmy Carter and Ronald Reagan were a series of steps towards deregulation of the economy. For years, it was argued, the heavy hand of government in a range of industries from airlines to telecommunications, from trucking to finance, had curtailed competition and deprived the consumer of the benefits of the market system. The first of the industries to be fully deregulated on Capitol Hill, through an alliance between Senator Edward Kennedy and the Carter White House, was the airlines in 1978. The results were dramatic. A series of new discount airlines, unencumbered by entrenched route structures, with names like Air Florida, People Express, Republic and Piedmont, challenged the traditional giants such as Pan American

World Airways and American Airlines, forcing them to cut both domestic and international fares.

The result of cutprice competition among the airlines was a severe shakeout. Traditional airlines found their profit margins crushed and the weaker ones were forced into bankruptcy. On the lucrative transatlantic route an early cut price pioneer, Laker Airways, collapsed in 1979; its demise was later followed by the "Big Orange" Braniff. Other formerly profitable airlines like Pan American and Eastern found the ruthless competition hard going and had to pare back routes and trim employee benefits to survive. Even some of the architects of the scheme, such as Professor Alfred Kahn, who served the Carter administration in a variety of economic advisory posts, were to argue later that deregulation in the airlines had gone too far.

However, by now Washington had the deregulation bug and the supply-side minded Reagan administration saw it as an important weapon in the crusade against big government. The crucial breakup of American Telephone and Telegraph (AT&T) in 1983 both opened up the long distance telephone service to competition and pitted two giants of America's high-tech revolution against each other. AT&T's Bell Laboratories quickly entered the market for personal computers, directly challenging International Business Machines (IBM) on its own turf. IBM and other high-tech companies moved in on the telecommunications industry, forging links with AT&T rivals such as the MCI Corporation.

Deregulation also became the watchword in the financial services industry, which had been kept under tight federal control since the 1930s, when the main concern had been to safeguard the banking and financial system after the traumas of the Great Depression. Over the last decade, however, the traditional barriers in financial services rapidly came down. Savings and loans institutions moved into banking; large banks such as Bank of America moved into stockbroking through the acquisition of companies such as discount brokers E.S.Schwab; retailing conglomerates such as Sears powered their way into investment banking and stockbroking; American Express became a force on Wall Street; and the rules and regulations which once prevented banks from crossing state lines came tumbling down.

As in the airline and telecommunications industries it was not a smooth transition. Savings and Loans had trouble in adjusting to their new roles, and many ran into difficulty. In two states, Ohio and Maryland, the problems of the Savings and Loans became a national story after their respective governors, Richard Celeste in Ohio and Harry Hughes in Maryland, both Democrats, were forced to call the first "bank holidays" since the Great Depression in order to organize rescue operations. In Chicago, America's largest lender to big corporations, Continental Illinois – which had expanded rapidly without a retail deposit base – was the subject of the biggest financial rescue in history when the Federal Deposit Insurance Corporation was forced to seize control to restore confidence in 1983. Ironically, the problems in the banking system actually helped to speed the process of deregulation. States, which historically had sought to preserve the independence of their finanical systems, welcomed interlopers from New York and California with open arms when institutions in their own states became overstretched in the more open financial system.

Decline in Manufacturing

The takeover fever which characterized the decade 1975-85 was not simply a bout of "speculative froth." It was a reflection of profound changes in the profile and shape of the American economy. "For much of the last 120 years, manufacturing led the growth of the American economy," observed the team of economists at Data Resources Inc in their landmark 1984 report on the state of US industry. During the years after the completion of the railroads and the electricity grid much of America's economic growth, innovation and capital investment went into the basic manufacturing industries: steel, machinery, automobiles, appliances, chemicals and most recently computers. In addition there was more modest growth in textiles, chemicals, clothing, paper and food processing. Indeed, in the period until 1966 manufacturing substantially outpaced the creation of wealth in the economy as a whole.

The dominance of manufacturing began to fade in the early 1970s. By 1982 there had been dramatic declines in the productive capacity of many of the nation's most important industries. The sharpest setbacks were in cotton fabrics and leather, which plummeted some 25 per cent. The steel industry – the engine of the American economy – dropped 16 per cent in its contribution to total manufacturing output. Other important industries including motor cars, appliances, television and radio and non-ferrous metals struggled to stand still. Slower growth, of less than 10 per cent, was recorded in petroleum products, shipbuilding, railroad equipment, mobile homes, lumber, tires and metal cans.

Nowhere is America's manufacturing decline more starkly reflected than in the steel industry. The years of the Carter and Reagan administrations were marked by instability in the domestic economy and a roller-coaster ride for the dollar which left big steel in dire trouble. The industry's plight provided the most graphic illustration of the country's changing economic landscape. It was two days after Christmas in 1982 that economics caught up with Bethlehem Steel's plant at Lackawanna, New York, after 82 years of protion. The plant along the banks of Lake Erie, which had once employed 22,000 workers, was closed without consultation, putting 6,000 of the remaining 7,300 members of the United Steel Workers union out of work.

Symptomatic of the steel crisis, the Youngstown plant in Ohio stands silent and deserted after closure toward the end of 1977 with the loss of 5,000 jobs.

UPI-Bettmann Newsphotos/BBC Hulton Picture Library

The Lackawanna closure was the latest in a string of steel casualties in the late 1970s and early 1980s which reads like a memorial to the booming days of American manufacturing industry. In 1982 McLouth Steel, the medium sized Detroit manufacturer, went bankrupt. National Steel, desperate to be rid of the Weirton plant in West Virginia, sold it off to the workers. United States Steel closed plants from Fairfield, Alabama, to Youngstown, Ohio. Wheeling Pittsburgh – which poured resources into modernization – declared bankruptcy in 1985 in an effort to curtail the wages and benefits of its workers.

The closure of steel towns, grown prosperous on the furnaces and the rolling mills, can have a paralysing effect on their communities. In Lackawanna, for instance, 65 per cent of the city's revenues were drawn from taxes levied on Bethlehem Steel. The drab town which borders the steel plant has seen its population drift away, the numbers dropping from 30,000 to 20,000 over two decades. Towns such as Lackawanna in New York and Monessen in the desolate valley of the Monongahela River in Pennsylvania have died a slow death. Once thriving bars have long been shuttered up; gas stations and car dealers have long ago closed down and other service jobs have just faded away.

Bethlehem's Lackawanna plant, which occupied a 600-acre, three-mile long site on the shores of Lake Erie – some five miles from Buffalo – has become a symbol of industrial obsolescence. Because of the prohibitive costs of dismantling closed mills and furnaces, the plant has become a prime exhibit of industrial archaeology, spanning a period of 80 years from the heyday of the blast furnace to the advent of the "scrubber" – the atmospheric cleaning equipment required in the late 1970s to meet modern environmental standards.

The collapse of Lackawanna and plants like it throughout America's "Rustbelt" bear witness to the economic hardships of their time. In the late 1970s industry was forced to cope with double digit inflation, surging fuel bills and unprecedented financing costs. Although the sickly dollar made American goods competitive with the rest of the world, economic and financial circumstances were not conducive to increasing exports. Besides, the nation's high labor costs and outmoded plant and equipment made it a poor competitor with many of its major trading partners. In the early 1980s American steel producers first had to deal with the deepest recession since the 1930s in 1981-82, as Draconian measures were taken to reduce inflation, and then a surging dollar, which made imports more competitive and rendered it impossible to sell US steel abroad.

Thus the two key economic factors in the decline of the steel and other manufacturing industries in the last decade were poor growth rates and deteriorating international trade. Each of the seven recessions which America has experienced since the 1950s has led to an erosion of industrial production. There were three recessions in the decade under study here: November 1973 to March 1975, January 1980 to July 1980, and July 1981 to November 1982. Each took a severe toll on production, profits and investment. The speeded-up business cycle, together with its increased severity in recent years, damaged the ability of companies to make profits and therefore to modernize through new investment. With the notable exception of the boom year 1984, growth in the gross national product was falling, from a 3.7 per cent average rate in the years 1967 to 1973 to 2.2 per cent in the period 1974 to 1982.

International competition was the other factor which took its toll on American manufacturing. In 1965 just 4.3 per cent of the available goods for sale on the American market were imported. By 1980 this figure had surged to 13.5 per cent, and continued to rise strongly as the dollar soared in the early 1980s. Exports rose over the same 15-year period from 5.1 per cent of US factory shipments in 1965 to 10.7 per cent by 1980. But despite this rise the United States' overall share of world manufacturing was on a downward spiral and had fallen 15.2 per cent by 1980. In more recent years this trend has accelerated as the Japanese have succeeded in taking an increasing share of world markets.

These macro-economic factors combined with more localized conditions to produce the disasters of Lackawanna and Detroit. While investment in new plant and machinery was near the normal rate of the previous two decades during the period 1975 to 1985, investment by America's competitors such as Japan was much greater. Among the chief reasons for this were the relatively high cost of capital

in the United States and restrictive depreciation rules. It was not until the passage of President Reagan's Economic Recovery Act of 1981, which included generous new depreciation rules, that American firms were able to enjoy better investment prospects. By then, however, the nation's traditional manufacturing base had been so decimated it was of little use.

The New Growth Industries

The corollary of the decline of manufacturing industry throughout this period was the boom in service industries and high technology. As America became a more affluent society from the 1960s and disposable incomes rose, the pattern of consumer behavior changed. Initially consumers demanded more food, better clothes, housing and consumer durables. At even higher levels of income, service becomes more greatly valued. Consumers seek to take their food in restaurants rather than at home, the public requires longer years of education to cope with a more technologically complex society and to prepare for a higher quality of life. The consumer demands better health care and the social services sector of the economy becomes more important. Industry also looks to more sophisticated services ranging from legal and accounting to consulting, computing and technological. The increasing sophistication of the consumer and industry required a more information-orientated society. Hence the boom in communications and computers with the public looking for ever more mature hardware and ever better software.

As basic industry declined, manufacturing built around the booming service and high-tech sectors of the economy blossomed. The assembly and manufacture of electronic components from Route 128 in Massachusetts to Silicon Valley in California surged 129 per cent between the early 1970s and early 1980s. The production of plastics climbed 125 per cent, office equipment 87 per cent, communications equipment 59 per cent, chemical products 63 per cent and synthetic materials 77 per cent. Many of these growth-hungry sectors were built on the demands for better services and information.

The race to conquer new frontiers in space and the development of an increasingly modern defense policy, culminating with President Reagan's Strategic Defense Initiative research program, contributed to the rise of the high-tech sector. The first flight of the Space Shuttle in 1982 rekindled an interest in the space program not seen since the 1960s and the Herculean effort to get a man on the moon. Communications satellites were launched into space on the evening news, astronauts conducted repairs of equipment with jet packs on their backs, like characters from Buck Rodgers, while, down on the ground, ordinary Americans, searching for ever greater dollops of entertain-

ment and information, installed satellite dishes in their back gardens which enabled them to pick up dozens of television broadcasts from around the nation.

The development of the Space Shuttle, the first reuseable space craft, together with the development of a new generation of strategic weapons from the MX intercontinental missile to the B-1 strategic bomber, led to the expansion of new aerospace boom towns in California. The microchip spawned the exponential growth of towns like San Jose in the Silicon Valley, and the development of an advanced aerospace industry brought life to the Mojave Desert. Towns such as Palmdale, California, just a few miles from Edwards Air Force Base, where the shuttle made its first landing and the B-1 bomber was tested, grew out of the desert as the aerospace pioneers such as the Rockwell Corporation and McDonnell Douglas moved in. The rolling hills of sand and cactus gave way to sleek factories and rows of modern town houses for the tens of thousands of workers who moved to Palmdale, and communities like it, from around the country. For every crumbling Lackawanna there was a Palmdale to take its place.

The city which best represented America's second industrial revolution was Houston, Texas. In their 1982 book *The Deindustrialization of America* Barry Bluestone and Bennett Harrison argued that "Houston is what reindustrialization is all about. This exploding metropolis and cities like it have been able to attract billions of dollars of investment in

Expansion of the defense and space industries gave rise to aerospace boom towns such as Culver City, California, where Hughes Helicopters are located.

Hughes Helicopters

NASA

practically no time at all." Between 1971 and 1978, the authors noted, ninety-nine large firms moved into the city. This influx of firms meant that, despite the half-a-million new residents who flocked into the Texan city in the 1970s, unemployment rates remained below 4 per cent against a near double-digit jobless rate in many of the eastern industrial cities.

Houston's boom was initially based on the energy turmoil of the late 1970s and the early 1980s since most of the largest oil companies from Exxon to Texaco have head-quarters there. However, through its favorable tax struc-ture it also grabbed more than its fair share of the aerospace business – drawn by the Johnson Space Center – and semi-conductors too. Houston's populatioon increased some 45 per cent over the last ten years while Rustbelt cities such as St Louis saw a 27 per cent decline.

The speed of the transformation in the shape of American industry over the decade 1975 to 1985 can be directly related to changing economic conditions. Without the oil crisis and the energy mania it generated, Houston would have not been the boom town it became. Similarly, without the enormous fluctuations seen in the United States dollar over the period the decline in traditional manufacturing industry in cities such as St Louis would not have been so rapid. It was the fast changing economic scene which generated the shifting industrial landscape.

Texaco

Drilling for oil in Cook Inlet, Alaska. Huge oil price increases in the 1970s spurred the search for new local supplies in order to reduce costly imports.

Coping with the Oil Crisis

The oil crisis which afflicted the United States and the Western economies in the 1970s was clearly the most traumatic event of the period. It brought in its wake unprecedented inflation in modern times and led to in-flationary expectations which sent interest rates soaring. In 1975 the consumer prices index rose 7 per cent, reflecting the 1973-74 oil price shock. Inflation temporarily subsided in 1976 and 1977 before surging to 9 per cent in 1978 and 13.3 per cent in 1979. The Carter administration was forced to deal with the consequences of both the 1973-74 price hikes (in the wake of the Yom Kippur War) and the further oil price and supply disruption caused by the fall of the Shah of Iran. It adopted a two-pronged approach, involving energy conservation accompanied eventually by tighter fiscal and monetary policies.

The administration moved energy conservation to the top of the economic and political agenda in a policy switch which would make economic management considerably more easy for its successors. In an address to the nation on

The Space Shuttle Columbia rises into the early morning sky, January 1986. Although spending on space research has increased in recent years, technical problems have dogged the Shuttle program.

April 17, 1977 President Carter warned: "The energy crisis has not yet overwhelmed us, but it will if we do not act quickly. It is a problem we will not be able to solve in the next few years, and it is likely to get progressively worse through the rest of this century. Our decision about energy will test the character of the American people and the ability of the President and the Congress to govern this nation. This difficult effort will be the 'moral equivalent of war,' except we will be uniting our efforts to build and not destroy."

In 1973 when the oil crisis arose, the United States was importing some 35 per cent of its oil. When Jimmy Carter assumed office in 1977 this figure had risen to 50 per cent or nine million barrels of oil every day. The Carter plan led to the establishment of a new Department of Energy to take responsibility for energy policy, which at the time was being made by no less than 50 disparate agencies and departments spread through the federal government. It stressed conservation in both the home and business place, and sought to bring domestic oil prices up to international levels.

It was, however, a long-term policy which failed to halt the inflation sweeping through the economy. By requiring domestic producers of natural gas to charge more market-oriented prices the administration in effect added tempor-arily to the price spiral imported from abroad. Similarly, conservation was not simply a matter of lowering thermo-

MERGER MANIA

The turbulent economic conditions of the decade 1975 to 1985 brought with them a bout of "megamergers" which had the financial markets and the American public gasping for breath. Merger mania was nothing new: its early manifestations date back to the turn of the century as the American economy recovered from the depression of 1893.

What was remarkable about the mergers of 1975 to 1985, however, was their enormous size. It was the decade when the billion dollar merger became commonplace and the multibillion dollar deal almost routine. It was the decade in which one of the "Seven Sisters" of the oil industry, Texaco, gobbled up another, Gulf Oil, in a spectacular $13 billion deal at a time when no company, however large, was safe from predators. While the number of merger transactions remained relatively constant throughout the period at 2,000 to 2,500 a year, the size of the deals escalated as the decade progressed. The average annual reported value of mergers in the period 1981 to 1984 was some 48 per cent greater than the average of any four years in the late 1960s and early 1970s.

The fashions in mergers came in a series of waves. In the 1970s the oil giants, flush with cash, splurged their profits by buying into new industries. Mobil plunged into department stores, Exxon into office machines and Atlantic Richfield into mineral resources. But as the fat profits in oil were reduced in the energy glut of the early 1980s, it was the oil companies which found themselves the takeover targets.

In the food industry, takeovers became the norm as one household name swallowed another. In a lightning series of raids on its competitors between 1982 and 1984, General Foods bought Entenmann's baked goods, Monterey Cheese, Peacock ·Foods, pasta maker Ronzoni Foods and the bakery firm Oroweat Foods. The food industry had discovered economies of scale in consumer marketing and General Foods and other industry leaders such as Nabisco and Quaker Oats were not going to be left behind.

The media which reported with such glee on the big takeovers then found themselves surrounded. Rupert Murdoch, the boundlessly enterprising Australian publisher, having added the *New York Post* and *Chicago Sun Times* to his American empire, set his sights in the 1980s on creating his own television network. He first purchased six Metromedia stations

across the country and then went into the movie business with the takeover of Twentieth Century-Fox. CBS fended off Ted Turner's emergent cable television empire in a bitter battle as the American Broadcasting Corporation, fearful of an unfriendly bidder, sought shelter with the smaller Capital Cities Communications.

But the battle which attracted most attention was the fight for control of the Martin Marietta Corporation in the summer of 1982. What began with a raid by the ambitious businessman William Agee and his Bendix Corporation on the missile manufacturer Marietta ended in a dogfight, with Bendix the $1.9 billion eventual victim of Allied Corporation. Marietta, supported by the larger defense giant United Technologies, turned the tables on Agee, who was eventually forced to agree terms with the new player, Edward Hennessy of Allied Corporation. Because of the ruthless way in which the merger was fought it became known as the "Pac-Man" battle after a video game in which an open mouth swallows all obstacles in its path.

The battle for Martin Marietta was quickly followed by the emergence of a new breed of corporate raiders. Men like T. Boone Pickens, scourge of the oil companies, became national figures as they

T. Boone Pickens (above) epitomized the corporate raider of the 1980s, and Rupert Murdoch (below) expanded his media empire.

imposed their will on supposedly dauntless captains of industry. Pickens, the chairman of the small Amarillo based Mesa Petroleum, portrayed himself as a populist hero conquering the citadels of entrenched interests.

"I am the champion of the small stockholder," declared Mr Boone Pickens in March 1985. "Many American companies are hopelessly undervalued and I blame their management entirely." In a whirlwind series of deals, Pickens bought up stakes in a half-dozen major oil companies including such giants as Phillips, Cities Services, Superior Oil and Gulf – and then stood back as the bidding war broke out. When it was all over his company Mesa and its 750,000 shareholders were some $13 billion richer.

The corporate raiders led by Pickens and joined by other raiders such as New York financier Carl Icahn, the Anglo-French businessman Sir James Goldsmith and the Los Angeles tycoon Saul Steinberg, spread their net far beyond the oil industry. Icahn won a notorious battle for control of Trans World Airways against the airline magnate Frank Lorenzo of Texas Air. Sir James Goldsmith forced the St Regis Corporation into the arms of Champion International before fixing his gaze on a bigger prize, the paper concern Crown Zellerbach. Steinberg, meanwhile, gave Walt Disney a scare.

Wall Street lawyers specializing in takeover defenses found themselves in constant demand. "I get calls every day from some company president who says 'Help! We're being taken over'," one Wall Street lawyer told *Business Week* in March 1985. To protect themselves against raiders, companies put together so called "poison pills" and "shark repellants." These ranged from new share issues to "golden parachutes" for directors, both of which were designed to make it difficult for the raiders.

However, despite the enthusiasm for mergers, the decade produced mixed results. In the years 1980 to 1985 the number of divestitures – takeovers being undone – jumped some 29 per cent to a value of $29.4 billion. Big may have appeared beautiful, but it did not always work out that way. Mobil Oil had sunk $1.8 billion into buying Marcor Inc, owners of the department store chain Montgomery Ward, but the oil giant's profits from the retailer in nine years totalled a paltry $17 million. In 1985 Mobil announced that it was writing down the value of its store chain by $500 million and was putting Montgomery Ward back up for sale. This was just one among very many mergers which simply failed to live up to its promise.

*Congressmen Jack Kemp (above left) and William Roth
(above right) championed the big tax cuts of 1981.*

stats as the president implied in his exhortations to the nation. It required corporations to install sophisticated new equipment and motor manufacturers to invest in production lines for a new generation of more fuel efficient cars to supplant the gas guzzlers of old. These costs were inevitably passed on to the consumer, making inflation even worse.

To accommodate the economic disruption caused by the oil crisis and to keep the economy moving the Federal Reserve Board, then in the hands of President Carter's appointee, a Democratic businessman named G. William Miller, created money at a fast rate. With inflation surging and the money supply growing, foreign investors took a dim view of the American economy and its dependence on strategically vulnerable foreign oil supplies. They began to sell dollars. This imperative on the foreign exchanges and domestic bond markets forced an abrupt change of direction. It came in the shape of the looming six-feet seven-inch frame of Paul Volcker, the new incumbent in the Federal Reserve, who joined in the summer of 1979 after Miller was switched to the US Treasury.

On Saturday October 6, 1979, while official Washington and the White House were preoccupied with a Papal visit to the nation's capital, Volcker called correspondents to the Federal Reserve at 6pm that evening and put America on a new monetary standard. Inflation would be squeezed out of the economy by a tighter monetary policy to be exercised by monitoring bank reserves. Energy conservation and pay policy were simply not doing the job of restraining inflation. With prices rising at the alarming rate of 18 to 20 per cent in the early months of 1980, election year, even more Draconian action was called for.

In March 1980 President Carter, with the collaboration of the Federal Reserve, stiffened his resolve to beat back inflation with higher interest rates, direct controls on credit, including credit cards, and a fiscal package aimed at balancing the budget. As a result interest rates surged above 20 per cent and investment and production in the economy ground to a halt. By June 1980 the impact of the

Carter package on industry and employment was so severe that the president and his advisers were forced into another policy reversal in an effort to avoid an election debacle in November. The tough credit controls were removed and interest rates reduced.

But the battle against inflation had taken its toll. Economic policy zig-zags, the difficulty in achieving budget cuts, and disputes with Congress over energy policy had all created the impression of an administration which had lost control of economic policymaking. More seriously, however, over the longer run the uncertainty of inflation and high interest rates had created a climate in which the pace of America's manufacturing decline accelerated.

Reagan's Bold Approach

President Carter's record of economic mismanagement provided an easy target for the Republican presidential nominee Ronald Reagan in the 1980 election. Although Reagan's own optimistic brand of economic thinking had been labelled as "voodoo economics" by a primary opponent, George Bush, early in the election year, the upbeat message found a resonance among the American people. Reagan argued it was possible to have it all: lower taxes, a balanced budget and bigger defense spending.

The Reagan economic team decided to strike while the iron was hot. In March 1981 it announced a grandly confident program of tax cuts and domestic budget reductions. On the budget front the Reagan team sought to sweep away the array of social programs which had become part of the federal government since Lyndon Johnson's Great Society almost two decades earlier – leaving behind a "safety net" for the old, infirm and least well off. The budget also proposed a vast shift of resources from the domestic to the defense sector.

On the revenue side of the equation the Reagan team produced a comprehensive batch of tax reductions. Personal income tax rates would be cut by 25 per cent; the top rate of tax would be cut from 70 per cent to 50 per cent and a new formula for speedy depreciation of assets by American business was introduced in the hope of speeding new investment for American business. This attempt to encourage growth through bold tax reductions was dubbed "supply-side" economics. It was the antithesis of the demand management policies which American presidents had followed since the end of the Second World War. By stimulating more growth, the tax reductions would, it was claimed, generate new revenues and help pay for increased defense expenditure.

In the first dramatic seven months of the Reagan presidency the main elements of what the press came to call "Reaganomics" were put into place by a Congress determined to try something new after the failures of the Carter

years and spurred on by President Reagan's personal popularity. Herbert Stein, who served as chairman of the Council of Economic Advisers from 1972 to 1974, summed up Reaganomics in his 1984 study *Presidential Economics*.

Dr Stein wrote: "The 1981 tax legislation would reduce receipts by over $100 billion, or four per cent of the GNP, in fiscal year 1985. The President celebrated the budget as a great triumph. And up to a point it was. Three main items of the conservative agenda had been achieved in less than seven months – a big tax cut, a big increase in defense appropriations and an encouraging cut in non-defense spending. But one haunting, traditionally conservative message remained. Where was the money coming from?"

No sooner was the ink dry on the bill than the flaws in the Reagan program became apparent. The stock market fell, unemployment rose sharply and industrial production plunged. Far from tapping new growth resources the American economy was heading for its worst recession since the 1930s. While the level of inflation dropped sharply to 8.9 per cent in 1981, and to just 3.9 per cent in 1982, the unemployment rate rose from 7.5 per cent of the workforce in 1981 to a post-war peak of 10.6 per cent in November 1982. Accompanying the high unemployment was acute nervousness on the financial markets as a result of a federal budget deficit which soared toward $200 billion and an emerging problem for America's banking system as first Mexico and then other big debtor countries found they could no longer afford to make repayments on their mountain of international debt.

In 1983 and 1984 the fiscal stimulus provided by the Reagan cuts led to a reawakening of the economy. While the traditional industries such as steel continued to struggle, the Reagan tax cuts encouraged a strong increase in industrial investment, particularly by small and medium sized corporations. It was a boom era for the new high

technology computer companies such as Apple and Kaypro. The Reagan boost to defense spending provided new jobs in advanced weapons from the General Dynamics shipyards in Norfolk, Virginia, to the Rockwell International production line for the B-1B strategic bomber in California. As the deficits mounted, the jobless rate began to tumble to 8.1 per cent by the end of 1983 and to 7 per cent by 1985.

But the Reagan boom, while securing the president a landslide election victory in 49 states in 1984, left the economy with serious long-term structural problems. In 1984 the free-enterprise Reagan administration was forced to bail out and take into public ownership Continental Illinois Bank of Chicago, at the time the sixth largest bank in the nation with assets in the tens of billions. Continental Illinois' problems were symbolic of a banking system which, like the federal government, had become overstretched in the boom years. In states from Ohio to Maryland the Savings and Loan companies, homes for the small savers, faced runs by depositors as a result of loss of confidence. In 1985 the world's largest financial institution, Bank of America, was forced to cut its dividend rate to shareholders after its profits were wiped out by loan losses.

These problems in the financial sector were mirrored in the national economy. The budget deficits, despite frequent attempts at trimming them, soared to $200 billion a year. Interest rates rose and vast amounts of international savings were drawn into New York, sending the dollar soaring. In the early months of 1985 the superdollar was worth more than twice its value when President Reagan took office.

The impact of the strong currency on America's manufacturing base was disastrous. Cheap imports flooded onto the local market and exporting industries found they could no longer compete abroad. The deindustrialization of America's Rustbelt continued apace and even the booming service and high technology sectors found the going tough. The United States once again found itself staring into the abyss of recession.

Apple Computers

The production line of Apple Computers. Such companies benefited from the "information revolution" wrought by the microchip.

Chapter 4

Changes in Society

By the 1980s the United States was increasingly a nation of varied ethnic origins whose citizens required many specialized services. By this time, too, blacks had made impressive gains since the 1960s in politics and education — but fundamental problems remained, many deriving from high unemployment and low income. The National Organization for Women fought for greater women's rights; but while notable advances were undoubtedly made, there were strict limits to the extent of change permitted, as the campaign for the Equal Rights Amendment showed. In an era of intense feminist activity, conservative instincts remained strong.

Pluralism and Fragmentation

In the fall of 1976 Alex Haley published a historical novel entitled *Roots: Saga of an American Family*, based on research into his own family history. *Roots* was the tale of a young African forcibly transported to slavery in colonial America and of the struggles of his descendants to survive and finally prosper in the New World. The success of *Roots* was extraordinary, especially as a television series. More than 130 million Americans viewed at least part of the eight-day series, the largest audience for any program to that time. By March, 1977 the book had gone through fourteen printings and sold more than 750,000 copies.

The strong identification of so many blacks and whites with history seen through the eyes of an oppressed minority, was testimony to the resonance of Haley's novel and to the social and political changes that had taken place in America since the 1950s. Among other things it signified a widening acceptance of the pluralistic character of American society.

In the 1960s the federal government, responding to years of civil rights agitation, began to pass legislation designed to eliminate legal discrimination against blacks and other minorities. In 1965, black voting rights were protected. Also in 1965 an immigration act repealed the exclusionary policies of the 1920s. This new law removed quotas favoring immigrants from northern and western Europe over those from the third world. Taking effect in 1968, it greatly altered the nature of subsequent immigration.

The protests of the 1960s focused attention on the diversity of "American experiences." Recognition of the nation's continued cultural diversity contradicted the "melting pot" analysis after the Second World War by scholars attempting to define America's unique character. The emphasis on racial and ethnic pride of the late 1960s set the stage for the popular embrace of *Roots*, popularized genealogical study and reinforced the perception of Amer-

icans as a pluralistic people. Changes in immigration policy attempted to redress past injustices and affirmed the goal of diversity. They led to even more dramatic changes in the composition of the American population and raised important questions about accommodations to pluralism in politics and culture.

Between 1970 and 1980 the American population experienced its second lowest growth rate in history, increasing 11.5 per cent to over 226 million people. Immigrants accounted for just over one-third of this increase. The foreign born proportion of the population, falling for more than a generation to a low of under 5 per cent in 1970, rebounded to over 6 per cent by 1980. More significantly, most of the newcomers were not European. By 1980, 85 per cent of the new immigrants were from Latin America, Asia or Africa. Europeans accounted for almost one-third of those entering in 1970 but only 13 per cent in 1979. The character of immigration was changing, and since native-born Americans had fewer children during the 1970s, so were the ethnic characteristics of the nation as a whole.

Non-white Americans (including Hispanics) accounted for more than 20 per cent of the population by 1980, the highest proportion recorded since the Civil War. Although the number of Asians grew most rapidly, almost doubling during the 1970s, their numbers remained small, slightly over 1 per cent of the population. The notable progress of many Asian immigrants in business and science was at least partly attributable to the training and experience which many brought with them. There was wide variety in their make-up, however, ranging from Koreans, the majority of whom were educated people coming from professional or managerial jobs, to the Vietnamese boat people of 1979 who came with less education and fewer skills.

The Hispanic population grew by just over 60 per cent during this period, but its size gave the increase greater impact. The 1980 census reported more then 14.5 million Hispanics, representing almost 6.5 per cent of the population. The greatest number were Mexican-Americans, followed by Cubans and Puerto Ricans.

Mexican-Americans settled primarily in the Southwest, in California and Texas; Cubans mainly in Florida, with a growing Cuban community in New Jersey. Puerto Ricans concentrated in the New York metropolitan area, with newer small Puerto Rican enclaves in Connecticut, Massachusetts, New Jersey and Pennsylvania. Mexican-Americans and Puerto Ricans tended to be younger than the general population. Compared to other Hispanics, Cubans reflected more middle-class attributes – lower fertility, higher educational levels, lower unemployment, higher rates of home ownership, and higher median family income.

The differences to be found among Cubans illustrate the difficulty of generalizing about Hispanics. The post-

Left: New York's Chinatown has a distinctive character that derives from its original immigrant population. A banner proclaims opposition to Red China's admission to the UN. Below: Mexicans provide an important source of labor in California.

Tom Bradley (left), Mayor of Los Angeles, is a symbol of black advancement. Generally, however, blacks have lower incomes than whites, and black unemployment is twice as high as that for whites. Right: A protest march by the unemployed, 1981.

DC 37 SAYS: MONEY FOR HUMAN NEEDS NOT WAR MACHINES

revolutionary Cuban immigration, beginning in 1959, was almost entirely white (94 per cent), well-educated (an average of 14 years of schooling), and averaged 34 years of age. They came mainly from the politically moderate to conservative Cuban middle and upper classes. The second wave during the mid-1960s included fewer whites (80 per cent), and was younger and more working class. The largest single influx of Cubans, in 1980, included even fewer whites (60 per cent), was much younger and much poorer than preceding groups. Different groups of Cubans accordingly faced different problems inside the United States.

Although groups from Hispanic nations shared important aspects of culture, particularly their common language, class differences affected their adjustment to American society. Middle and upper class Hispanics were generally more educated and had a greater command of English. Thus, although the Spanish language provided a common bond, lower class Hispanics were more directly affected by decisions concerning bilingual public education than were the more affluent. Similar problems divided the adjustment experience and interests of Asian groups such as the Vietnamese. Earlier, better educated and wealthier Vietnamese immigrants were less likely to need bilingual classroom instruction than were later arrivals.

Bilingual education was one of the most controversial issues accompanying the new emphasis on pluralism. The first legislation to encourage such programs was passed in the late 1960s. By 1980 there were about 700 bilingual programs in 68 different languages in the public schools of the United States. As the number of Americans speaking limited English or no English at all increased in cities like Los Angeles and Miami, groups fearing the loss of "purity" in American culture began to call for legislation that would formally establish English as the official language of the nation.

In 1980 voters in Dade county, Florida, where one-third of Miami's population was Hispanic, passed an ordinance prohibiting the use of county funds for bilingual programs. The drive to legislate an official American language reached the national level in 1983 when former Senator S. I.

Hayakawa of California founded "US English" with the goal of ending "the automatic acceptance of rival languages in public life" to ensure that "English is, and ever must remain, the only official language of the United States." In the fall of 1985 Education Secretary William J. Bennett indicted "bilingual only" federal policy as detrimental to Hispanic adjustment. This reaction reflected part of the growing apprehension over the possible fragmentation of American culture.

The Position of Blacks

While foreign immigration altered American culture, other modifications came from within. By 1975 the character of the civil rights movement was changing. In most areas discriminatory laws had been overturned and, except among obdurate segregationists, integration, at least in principle, had become an accepted goal. The 1965 voting

rights act facilitated impressive gains in black political power. The number of blacks holding elective office rose from 103 in 1964 to 1,400 in 1970, and then to almost 5,600 by 1984. Two-thirds of these officeholders were in the South. The number of black mayors increased from none in 1965 to over 200 in 1984, with several presiding over major cities like Los Angeles, Atlanta, New Orleans, Birmingham, Chicago and Philadelphia. Yet, as with much of the progress made by blacks during these years, these were qualified victories. Although 12 per cent of Americans were black in 1984, only 1 per cent of political officeholders were. In Newark, New Jersey, Gary, Indiana, and Detroit, Michigan, black mayors administered cities in deep decline.

There was substantial achievement in black education. By the late 1970s a generation of struggle had raised the percentage of black young adults holding high school degrees to nearly that of their white counterparts. This was true even though the high school drop-out rate remained higher for blacks than for whites. Improvement at the college level was equally marked: by 1980 the proportion of blacks on campus was nearly the same as their proportion in the national population.

Yet progress in politics and education did not generally translate into economic gains. Black family income remained well below that of whites. In response to advances made under job training and placement, affirmative action and other Great Society programs, black median income rose to within 65 per cent of white income by 1975. Policy reversals and economic recession in the 1980s, however, once again increased the gap, so that by 1984 black relative income stood below the 1960 level of 55.4 per cent. Black unemployment during the 1970s and 1980s remained double that for whites, as it had been since 1954. By the mid-1980s the percentage of unemployed blacks rose to levels approximating national unemployment rates during the Depression of the 1930s. In many central cities over 50 per cent of black men searched in vain for work. Many more were so discouraged that they dropped out of the work force altogether. Including these discouraged workers, 1980 national black unemployment was estimated at 25 per cent. The 1982 recession increased this figure.

The continued discrepancy between black and white was obscured by the growing visibility of a successful black middle class. The positive effect of education was most apparent for a few blacks with notable achievements in government, the professions and in business. The income gap between educated blacks and whites of similar background narrowed so that by the mid-1980s college-educated blacks and college-educated whites earned similar entry level salaries. The more education black workers had, the more likely they were to earn incomes comparable to their white counterparts.

Much of this advance in black earnings and occupational opportunities was the direct or indirect result of affirmative action programs. One study conducted by the Depart-

ment of Labor estimated that companies with affirmative action programs increased their minority hiring at a rate nearly twice that of other firms. Skilled, professional and managerial blacks especially benefited from such hiring. During the early 1980s the federal government eased its pressure on private enterprise, allowing most government contractors to discontinue these programs.

Simultaneously there was a cutback in programs geared to assist the poor, many of whom were black. Reductions in federal aid to dependent children, the food stamp program, eduction grant programs, federal programs for job training, and medical aid programs made the lives of poor people more precarious. The virtual elimination of federally assisted legal aid programs significantly quieted the legal voice of the poor. Studies showed a rise in the percentage of the population in poverty, especially among blacks, by 1985. This was a marked reversal in trends showing a decline in poverty during the 1970s.

Improved opportunity for a few fortunate minorities and decreased aid for the masses in poverty reinforced a growing divergence between the circumstance of the black middle class and those of the black lower class. The potential for fragmentation increased as economic differences were compounded by a growing ethnic diversity, as Haitians and dark-skinned Latinos were added to the black population. By the late 1970s some observers feared the widening gap would create a permanent "black underclass."

This fear was heightened by the rise in the number of households headed by single black women, from about one-quarter in 1965 to almost one-half by 1982. The plight of black female household heads was only an exaggeration of that for all female heads of families, at least one-third of whom lived below the poverty line by the 1980s. The rise in male unemployment and aid policies in over half of the states which gave assistance only to families with no fathers present contributed to the growing number of female-headed families. Lower wages for women workers, about 60 per cent of that paid to their male counterparts, and the dramatic increase in the number of mothers in the work force, made poverty a women's issue.

Greater Opportunities for Women

Under pressure from civil rights and women's groups, federal employment regulations were strengthened by the passage of the Equal Employment Opportunity Act of 1972. Thereafter, female workers made inroads into many male-dominated careers. One key legal case was brought against American Telephone and Telegraph. AT&T was charged with the systematic exclusion of minorities and women from higher-level management positions and in 1973 the court ordered the company to rectify its hiring practices. Within two years the Department of Labor increased the

In the 1970s women increasingly took jobs previously done by men. Clockwise from top left: a woman coal-miner, apprentice engineers, a female construction worker and woman mechanic.

number of training grants provided to labor unions to expand work opportunities for minorities and women. In 1978 the federal government set goals and time tables for the growth of job opportunities for minorities and women in the construction trades.

The impact of these efforts was quickly felt. Between 1972 and 1980 the number of women in skilled jobs nearly doubled, many in traditionally male occupations. For example, there were practically no women in the coal industry before 1972, but by 1980 women held some 3,000 jobs in the largest mining companies. Despite these efforts, most work in the early 1980s remained segregated by gender. Ninety-nine per cent of all secretaries were women, while a comparable percentage of firefighters were men.

Male occupations continued to pay higher wages. Moreover, as women moved into many positions, job titles were changed and wages lowered. Conversely, wages tended to increase as men took jobs in areas traditionally held by women. To combat this situation, some suggested that work be evaluated to determine a scale by which different jobs could be rated according to their worth. Jobs of similar worth could then carry similar wages.

In 1982 the Illinois Commission on the Status of Women suggested that a secretary and an electrician performed roughly comparable work; therefore the secretary's salary, about half that of the electrician, should be raised. A study commissioned by the Washington state government found that there was a 20 per cent salary advantage for those who worked in traditionally male occupations over those who held traditionally female jobs. This was true even when the jobs involved similar skills, intelligence, responsibility and working conditions.

Accepting the comparable worth concept, in 1983 a US

District Court ruled that the state of Washington must pay state-employed secretaries and truck drivers at a comparable rate. Even though similar rating systems are used for military and civilian federal employment, critics argued that the plan was unworkable and too costly. The notion was rejected by Clarence M. Pendelton, the conservative black chairman of the Reagan Civil Rights Commission, who derided the comparable worth concept as "probably the looniest idea since 'looney tunes' came to the screen." In the late summer of 1985 a federal court of appeals reversed the Washington decision, declaring that the presence of a wage gap did not prove an intention to discriminate.

ERA and the Anti-abortion Campaign

Comparable worth was one of several programs supported by the women's movement that met with frustration by the mid-1980s. The most celebrated campaign during this period was the drive for an Equal Rights Amendment to the Constitution which would guarantee women equal protection in law. The campaign was spearheaded by the National Organization for Women, founded in 1966, which had become the most influential feminist group in the country. Passed easily by Congress in 1972, the ERA became the major battle ground for women's rights. Opposition to the ERA arose from several groups. The Mormon church predicted it would destroy the family. Conservative politicians, especially in the South, blocked ratification in their states on the grounds that the amendment would subvert basic American values.

Conservative women organized opposition to the ERA, fearing that its passage would undermine traditional gender roles and protections. They foresaw dire consequences – unisex public bathrooms, the institution of a military draft for women, the devaluation of motherhood – if the amendment passed. Nor was the ERA universally supported by feminists. Some feminist lawyers argued that it was unnecessary and that existing provisions in the Constitution, if properly interpreted, would protect the rights of women. ERA advocates countered that since the court had not made such interpretations in the past, there was no reason to assume they would in the future if a specific amendment were not passed to make such interpretations unavoidable.

Despite opinion polls during the 1970s showing that the ERA was supported by a majority of Americans, and a brisk start, with twenty-two states ratifying it in the first year, the amendment fell three states short of the thirty-eight necessary for passage. An extension of the time limit for ratification in 1979 prolonged the struggle, but time ran out in the summer of 1982.

Simultaneously, feminists became concerned about the spread of anti-abortion sentiment led by many of the same groups which successfully opposed the ERA. The Supreme Court in *Roe v. Wade* in 1973 ruled that during the first three months of pregnancy, abortion was a matter between a woman and her doctor, not subject to governmental prohibition. Almost immediately, anti-abortion forces organized opposition to the decision, calling for a constitutional amendment to outlaw abortion and local legislation to limit its impact. Their most important success was legislation which restricted the use of federal funds for abortion through the medicaid program for the poor.

In the wake of the defeat of ERA and the rising influence

The campaign for the Equal Rights Amendment received enthusiastic support from feminist groups, which took part in a rally in Washington in 1979.

"I do not believe my daughter should have fewer rights than my sons."

President Jimmy Carter

The Equal Rights Amendment

Equality of Opportunity **ERA** Quality of Achievement

of anti-abortion forces, the National Organization for Women redoubled its efforts in the political arena, determined to elect more women to public office before mounting another ERA campaign. The National Women's Political Caucus, established in 1971, was instrumental in encouraging and supporting women candidates, and the 1970s saw more women in public office than ever before. By 1980 there were women in every state legislature in the country, almost three times as many as in 1968, and women served as chief executives of several cities and states. On closer examination, however, these numbers were not encouraging to feminists. Some of the women in public office were political conservatives who did not support the ERA or share NOW's visions.

The national elections of 1980 and 1984 were especially discouraging to women's rights advocates. Ronald Reagan's sweeping victory over President Jimmy Carter in 1980 revealed the power of the "New Right," a well-financed coalition of conservative political and fundamentalist religious groups. The Republican national convention of that year rejected the two major campaigns of the feminist movement, the ERA and abortion rights. The party pledged itself to work for a constitutional amendment to ban

Left: Despite Carter's support, the ERA gained insufficient state backing. Below: Women in conference, with Betty Friedan to the right of the podium.

abortion and for the appointment of federal judges who opposed abortion. This stand contradicted popular opinion expressed in 1982 when an Associated Press/NBC News poll found that 75 per cent of all Americans opposed an anti-abortion amendment, while only 19 per cent favored it. Reagan's victory in 1980, based largely on his personal appeal and popular disenchantment with Carter's handling of the Iran hostage situation, may have obscured the ambivalence felt by many Americans toward Reagan policies, but it reflected the growing political strength of conservatives. The defeat of several liberal politicians in state and local elections made it more difficult for liberal officeholders to speak out. Feminist issues received declining support at the federal level of government.

The Gender Gap

Despite the rise in political power of American conservatism, Republicans became concerned about what the press dubbed the "gender gap," a recognition of a divergence between the attitudes and interests of men and women. A Gallup poll taken in January, 1983 showed that men were more likely than women to support the president's policies. Republican women were less likely than Republican men to approve of the president's performance in office. Reagan's appointment of a few women to highly visible positions in the administration, and of Sandra Day O'Connor as the first female justice of the Supreme Court, seemed to show awareness of the political consequences of the gender gap.

The Democratic party hoped to capitalize on the gender gap during the presidential election of 1984. Former Vice President Walter Mondale chose Congresswoman Geraldine Ferraro of New York as his vice presidential running mate, the first woman so selected by a major party. Women generally responded warmly to Ferraro and were more likely than men to vote Democratic, but Reagan's popularity carried him to a landslide victory. Many responded to the rise of conservative politics and the defeat of the Mondale-Ferraro candidacy by joining the progressive women's movement. By the mid-1980s NOW, the National Women's Caucus, and the National Abortion Rights Action League all reported substantial growth in membership.

In 1981, Betty Friedan, early spokeswoman for the feminist cause and one of the founders of NOW, published *The Second Stage.* Sharply critical of some feminist groups, Friedan argued that the feminist movement had often aided the conservative preemption of family issues by replacing the "feminine mystique" which had limited women to dependent roles with an equally destructive "feminist mystique" which denigrated the woman's role within the family. The new stage, she believed, would go beyond the women's movement to recognize the diversity in women's roles and issues. Men and women would be united in a

UPI-Bettmann Newsphotos/BBC Hulton Picture Library

The appointment of Sandra Day O'Connor as first woman justice of the Supreme Court acknowledged women's enhanced status in public life.

movement to change society's institutions, making equal rights in politics, work and the family available to all. The strong political differences between women were reflected in reactions to Friedan's words, which were variously received as a call to more radical reform, a retreat which put women back into the home, or a recognition of the differences in women's needs and interests. Critics accused her of acquiescing in the rise of conservatism.

The Unemployment Crisis

As the debate continued among feminists the appeal of conservative politics was enhanced by economic uncertainty. After almost a century of struggle, many industrial workers had the prospect of occupational and social stability. Union benefits allowed for adequate medical care and a modest retirement. But from the early 1970s a shift in the economic base profoundly affected American workers and their expectations for the future. The decline of steel and other heavy industry resulting from the growth of foreign competition, the internationalization of American corporations, and corporate managerial and investment decisions precipitated a crisis in northern industrial cities as plants closed or cut back their labor force, putting thousands out of work.

HUD

*Unionists demonstrate in Washington. High
unemployment coupled with cuts in welfare programs
led to criticism of economic policy.*

During the recession of 1982 the unemployment rate reached almost 11 per cent (up from 3.5 per cent in 1969), the highest since the 1930s. Even during the recovery period of 1984 national unemployment stood above 7 per cent, with much higher rates for minorities and in major industrial cities. Conservative advisory groups like the Heritage Foundation suggested that these older industrial "Frostbelt" or "Rustbelt" cities had outlived their usefulness and might be abandoned in favor of "Sunbelt" cities which benefited from warmer winters and the resulting lower energy costs. Unemployed industrial workers were told to retrain themselves and to relocate in the prospering areas farther south. Computers and related industries, collectively referred to as high tech, were seen as the wave of the future and the new hope of those whose skills in heavy industry no longer appeared useful.

Thousands of Americans left the urban Northeast for the metropolitan areas of the South and the Southwest to search for jobs. Many industries had migrated south seeking lower labor costs. Labor unions which were strong in the North and Midwest had little power in the sunbelt. Southern right-to-work laws prohibiting the closed shop and low corporate taxes were additional enticements for businesses. Unionized workers who had achieved a mea-

sure of economic security were particularly imperilled. Other businesses, finding economic conditions and a political climate which gave them an advantage in their dealings with powerful labor unions, seized the opportunity to press employees for concessions. These concessions were needed, it was said, to preserve jobs in the ailing industrial cities of the North. Yet thousands of jobs were lost as companies closed their doors in favor of more profitable climates elsewhere in the nation or abroad.

The fortunate were able to find new jobs after the round of plant closings in the early 1980s. Most, however, suffered from the phenomenon of "job skidding," taking employment in high tech fields or in the growing service sector, accepting lower wages and inferior employee benefits. In 1983 a former steelworker who found work in the electronics components industry was likely to earn only 60 per cent of his former wage and receive minimal benefits. Those workers who were less fortunate found only part-time employment.

During the 1980s the largest increase in jobs came in part-time employment, which carried few or no benefits. These workers were only one step away from poverty at a time when government support to the poor was shrinking dramatically. As the unemployment figures grew, the numbers of those so discouraged that they no longer sought work also increased. Older workers, 45 years and over, were especially hard-hit. Less likely to be hired by firms offering training for new workers, many were forced into a precarious early retirement supplemented by occasional or part-time employment. Ironically, however, rising unemployment actually benefited some consumers by driving down high rates of inflation.

Federal policy changes after 1980 did little to address the problems of dislocated workers losing their grip on middle class status. The economic philosophy of the Reagan administration emphasized incentives to business in the hope of stimulating investments and creating new private sector jobs. The Comprehensive Employment and Training Act (CETA), established in the early 1970s to provide training and employment, began to be phased out in 1981. The loss of hundreds of thousands of public sector CETA jobs worsened the unemployment problem. Indirectly recognizing the intransigence of high unemployment, the "full employment unemployment rate" was renamed the "inflation threshold unemployment rate" and set by the Council of Economic Advisors in 1983 at 7 per cent. Eight million workers could be out of work under conditions which were once called "full employment."

Changes in the tax code further eroded the position of workers. The Economic Recovery Tax Act of 1981 sought to encourage saving and to discourage consumption. The effect was an upward redistribution of income. Between 1979 and 1984 the effective tax rate for those earning under $10,000 a year increased by about 2 per cent while the rate for those earning over $35,000 declined by just 0.5 per cent.

Top picture: UPI-Bettmann Newsphotos/BBC Hulton. Bottom picture: Moorland-Springarn Research Center, Howard University.

Although contraction in the economy and changes in economic policy had an immediate impact on the working class, the young, the educated and upwardly mobile people felt the effect as well. Liberal arts college graduates found the professional job market shrinking or closed altogether. The economic shift from industrial production to service jobs and information management encouraged a dramatic rise in the numbers of college students majoring in computer science, business administration, law and engineering. As the job market became more competitive, even for these advantaged job seekers, many became more defensive in their career decisions.

Books in the 1970s entitled *Looking Out for Number One* and *Winning by Intimidation* reflected the mood of these graduates who, by virtue of their privileged position, should have felt economically secure but did not. This new young upwardly mobile ("Yuppie") generation, acknowledged little personal responsibility for past injustice and found its redress too costly. Many joined other conservatives in questioning the wisdom and fairness of social programs to redress historic racial and gender inequities. More generally, the contraction of the middle class, fiscal and tax policies, structural economic changes, a mounting national debt, economic recession and unemployment created a sense of precariousness which spawned support for conservative policies. Younger people chafed at having to pay into a federal retirement fund supporting an expanding elderly population. Proposals were voiced for a major overhaul of the social security system. Only through determined organization did the elderly stave off threats to the benefits upon which most depended.

Conservative groups sought to reverse what they saw as a generation of excessive change. Religious fundamentalists, some of whom adopted the umbrella term "moral majority," sought a return to the "traditional family" away from the feminist agenda or from the reforms of the Great Society. For some, affirmative action or busing to promote racial

Above: Fires burn out of control during race riots which erupted in Miami in 1980. Left: The Rev Jesse Jackson sought to promote the fortunes of minority groups in his 1984 campaign for the Democratic presidential nomination.

integration in the public schools was the problem. Many believed that social reform had moved too far too fast and that the scales of social justice had tipped in the direction of the "formerly disadvantaged," creating victims of a new "reverse discrimination."

A Variety of Views

The focus on pluralism in American culture which grew out of the civil rights era facilitated the celebration of diversity. Ethnic festivals and celebrations, and broadening American tastes in food and fashion, symbolized the growing cosmopolitanism. But Ku Klux Klan campaigns against Vietnamese immigrant fishermen competing for fishing grounds in Corpus Christi, Texas, or the economic and racial tensions which pitted blacks against Latinos in the rioting in Miami, Florida, in 1980 suggested the negative side of American diversity.

Responses to perceptions of excessive change varied. Extreme solutions were alluded to by groups on the far

right espousing racial purity and "white power." More moderate opinion called for selective immigration policies favoring those with high levels of education and skill and cutting off illegal immigration. On the other end of the political spectrum were those who believed efforts toward social justice had not gone far enough. In 1984, Jesse Jackson, the first serious black candidate for the presidential nomination, called for an alliance of those "shut out" of American society in a "rainbow coalition" to assert political power in favor of the positive aspects of pluralism. Yet there was great divergence among the potential components of this coalition. Jackson's campaign actually heightened national and international tension between blacks and Jews, sorely testing traditional alliances between these groups.

Within the black community argument over strategies for the future continued amid sharpened class and political divisions, with a small but well-publicized black conservative voice challenging the wisdom of past social policy and the legitimacy of traditional black civil rights leadership. Among women, differences remained over the effectiveness, the methods and the goals of the feminist movement, although the 1985 election of the activist-oriented Eleanor Smeal to the presidency of NOW appeared to be an important signal for the future of that organization.

Differences between and within these groups closely paralleled their different positions in the changing structure of society itself. For those who believed that they had lost ground, to women, immigrants or blacks, the stress of competition for seemingly shrinking resources often fragmented potential alliances. For them, conservatism seemed to promise a return to times when they could count on the advantage of race, or gender, to provide stability and certainty. To some blacks who benefited from the progress

Suspected illegal immigrants are searched at a US border patrol. California was the preferred route for many of those seeking illegal entry.

Camera Press

toward racial fairness, a new meritocracy and its emphasis on individualism appeared to offer a route to economic success, the consolidation of gains already made, and the assurance that their progress was deserved, not the result of special favors. For many women the call for a return to "traditional" family values argued for the importance of their primary roles as mothers and homemakers, even as it raised disturbing problems for women working outside the home. Under these circumstances the rainbow coalition was difficult to achieve in the political season of 1984.

The growth of American pluralism and the general acceptance of the pluralistic nature of the nation's character in the 1970s and 1980s was, then, a painful and confusing process. It was marked by immigration policies which increased racial and ethnic diversity, educational policies which recognized and encouraged diversity, and attempts to accommodate the demands of the women's movement to the variety of women's experience. Recognizing the diversity of American experience also focused attention on unequal opportunities for achievement and advancement.

In the face of economic insecurities in the early 1980s, there was growing conservative opposition to further changes in the structure of opportunities. Conflicts between these forces and beliefs often led to contradictory policies. Some Cubans arriving by boatlift were welcomed as political refugees while threats were made to turn back boatloads of Haitians. Unwelcome immigrants were placed in detention camps. Legislation was proposed which would give amnesty to many Mexican immigrants who had been working illegally in America while measures were introduced to cut off illegal immigration. Conservatives fought the ERA and the Supreme Court's declaration of women's right to abortions, as threats to the family, but supported cuts in programs which provided food for infants and expectant mothers. Meanwhile, economic necessity and expanded choices brought more married women into the work force.

It seemed likely that these trends would, in the next few years, not only continue but accelerate. Optimists and boosters would proclaim that the United States was more than ever a "nation of nations." Their speeches and articles would dwell upon the success achieved by certain immigrant groups, notably those from Asia, or by individuals such as Mayor Henry Cisneros of San Antonio, Texas, and Senator Daniel Inouye of Hawaii. Pessimists and doubters, on the other hand, would emphasize the strains placed upon the United States by a miscellaneous polygot population. "Melting pot," "salad bowl," or even "trash bin:" the various metaphors indicated the variety of perceptions. Was diversity widening the gap between haves and have nots? Would the 1980s witness fragmentation even among traditional allies? Was pluralism, and the prospect of its continuance, a mark of vitality, a severe challenge to national unity, or something of both?

Chapter 5

THE NATIONAL SPIRIT

A decade after the Bicentennial, the United States seemed to exhibit confidence and optimism under the leadership of an amiable president keen to see America "walk tall" in the world. Conservative forces were in the ascendant, liberalism in retreat. Yet the mood of the nation was not easily categorized. To what extent did it differ from previous eras in the nation's history? Why did the so-called "Reagan Revolution" attract doubt and dissent from a number of articulate conservatives? And how did such components of popular culture as literature, movies, TV and the theater reflect the character of the times?

Aspects of Americana

In the 1980s as in the 1970s, the United States seemed to be caught up in an unending series of commemorations. 1982-83 was widely marked as the 50th anniversary of the election and inauguration of Franklin D. Roosevelt. 1984-85 brought celebrations and symposia featuring the 40th anniversary of the last great conflicts of the Second World War, the dropping of the atom bombs on Hiroshima and Nagasaki, the collapse of Germany and Japan. 1985 was noted as the centennial of the Statue of Liberty in New York harbor, and of the completion of the giant obelisk known as the Washington Monument, in the nation's capital.

Bicentennial activities were also conspicuous. In 1976 there was a nationwide celebration of the 1776 Declaration of Independence – the point at which the rebelling colonies formally announced their break with the mother country. Various events of the ensuing War of Independence were restaged, and made the occasion for bouts of oratory. Among these was the bicentennial of the victory of General Washington's Franco-American army over Lord Cornwallis at Yorktown, Virginia, in 1781. Two years later, the 1783

Peace of Paris was duly assessed and savored, for this treaty not only recognized the reality of American independence but gained from the British almost everything that the most wildly optimistic colonists could have wished.

The historical pageant rolled on. In the mid-1980s Chief Justice Warren Burger, chairman of a bicentennial commission to honor the 1787 Constitution, showed a bustling determination to remind the entire population that theirs was a heritage of "laws, not of men."

The mood of all these anniversaries was for the most part proudly cheerful, a time for firework displays, parades and patriotic speeches. America, as President Ronald Reagan proclaimed, was living up to his historic mission: "walking tall," in his words. Such too was the mood of the crowds that attended the 1984 Olympic Games in Los Angeles. Every American medallist, and there were a great many, was applauded to the skies. (The Soviet Union boycott, evident in competition, little affected spectator enthusiasm.)

Ronald Reagan's admirers, and even some of his critics, pointed to the contrast between the doom-and-gloom atmosphere of the Carter years and the new spirit of can-do boosterism that accompanied Reagan's election victory of November 1980. In November 1984 the electorate, voting him back for a second term, could be seen as endorsing

The Bicentennial celebrated heroes and events. Above: Re-enactment of the occasion when Washington led the Charlestown Militia to Prospect Hill and raised the colonial flag. Left: Uncle Sam in Wisconsin.

their support for the traditional values Reagan exemplified: freedom, optimism, strength, private enterprise, church, family, and flag. America was "back," according to his supporters, the leader among nations, with nothing in the record to be ashamed of, and nothing to correct except the drift of the previous few decades toward big government, high taxes, welfarism, and military and diplomatic weakness in the face of world communism.

How else could one interpret the humiliating defeat of the Democratic candidates, Walter Mondale and Geraldine Ferraro, in 1984? The incumbent president had insisted that government was not the solution to America's problems, but itself the major problem. Sure enough, the District of Columbia, home of the nation's paper-pushing bureaucrats, had been almost the only bit of the country to back the Mondale-Ferraro ticket. This was proof-positive, for Reaganite Republicans, that the lessons of the past remained fundamental for the America of today.

Every so often magazines and newspapers would run an article with some such title as "Where Have All The Heroes Gone?" – the implication being that the United States had lost its appetite for greatness. During the decade 1975-85 the question was frequently put, and with increasing frequency answered in the affirmative. An upsurge of nostalgic emotion occurred in 1979, with the death from cancer of Hollywood's beloved old tough-guy star John Wayne. In that year Ronald Reagan, reasserting his bid for the Republican presidential nomination, recollected for *Reader's Digest* how Wayne had once told his fellow-actor: "That little clique back there in the East has taken great personal satisfaction reviewing my [conservative] politics instead of my pictures." One day, "Duke Wayne" prophesied to Reagan, "those doctrinaire liberals will wake up to find the pendulum has swung the other way."

Lo and behold, had it not come to pass? Was not that in truth the message of the innumerable symposia convened in 1984 to discuss George Orwell's gloomily prophetic fantasy *1984*? Orwell, it was said, might have been correct about the menace of totalitarianism, but had been proved quite wrong about the vitality and prosperity of the "free world." The year had arrived, only to reveal the basic flaws in Orwellian pessimism. American involvement in the Vietnam War appeared to some during the mid-1970s as a meaningless nightmare, a "quagmire," analogous to the mood of *1984*. "Stateside" America seemed unwilling to talk about the debacle, or to acknowledge the existence of Vietnam veterans. Yet despite official indifference a Vietnam Memorial was constructed in Washington, close to the Lincoln Memorial and to the White House. Within a few years it was a place of pilgrimage, and the veterans themselves were beginning to "walk tall."

"The Great Communicator" charms the media. The president's cheerful, avuncular manner was particularly persuasive on television.

Liberals under Attack

A fairly good case can be made for arguing that John Wayne's rather than Orwell's predictions came true. The "liberals," that is, can be shown as having been ousted by the conservatives. Karl Marx loses out to Adam Smith, statism to libertarianism, the spenders of other people's money to the producers of America's wealth. An indignant view of the situation in 1975 was expressed in Pat Buchanan's *Conservative Votes, Liberal Victories: Why the Right Has Failed*. Buchanan, a former speech-writer for Richard Nixon, maintained that his former chief's shrewd insights had been negated by the "pressure of millions dependent upon federal checks and federal benefits, and the entrenched and unresponsive power of the media, the bureaucracy and the courts."

The American public was resoundingly conservative. Its wishes, said Buchanan, were ignored by an "unelected oligarchy ... insulated from the electorate and the common man." This oligarchy was concentrated in the "megalopolis" of the North-East, from Boston to Washington D.C. Here were to be found the institutions of a decadent elite: Ivy League universities (headed by Harvard, Yale, and Princeton); lofty "social engineers" directing the great foundations such as Ford and Rockefeller; the headquarters of the national TV networks; their dangerous "liberal" associates staffing the *New York Times* and *Washington Post*; think-tanks such as Brookings in Washington D.C.; and countless federal or congressional appointees, proliferating useless if not pernicious regulations.

A similar analysis with a regional emphasis was offered, also in 1975, by Kevin Phillips, another previous worker for the Nixon White House. In *Mediacracy: American Parties and Politics in the Communications Age*, Phillips focussed upon the (to him) alarming growth and dominance of the

"knowledge industry" of "educators, consultants and media executives." Concentrated in the North and East, they were manipulators and parasites, out of touch with rugged individualists, the true Americans, of the South and West. Writers like Phillips portrayed a nation split between exploitative "Yankees" and honest-to-God "Cowboys."

Even those with no ideological bent felt a need to reconstruct the nation's socio-economic map. Wealth and population were shifting in a south-westerly direction. The process was symbolized by the emigration of north-eastern baseball clubs, starting in the late 1950s. Thus the Brooklyn Dodgers went to Los Angeles, the New York Giants to San Francisco, the Boston Braves first to Milwaukee and then to Atlanta, Georgia; and, by a nice irony, the Washington Senators were transformed into the Texas Rangers. The teams were where the money, the sunshine and the enthusiasm beckoned. Why should not politics be enabled to obey the same natural impulses? For millions of people, old conceptions failed to correspond to new reality.

Rethinking the Mix

In *The Nine Nations of North America* (1981) the journalist Joel Garreau reinterpreted geography, bringing Canada and Mexico into the picture. The Far West coast, from central California to Alaska, he designated as "Ecotopia." The great central valley, stretching from Texas north to Lake Winnepeg, was "The Bread-basket." The old industrial region of the central and midwestern states was "The Foundry." There was a "MexAmerica" and a "Dixie." These were understandable enough divisions. More revealing of a desire to rethink the national mix (and perhaps of uncertainty as to how to go about the task) was the inclusion of a chapter called "Aberrations" – outlying oddities such as Alaska and Hawaii that were hard to fit into a meaningful scheme. The shock for metropolitan North-Easterners was to discover that the aberrations included New York City and Washington D.C. Mr Garreau wondered "why the idea that gathering continental power in one place" – Washington – "was once considered reasonable, possible, and in the best interests of the majority." Whatever the reason, "that it has gone awry is undeniable." Washington does not serve the best interests of the far-flung American people. "Only the residents of Washington, reaping the benefits of being at the center of the Imperium, fail to view this as bizarre."

Since middle-of-the-road citizens thought in this vein, it is not surprising that more committed conservatives should push the argument further. Or that, since most of these articulate characters were themselves in the business of communication, they should denounce the liberal elite and seek to replace it with more satisfactory voices. One step was the funding and launching of publications that could counteract the "liberal" near-monopoly. Some magazines – *National Review, Human Events* – had an older history. They were joined by fresh periodicals such as Richard A. Viguerie's *Conservative Digest* (1975). Conservative opinion was expressed with new vigor and funding on university campuses. And it gained ground in intellectual circles through the establishment of periodicals like the *New Criterion*, or the change in editorial policy of older ones like New York's monthly *Commentary*, which for some twenty years after its founding in 1945 was basically "liberal" in sentiment but which by the mid-1970s was taking a hard line on perceived weaknesses in American behavior, private and public, domestic and foreign.

The national swing toward "conservatism" was sometimes deplored and sometimes welcomed, in scores of journalistic assessments. Few denied that a large-scale adjustment appeared to be taking place. Thus campuses were markedly less agitated than in the previous decade. Politically or economically radical groups were less in evidence. Students, it was claimed, were concerned now to find employment within the system, not to drop out in search of alternative ways of life. Vocational degrees, notably accountancy, soared in popularity. Medicine and law retained their appeal for ambitious young Americans; competition for them was even heightened by the entry of large numbers of women for whom these avenues had once appeared closed.

Intellectual positions that could be called "conservative" were likewise, it seemed, in the ascendant. Robert Nozick, a Harvard philosopher, won prizes and a great deal of attention with a book entitled *Anarchy, State, and Utopia* (1974), in which he contended that on moral and other grounds, minimal state control over citizens' lives was not only preferable but essential for any society deserving to be called "free." His position differed fundamentally from that of an elder colleague, John Rawls, whose *Theory of Justice* (1971), under formulation since the 1950s, strove to reconcile individualism and social justice. Milton Friedman and George Stigler, redoubtable exponents of private enterprise, both won Nobel prizes for economics. Except for the irrepressibly fluent John Kenneth Galbraith, most of Friedman and Stigler's one-time adversaries in the economics profession sounded rather muted and uncertain of their own tenets.

At least, they did not produce very emphatic rebuttals. The initiative seemed to lie with what Malcolm Bradbury wittily dubbed the "sado-monetarists." So Milton and Rose Friedman's *Free to Choose: A Personal Statement* (1980) became a bestseller. Ronald Reagan praised the book as "superb"; the columnist William F. Buckley Jr called it a "motherlode of economic and social wisdom. ... An important, shrewd, omnicompetent, readable guide to reasoned thought for those who choose to be free." Even the *New York Times Book Review* saluted the Friedmans' defense of the market economy – Adam Smith's "invisible hand" – as "noteworthy for ... clarity, logic, candor."

The glorification of private enterprise became a prime concern of energetic new Washington think-tanks, notably the Heritage Foundation and also the American Enterprise Institute for Public Policy Research. They provided temporary or more permanent homes for a variety of scholar-celebrities such as Jeane Kirkpatrick, President Reagan's former Ambassador to the United Nations. Michael Novak, a senior fellow at American Enterprise, had once been known as a lively critic of "WASP" privilege (in *The Rise of the Unmeltable Ethnics*). By the end of the 1970s he was an ardent advocate of "democratic capitalism." Two conferences that he organized led to the publication of semi-theological analyses on *The Denigration of Capitalism* and *Capitalism and Socialism* (1979), representing a brand of intellectual Roman Catholic conservatism not vastly different from that of William Buckley.

In Praise of Capitalism

The thesis of such publications was that, for various unfortunate reasons, capitalism in America found itself on the defensive. Instead of extolling its virtues, and exposing the errors and crimes of left-wing, "unfree" economies, Americans had tended to apologize for the supposed deficiencies of their own system. Friedman, Novak, and others were joined by George Gilder, author of *Wealth and Poverty* (1981) – a book heralded by David Stockman, then director of the Reagan Office of Management and Budget, as "Promethean in its intellectual power." *Wealth and Poverty*, said Stockman, "shatters once and for all the Keynesian and welfare state illusions that burden the failed conventional wisdom of our era." Stockman, be it noted, had once been a pupil at Harvard of the "Keynesian" economist J. K. Galbraith.

In Gilder's glowing account, true capitalists were dynamic, risk-taking, and altruistic. They created wealth, as distinct from the static, socially useless riches of "an Indian rajah or an Arabian prince." The adventurous, red-blooded, "charismatic" American capitalist supplied goods because he felt impelled to do so. Excitement, not profit, was his primary motive. "Individuals with cash comprise the wild card – the mutagenic germ in capitalism." If they became wealthy, why should they not? The whole society benefitted from this happy-go-lucky pioneering spirit. But liberals, many of them scions of rich old families who had given up striving, had managed to promote a national "war against wealth." In Gilder's view, "the idea that all wealth is acquired through stealing is popular in prisons and at Harvard." Suspicion of those who produce wealth had become "the racism of the intelligentsia."

It also followed for Gilder that the pioneering entrepreneur needed the protection and spur of marriage and family. The duty of the male was to bring home the bacon, we might say, and of the female to cook it for her husband and children. Feminists were among the enemies of American progress: instead of counting the blessings of women, and noting the consequences of broken homes and egocentric pursuits, they swelled the ranks of the horde of American nay-sayers (including much of the black population) obsessed with the notion that society was discriminating against them. George Gilder thus shared at least some attitudes with "neo-conservatives" such as Robert Nisbet, Daniel Bell, Irving Kristol, Nathan Glazer, Daniel P. Moynihan and Norman Podhoretz; with William Buckley and his fellow-columnist George Will; with opponents of the Equal Rights Amendment such as Phyllis Schlafly, leader of the Roman Catholic Eagle Forum; and to some degree with the "video-evangelism" proclaimed by a new breed of immensely prominent fundamentalist ministers.

Of these, one of the most politically active was the Rev. Jerry Falwell, creator of the "Moral Majority" in 1979. Falwell's intention, as summarized by the *Conservative Digest*, was "to mobilize ... Americans to work for pro-God, pro-family policies in government." Falwell, and other ministers of the "electronic church" like Pat Robertson of the Christian Broadcasting Network, claimed a constituency of born-again Protestants, right-thinking Catholics, and conservative Jews and Mormons, large enough to enable them to take over the country. In combination, claimed their spokesmen, they could bend Congress and the White House to their collective, democratic will. They had the votes, the money, the program and the purpose.

Indeed, it did seem at times that the two ends of Pennsylvania Avenue were the ready servants of a massive, confident, nationwide conservative coalition. Members of Congress hesitated to offend the Moral Majority, the National Rifle Association, the National Right to Life (anti-abortion) Committee, or the National Right to Work (anti-unionist) Committee. The Reagan administration seemed positively eager to endorse such positions. Despite having been shot by a would-be assassin (as had nearly happened twice to President Ford), Ronald Reagan declared his opposition to legislation imposing controls on handguns. He was equally clear in expressing disapproval for legalized abortion. In both his first and second term, President Reagan's appointments were consistently slanted against federal regulations, whether designed to protect the environment or to extend welfare provisions.

His second Attorney-General, Edwin A. Meese, finally confirmed in office in 1985, made plain the administration's aim to promote "law and order" and to "conservatize" the federal judiciary as well as the government. Five of the nine Supreme Court justices in 1985 were aged 75 or over. The likelihood was that, by appointing relatively youthful replacements, Reagan would bequeath to his successors for decades to come a court as emphatically conservative as that of the Earl Warren era had been "liberal." In a climate of that nature, it was predicted, the trend toward capital

Camera Press

Above: An anti-porn march in New York, with liberal morality under attack. Below: Sylvester Stallone as Rambo, super-patriot on a rescue mission to Vietnam.

AP

punishment would continue. "Excessive" protection of the rights of suspects would be curtailed in the interests of conviction; for Attorney-General Meese contended that arrested suspects were naturally those who knew most about the offense in question. It was time to punish culprits instead of mollycoddling them.

The public for the most part apparently agreed. At any rate, there was wild initial enthusiasm for the action of a young white man in the New York subway who, hustled by some black teenagers, pulled out a pistol and wounded each of them. There was a still greater surge of approval for the film *Rambo: First Blood II* (1985). Audiences across the land cheered the exploits of the hero, played by Sylvester Stallone, who goes back to Vietnam and singlehandedly rescues long-held American prisoners – slaying a multitude of the enemy in the process.

Echoes From the Past

It is easy to conclude that where so many movements are headed in the same general direction, and with so little coherent opposition, a shift of major proportions must be under way. Perhaps, we may think, it would be too simple to call the change the "Reagan Revolution." President Reagan might arguably be the beneficiary rather than the leader of such a revolution, even if we take into account his pronouncements as Governor of California, back in the 1960s. After all, was not Jimmy Carter also a conservative, in most respects? Carter too, we must remember, was fiscally cautious, yet also embarked on a rapid and substantial build-up of the armed forces, and was himself trained as a career officer in the Navy. Carter too had started out in small-town America, and made a success in agribusiness. Carter, securely married, was not only a regular churchgoer, with an evangelist sister, but a "born-again" Christian.

To bring up that sort of consideration, though, is to begin to ask how much in the mood of recent America is actually new or deepseated. Take for instance this statement:

Liberals whose hair is growing thin and the lines of whose figures are no longer what they were, are likely to find themselves today in the unhappy predicament of being treated as mourners at their own funerals. When they pluck up heart to assert that they are not yet authentic corpses, but living men with brains in their heads, they are pretty certain to be gently chided and led back to the comfortable armchair that befits senility.

It is not as pithy as Irving Kristol's definition ("A conservative is a liberal who has been mugged"), and more genial in tone than many Reagan-era epitaphs for liberalism. Otherwise it could well belong in the 1980s. But in fact the passage was composed in the late 1920s by the

liberal-radical scholar Vernon L. Parrington, as part of his *Main Currents in American Thought*.

"Conservative" pronouncements of the Carter-Reagan years in fact constantly refer to traditional American viewpoints, or perhaps unconsciously echo ancestral arguments. Milton Friedman is among several authors to revive a century-old essay on "The Forgotten Man" by the Yale sociologist William Graham Sumner. Sumner was an unabashed defender of the Darwinian vision of life as a struggle for the survival of the fittest. His "Forgotten Man" was therefore not the underprivileged, unemployed American victim of circumstance evoked by Franklin D. Roosevelt during the New Deal. Sumner's "Forgotten Man" was the middle-class, law-abiding, industrious citizen, X. Reformers and do-gooders such as A and B are always, in Sumner's universe, scheming to take away X's hard-earned money through taxation, and redistribute his income for the benefit of the *un*deserving poor man, D. In a remarkably "modern" essay, "The Absurd Effort to Make the World Over" (1894), Sumner had ridiculed the presumption that it was wrong for a few people to hold a great deal of wealth. The "Captains of Industry" deserved their success. Their opulence increased the total sum of national wealth.

Other ideas as to the role of philanthropy in American life, which had led to such spectacular gifts as the Hirshhorn Museum, and the new East Wing of the National Gallery, in Washington D.C., had also long been embedded in the American character. In the 1880s the multimillionaire Andrew Carnegie had worked out his creed of giving, or "Gospel of Wealth," according to which people should be at liberty to acquire wealth, and to decide for themselves without government compulsion on how to dispose of their fortunes; but that they did have a social responsibility, as "stewards" or trustees of their own money, to return the bulk of it to the society that had enabled them to prosper so mightily. Carnegie, in common with Sumner and most conservatively inclined Americans of the Gilded Age, strongly disapproved of what he termed "indiscriminate charity":

> It were better for mankind that the millions of the rich was thrown into the sea than so spent as to encourage the slothful, the drunken, the unworthy. Of every thousand dollars spent in so called charity to-day, it is probable that $950 is unwisely spent; so spent, indeed, as to produce the very evils which it proposes to mitigate or cure.

A conservative of the 1980s might not be so blunt, but he could readily identify with the free-market precepts of the old captains of industry. In truth, Ronald Reagan showed he stood on that ground in 1964, in the course of a highly-praised speech on behalf of Senator Barry Goldwater. "The real destroyer of the liberties of the people," Reagan said (supposedly quoting from the ancient Graeco-Roman historian Plutarch), "is he who spreads among them bounties, donations and benefits." The same message was

The East Building of Washington's National Gallery of Art was built with funds provided by Paul Mellon, the late Ailsa Mellon and the Andrew Mellon Foundation. It was opened in 1978.

conveyed subsequently by President Reagan, for instance in his first inaugural address of January 1981: "It is no coincidence that our present troubles parallel ... the intervention and intrusion in our lives that result from unnecessary and excessive growth of government."

Thomas Jefferson and Andrew Jackson, patron saints of the Democratic party, would applaud such sentiments. So too could that arch-individualist Henry David Thoreau. In his essay on "Civil Disobedience" (1848) Thoreau cited Jeffersonian and Jacksonian slogans ("that government is best which governs least"), and insisted that, properly interpreted, their true meaning was "that government is best which governs not at all."

If the beliefs of the "Reagan Revolution" were then so deeply engrained in the nation's ideology, a conservative might feel an added confidence in the rightness of his position. Americans of his persuasion might conclude that they were merely restoring the nation to its historic direction. The "liberalism" of the first two-thirds of the 20th century could be perceived as not the norm but merely an incidental if unduly prolonged departure from America's historic goals. In that case perhaps the trend should be described as a "Counter-Revolution."

Defining Key Terms

There was an extraordinary lack of consensus on just what was going on below the surface of political or cultural events. One puzzle that we have avoided so far is to define the meanings of "liberal" and "conservative." "Liberal" was somewhat easier to define than "conservative," since it has become a term of abuse, an affiliation to deny or to pin on

other people rather than to claim as an honorable and viable stance. But what of the "conservative"? On close inspection there was far less common ground than the word might seem to imply. One commentator, Alan Crawford, distinguishes between sundry organizations of the "New Right," and the "neo-conservative" intellectuals. Spokesmen like Patrick Buchanan and Kevin Phillips tended to dismiss intellectuals like Kristol and Moynihan, or columnists like Buckley and Will, as "chiefs without Indians," egghead theorizers still half-committed to "liberal" attitudes on social security or capital punishment or other vexed issues.

Again, a broad spectrum of conservatives voiced disapproval of the Reagan administration, almost as sharply as they had done when Carter was in the White House. Some grumbled that the Reaganites had too readily given up the fight for a less-governed, entrepreneurially liberated land. They were attacked as compromisers, centrist politicians lacking in genuine conservative commitment. According to some embittered New Rightists, the revolutionary or counter-revolutionary drive had ground to a halt. Others, including the neo-conservative intellectuals associated with *Commentary*, were also on the whole disappointed by the failure (as they saw it) of the White House to follow any consistent, rational policy, let alone offer a consistent conservative one.

In 1985 – yet another anniversary – *Commentary* produced a special issue which looked back to the magazine's founding in 1945, immediately after the Second World War. The first editor had announced some goals for the nation to follow in domestic and foreign affairs. Now, forty years on, the magazine printed the responses of twenty-nine mainly neo-conservative pundits. Contributors were asked to review the original set of goals and assess how far they had

been pursued or attained. Their mood was on the whole somber. They were not greatly impressed with America's performance, including that of the Reagan administration.

There was more variety of viewpoint in a 50th anniversary special issue of the magazine *Partisan Review* (1984), yet also a good deal of head-shaking. Certain contributors felt that *Partisan Review* had not lived up to its responsibility as a voice of conscience for American intellectuals. Certain others suggested the *Review* had upheld the wrong ideals, and clung blindly to them. In "Reflections of a Neoconservative," Irving Kristol confessed it was hard to say what "conservative" – or for that matter "radical" or "modernist" – meant, although they were all in constant use. His own preferences, he explained, lay toward "premodern" ideas. He had decided that Jane Austen was a greater novelist than Proust or Joyce, "that Aristotle is more worthy of study than Marx; ... that the Founding Fathers had a better understanding of democracy than any political scientists since. . . . Well, enough. As I said at the outset, I have become conservative, and whatever ambiguities attach to that term, it should be obvious what it does *not* mean."

Is it possible to define the key terms more clearly? Such was the aim of two young Cato Institute analysts, in *Beyond Liberal and Conservative: Reassessing the Political Spectrum* (1984). They suggested that in order to make sense of the evolution of American attitudes, a "four-part matrix" was needed instead of the trite and misleading liberal-conservative dualism. Their four categories are

Star Wars, *a huge box-office success, set a new trend in science-fiction movies with fast-moving plot and spectacular special effects.*

liberal, *libertarian*, *populist*, and *conservative*. The division is explained thus:

> Liberals support government economic intervention and expansion of personal freedoms; conservatives oppose both. Libertarians support expanded individual freedom but oppose government economic intervention; populists oppose expansion of individual freedom but support government intervention in the economy.

This scheme of definitions does help in understanding a range of socio-economic issues, and the apparently confusing or contradictory alignments within American politics. We shall come back later to some of its wider implications.

One of its uses, obviously, is to emphasize the complexity of the American scene. Even President Reagan, jovial and boosterish, did not claim that everything was right with the nation. While few people were totally negative, very few were euphoric about the economy, or the prospects for peace, or homicide rates, or traffic in drugs, or national homogeneity in face of ethnic re-alignments. Thus, it was predicted that in California, by 2000 AD, white native Americans would be in the minority – outnumbered by Hispanic and Asiatic inhabitants. The mid-1970s brought a new concern for *scarcity*, where in the previous years American talk had nearly all been of *abundance*. Such talk was prompted by the OPEC oil crisis. Yet *scarcity* became a shorthand term for a host of associated worries. Commentators prophesied an actual drop in the future standard of living for Americans. They would, it was said, have less home living space than their parents, at least in the urban areas that were absorbing the bulk of American population. More and more of their income would go to the support of the aging.

Another key term, borrowed from thermodynamics but widely applied in other contexts, was *entropy*: the concept, that is, of an irrecoverable diminution of the world's supply of effective energy. Television executives, for example, referred to the "entropy factor" governing the life-span of even the most popular programs. Little by little such programs lost their appeal for the viewing public. The energy-drain could be retarded by imaginative producers, but only for a while: decline and eventual demise were in the nature of things.

Realism or Pessimism?

There was certainly an apocalyptic strain both in public discourse and in popular as well as highbrow culture. There were fewer alarm-and-despondency scenarios, perhaps, than in the early 1970s, although the prospect of nuclear war remained as ominous as before. Films like *Star Wars*, *Close Encounters of the Third Kind*, *E.T.*, and *Back to the Future*, indeed managed to fantasize reassuringly about time-warps, high technology, and creatures from outer space. There was a crop of relatively cheerful stories and articles about the teen-age "preppies" and "Valley Girls," and about the young, upwardly mobile, career-oriented "Yuppies" of the 1980s.

For the historian Christopher Lasch, however, this was *The Culture of Narcissism*, self-centered and materialistic. The consumerist ambitions and fads of the "baby-boom" adults of the 1980s were sharply satirized in the *Doonesbury* strip cartoons of the Canadian-born Gary Trudeau, and in the *"Washingtoon"* series of Mark Alan Stamaty, whose character Bob Forehead, a "John F. Kennedy look-alike," has virtually no mind of his own, simply an appetite for votes and celebrity. James Fallows, a Washington editor of the *Atlantic Monthly*, expressed alarm at these tendencies ("The Case Against Credentialism") in the magazine's December 1985 issue. Fallows was one of a number of commentators worried by his society's growing emphasis upon the service sector of the economy rather than upon manufacturing: upon the cosy privilege of the corporate business structure instead of the perils of old-fashioned entrepreneurial enterprise. He noted the tenfold expansion of business schools since the 1960s, and the expectation of business school graduates that they would, given their MBAs and other approved credentials, wind up in well-paid, standardized mediocrity.

Diagnoses of American high culture were apt to sound equally cheerless. The widely admired and cosmopolitan scholar George Steiner, domiciled in Europe but a frequent visitor to the United States, wrote a paper for a 1980 symposium on "Art and Life in America." His theme was the inferior quality of American high culture when compared to that of Europe or even of societies within the Soviet bloc. Right up to the present, American philosophy was for Steiner "thin stuff." American music was "of an essentially provincial character." Much of American mathematical thought had been developed by foreigners. In painting, dance, architecture, etc., Steiner doubted whether the American contribution was more than an appendix – admittedly, in sometimes extreme form – to the great basic innovations of European modernism.

In literature, he conceded, American achievement seemed more notable. "The general terrain of the novel in the mid-twentieth century," according to Steiner, "has been widely governed and, at vital points, redrawn by American novelists and masters of the short story." Nevertheless for him the greatest figures – Thomas Mann, Franz Kafka, James Joyce, Marcel Proust – were *not* Americans. As for poetry, the stature of such outstanding figures as Robert Frost, Wallace Stevens, and Robert Lowell, was hard to estimate – and they were all dead. And, even conceding that American performance in literature might be more solid than in other areas of culture, did the population as a whole really care about the activities of living artists, writers and intellectuals? Did the latter themselves feel they were

engaged in difficult, often unpopular, yet profoundly serious tasks?

Not in Steiner's view. He saw America as full of excellent museums and research libraries. Such a culture was, in his words, heavily custodial: American "institutions of learning and of the arts constitute the great archive, inventory, catalogue, store-house, rummage-room of western civilization. . . . Together, curators, restorers, librarians, thesis-writers, performing artists in America underwrite, reinsure the imperilled products of the ancient Mediterranean and the European spirit." In short, the United States had become an elderly culture without ceasing to be a derivative one. Its corporate civilization somehow dulled and homogenized individual creativity. So, paradoxically, did the willingness of late-20th century America to applaud the newest cultural novelty, in whatever form of art.

Not surprisingly, George Steiner's opinions (first printed in the magazine *Salmagundi*, nos. 50-51, and discussed in nos. 52-53) annoyed some of his audience. It was complained that he was repeating ancient and snobbish European prejudices. Was there so much difference between the circumstance of the two continents? If high culture could only flourish in warped and reactionary milieux, was the price worth paying? What of the popular or "lively" arts in America – jazz and subsequent developments in music, the comic book and strip cartoon, the vast and varied outreach of the movies? Still, most of the comments seemed to accept that American culture's newest manifestations were a disappointment.

Concern at Cultural Trends

Perhaps certain American pundits were ready to assent to some of Steiner's critique because they had been saying similar things themselves. Thus a series of 1983 *New Yorker* articles on the publishing industry indicated that once-distinguished houses were apt to disappear into large conglomerates, and thereby to become increasingly standardized and dehumanized. In this world, publishers were more and more hesitant to bring out truly unusual work, while writers were understandably tempted to model themselves on the minority of successful authors. The little group of top authors received huge advances for their novels or their inspirational or humorous or historical treatments. Celebrities were almost guaranteed large returns, even if their books were of the "told-to" variety. At the top of the fiction bestseller list in November 1985 was *Texas*, by the ever-popular James Michener. Not far behind came *Contact*, by the physicist-TV personality Carl Sagan, trying his hand at fiction. Pressing on their heels were works by such sure-fire novelists as Stephen King, Irving Stone and Howard Fast.

Basically the same list could have been compiled at any time in the previous decade. The leading non-fiction bestseller was *Elvis and Me*, by Priscilla Beaulieu Presley. The next four items were autobiographies, by the entertainer Shirley MacLaine, the test pilot Chuck Yeager, Lee Iacocca of Chrysler Motors, and the sports commentator Howard Cosell. Pushing up on to the list were new memoirs, each apparently ghost-written, from Geraldine Ferraro and John DeLorean ("The automobile entrepreneur tells how he became a born-again Christian after being arrested for drug trafficking"). Two titles dealt with success in business. Two others offered gossip about the late Marilyn Monroe and about the domestic life of Senator Teddy Kennedy.

The offerings of the major book clubs provided greater variety and intellectual challenge. Yet a cynic could feel that they too followed the same overall pattern: well-packaged, predictable products, scrabbling for a modest share of attention in a society where most people virtually ceased to read books, other than instruction manuals, once their schooldays were behind them. Books did continue to be published, and good ones. Yet in this dismal reckoning, only a favored few authors would ever get into the big time. Lewis Hyde, in *The Gift: Imagination and the Erotic Life of Property* (1983), argued that a book, like any other work of art, is a gift, not a commodity: "Or, to state the modern case with more precision, that works of art exist simultaneously in two 'economies,' a market economy and a gift economy." Hyde maintained that the gift economy was the more powerfully enduring: "a work of art can survive without the market, but where there is no gift there is no art."

But why should any significant amount of art survive in such circumstances? Surely most books *were* commodities, and so regarded by most potential readers? That at any rate was the interpretation of current American culture expounded in Charles Newman's *The Post-Modern Aura* (1984). For Newman, market forces determined the output of American literature, painting, sculpture and the like, just as with other products of consumerism. The process debased the standards of all but a tiny fraction of creative figures. The results might *look* good: but, as with the tomatoes or apples on display in supermarkets, they had been bred for appearance, picked too soon, artificially ripened, and were almost without flavor.

Chroniclers of American culture might find apparent corroboration in various fields. Some of them pointed to the ailing state of the American theater. Tennessee Williams died in 1983, having written nothing of weight for at least a decade. His once-great contemporary Arthur Miller seemed to be living on past glories. Broadway was economically in the doldrums, and heavily reliant upon foreign imports or upon revivals of old hits. If its plight was partly due to the greater appeal of cinema, why was the stage still vital in other countries? Why, according to the more acerbic critics, were American movies so adolescent in conception? Did the word "adult" in the American context merely signify something pornographic, as in "adult movie"?

In fact, contemporary American culture at all levels caused widespread concern. If highbrow critics denounced rampant commercialism, middlebrow Americans often expressed dismay at the violence and coarseness of popular entertainment. Profane language was almost commonplace in American movies, which had once erred in the other direction – excessive prudishness. Wives of some prominent figures on Capitol Hill launched a movement to counter the sexual explicitness of the rock-group lyrics listened to by teenagers. Nudity, homosexuality and sexual aggressiveness had become standard fare for stage and screen. It began to seem that almost every successful film involved shootings and beatings, made hideously "real" by cinematic trickery: bullets apparently puncturing flesh, gouts of blood, stabbings and stranglings galore. Television was not much better. Even in such programs as *Hill Street Blues*, *Cagney and Lacey*, and *Miami Vice*, which presented police teams as brave and basically decent people, the public they serve tended to be depicted as crazy, greedy and vicious.

Alternatively, some people feared that cultural preferences were too immature, or too conventional. Many grown-ups, after all, read little or nothing except comic-books. Many, to the sorrow of their cultivated fellows, wrote and spoke in clichés. The jargon of the services, of business and of the bureaucracy could be thought even more deplorable than the profanity and obscenity of ordinary speech, which was at least vivid. The dead language of "at this point in time," and of verbs like "to prioritize," "to interface," "to impact," "to caveat," irritated the sensitive as much as did the playing of canned music in elevators, supermarkets and waiting rooms. In interviews the young, and their athlete heroes, often seemed unable to say twenty words without interpolating a "you know."

The Positive Side of the Picture

Altogether, then, it was easy to conclude that American culture was in poor shape, and worsening steadily. The contrary case could, however, take note of more reassuring factors. Some of the most persuasive testimony came from the veteran writer Leslie Fiedler. For example, in his *What Was Literature? Class Culture and Mass Society* (1982), Fiedler refused to accept the familiar highbrow-lowbrow distinction. The very idea of "classic" literature for him was associated with "class" and with the "classroom." The academic elders had taken upon themselves the task of deciding on a merit ranking of authors. That was bad enough. But they had compounded the offense by awarding points for displays of high culture: polysyllabic diction, obscure references likely to make sense only to professional scholars, quotations in foreign and preferably ancient languages. Why should some self-appointed priesthood try to tell Americans what they were to read and what they

NY Convention and Visitors Bureau

Live theater offered diverse alternatives to TV's blandness and musicals remained as popular as ever.

were to think about it? What had actually been happening, Fiedler argued, was that taste was formed by the enthusiasms of the young. Their response to stories, poems or music was instinctive. They were not hampered by preconceptions as to proper standards. In effect they were educating the educators.

In *What Was Literature?* Leslie Fiedler focussed upon a few immensely popular works, including Margaret Mitchell's *Gone With the Wind* and Alex Haley's *Roots*. *Gone With the Wind* had maintained its appeal for half a century. *Roots*, of more recent vintage, had stirred the imagination of millions of people, of every racial stock. Their importance as guides to and shapers of American culture was surely undeniable? Why then exclude such products from consideration as "serious" contributions? Or why be disdainful about the place of movies or TV or even supposedly "junk" literature, in seeking to understand the United States? Even academe had come to realize that *Birth of a Nation*, Chaplin and Buster Keaton comedies, or the hard-boiled fiction of Dashiell Hammett and Raymond Chandler, once regarded as "mere entertainment," were now under close, admiring scrutiny by highbrows. That being so, it seemed reasonable to bet that some of the mass culture of 1975-85 would impress the critics of a future generation.

In the meantime, despite the negative reactions of some analysts, there were things to be said *in favor* of almost every aspect of late-20th century American culture. Primary and secondary education might be falling dangerously short, especially in the teaching of science and mathema-

tics; nevertheless the United States continued to win the lion's share of Nobel awards for scientific and medical research. Scholars in humanities and social sciences worried that they were becoming over-specialized, obsessed with statistical data, and therefore losing touch with the general public, not to mention their potential students. The "publish-or-perish" rule of academe, it was said, impelled faculty members to churn out articles and books in excess of any conceivable need. True enough. Yet the standard of the best American scholarship was very high. There was a large number of first-rate American learned periodicals; and every year saw the publication of thirty or forty books that contrived to be learned *and* fresh *and* readable. There were, for example, magnificent examples of biography, such as Louis Harlan's life of Booker T. Washington, Leon Edel on the novelist Henry James, and Ronald Steel's *Walter Lippmann and the American Century*.

Again, the publishing industry might be dominated by big business, and by a little group of established authors. But that was, if unfortunate, nothing new. At least some of the famous writers – say, Saul Bellow, Norman Mailer, John Updike, William Styron, Philip Roth, Gore Vidal – were far from negligible. Nor were they look-alikes: they differed greatly from one another, sometimes trenchantly so.

To a growing extent, the new reputations were being made by women writers, several of them (Toni Morrison, Alice Walker) black. The feminist approach, apparent on campuses and elsewhere from the 1960s, was often treated in its early phases as a temporary fad. But it did not go away. Stories, fiction, history, sociology and psychology: all revealed a plenitude of new voices, eager to state hitherto neglected truths as to the condition of half the human race.

Not everyone was delighted with this particular trend, but by 1985 few expected it to disappear. However reluctantly in some quarters, the nation began to take for granted that women artists and authors would be joined by others in law, medicine and every other profession and calling. It was indeed widely expected that the major parties would make a habit of nominating women as vice-presidential candidates. Sooner or later, probably sooner, a woman would become president. Such a development would have seemed unthinkable to most people not many years earlier.

Sci-fi, Comic-Books and Humor

On the cultural plane, commentators such as Fiedler also rightly stressed the vitality in the United States of the various branches of science-fiction. Some of this fantasy literature had first begun modestly or scruffily enough in pulp magazines, catering to "fans" rather than readers. The fans indeed remained a large and loyal group, some of them devoted to comic-book "fanzines" with titles like *West Coast*

Avengers, Iron Man, Dalgoda, Grimjack, Conan the Barbarian, and *Saga of the Swamp Thing*. Comics of that kind accounted for 95 per cent of the market. While sometimes inventive and stylishly drawn, they were as a rule bound by their imitative conventions. "If you've seen one, you've seen them all" was the kind of criticism they provoked. To that extent they looked like one more bit of evidence for an indictment of semi-literate mass culture. It is often said that just as in Gresham's Law bad currency drives out good, so in matters of taste trash drives out worthwhile stuff. Or, in more modern terminology, the Law of Entropy operates to dissipate quality, as part of a one-way process of decline.

However, a more cheering outcome can also be detected, in comic-books no less than in other sides of American life of the present day. In a sense it represents a backlash or counter-attack – a determined effort by artists and consumers to reverse the tide. Yet something rather different is at work. The rich potential living within the trashy mass-product is perceived by a few imaginative souls, who then take advantage of the consumer economy's appetite for novelty to produce daringly fresh material. They can do so in part because the mass audience itself becomes sophisticated. In other words, the very stultifications of mass consumption may generate an avante-garde within the culture.

Something of the sort appears at any rate to have happened with comic-books. By the 1980s these were increasingly sold in specialist stores – a thousand or more of them spread around the shopping malls of the United States. Within such a cult, it was feasible to design experimental comics for a readership of only a few thousand copies. An example of this world-within-a-world was a twice-yearly magazine named *Raw*. One strip in the magazine, "Maus," is a fantasy on German concentration camps, with the Jews drawn as mice and their Nazi guards as sadistic cats. Another avante-garde comic, *American Splendor*, began in 1976 and deliberately confined its story-strips to working-class life in Cleveland, Ohio – the magazine's home.

A similar tendency seems to have governed the kindred world of science-fiction or "sci-fi." Much of it was standard fare, manufactured according to set formulae for an undiscriminating audience (as with a great deal of the output of crime and suspense fiction). Yet there was, too, a sizeable readership of sci-fi buffs, often more concerned with philosophical problems than with stunt-technology. What-if, for instance, the Germans and Japanese had been the victors in the Second World War, and had carved up the eastern and western states of America into occupation zones? This was the supposition of the brilliant science-fiction writer Philip K. Dick in *The Man in the High Castle* (1962). Several of his subsequent tales imagined alternative existences, on earth and in outer space.

Kurt Vonnegut continued to work the zone between "reality" and science-fiction, as did the anthropologically-

THE VIETNAM MEMORIAL

The Vietnam Memorial in Washington D.C. was dedicated in November 1982 in honor of the 58,000 American men and women who died in that war. It came into being as the inspiration – some would say the obsession – of a former infantry corporal, Jan C. Scruggs. Scruggs, the son of a milkman in small-town Maryland, had gone to a showing of *The Deer Hunter*. The film haunted him, especially for its portrayal of blue-collar Americans, their inarticulate patriotism, and the failure of their civilian associates to comprehend where they had been and what they had done. Scruggs made his mind up that a memorial should be erected – a national memorial, in the nation's capital.

During 1979 Scruggs launched his campaign. Launched may be too grand a word. Though he was soon joined by two other veterans, an ex-Air Force officer named Bob Doubek, and Jack Wheeler, a graduate of West Point, their early months of effort were discouraging in the extreme. Their estimate was only too correct: Vietnam was the conflict that most people did not want to talk about. Vietnam veterans were far more of a "lost generation" than Americans of the Ernest Hemingway generation, on whom that label was fixed. Hemingway and his contemporaries came home as victors, feted and paraded. The troops from Vietnam found that their own experiences were being ignored, in a kind of conspiracy of silence. Or, still worse, they were sometimes treated as killers and criminals.

As a result Jan Scruggs and his comrades made little headway at the outset. They established a Vietnam Veterans Memorial Fund and appealed for donations. Less than $150 came in during the first month. They persevered and little by little rallied support, initially from Senators Charles C. McC. Mathias of Maryland and John W. Warner of Virginia. They

devised an ambitious timetable, requiring them to fasten upon a site, raise several million dollars and complete construction by Memorial Day, 1982.

Their seriousness and boldness paid off. With senatorial aid they managed to gain an allocation of two acres in Constitution Gardens, close to the Lincoln Memorial. Money contributions began to come in, at this stage all from ordinary citizens: corporate generosity came later. There were heartfelt messages along with the checks and money orders:
"Those boys, God Bless, were give a very *Rotten* deal."
"I hope your memorial can heal many of the hurts that that unfortunate war has caused. It lies there like unfinished business."

The theme of the campaign was indeed reconciliation. They met hostility from angry opponents of the war. "I am getting very very tired," wrote one, "of hearing about the poor Vietnam veterans." And, as their program developed, they ran into some bitter complaints from people who

thought the memorial was too apologetic, too modernistic.

This protest focused on the design for the Memorial chosen from 1,421 entries in an open competition, judged by a panel of eminent artists. The winner turned out to be Maya Ying Lin, a Yale student of Chinese parentage. Her design – a widely angled set of black granite slabs, inscribed with the names of the dead in chronological order, and sunk below ground level – was denounced by one furious veteran as "a black gash of shame." The conservative *National Review* called the design "Orwellian glop" and hoped that President Reagan would prevent it from being built.

In fact he and his administration tended to remain non-committally aloof from the various controversies swirling around the project. Maya Lin's basic design was accepted. The only compromise, offered to appease critics, was the addition of a bronze statue of three soldiers (one white, one black, one Hispanic), and an American flag – these set a little distant from the granite wall.

Miraculously, the wall was finished and landscaped by the set date. Its formal dedication, on a somber November day, was a day of choking emotion and pride for thousands of veterans and their families. Some bore militant slogans ("Next Time, Let Us Win It") or names of camps and battlegrounds. Other messages were ironic, or merely sad: "2nd Place, South-East Asia War Games, 1961-1974" and "Never Again." The crowds embraced and wept, milling in front of the grimly beautiful tally of the dead, their faces reflected in the shining stone.

Ever since that day the crowds have kept coming, day and night – leaving mementoes, touching the incised names with their fingers, testifying with deep emotion to grief, bewilderment, kinship, unity: all the great bundle of feelings that make up the spirit of a nation, and its need to attain a catharsis, or at least reach a truce, over one of the most agonizingly inconclusive episodes in the American past.

trained author Ursula LeGuin. The expatriate novelist Russell Hoban, living in London, incorporated linguistic experiments in his fables (as in *Riddley Walker*, 1980); so, in *Stars in My Pockets Like Grains of Sand* (1985), did the resourceful Samuel R. Delany. Ishmael Reed, like Delany a black American, played dazzling tricks upon time and space, and the white ethic, in such surrealistic novels as *Flight to Canada* (1976) and *The Terrible Twos* (1982).

Present in much of this fare, highbrow and lowbrow, is a serious respect for the unserious: in other words, for humor. Humor has of course many forms. Some of them have been called "sick;" examples include the spreading popularity of valentines and other greeting cards which purvey messages of gross insult. Some American aspects – humor in the guise of "good-humor" – seem emptily jovial, as with the first-naming familiarity of utter strangers, the yellow "Smile" badges, and the constant injunction to "have a nice day."

Craving for Entertainment

The 1970s and 1980s witnessed, too, a rapid spread of the "roast" – a public occasion in which famous people, especially those in politics, open themselves to mockery from journalists and other licensed jesters. Presidents Ford, Carter and Reagan and their senior assistants were all subjected to the ritual. All obviously felt obliged to pretend to be delighted at this exposure. They, and their script-writers, strove to convey appreciative aplomb, firing back equivalent one-liners, as if the nation's role models were and ought to be its chief comedians, headed by George Burns and Bob Hope. Did Gerry Ford fall over things? Did Jimmy Carter lust in his heart for other women than Rosalynn (as he ill-advisedly confessed to a magazine interviewer)? Did Ronald and Nancy confuse Hollywood with the real world? They all twinkled back at their accusers, sometimes roguishly admitting the charges against them. If this was the price to be paid for the glamor of celebrity, it was one they accepted with every appearance of pleasure.

Fortunately, there were several more genuine and more attractive manifestations of the American craving for entertainment. Syndicated columnists – Art Buchwald, Calvin Trillin, Ellen Goodman – managed to maintain a high level of sprightly good sense. So did Russell Baker, who was also the author of *Growing Up* (1982), a beautiful account of his early life, and Baker's *New York Times* colleague William Safire, the compiler of a diverting weekly essay on current uses and abuses of the American language. On the plane of wit, John Updike's *New Yorker* reviews were radiantly sympathetic, while Gore Vidal's pieces in the *New York Review* were often wickedly amusing. At its best, indeed, the *New Yorker* was a compendium of excellent visual and written humor.

One of the most cheering successes was registered by the Minnesota humorist Garrison Keillor, whose book *Lake Wobegon Days* climbed swiftly to the top of the 1985 bestseller lists, overtopping more predictable items. For some years Keillor had directed and written a weekly radio program, *Prairie Home Companion*, aired over National Public Radio. It was a gentle, affectionate take-off of old-time radio, in the days before television. *Prairie Home Companion* offered music and songs, genuine birthday and other greetings with a strong family atmosphere, spoof advertisements for non-existent products and monologues about earlier days in the imaginary small town of Lake Wobegon by Keillor himself. His sketches began to appear in the *New Yorker*, and then as the bestselling book. As recordings they are even better than in print. Keillor presents himself and his fellow Minnesotans as provincial, awkward, sometimes foolish and petty, yet basically decent. His own youthful aspirations are often gloriously comical. But as with all true humor, there is a poignant touch of sadness – of "alas, the fleeting years."

Keillor's monologues are about the past. Their nostalgia has a tinge of sadness because he seems to be talking of a bygone America more wholesome than today's corporate, consumer-oriented urban scene. In fact a good deal of late-20th century American culture projects this wistful admiration for the values of yesteryear. It underlies the appetite for anniversaries noted at the beginning of this article. Each becomes a tribute to the past in the process of celebrating the present. Yes, each asserts, the nation has traveled a long way over the years. But each celebration implicitly asks, has the route always led upwards?

Enduring Attitudes

In their most positive and reasonable moods, Americans of the decade 1975-85 tried to reconcile pride in change and movement with the conviction that they were still drawing sustenance from a past record of solid merit. In this spirit did Americans willingly support museums and flock to commemorative parades. Despite the fascination with computers, microwave ovens and other gadgets of a high-tech civilization, never had the nation paid so much respect to the preservation of its material heritage.

Something similar may well help to explain the apparently contradictory analysis of contemporary conservatism. The terms, we have seen, are blurred. In the 1980s, it seems that "liberal" is, perhaps temporarily, out of vogue. Polls indicated, however, that politicians of various stripes liked to call themselves "progressive" and also "moderate." Perhaps this means that their impulse is always toward the middle of whatever they take to be public sentiment. In that regard conservatism is safe middle ground, for at least two

Rafer Johnson lights the Olympic torch at Los Angeles, where US success was even greater than usual, largely because of the Soviet boycott.

reasons. First, its very vagueness allows its champions to avoid committing themselves to any definite creed. They can change their minds. If for instance a major depression should afflict the American economy in the years ahead, conservatism could be turned inside out, like a reversible raincoat, in response to modified public demands. Whatever the rhetoric, the United States of the late-20th century was what it had long been, an odd amalgam of private enterprise and public direction, of individualism and community spirit.

The point is nicely made, we can remark in conclusion, in a 1985 article by the Harvard political economist Robert R. Reich. He identifies four fundamental "national parables" that have been invoked since the very beginning of American independence. He suggests that the nation's orators and aspirants for office have rung the changes on the four without ever needing a new set. They are: 1. *The Rot at the Top*; 2. *The Triumphant Individual*; 3. *The Benign Community*; 4. *The Mob at the Gates*.

Two of the four are optimistic, two pessimistic. *Rot at the Top* embodies fears of corruption and arrogance among men of privilege, whether on Wall Street or in Washington. It can be either reformist or reactionary. No. 4, *The Mob at the Gates*, could almost be labeled *Rot at the Bottom*. It speaks to the fears of Americans that their society is being undermined, perhaps by undesirable immigrants, or the Mafia, or ward bosses, or terrorists, muggers and people on

drugs. *The Triumphant Individual*, the saga of the self-made man (*Room at the Top*?), is in different ways that of Ford, Carter, Reagan, and indeed of Walter Mondale and Geraldine Ferraro, as well as of shop-floor-to-boardroom tycoon Lee Iacocca. *The Benign Community* is the small town from which several of the *Triumphant Individuals* started, just as it is Lake Wobegon, a place (in Keillor's words) that "exists so long as you don't go looking for it."

These are perhaps not the only scenarios current in late-20th century America. There are enduring visions of farms and of wilderness, and – at the opposite extreme – of the rapacious entrepreneurs and their love lives portrayed on television in *Dallas, Falcon Crest* and *Dynasty*. Benign communities are set in rural America; and audiences are supposed to disapprove of the bad behaviour of the rich in TV series, even while envying them a little.

In short, Reich's formulation does cover a great deal of American thinking and feeling about the strengths and potential weaknesses of the Republic. These reactions, especially vivid in the worlds of politics and entertainment, vary in emphasis from decade to decade. Yet in essence they are timeless. Any bold assertion as to a permanent regrouping of American opinion is therefore unwise. Yesterday's poorly regarded president (witness Dwight D. Eisenhower) may be transformed into today's hero. Conversely, yesterday's hero (John F. Kennedy) may be sharply devalued. In the same way, today's popular creeds may not survive any considerable strain, imparted by pressures upon the economy or by the nation's problems overseas. With reference to the current interpretations of "conservative" and "liberal" we might be wise to recall the satirical definition in Ambrose Bierce's *The Devil's Dictionary*:

> CONSERVATIVE: A Statesman who is enamored of existing evils, as distinguished from the Liberal, who wishes to replace them with others.

On January 28, 1986 the Space Shuttle Challenger exploded less than two minutes after takeoff, killing all on board. President Reagan led the nation in mourning, praising the astronauts' courage and saluting their memory. From left: Ellison Onizuka, Michael Smith, Sharon Christa McAuliffe, Francis Scobee, Gregory Jarvis, Ronald McNair and Judith Resnik.

The Constitution of the United States

We the People of the United States, in Order to form a more perfect Union, establish Justice, insure domestic Tranquillity, provide for the common defence, promote the general Welfare, and secure the Blessings of Liberty to ourselves and our Posterity, do ordain and establish this Constitution for the United States of America.

ARTICLE I

Section 1. All legislative Powers herein granted shall be vested in a Congress of the United States, which shall consist of a Senate and House of Representatives.

Section 2. The House of Representatives shall be composed of Members chosen every second Year by the people of the several States, and the Electors in each State shall have the Qualifications requisite for Electors of the most numerous Branch of the State Legislature.

No Person shall be a Representative who shall not have attained to the age of twenty five Years, and been seven Years a Citizen of the United States, and who shall not, when elected, be an Inhabitant of that State in which he shall be chosen.

Representatives and direct Taxes shall be apportioned among the several States which may be included within this Union, according to their respective Numbers, which shall be determined by adding to the whole Number of free Persons, including those bound to Service for a Term of Years, and excluding Indians not taxed, three fifths of all other Persons. The actual Enumeration shall be made within three Years after the first Meeting of the Congress of the United States, and within every subsequent Term of ten Years, in such Manner as they shall by Law direct. The Number of Representatives shall not exceed one for every thirty Thousand, but each State shall have at Least one Representative; and until such enumeration shall be made, the State of New Hampshire shall be entitled to chuse three, Massachusetts eight, Rhode-Island and Providence Plantations one, Connecticut five, New-York six, New Jersey four, Pennsylvania eight, Delaware one, Maryland six, Virginia ten, North Carolina five, South Carolina five, and Georgia three.

When vacancies happen in the Representation from any State, the Executive Authority thereof shall issue Writs of Election to fill such Vacancies.

The House of Representatives shall chuse their Speaker and other Officers; and shall have the sole Power of Impeachment.

Section 3. The Senate of the United States shall be composed of two Senators from each State, chosen by the Legislature thereof, for six Years; and each Senator shall have one Vote.

Immediately after they shall be assembled in Consequence of the first Election, they shall be divided as equally as may be into three Classes. The Seats of the Senators of the first Class shall be vacated at the Expiration of the second Year, of the second Class at the Expiration of the fourth Year, and of the third Class at the Expiration of the sixth Year, so that one third may be chosen every second Year; and if Vacancies happen by Resignation, or otherwise, during the Recess of the Legislature of any State, the Executive thereof may make temporary Appointments until the next Meeting of the Legislature, which shall then fill such Vacancies.

No Person shall be a Senator who shall not have attained to the Age of thirty Years, and been nine Years a Citizen of the United States, and who shall not, when elected, be an Inhabitant of that State for which he shall be chosen.

The Vice President of the United States shall be President of the Senate, but shall have no Vote, unless they be equally divided.

The Senate shall chuse their other Officers, and also a President pro tempore, in the Absence of the Vice President, or when he shall exercise the Office of President of the United States.

The Senate shall have the sole Power to try all Impeachments. When sitting for that Purpose, they shall be on Oath or Affirmation. When the President of the United States is tried the Chief Justice shall preside: And no Person shall be convicted without the Concurrence of two thirds of the Members present.

Judgment in Cases of Impeachment shall not extend further than to removal from Office, and disqualification to hold and enjoy any Office of honor, Trust or Profit under the United States: but the Party convicted shall nevertheless be liable and subject to Indictment, Trial, Judgment and Punishment, according to Law.

Section 4. The Times, Places and Manner of holding Elections for Senators and Representatives, shall be prescribed in each State by the Legislature thereof; but the Congress may at any time by Law make or alter such Regulations, except as to the Places of chusing Senators.

The Congress shall assemble at least once in every Year, and such Meeting shall be on the first Monday in December, unless they shall by Law appoint a different Day.

Section 5. Each House shall be the Judge of the Elections, Returns and Qualifications of its own Members, and a Majority of each shall constitute a Quorum to do Business; but a smaller Number may adjourn from day to day, and may be authorized to compel the Attendance of absent Members, in such Manner, and under such Penalties as each House may provide.

Each House may determine the Rules of its Proceedings, punish its Members for disorderly Behaviour, and, with the Concurrence of two thirds, expel a Member.

Each House shall keep a Journal of its Proceedings, and from time to time publish the same, excepting such Parts as may in their Judgment require Secrecy; and the Yeas and Nays of the Members of either House on any question shall, at the Desire of one fifth of those Present, be entered on the Journal.

Neither House, during the Session of Congress, shall, without the Consent of the other, adjourn for more than three days, nor to any other Place than that in which the two Houses shall be sitting.

Section 6. The Senators and Representatives shall receive a Compensation for their Services, to be ascertained by Law, and paid out of the Treasury of the United States. They shall in all Cases, except Treason, Felony and Breach of the Peace, be privileged from Arrest during their Attendance at the Session of their respective Houses, and in going to and returning from the same; and for any Speech or Debate in either House, they shall not be questioned in any other Place.

No Senator or Representative shall, during the Time for which he was elected, be appointed to any civil Office under the Authority of the United States, which shall have been created, or the Emoluments whereof shall have been encreased during such time; and no Person holding any Office under the United States, shall be a Member of either House during his Continuance in Office.

Section 7. All Bills for raising Revenue shall originate in the House of Representatives; but the Senate may propose or concur with amendments as on other Bills.

Every Bill which shall have passed the House of Representatives and the Senate, shall, before it become a Law, be presented to the President of the United States; If he approve he shall sign it, but if not he shall return it, with his Objections to that House in which it shall have originated, who shall enter the Objections at large on their Journal, and proceed to reconsider it. If after such Reconsideration two thirds of that House shall agree to pass the Bill, it shall be sent, together with the Objections, to the other House, by which it shall likewise be reconsidered, and if approved by two thirds of that House, it shall become a Law. But in all such Cases the Votes of both Houses shall be determined by yeas and Nays, and the Names of the Persons voting for and against the Bill shall be entered on the Journal of each House respectively. If any Bill shall not be returned by the President within ten Days (Sundays excepted) after it shall have been presented to him, the Same shall be a Law, in like Manner as if he had signed it, unless the Congress by their Adjournment prevent its Return, in which Case it shall not be a Law.

Every Order, Resolution, or Vote to which the Concurrence of the Senate and House of Representatives may be necessary (except on a question of Adjournment) shall be presented to the President of the United States; and before the Same shall take Effect, shall be approved by him, or being disapproved by him, shall be repassed by two thirds of the Senate and House of Representatives, according to the Rules and Limitations prescribed in the Case of a Bill.

Section 8. The Congress shall have Power To lay and collect Taxes, Duties, Imposts and Excises, to pay the Debts and provide for the common Defence and general Welfare of the United States; but all Duties, Imposts and Excises shall be uniform throughout the United States;

To borrow Money on the credit of the United States;

To regulate Commerce with foreign Nations, and among the several States, and with the Indian Tribes;

To establish a uniform Rule of Naturalization, and uniform Laws on the subject of Bankruptcies throughout the United States;

To coin Money, regulate the Value thereof, and of foreign Coin, and fix the Standard of Weights and Measures;

To provide for the Punishment of counterfeiting the Securities and current Coin of the United States;

To establish Post Offices and post Roads;

To promote the Progress of Science and useful Arts, by securing for limited Times to Authors and Inventors the exclusive Right to their respective Writings and Discoveries;

To constitute Tribunals inferior to the supreme Court;

To define and punish Piracies and Felonies committed on the high Seas, and Offences against the Law of Nations;

To declare War, grant Letters of Marque and Reprisal, and make Rules concerning Captures on Land and Water;

To raise and support Armies, but no Appropriation of Money to that Use shall be for a longer Term than two Years;

To provide and maintain a Navy;

To make Rules for the Government and Regulation of the land and naval Forces;

To provide for calling forth the Militia to execute the Laws of the Union, suppress Insurrections and repel Invasions;

To provide for organizing, arming, and disciplining, the Militia, and for governing such Part of them as may be employed in the Service of the United States, reserving to the States respectively, the Appointment of the Officers, and the Authority of training the Militia according to the discipline prescribed by Congress;

To exercise exclusive Legislation in all Cases whatsoever, over such District (not exceeding ten Miles square) as may, by Cession of Particular States, and the Acceptance of Congress, become the Seat of the Government of the United States, and to exercise like Authority over all Places purchased by the

Consent of the Legislature of the State in which the Same shall be, for the Erection of Forts, Magazines, Arsenals, dock-Yards, and other needful Buildings;—And

To make all Laws which shall be necessary and proper for carrying into Execution the foregoing Powers, and all other Powers vested by this Constitution in the Government of the United States, or in any Department or Officer thereof.

Section 9. The Migration or Importation of such Persons as any of the States now existing shall think proper to admit, shall not be prohibited by the Congress prior to the Year one thousand eight hundred and eight, but a Tax or duty may be imposed on such Importation, not exceeding ten dollars for each Person.

The Privilege of the Writ of Habeas Corpus shall not be suspended, unless when in Cases of Rebellion or Invasion the public Safety may require it.

No Bill of Attainder or ex post facto Law shall be passed.

No Capitation, or other direct, Tax shall be laid, unless in Proportion to the Census or Enumeration herein before directed to be taken.

No Tax or Duty shall be laid on Articles exported from any State.

No Preference shall be given by any Regulation of Commerce or Revenue to the Ports of one State over those of another; nor shall Vessels bound to, or from, one State, be obliged to enter, clear or pay Duties in another.

No Money shall be drawn from the Treasury, but in Consequence of Appropriations made by Law; and a regular Statement and Account of the Receipts and Expenditures of all public Money shall be published from time to time.

No Title of Nobility shall be granted by the United States: And no Person holding any Office of Profit or Trust under them, shall, without the Consent of the Congress, accept of any present, Emolument, Office, or Title, of any kind whatever, from any King, Prince, or foreign State.

Section 10. No State shall enter into any Treaty, Alliance, or Confederation; grant Letters of Marque and Reprisal; coin Money; emit Bills of Credit; make any Thing but gold and silver Coin a Tender in Payment of Debts; pass any Bill of Attainder, ex post facto Law, or Law impairing the Obligation of Contracts, or grant any Title of Nobility.

No State shall, without the Consent of the Congress, lay any Imposts or Duties on Imports or Exports, except what may be absolutely necessary for executing its inspection Laws: and the net Produce of all Duties and Imposts, laid by any State on Imports or Exports, shall be for the Use of the Treasury of the United States; and all such Laws shall be subject to the Revision and Controul of the Congress.

No State shall, without the Consent of Congress, lay any Duty of Tonnage, keep Troops, or Ships of War in time of Peace, enter into any Agreement or Compact with another State, or with a foreign Power, or engage in War, unless actually invaded, or in such imminent Danger as will not admit of delay.

ARTICLE II

Section 1. The executive Power shall be vested in a President of the United States of America. He shall hold his Office during the Term of four Years, and, together with the Vice President, chosen for the same Term, be elected, as follows

Each State shall appoint, in such Manner as the Legislature thereof may direct, a Number of Electors, equal to the whole Number of Senators and Representatives to which the State may be entitled in the Congress: but no Senator or Representative, or Person holding an Office of Trust or Profit under the United States, shall be appointed an Elector.

The Electors shall meet in their respective States, and vote by Ballot for two Persons, of whom one at least shall not be an Inhabitant of the same State with themselves. And they shall make a List of all the Persons voted for, and of the Number of Votes for each; which List they shall sign and certify, and

transmit sealed to the Seat of the Government of the United States, directed to the President of the Senate. The President of the Senate shall, in the Presence of the Senate and House of Representatives, open all the Certificates, and the Votes shall then be counted. The Person having the greatest Number of Votes shall be the President, if such Number be a Majority of the whole Number of Electors appointed; and if there be more than one who have such Majority, and have an equal Number of Votes, then the House of Representatives shall immediately chuse by Ballot one of them for President; and if no Person have a Majority, then from the five highest on the List the said House shall in like Manner chuse the President. But in chusing the President, the Votes shall be taken by States. the Representation from each State having one Vote; a quorum for this Purpose shall consist of a Member or Members from two thirds of the States, and a Majority of all the States shall be necessary to a Choice. In every Case, after the Choice of the President, the Person having the greatest Number of Votes of the Electors shall be the Vice President. But if there should remain two or more who have equal Votes, the Senate shall chuse from them by Ballot the Vice President.

The Congress may determine the Time of chusing the Electors, and the Day on which they shall give their Votes; which Day shall be the same throughout the United States.

No Person except a natural born Citizen, or a Citizen of the United States, at the time of the Adoption of this Constitution, shall be eligible to the Office of President; neither shall any person be eligible to that Office who shall not have attained to the Age of thirty five Years, and been fourteen Years a Resident within the United States.

In Case of the Removal of the President from Office, or of his Death, Resignation, or Inability to discharge the Powers and Duties of the said Office, the Same shall devolve on the Vice President, and the Congress may by Law provide for the Case of Removal, Death, Resignation or Inability, both of the President and Vice President, declaring what Officer shall then act as President, and such Officer shall act accordingly, until the Disability be removed, or a President shall be elected.

The President shall, at stated Times, receive for his Services, a Compensation, which shall neither be encreased nor diminished during the Period for which he shall have been elected, and he shall not receive within that period any other Emolument from the United States, or any of them.

Before he enter on the Execution of his Office, he shall take the following Oath or Affirmation:— "I do solemnly swear (or affirm) that I will faithfully execute the Office of President of the United States, and will to the best of my Ability, preserve, protect and defend the Constitution of the United States."

Section 2. The President shall be Commander in Chief of the Army and Navy of the United States, and of the Militia of the several States, when called into the actual Service of the United States; he may require the Opinion, in writing, of the principal Officer in each of the executive Departments, upon any Subject relating to the Duties of their respective Offices, and he shall have Power to grant Reprieves and Pardons for Offences against the United States, except in Cases of Impeachment.

He shall have Power, by and with the Advice and Consent of the Senate, to make Treaties, provided two thirds of the Senators present concur; and he shall nominate, and by and with the Advice and Consent of the Senate, shall appoint Ambassadors, other public Ministers and Consuls, Judges of the supreme Court, and all other Officers of the United States, whose Appointments are not herein otherwise provided for, and which shall be established by Law: but the Congress may by Law vest the Appointment of such inferior Officers, as they think proper, in the President alone, in the Courts of Law, or in the Heads of Departments.

The President shall have Power to fill up all

Vacancies that may happen during the Recess of the Senate, by granting Commissions which shall expire at the End of their next Session.

Section 3. He shall from time to time give to the Congress Information of the State of the Union, and recommend to their Consideration such Measures as he shall judge necessary and expedient; he may, on extraordinary Occasions, convene both Houses, or either of them, and in Case of Disagreement between them, with Respect to the Time of Adjournment, he may adjourn them to such Time as he shall think proper; he shall receive Ambassadors and other public Ministers; he shall take Care that the Laws be faithfully executed, and shall Commission all the Officers of the United States.

Section 4. The President, Vice President and all civil Officers of the United States, shall be removed from Office on Impeachment for, and Conviction of, Treason, Bribery, or other high Crimes and Misdemeanors.

ARTICLE III

Section 1. The judicial Power of the United States, shall be vested in one supreme Court, and in such inferior Courts as the Congress may from time to time ordain and establish. The Judges, both of the supreme and inferior Courts, shall hold their Offices during good Behaviour, and shall, at stated Times, receive for their Services, a Compensation, which shall not be diminished during their Continuance in Office.

Section 2. The judicial Power shall extend to all Cases, in Law and Equity, arising under this Constitution, the Laws of the United States, and Treaties made, or which shall be made, under their Authority;—to all Cases affecting Ambassadors, other public Ministers and Consuls;—to all Cases of admiralty and maritime Jurisdiction;—to Controversies to which the United States shall be a Party;—to Controversies between two or more States;—between a State and Citizens of another State;—between Citizens of different States;—between Citizens of the same State claiming Lands under Grants of different States, and between a State, or the Citizens thereof, and foreign States, Citizens or Subjects.

In all Cases affecting Ambassadors, other public Ministers and Consuls, and those in which a State shall be Party, the supreme Court shall have original Jurisdiction. In all the other Cases before mentioned, the supreme Court shall have appellate Jurisdiction, both as to Law and Fact, with such Exceptions, and under such Regulations as the Congress shall make.

The Trial of all Crimes, except in Cases of Impeachment, shall be by Jury; and such Trial shall be held in the State where the said Crimes shall have been committed; but when not committed within any State, the Trial shall be at such Place or Places as the Congress may by Law have directed.

Section 3. Treason against the United States, shall consist only in levying War against them, or in adhering to their Enemies, giving them Aid and Comfort. No Person shall be convicted of Treason unless on the Testimony of two Witnesses to the same overt Act, or on Confession in open Court.

The Congress shall have Power to declare the Punishment of Treason, but no Attainder of Treason shall work Corruption of Blood, or Forfeiture except during the Life of the Person attainted.

ARTICLE IV

Section 1. Full Faith and Credit shall be given in each State to the public Acts, Records, and judicial Proceedings of every other State. And the Congress may by general Laws prescribe the Manner in which such Acts, Records and Proceedings shall be proved, and the Effect thereof.

Section 2. The Citizens of each State shall be entitled to all Privileges and Immunities of Citizens in the several States.

A Person charged in any State with Treason, Felony, or other Crime, who shall flee from Justice, and be found in another State, shall on Demand of the executive Authority of the State from which he fled, be delivered up, to be removed to the State

having Jurisdiction of the Crime.

No Person held to Service or Labour in one State, under the Laws thereof, escaping into another, shall, in Consequence of any Law or Regulation therein, be discharged from such Service or Labour, but shall be delivered up on Claim of the Party to whom such Service or Labour may be due.

Section 3. New States may be admitted by the Congress into this Union; but no new State shall be formed or erected within the Jurisdiction of any other State; nor any State be formed by the Junction of two or more States, or Parts of States, without the Consent of the Legislatures of the States concerned as well as of the Congress.

The Congress shall have Power to dispose of and make all needful Rules and Regulations respecting the Territory or other Property belonging to the United States; and nothing in this Constitution shall be so construed as to Prejudice any Claims of the United States, or of any particular State.

Section 4. The United States shall guarantee to every State in this Union a Republican Form of Government, and shall protect each of them against Invasion; and on Application of the Legislature, or of the Executive (when the Legislature cannot be convened) against domestic Violence.

ARTICLE V

The Congress, whenever two thirds of both Houses shall deem it necessary, shall propose Amendments to this Constitution, or, on the Application of the Legislatures of two thirds of the several States, shall call a Convention for proposing Amendments, which, in either Case, shall be valid to all Intents and Purposes, as Part of this Constitution, when ratified by the Legislatures of three fourths of the several States, or by Conventions in three fourths thereof, as the one or the other Mode of Ratification may be proposed by the Congress; Provided that no Amendment which may be made prior to the Year One thousand eight hundred and eight shall in any Manner affect the first and fourth Clauses in the Ninth Section of the first Article; and that no State, without its Consent, shall be deprived of its equal Suffrage in the Senate.

ARTICLE VI

All Debts contracted and Engagements entered into, before the Adoption of this Constitution, shall be as valid against the United States under this Constitution, as under the Confederation.

This Constitution, and the Laws of the United States which shall be made in Pursuance thereof; and all Treaties made, or which shall be made, under the Authority of the United States, shall be the supreme Law of the Land; and the Judges in every State shall be bound thereby, any Thing in the Constitution or Laws of any State to the Contrary notwithstanding.

The Senators and Representatives before mentioned, and the Members of the several State Legislatures, and all executive and judicial Officers, both of the United States and of the several States, shall be bound by Oath or Affirmation, to support this Constitution; but no religious Test shall ever be required as a Qualification to any Office or public Trust under the United States.

ARTICLE VII

The Ratification of the Conventions of nine States, shall be sufficient for the Establishment of this Constitution between the States so ratifying the Same.

[Signatures omitted.]

Articles in addition to, and amendment of, the Constitution of the United States of America, proposed by Congress, and ratified by the several states, pursuant to the fifth article of the original Constitution.

AMENDMENT I

Congress shall make no law respecting an establishment of religion, or prohibiting the free exercise thereof; or abridging the freedom of speech, or of the press; or the right of the people peaceably to assemble, and to petition the Government for a redress of grievances.

AMENDMENT II

A well regulated Militia, being necessary to the security of a free State, the right of the people to keep and bear Arms, shall not be infringed.

AMENDMENT III

No Soldier shall, in time of peace be quartered in any house, without the consent of the Owner, nor in time of war, but in a manner to be prescribed by law.

AMENDMENT IV

The right of the people to be secure in their persons, houses, papers, and effects, against unreasonable searches and seizures, shall not be violated, and no Warrants shall issue, but upon probable cause, supported by Oath or affirmation, and particularly describing the place to be searched, and the persons or things to be seized.

AMENDMENT V

No person shall be held to answer for a capital, or otherwise infamous crime, unless on a presentment or indictment of a Grand Jury, except in cases arising in the land or naval forces, or in the Militia, when in actual service in time of War or public danger; nor shall any person be subject for the same offence to be twice put in jeopardy of life or limb; nor shall be compelled in any criminal case to be a witness against himself, nor be deprived of life, liberty, or property, without due process of law; nor shall private property be taken for public use, without just compensation.

AMENDMENT VI

In all criminal prosecutions, the accused shall enjoy the right to a speedy and public trial, by an impartial jury of the State and district wherein the crime shall have been committed, which district shall have been previously ascertained by law, and to be informed of the nature and cause of the accusation; to be confronted with the witnesses against him; to have compulsory process for obtaining witnesses in his favor, and to have the Assistance of Counsel for his defence.

AMENDMENT VII

In Suits at common law, where the value in controversy shall exceed twenty dollars, the right of trial by jury shall be preserved, and no fact tried by a jury, shall be otherwise re-examined in any Court of the United States, than according to the rules of the common law.

AMENDMENT VIII

Excessive bail shall not be required, nor excessive fines imposed, nor cruel and unusual punishments inflicted.

AMENDMENT IX

The enumeration in the Constitution, of certain rights, shall not be construed to deny or disparage others retained by the people.

AMENDMENT X

The powers not delegated to the United States by the Constitution, nor prohibited by it to the States, are reserved to the States respectively, or to the people.

AMENDMENT XI

The Judicial power of the United States shall not be construed to extend to any suit in law or equity, commenced or prosecuted against one of the United States by Citizens of another State, or by Citizens or Subjects of any Foreign State.

AMENDMENT XII

The Electors shall meet in their respective states and vote by ballot for President and Vice-President, one of whom, at least, shall not be an inhabitant of the same state with themselves; they shall name in their ballots the person voted for as President, and in distinct ballots the person voted for as Vice-President, and they shall make distinct lists of all persons voted for as President, and of all persons voted for as Vice-President, and of the number of votes for each, which lists they shall sign and certify, and transmit sealed to the seat of the government of the United States, directed to the President of the Senate;—The President of the Senate shall, in the presence of the Senate and House of Representatives, open all the certificates and the votes shall then be counted;—The person having the greatest number of votes for President, shall be the President, if such number be a majority of the whole number of Electors appointed; and if no person have such majority, then from the persons having the highest numbers not exceeding three on the list of those voted for as President, the House of Representatives shall choose immediately, by ballot, the President. But in choosing the President, the votes shall be taken by states, the representation from each state having one vote; a quorum for this purpose shall consist of a member or members from two-thirds of the states, and a majority of all the states shall be necessary to a choice. And if the House of Representatives shall not choose a President whenever the right of choice shall devolve upon them, before the fourth day of March next following, then the Vice-President shall act as President, as in the case of the death or other constitutional disability of the President—The person having the greatest number of votes as Vice-President, shall be the Vice-President, if such number be a majority of the whole number of Electors appointed, and if no person have a majority, then from the two highest numbers on the list, the Senate shall choose the Vice-President; a quorum for the purpose shall consist of two-thirds of the whole number of Senators, and a majority of the whole number shall be necessary to a choice. But no person constitutionally ineligible to the office of President shall be eligible to that of Vice-President of the United States.

AMENDMENT XIII

Section 1. Neither slavery nor involuntary servitude, except as a punishment for crime whereof the party shall have been duly convicted, shall exist within the United States, or any place subject to their jurisdiction.

Section 2. Congress shall have power to enforce this article by appropriate legislation.

AMENDMENT XIV

Section 1. All persons born or naturalized in the United States and subject to the jurisdiction thereof, are citizens of the United States and of the State wherein they reside. No State shall make or enforce any law which shall abridge the privileges or immunities of citizens of the United States; nor shall any State deprive any person of life, liberty, or property, without due process of law; nor deny to any person within its jurisdiction the equal protection of the laws.

Section 2. Representatives shall be apportioned among the several States according to their respective numbers, counting the whole number of persons in each State, excluding Indians not taxed. But when the right to vote at any election for the choice of electors for President and Vice President of the United States, Representatives in Congress, the Executive and Judicial officers of a State, or the members of the Legislature thereof, is denied to any of the male inhabitants of such State, being twenty-one years of age, and citizens of the United States, or in any way abridged, except for participation in rebellion, or other crime, the basis of representation therein shall be reduced in the proportion which the number of such male citizens shall bear to the whole number of male citizens twenty-one years of age in such State.

Section 3. No person shall be a Senator or Representative in Congress, or elector of President and Vice President, or hold any office, civil or military, under the United States, or under any State, who, having previously taken an oath, as a

member of Congress, or as an officer of the United States, or as a member of any State legislature, or as an executive or judicial officer of any State, to support the Constitution of the United States, shall have engaged in insurrection or rebellion against the same, or given aid or comfort to the enemies thereof. But Congress may by a vote of two-thirds of each House, remove such disability.

Section 4. The validity of the public debt of the United States, authorized by law, including debts incurred for payment of pensions and bounties for services in suppressing insurrection or rebellion, shall not be questioned. But neither the United States nor any State shall assume or pay any debt or obligation incurred in aid of insurrection or rebellion against the United States, or any claim for the loss or emancipation of any slave; but all such debts, obligations and claims shall be held illegal and void.

Section 5. The Congress shall have power to enforce, by appropriate legislation, the provisions of this article.

AMENDMENT XV

Section 1. The right of citizens of the United States to vote shall not be denied or abridged by the United States or by any State on account of race, color, or previous condition of servitude.

Section 2. The Congress shall have power to enforce this article by appropriate legislation.

AMENDMENT XVI

The Congress shall have power to lay and collect taxes on incomes, from whatever source derived, without apportionment among the several States, and without regard to any census or enumeration.

AMENDMENT XVII

The Senate of the United States shall be composed of two Senators from each State, elected by the people thereof, for six years; and each Senator shall have one vote. The electors in each State shall have the qualifications requisite for electors of the most numerous branch of the State legislatures.

When vacancies happen in the representation of any State in the Senate, the executive authority of such State shall issue writs of election to fill such vacancies: *Provided*, That the legislature of any State may empower the executive thereof to make temporary appointments until the people fill the vacancies by election as the legislature may direct.

This amendment shall not be so construed as to affect the election or term of any Senator chosen before it becomes valid as part of the Constitution.

AMENDMENT XVIII

Section 1. After one year from the ratification of this article the manufacture, sale, or transportation of intoxicating liquors within, the importation thereof into, or the exportation thereof from the United States and all territory subject to the jurisdiction thereof for beverage purposes is hereby prohibited.

Section 2. The Congress and the several States shall have concurrent power to enforce this article by appropriate legislation.

Section 3. This article shall be inoperative unless it shall have been ratified as an amendment to the Constitution by the legislatures of the several States, as provided in the Constitution, within seven years from the date of the submission hereof to the States by the Congress.

AMENDMENT XIX

The right of citizens of the United States to vote shall not be denied or abridged by the United States or by any State on account of sex.

Congress shall have power to enforce this article by appropriate legislation.

AMENDMENT XX

Section 1. The terms of the President and Vice President shall end at noon on the 20th day of January, and the terms of Senators and Representatives at noon on the 3d day of January, of the years in which such terms would have ended if this article had not been ratified; and the terms of their successors shall then begin.

Section 2. The Congress shall assemble at least once in every year, and such meeting shall begin at noon on the 3d day of January, unless they shall by law appoint a different day.

Section 3. If, at the time fixed for the beginning of the term of the President, the President elect shall have died, the Vice President elect shall become President. If a President shall not have been chosen before the time fixed for the beginning of his term, or if the President elect shall have failed to qualify, then the Vice President elect shall act as President until a President shall have qualified; and the Congress may by law provide for the case wherein neither a, President elect nor a Vice President elect shall have qualified, declaring who shall then act as President, or the manner in which one who is to act shall be selected, and such person shall act accordingly until a President or Vice President shall have qualified.

Section 4. The Congress may by law provide for the case of the death of any of the persons from whom the House or Representatives may choose a President whenever the right of choice shall have devolved upon them, and for the case of the death of any of the persons from whom the Senate may choose a Vice President whenever the right of choice shall have devolved upon them.

Section 5. Sections 1 and 2 shall take effect on the 15th day of October following the ratification of this article.

Section 6. This article shall be inoperative unless it shall have been ratified as an amendment to the Constitution by the legislatures of three-fourths of the several States within seven years from the date of its submission.

AMENDMENT XXI

Section 1. The eighteenth article of amendment to the Constitution of the United States is hereby repealed.

Section 2. The transportation or importation into any State, Territory, or possession of the United States for delivery or use therein of intoxicating liquors, in violation of the laws thereof, is hereby prohibited.

Section 3. This article shall be inoperative unless it shall have been ratified as an amendment to the Constitution by conventions in the several States, as provided in the Constitution, within seven years from the date of the submission hereof to the States by the Congress.

AMENDMENT XXII

Section 1. No person shall be elected to the office of the President more than twice, and no person who has held the office of President, or acted as President, for more than two years of a term to which some other person was elected President shall be elected to the office of the President more than once. But this Article shall not apply to any person holding the office of President when this Article was proposed by the Congress, and shall not prevent any person who may be holding the office of President, or acting as President, during the term within which this Article becomes operative from holding the office of President or acting as President during the remainder of such term.

Section 2. This Article shall be inoperative unless it shall have been ratified as an amendment to the Constitution by the legislatures of three-fourths of the several States within seven years from the date of its submission to the States by the Congress.

AMENDMENT XXIII

Section 1. The District constituting the seat of Government of the United States shall appoint in such manner as the Congress may direct:

A number of electors of President and Vice President equal to the whole number of Senators and Representatives in Congress to which the District would be entitled if it were a State, but in no event more than the least populous State; they shall be in addition to those appointed by the States, but they shall be considered, for the purposes of the election of President and Vice President, to be electors appointed by a State; and they shall meet in the District and perform such duties as provided by the twelfth article of amendment.

Section 2. The Congress shall have power to enforce this article by appropriate legislation.

AMENDMENT XXIV

Section 1. The right of citizens of the United States to vote in any primary or other election for President or Vice President, for electors for President or Vice President, or for Senator or Representative in Congress, shall not be denied or abridged by the United States or any State by reason of failure to pay any poll tax or other tax.

Section 2. The Congress shall have the power to enforce this article by appropriate legislation.

AMENDMENT XXV

Section 1. In case of the removal of the President from office or of his death or resignation, the Vice President shall become President.

Section 2. Whenever there is a vacancy in the office of the Vice President, the President shall nominate a Vice President who shall take the office upon confirmation by a majority vote of both houses of Congress.

Section 3. Whenever the President transmits to the President pro tempore of the Senate and the Speaker of the House of Representatives his written declaration that he is unable to discharge the powers and duties of his office, and until he transmits to them a written declaration to the contrary, such powers and duties shall be discharged by the Vice President as Acting President.

Section 4. Whenever the Vice President and a majority of either the principal officers of the executive departments or of such other body as Congress may by law provide, transmit to the President pro tempore of the Senate and the Speaker of the House of Representatives their written declaration that the President is unable to discharge the powers and duties of his office, the Vice President shall immediately assume the powers and duties of the office as Acting President.

Thereafter, when the President transmits to the President pro tempore of the Senate and the Speaker of the House of Representatives his written declaration that no inability exists, he shall resume the powers and duties of his office unless the Vice President and a majority of either the principal officers of the executive department or of such other body as Congress may by law provide, transmit within four days to the President pro tempore of the Senate and the Speaker of the House of Representatives their written declaration that the President is unable to discharge the powers and duties of his office. Thereupon Congress shall decide the issue, assembling within forty-eight hours for that purpose if not in session. If the Congress within twenty-one days after receipt of the latter written declaration, or, if Congress is not in session, within twenty-one days after Congress is required to assemble, determines by two-thirds vote of both Houses that the President is unable to discharge the powers and duties of his office, the Vice President shall continue to discharge the same as Acting President; otherwise, the President shall resume the powers and duties of his office.

AMENDMENT XXVI

Section 1. The right of citizens of the United States, who are 18 years of age or older, to vote shall not be denied or abridged by the United States or any state on account of age.

Section 2. The Congress shall have the power to enforce this article by appropriate legislation.

Bibliography

Chapter 1: A DECADE OF TRANSITION

Abernathy, M. Glenn, Hill, Dilys M., & Williams, Phil, eds., *The Carter Years: The President and Policy Making* (New York & London, 1984)

Carter, Jimmy, *Keeping Faith: Memoirs of a President* (New York, 1982)

Dallek, Robert, *Ronald Reagan: The Politics of Symbolism* (Cambridge, Mass., 1984)

Ford, Gerald R., *A Time to Heal: The Autobiography of Gerald R. Ford* (New York, 1979)

Hargrove, Erwin C. & Nelson, Michael, *Presidents, Politics and Policy* (Baltimore, 1984)

Palmer, John L. & Sawhill, Isabel V., *The Reagan Record* (Cambridge, Mass., 1984)

Pardon of Richard Nixon and Related Matters: Hearings Before the Sub-Committee on Criminal Justice of the Committee of the Judiciary of the House of Representatives (Washington DC, 1975)

Ranney, Austin, ed., *The American Elections of 1980* (Washington DC & London, 1981)

Reeves, Richard, *A Ford, Not a Lincoln* (New York & London, 1975)

Talbott, Strobe, *Deadly Gambits: The Reagan Administration and the Stalemate in Arms Control* (New York, 1984)

Wayne, Stephen J., *The Legislative Presidency* (New York, 1978)

Chapter 2: FOREIGN POLICY AFTER VIETNAM

Barnet, Richard J., *The Alliance: America, Europe, Japan – Makers of the Post-War World* (New York, 1983)

Brzezinski, Zbigniew, *Power and Principle: Memoirs of the National Security Adviser* (New York, 1983)

Carter, Jimmy, *Keeping Faith: Memoirs of a President* (New York, 1982)

Ford, Gerald R., *A Time to Heal: The Autobiography of Gerald R. Ford* (New York, 1979)

Garthoff, Raymond L., *Détente and Confrontation: American-Soviet Relations from Nixon to Reagan* (Washington DC, 1985)

Haig, Alexander M. Jr., *Caveat: Realism, Reagan, and Foreign Policy* (New York, 1984)

Hoffman, Stanley, *Dead Ends: American Foreign Policy in the New Cold War* (Cambridge, Mass., 1983)

LaFeber, Walter, *Inevitable Revolutions: The United States in Central America* (New York, 1983)

Talbott, Strobe, *Deadly Gambits: The Reagan Administration and the Stalemate in Arms Control* (New York, 1984)

Vance, Cyrus, *Hard Choices: Critical Years in America's Foreign Policy* (New York, 1983)

Chapter 3: THE ECONOMIC LANDSCAPE

Bluestone, Barry, & Harrison, Bennett, *The Deindustrialization of America* (New York, 1982)

Boesky, Ivan, *Merger Mania* (New York, 1985)

Carter, Jimmy, *Keeping Faith* (New York, 1982)

Delamaide, Darrell, *Debt Shock* (Garden City, N.Y., 1984)

Diebold, John, *Making the Future Work* (New York, 1984)

Eckstein, Otto, Caton, Christopher, Brinner, Roger, & Duprey, Peter, *The DRI Report on US Manufacturing Industries* (New York, 1984)

Economic Report of the President, February 1984 (Washington DC, 1984)

Economic Report of the President, February 1985 (Washington DC, 1985)

Friedman, Milton & Rose, *Free to Choose* (New York, 1980)

Gilder, George, *Wealth and Poverty* (New York, 1981)

Jarvis, Howard, with Pack, Robert, *I'm Mad As Hell* (New York, 1979)

Lampert, Hope *Till Death Do Us Part* (San Diego, Cal., 1983)

Lawrence, Paul R., & Dyer, Davis, *Renewing American Industry* (New York, 1983)

Reich, Robert B., *The Next American Frontier* (New York, 1983)

Stein, Herbert, *Presidential Economics* (New York, 1984)

Chapter 4: CHANGES IN SOCIETY

Deckard, Barbara Sinclair, *The Women's Movement* (New York, 1983)

Friedan, Betty, *The Second Stage* (New York, 1981)

Harrington, Michael, *The New American Poverty* (New York, 1984)

Hayden, Tom, *The American Future* (Boston, 1980)

Parrillo, Vincent N., *Strangers to These Shores* (New York, 1980)

Wilson, William Julius, *The Declining Significance of Race* (Chicago, 1978)

Yetman, Norman R., ed., *Majority and Minority* (Boston, 1985)

Chapter 5: THE NATIONAL SPIRIT

Abbott, Philip, *Furious Fancies: American Political Thought in the Post-Liberal Era* (Westport, Conn., 1980)

Carroll, Peter N., *It Seemed Like Nothing Happened: The Tragedy and Promise of America in the 1970s* (New York, 1982)

Crawford, Alan, *Thunder on the Right: The "New Right" and the Politics of Resentment* (New York, 1980)

Garreau, Joel, *The Nine Nations of North America* (Boston, 1981)

Greenawalt, Kent, *Discrimination and Reverse Discrimination* (New York, 1983)

Harris, Marvin, *America Now: The Anthropology of a Changing Culture* (New York, 1981)

Lieberman, Jethro K., *The Litigious Society* (New York, 1983)

Newman, Charles, *The Post-Modern Aura* (Evanston, Ill., 1985)

Phillips, Kevin P., *Post-Conservative America: People, Politics and Ideology in a Time of Crisis* (New York, 1983)

Scruggs, Jan C., and Swerdlow, Joel L., *To Heal a Nation: the Vietnam Veterans Memorial* (New York, 1985)

Sims, Norman, ed., *The Literary Journalists* (New York, 1984)

General Bibliography

Reference

Adams, James T., ed., *Atlas of American History* (New York, 1943)

Adams, James T. (vols. 1-5), Hopkins, Joseph G.E., & Andrews, Wayne (vol. 6), eds., *The Dictionary of American History* (New York, 1940-62)

American Heritage Pictorial Atlas of U.S. History (New York, 1966)

Bartlett, Ruhl J., ed., *The Record of American Diplomacy* (4th edn., New York, 1964)

Bemis, Samuel F., & Griffin, Grace G., eds., *Guide to the Diplomatic History of the United States, 1775-1921* (Washington, DC, 1935)

Boorstin, Daniel J., ed., *The American Primer* (2 vols., New York, 1966, 1968)

Commager, Henry Steele, ed., *Documents of American History* (9th edn., New York, 1973)

Commons, John R., *et al.*, *Documentary History of American Industrial Society* (10 vols., Cleveland, 1910-11)

Freidel, Frank, *Harvard Guide to American History* (rev. edn., 2 vols., Cambridge, Mass., 1974)

Garraty, John A., & Sternstein, Jerome L., eds., *Encyclopedia of American Biography* (New York, 1974)

Gohdes, Clarence, *Bibliographical Guide to the Study of the Literature of the United States of America* (3rd edn., Durham, N.C., 1970)

Hart, James D., comp., *Oxford Companion to American Literature* (rev. edn., New York, 1965)

Johnson, Allen, & Malone, Dumas, *et al.*, eds., *Dictionary of American Biography* (20 vols., plus supplements 1-2, New York, 1928-58)

Johnson, Thomas H., comp., *Oxford Companion to American History* (New York, 1966)

Lamar, Howard R., ed., *The Reader's Encyclopedia of the American West* (New York, 1977)

Morris, Richard B., ed., *Encyclopedia of American History* (rev. edn., New York, 1970)

Thernstrom, Stephan, *et al.*, eds., *Harvard Encyclopedia of American Ethnic Groups* (Cambridge, Mass., 1980)

Van Doren, Charles, *et al.*, eds., *Webster's Guide to American History* (Springfield, Mass., 1971)

Welland, Dennis, ed., *The United States: A Companion to American Studies* (London, 1974)

Architecture, Art, Music

Burchard, John, & Bush-Brown, Albert, *The Architecture of America: A Social and Cultural History* (Boston, 1966)

Kauffmann, Edgar, Jr., ed., *The Rise of an American Architecture* (New York, 1970)

Richardson, Edgar P., *Painting in America: From 1502 to the Present* (New York, 1965)

Roth, Leland M., *A Concise History of American Architecture* (New York, 1979)

Sablosky, Irving L., *American Music* (Chicago, 1969)

The Constitution

Kelly, Alfred H., & Harbison, W.A., *The American Constitution* (4th edn., New York, 1970)

Swisher, Carl B., *American Constitutional Development* (2nd edn., Boston, 1954)

Economic & Social History

Chandler, Alfred D., Jr., *The Visible Hand: The Managerial Revolution in American Business* (Cambridge, Mass., 1977)

Faulkner, Harold U., *American Economic History* (8th edn., New York, 1960)

Fox, Richard W., & Lears, T.J. Jackson, eds., *The Culture of Consumption: Critical Essays in American History, 1880-1980* (New York, 1983)

Jackson, Kenneth T., *Crabgrass Frontier: The Suburbanization of the United States* (New York, 1985)

Kirkland, Edward C., *A History of American Economic Life* (4th edn., New York, 1969)

Patterson, James T., *America's Struggle against Poverty, 1900-1980* (Cambridge, Mass, 1981)

Rorabaugh, W.J., *The Alcoholic Republic: An American Tradition* (New York, 1979)

Education

Calhoun, Daniel, ed., *The Educating of Americans: A Documentary History* (Boston, 1969)

Knight, Edgar W., *Education in the United States* (3rd edn., Boston, 1951)

Rippa, S. Alexander, *Education in a Free Society: An American History* (2nd edn., New York, 1971)

Welter, Rush, *Popular Education and Democratic Thought in America* (New York, 1962)

Family & Generation

Achenbaum, W. Andrew, *Old Age in the New Land: The American Experience since 1790* (Baltimore, 1978)

Bremner, Robert H., et al., eds., *Children and Youth in America: A Documentary History, 1600-1973* (3 vols., Cambridge, Mass., 1970-74)

Fischer, David H., *Growing Old in America* (New York, 1977)

Kett, Joseph F., *Rites of Passage: Adolescence in America, 1790 to the Present* (New York, 1977)

Kettner, James H., *The Development of American Citizenship, 1608-1870* (Chapel Hill, N.C., 1978)

Wishy, Bernard, *The Child and the Republic: The Dawn of Modern American Child Nurture* (Philadelphia, 1968)

Foreign Policy

Bailey, Thomas A., *A Diplomatic History of the American People* (9th edn., New York, 1974)

Combs, Jerald A., *American Diplomatic History: Two Centuries of Changing Interpretations* (Berkeley & Los Angeles, 1983)

De Conde, Alexander, *A History of American Foreign Policy* (2nd edn., New York, 1971)

Gaddis, John L., *Russia, the Soviet Union, and the United States: An Interpretive History* (New York, 1978)

LaFeber, Walter, *The Panama Canal: The Crisis in Historical Perspective* (New York, 1978)

May, Ernest, *Imperial Democracy: The Emergence of America as a Great Power* (New York, 1961)

Historiography

Bernstein, Barton J., ed., *Towards a New Past: Dissenting Essays in American History* (New York, 1968)

Cunliffe, Marcus, & Winks, Robin, eds., *Pastmasters: Essays on American Historians* (New York, 1969)

Degler, Carl, ed., *Pivotal Interpretations of American History* (2 vols., New York, 1966)

Garraty, John A., ed., *Interpreting American History: Conversations with Historians* (New York, 1970)

Loewenberg, Bert J., *American History in American Thought: Christopher Columbus to Henry Adams* (New York, 1972)

Sternsher, Bernard, *Consensus, Conflict, and American Historians* (Bloomington, Ind., 1975)

Humor

Blair, Walter, & Hill, Hamlin, *America's Humor: From Poor Richard to Doonesbury* (New York, 1978)

Immigration

Handlin, Oscar, *The Uprooted* (Boston, 1951)

Jones, Maldwyn A., *American Immigration* (Chicago, 1960)

Wittke, Carl, *We Who Built America* (rev. edn., Cleveland, 1967)

Indians

Berkhofer, Robert F., Jr., *The White Man's Indian: Images of the American Indian from Columbus to the Present* (New York, 1978)

Dippie, Brian W., *The Vanishing American: White Attitudes and U.S. Indian Policy* (Middletown, Conn., 1982)

Prucha, Francis P., *The Great Father: The United States Government and the American Indians* (2 vols., Lincoln, Neb., 1984)

Intellectual History

Barker, Charles A., *American Convictions: Cycles of Public Thought, 1600-1850* (Philadelphia, 1970)

Curti, Merle, *Human Nature in American Thought: A History* (Madison, Wis., 1980)

Curti, Merle, *The Growth of American Thought* (3rd edn., New York, 1964)

Higham, John, & Conkin, Paul K., eds., *New Directions in American Intellectual History* (Baltimore, 1979)

Kennedy, David M., & Robinson, Paul A., eds., *Social Thought in America and Europe: Readings in Comparative Intellectual History* (Boston, 1970)

Parrington, Vernon L., *Main Currents in American Thought: An Interpretation of American Literature from the Beginnings to 1920* (3 vols., New York, 1927-30)

Perry, Lewis, *Intellectual Life in America* (New York, 1984)

Interpretative Studies

Arieli, Yehoshua, *Individualism and Nationalism in American Ideology* (Cambridge, Mass., 1964)

Boorstin, Daniel J., *The Americans* (3 vols., New York, 1958-73)

Brogan, Hugh, *The Longman History of the United States of America* (London & New York, 1985)

Burns, James M., *The American Experiment: The Vineyard of Liberty* (New York, 1982)

Degler, Carl N., *Out of Our Past* (rev. edn., New York, 1970)

Jones, Maldwyn A., *The Limits of Liberty: American History, 1607-1980* (New York, 1983)

Kammen, Michael G., *People of Paradox: An Inquiry Concerning the Origins of American Civilization* (New York, 1972)

Pole, J.R., *Paths to the American Past* (New York, 1979)

Pole, J.R., *The Pursuit of Equality in American History* (Berkeley & Los Angeles, 1978)

Potter, David M., *People of Plenty: Economic Abundance and the American Character* (Chicago, 1954)

Scott, William B., *The Pursuit of Happiness: American Conceptions of Property from the Seventeenth to the Twentieth Century* (Bloomington, Ind., 1977)

Wiebe, Robert H., *The Opening of American Society: From the Adoption of the Constitution to the Eve of Disunion* (New York, 1984)

Wilkinson, Rupert, *American Tough: The Tough-Guy Tradition and American Character* (Westport, Conn., 1984)

Journalism

Mott, Frank L., *American Journalism: A History, 1690-1960* (3rd edn., New York, 1962)

Weisberger, Bernard A., *The American Newspaperman* (Chicago, 1961)

Labor

Brody, David, ed., *The American Labor Movement* (New York, 1971)

Foner, Philip S., *History of the Labor Movement in the United States* (3 vols., New York, 1947-64)

Gutman, Herbert G., *Work, Culture and Society in Industrializing America: Essays in Working Class and Social History* (New York, 1977)

Leab, Daniel J., ed., *The Labor History Reader* (Urbana, Ill., 1985)

Rayback, Joseph G., *History of American Labor* (rev. edn., New York, 1966)

Literature

Cunliffe, Marcus *The Literature of the United States* (rev. edn., Harmondsworth, Middlesex, 1967)

Spiller, Robert E., *et al.*, *Literary History of the United States* (3 vols., 4th rev. edn., New York, 1974)

Politics & Political Thought

Boorstin, Daniel J., *The Genius of American Politics* (Chicago, 1953)

Chambers, William N., & Burnham, Walter D., eds., *American Party Systems: Stages of Development* (2nd edn., New York, 1974)

Diggins, John P., *The Lost Soul of American Politics: Virtue, Self-Interest, and the Foundations of Liberalism* (New York, 1984)

Gatell, Frank O., *et al.*, eds., *Readings in American Political History* (New York, 1972)

Hartz, Louis, *The Liberal Tradition in America* (New York, 1955)

Hofstadter, Richard, *The American Political Tradition and the Men who made it* (rev. edn., New York, 1973)

Kelley, Robert, *The Cultural Pattern in American Politics: The First Century* (New York, 1979)

Roche, John P., ed., *American Political Thought: From Jefferson to Progressivism* (New York, 1967)

Schlesinger, Arthur M., Jr., ed., *History of U.S. Political Parties* (4 vols., New York, 1973)

The Presidency

Bach, Stanley, & Sulzner, George T., eds., *Perspectives on the Presidency* (Lexington, Mass., 1974)

Cunliffe, Marcus, *American Presidents and the Presidency* (New York, 1969)

Neustadt, Richard E., *Presidential Power* (New York, 1960)

Schlesinger, Arthur M., Jr., & Israel, Fred L., *History of American Presidential Elections, 1789-1968* (4 vols., New York, 1971)

Racial & Ethnic

Franklin, John Hope, *From Slavery to Freedom* (4th edn., New York, 1974)

Gutman, Herbert G., *The Black Family in Slavery and Freedom, 1750-1925* (New York, 1976)

Levine, Lawrence W., *Black Culture and Black Consciousness: Afro-American Folk Thought from Slavery to Freedom* (New York, 1977)

Meier, August, & Rudwick, Elliott M., *From Plantation to Ghetto: An Interpretive History of American Negroes* (New York, 1966)

Takaki, Ronald T., *Iron Cages: Race and Culture in Nineteenth-Century America* (New York, 1979)

Religion

Ahlstrom, Sydney E., *A Religious History of the American People* (New Haven, Conn, 1972)

Olmstead, Clifton E., *Religion in America, Past and Present* (Englewood Cliffs, N.J., 1961)

Smith, Hilrie S., Handy, Robert T., & Loetscher, Lefferts A., *American Christianity: An Historical Interpretation with Representative Documents* (2 vols., New York, 1960-63)

Smith, James W., & Jameson, A. Leland, eds., *Religion in American Life* (4 vols., Princeton, 1961)

The South

Clark, Thomas D., *The Emerging South* (2nd edn., New York, 1968)

Woodward, C. Vann, *The Burden of Southern History* (Baton Rouge, 1960)

Sport, Leisure, Entertainment

Dizikes, John, *Sportsmen and Gamesmen* (Boston, 1981)

Sklar, Robert, *Movie-Made America: A Cultural History of American Movies* (New York, 1975)

The Supreme Court

McCloskey, Robert G., *The American Supreme Court* (Chicago, 1960)

Pollak, Louis H., ed., *The Constitution and the Supreme Court: A Documentary History* (2 vols., Cleveland & New York, 1966)

Warren, Charles, *The Supreme Court in United States History* (2 vols., Boston, 1937)

Transport, Communications, Media

Crouch, Tom D., *A Dream of Wings: Americans and the Airplane* (New York, 1981)

Czitrom, Daniel, J., *Media and the American Mind: From Morse to McLuhan* (Chapel Hill, N.C., 1982)

Emme, Eugene M., *A History of Space Flight* (New York, 1965)

Fuller, Wayne E., *The American Mail: Enlarger of the Common Life* (Chicago, 1972)

Rae, John B., *The American Automobile: A Brief History* (Chicago, 1965)

Stover, J.F., *American Railroads* (Chicago, 1961)

Urban History

Callow, Alexander B., Jr., *American Urban History: An Interpretive Reader with Commentaries* (New York, 1969)

Glaab, Charles N., & Brown, A. Theodore, *A History of Urban America* (New York, 1967)

Wakstein, Allen M., ed., *The Urbanization of America: An Historical Anthology* (Boston, 1970)

War & Peace

Brock, Peter, *Pacifism in the United States: From the Colonial Era to the First World War* (Princeton, 1968)

Leonard, Thomas C., *Above the Battle: War-Making in America from Appomattox to Versailles* (New York, 1978)

Lynd, Staughton, ed., *Nonviolence in America: A Documentary History* (Indianapolis, 1966)

Mahon, John K., *History of the Militia and the National Guard* (New York, 1983)

Millis, Walter ed., *American Military Thought* (Indianapolis, 1966)

Sprout, Harold & Margaret, *The Rise of American Naval Power, 1776-1918* (Princeton, 1942)

Weigley, Russell F., *History of the United States Army* (New York, 1967)

Williams, T. Harry, *The History of American Wars: From 1745 to 1918* (New York, 1981)

The West

Bartlett, Richard A., *The New Country: A Social History of the American Frontier, 1776-1890* (New York, 1975)

Billington, Ray A., *Westward Expansion: The History of the American Frontier* (3rd edn., New York, 1967)

Clark, Thomas D., *Frontier America: The Story of the Westward Movement* (2nd edn., New York, 1969)

Women

Banner, Lois W., *American Beauty* (New York, 1983)

Degler, Carl N., *At Odds: Women and the Family in America from the Revolution to the Present* (New York, 1980)

Kessler-Harris, Alice, *Out to Work: A History of Wage-Earning Women in the United States* (New York, 1982)

Sinclair, Andrew, *The Emancipation of the American Woman* (rev. edn., New York, 1965)

Welter Barbara, ed., *The Woman Question in American History* (Hinsdale, Ill., 1973)

Index

Roman numerals designate volume numbers
Page numbers in italics refer to captions

AAA, see Agricultural Adjustment Act
Abbot, Joel, IV 59
"ABC-1" plan (Second World War), XV 129; XVI 12, 13
ABC powers, XII 29
Abe, Nobuyuki, XV 125
Abel, Rudolf, XVIII 81
Aberdeen, George Hamilton Gordon, 4th Earl of, V 64, *64*
Abernathy, Ralph, XIX 55
Abilene, Kansas, IX 44, 45, 46, 54, *54*, 55, 62, 63; XVII 68, *68*
Abilene Trail, IX 45
Abolition movement, III 140; IV 104, 109, 122, 123; V 44, 48, 71, 72, 91; VI 24, 26, 28, 37, 56, 57; W. L. Garrison, VI 61, 68, 70–71; and Christianity, VI 62; Enlightenment, VI 62; Quakers, VI 62–63; Methodists, VI *62*, 63; abolition of northern slavery, VI 63–64; Thomas Jefferson, VI 65; weakening of, VI 65; "gradualism," VI 65; aided by communications revolution, VI 68, 72, *73*; B. Lundy, VI 68, 70; Tappan brothers, VI 71–72; abolition in British West Indies, VI 71; American Anti-Slavery Society, VI 71–72; organization of, VI 72; petition campaign, VI 72, 74, *76*, 77; confrontation tactics, VI 74–75, 81; reaction against, VI 77–78, *79*; racial equality, VI 78; radical party of, VI 81; ecclesiastical party of, VI 81; political party of, VI 81; Afro-American party, VI 81, 82–83; respectable element in politics, VI 91; see also Negroes; Slavery
Abraham, Plains of, I 98, *98*
Abraham Lincoln Battalion (Spanish Civil War), XV 86, 88, 89, *89*; see also Spanish Civil War
Abrams, Creighton, XVIII 121
Abstract expressionism, XVII 91, *92*, 94, *94*, 95–96, 97; see also Action painting; New York School
"Academies," IV 86, 95; X 88; see also Education
Acadia, I 28, 85, 96
Ace (First World War), XII 85, *85*, 87, *87*
Acheson, Dean, XVII 73; Alger Hiss, XVII 40; postwar Europe, XVIII 29; German rearmament, XVIII 35; on China, XVIII 46, 47, 48–49; Korea, XVIII 50, 51, 53; and General MacArthur, XVIII 58; and J. F. Dulles, XVIII 61; on Joseph McCarthy, XVIII 64
Acker, John C., XII 67
Across The Continent, IX 138, *138*
Across The Wide Missouri, XVII 105
Act to Expedite the Strengthening of National Defense (1940), XV 127
Action painting, XVII 91, 92, 94, 95
Adairsville, Battle of (1864), VII 120
Adam of Bremen, I 19
Adams, Abigail, III 92, 139–140
Adams, Cassily, IX *138*, 139
Adams, Charles Francis, VI 89; VII 100, *101*, 102
Adams, Charles Kendall, X 88, 92
Adams, Franklin P., XI 124
Adams, Henry, VII 102; X 42; XI 102, 103, *103*, 104–105
Adams, John (president), II *48*, *53*; on James Otis, I 126; defense of T. Preston, I *130*; Declaration of Independence, II *10*, 12, *13*; views on independence, II 16, 19, 126; on George Washington, II 25, 109; theories of government, II 47–48, 51; on War of Independence, II 34, 84–85, 104; Pennsylvania constitution, II 56, 58; Treaty of Paris, II *130*, *130*, 139; on foreign affairs, II 134; III 20; vice president, III 35, 46; presidential candidate, III 54; president, III 55–56, 58, 73, 135; 1800 election, III 60–62, *62*; defeat, III 65; "midnight appointments," III 78; on national consciousness, III 90; on language, III 94; on education, IV 86
Adams, John Quincy (president), II *53*; III 109; Florida question, III 130–131; Latin America, III 131; president, IV 28–29, *29*; Oregon question, V 52, 53; defense of J. Cinque, VI *35*; attack on "gag rule," VI 76; Missouri debates, VI 86, 104
Adams, Samuel, agitator, I 120; II 87; "Boston Massacre," I 130, 132, *132*; Boston Tea Party, I 133; II 16; Continental Congress, II *13*; on independence, II 19; Revere's ride, II 22, 23; Articles of Confederation, II 58; Constitutional Convention, III 24; on Constitution, III 30
Adams, Sherman, XVII 73, 75, 85, *85*
Adams-Onis Treaty (1819), III 131
Addams, Jane, X 118; XI 56, *94*; XII 55, 118; XV 17
Adder's Den, VII 135
Address of the Southern Delegates in Congress, VI 91
Address to the Slaveholding States, VI 134
Ade, George, XI 124
Adenauer, Konrad, XVIII 68, *68*
Adler, Dankmar, X 96
Admiralty Islands, XVI 41
Adventures of Augie March, The, XVII 104, 105
Adventures of a Young Man, XIV 88
Adventures of Huckleberry Finn, The, X 101; XVII 105
Adventures of Tom Sawyer, The, X 26
Advertisements for Myself, XVII 104
Advertising, and American Tobacco Co., VIII 124; Ford Motor Co., XI 17; rise of brand names. XI 23, *23–24*, 25; First World War, XII 125; and behaviourist psychology, XIII 49–50, *49–50*; during Great Depression, XIV *18*, 19, and McCarthyism, XVII 48; in 1950s, XVII *118*, 121
Aerial warfare, in First World War, XII 84–85, *84*, *85*; Second World War, XVI 10, *10*, 15, *72*, 74, *75*, 85, 90; see also Air power
Aerospace industry, XIX 88, 93; see also Industry
Aetna Life Insurance Company, XIII 136
Affluent Society, The, XVII 107
Afghanistan, XX 32–33
AFHQ, see Allied Force Headquarters
AFL, see American Federation of Labor
Africa, I 10, 13; VI 28, 30; XIII 99; XVI 15; XX 26–27, 29, 39
African Methodist Episcopal Church, VI 68, *69*

Afro-American Council, VIII, 108
Against the American Grain, XVII 124
Agassiz, Louis, IV 87; X 97
Agee, James, XIV 56
Age of Reason, The, III 138
Age of Reform, The, XVII 107
Agnew, Samuel, VI 34
Agnew, Spiro (vice president), XIX 46, 104, 110, 111, 125
Agrarian movements, X 127, *129*, 131–132, *131*; see also Agriculture
Agricultural Adjustment Act (1933), XIV 34, *35*, 47, 117–120, *118*, 124, 128
Agricultural Adjustment Act (1938), XIV 126, 128
Agricultural and Mechanical colleges, see Land-grant colleges
Agriculture, I 62, 102, 104; III 17; V 34; 1812 depression, III 119; in early nineteenth century, IV 39; commercialization of, IV 48, 68, *69*, 70; in the South, VI 40, 45–46, *46*, 48; specialization, VI 42; effect of westward movement on, VI 46; in West, IV 68, 70, 76; IX 10, 11, 13; in Great Plains, IX 92, 94–97, *95*, 99, *99*; effect of Reconstruction on, VIII 55, 57–59; in New South, VIII 126, 128; production, 1870–1900, X 10; industrialization of, X 22; 1887 drought, X 126; Farmers' Alliance, X 126, 131–132; the Grange, X 127, *129*, 131, *131*; and Populist party, X 132–134, *133*, 136–141 *passim*; in Harding era, XIII 126; 1920s depression, XIII, 50, 64, 134–136, *135*; McNary-Haugen bill, XIII 124; Agriculture Marketing Act, XIII 127; FCA, XIV 34; Resettlement Administration, XIV 49; FSA, XIV 65; in 1930s, XIV 116, 117, *117, 120, 121, 129–130*; AAA, XIV 117–120; tenancy, VIII 55, 57–58, 126, 128; XIV 119–120, *120*, 124, *124*; Dust Bowl, XIV 122–123, *123*; Brannan plan, XVII 25; poverty in 1950s, XVII 116; see also names of individual crops; Plantations; Sharecropping; Tenancy
Agriculture Marketing Act (1929), XIII 127, 136; XIV 116
Aguinaldo, Emilio, XI *36*
AIM, see American Indian Movement
Airborne operations (Second World War), XVI 82
Air brake, X 28
Air-Conditioned Nightmare, The, XVII 104
Aircraft carriers, XVI 20, 26, 27, 28, *29*, 108, 110
Aircraft industry, XVI 52–53, *56, 57*; see also Aviation
Air Medal, XVI *79*
Air power, in First World War, XII 84–85, *84, 85*; Second World War, XV 35; XVI 15, 23; see also Aerial warfare
Airships, XV 93
Aitape, XVI 114
Aix-la-Chapelle, Treaty of (1748), I 91, 92
Akagi (carrier), XVI 28
Alabama, I 54, 89; III 128; statehood, III 133; V 48; plantation owners, VI 40; cotton, VI 43; secession convention, VI 125, 132, 134; secession ordinance, VI 134; Reconstruction, VIII 33, 42; Reconstruction constitution, VIII 42; railroad bond issues, VIII 42–43; Reconstruction politics, VIII 82, 84; convict leasing, VIII 132; Negro disfranchisement, VIII 135; iron industry, X 13; progressivism, XI 55; segregation, XVII 52
Alabama (ship), VII 107–108, *108*; 125–126
"Alabama Arbitration," VII 107–108; XV 14
Alabama Penny Savings and Loan Company, VIII 98
Alabama River, I 16
Alamo, V 41, 42, *43*; see also Mexican War
Alamogordo, New Mexico, XVI 128. 130
Alaska, I 35, 38, 39; XI 33, *33*, 74
Albany, New York, I 65, 70, 88, 89; III 136, *136*
Albany Regency, IV 24, 28
Albermarle, Duke of, I 74
Albers, Josef, XVII 90
Albert, Carl, XIX 46
Albert, Prince Consort (Britain), VII *103*
Alcalde, V 40, 122, 131, 138
Alcoholism, XI 92, 94
Alcorn, James, VIII 44–45, *45*
Alcott, Bronson, IV 88–89, 119, 120
Alcott, Louisa May, IV 88, 120
Alder Gulch, Montana, IX 77
Aldrich Commission, XI 67

Aldrin, Edwin, XIX 95, *96*
Aleutian Islands, XVI 25, 27, 28, 35
Alexander II (Russia), VII 107
Alexander of Tunis, Harold Rupert Leofric George Alexander, 1st Earl of, XVI 23, 36, 88, 90, 106
Alfonso II (ship), XI 35
Algeciras conference (1906), XI 77; XII 23
Alger, Horatio, X 97
Algeria, XVI 15, 76; XVIII 69
Algonquin, I 28, 37, 41, 48, 49, 51, 53, 79, *79*; see also Indians, American
Algonquin (ship), XII 53
Algonquin Circle, XIII 96
Alien and Sedition Acts (1798), III 58, 59, 78
Alien Property Custodian, XII 105
All American Indians, XIV 75; see also Football
Allegheny Portage Railroad, IV 51
Allegiance and Treason Resolves (1776), II 34
Allegory of Freedom, VIII *50*
Allen, Ethan, II 24, 25, *25*, 86
Allen, F. L., XIII 73, 74, 77; XIV 56
Allen, Gracie, see Burns and Allen
Allen, Hervey, XIV 90
Allen, O. K., XIV 43
Allen, Richard, VI 68
Allen, William Van, see Van Allen, William
Allen (ship), XII *68*
Allende, Salvador, XVIII 136
All God's Chillun Got Wings, XIII 98
Alliance for Progress, XVIII 85, 86
Alliance, Treaty of (1877), II 109
Alliance system, XII 13–14, *14*
Allied Force Headquarters (Second World War), XVI 74
Allied Powers (First World War), British view of, XII *11*; Italy joins, XII 20; and American neutrality, XII 33, 34, 35, 37, 114; secret compact with America, XII 44; Wilson's intervention, XII 49, 50; Russian Revolution, XII 53; press and propaganda, XII 58; debt, XII 61; state of war in 1917, XII 65, 69, 71; conflict with Pershing, XII 74; Supreme Commander, XII 84; losses, XII 98; secret treaties, XII 130; see also First World War
Allied Powers (Second World War), in peril, XVI 10; Lend-Lease, XVI 11; Operation Torch, XVI 15, 16, 80; D-Day preparations, XVI 88; bombing strategy, XVI 134; appraisal, XVI 135–140 *passim*; policy differences, XVIII 14; see also Second World War
Allied Supreme Command (Second World War), XVI 90
Allis-Corliss engine, XI *105*
All My Sons, XVII 103
All the King's Men, XVII 103
All Quiet on the Western Front, XIII 67
Allston, Washington, IV *130*
Almonte, Juan N., V 68, 70
Almshouses, IV 112, 114
"Alphabet agencies" (New Deal), XIV 56, 65, 133
Alpha mine, IX 80
Alternating current, X 32
Altgeld, John P., X 80, 85, 139
Aluminum, XI 82
Amalgamated Copper, X 19; XI 12
Amalgamated Clothing Workers of America, X 66
Amalgamation (miscegenation), VI 78
Amau, Eiji, XV 62
Ambassador of Good Will, The, XV 71
Ambon Island, XVI 25
Ambrose (ship), I 60
Amendments, constitutional, III 133, 134; XIV 53; see also individual amendments
America, origins of name, I 13; ethnological origins, I 35; European conception of, I 139; see also Central America; North America; South America
America and the Young Intellectual, XIII 70
America as a Civilization, XVII 108
America First Committee, XV 109, *109, 119*
America Goes to War, XV 79
"America-letter," IV 75
Americana, XIV 81
American Aero Squadron (First World War), XII 84
American Air Service (First World War), XII 85, *85*
American and Foreign Anti-Slavery Society, VI 82
American Anti-Slavery Society, VI 71–72, 82
American architecture, see Architecture
American art, see Art

American Association for Labor Legislation, XI 91, 92
American Association of University Women, XV 19
American bison, see Buffalo
American Board of Foreign Missions, V 54; XI 47
American Can, X 16
American Civil Liberties Union, XIII 112
American Civil War, see Civil War
American Colonization Society, VI 65, 68, 70
American Committee Against Militarism, XV 17
American Committee for the Outlawry of War, XV 17
American Commonwealth, The, XII 60
American Cottonseed-Oil Trust, X 19
American Crisis, The, II 40, *48*
American Democrat, The, IV 135
American Dictionary of the English Language, IV 84, *84*
American Dilemma, An, XVII 52
American Dream, The, XVII 121
American Expeditionary Force (First World War), XII 71, *72*, 73, 74, 76–80, *76–78*, 91–92, 95
American Farm Bureau Federation, XIV 116
American Federation of Labor, X 74; formation of, X 80, *80*; and Samuel Gompers, X 81, *81*; XIII 136; lobbying committee, X 81–82; social reform legislation, X 84; membership, XI 12–13, 99; aims, XI 94, 96; and socialism, XI 97; policy on Negroes, XI 100; First World War, XII 105, 116, 118; opposition to New Deal, XIV 109; failures, XIV 111; and CIO, XIV 112; corruption, XIV 114; and F. D. Roosevelt, XIV 136
American Fur Company, V 15
American Gothic, XIII *106*; XIV 82
American Home Squadron, V 83
American Humor, XIV 88
American imperialism, see Imperialism
American Indian Movement, XIX 62
American Indians, see Indians, American
American in Paris, An, XIII 92
Americanization, X 70, 72
American Landscape, XIV *87*
American Language, The, XIII 96
American League, XI 134; XIV 75; XVII 129; see also Baseball
American Legion, XV 79
American literature, see Literature
American Medical Association, XVII 26, 84; XIX 25, 40
American Mercury, XIII 70, 96, 105, *108*, 109, 111
American Missionary Association, VI 81
American party, see Native American party
American Peace Society, XII 129
American Philosophical Society, I 114; IV 85
"American plan," XIII 136
American Protective Association, X 72; XII 111
American Railway Union, X 139
American Red Cross, VII 32
"American Renaissance," IV 135, 141
American Revolution, see War of Independence
American River, V *121*, 122
American Slavery As It Is, VI 26, 72
American Smelting and Refining, X 19
American Society for the Promotion of Temperance, IV 115–116
American Sugar Refining Company, X 16, 19; X1 12
"American System," IV 23
American System of Manufacturing, XI 17; XIII 32
American Telephone and Telegraph Company, X 26; XIII 141
American Tobacco Company, VIII 124; X 16; XI 11, 12, 60
American Tragedy, An, XIII 72
American Traits, XI 122
American Union Against Militarism, XII 55
American War of Independence, see War of Independence
American Watch Company, IV 64
American Wheelman, X *123*
American Woolen Company, XI 98
Ames, Adelbert, VIII 40, 46, 85
Ames, Fisher, III 36, 45, 51, 55, 62, 137
Ames, Nathaniel, III 62
Ames, Oakes, IX 37
Ames, Oliver, IX 37
Amherst, Jeffrey Amherst, Baron, I 54, 97–99; II 29, 74, 78
Amherst College, IV 90; see also Universities and colleges

Amicus Curia briefs, XVII 21, 56
Amistad (ship), VI *35*
"Amos 'n' Andy," XIV 102, *103*
Amphibious vehicles, XVI 56, *80*, 82, 108
Ampudia, Pedrode, V 72, 76, 77
Amtracs, XVI 108
Anaconda, IX 84
Anarchism, X 80; XIII 13, 17
Anarchy, State and Utopia, XIX 140
Anaya, Pedro Maria, V 91, 92
Ancient Society, X 98
Anderson, Charles W., VIII 116
Anderson, Maxwell, XIII 67; XIV 91
Anderson, Robert, VI 134, 136, 137; VII *15*, 18
Anderson, Sherwood, XIII 66, 68, 70, 109; XIV 56, 80, 90
Andersonville, Georgia, VII 83, *83*; VIII 16
Andover, Massachusetts, I 62
André, John, II 115–116, *117*
Andrew, John A., VII 70
Andros, William, I 63
Angaur Island, XVI 113
Angell, James B., X 88
Angell, Norman, XII 13
Anglicans, I 75, 101, 109; see also Religion
Anglo-French Purchasing Mission, XV 115
Anglo-Japanese Alliance (1902), XV 20, 23, 46, 60
Anglo-Russian Entente (1907), XII 14
"Animal" dances, XI 126
Anna Christie, XIII 98
Annapolis Convention (1786), III 18, *19*
Annapolis Royal, Nova Scotia, I 79, 88
Anne, Queen (England), I *55*
Annie Get Your Gun, IX 133
Anshutz, Thomas, X *13*
Antelope, IX 12
Anthony, Scott, IX 102
Anthony, Susan Brownwell, IV *122*, 124
Anthony Adverse, XIV 90
Anthracite coal strike (1902), X 66; XI 60, *61*, 97; see also Strikes
Antiaircraft guns, XVI 53, 54
Antiballistic missiles, XIX 105; see also Ballistic missiles
Anti-Boycott Association, XI 97
Anti-Catholicism, IV 81; X 72; see also Roman Catholics
Anti-Comintern Pact (1936), XV 91
Anti-communist hysteria, X 78; 1950s, XVII 25, 26, 29, *36*; see also McCarthyism; Red scare
Anticosti Island, I 22
Antietam, Battle of (1862), VII *29*, 32, 72, *76*, 104, *140*
Anti-German hysteria (First World War), XII *122*, 123, *123*
Antilles, I 12; II 68
Antimasonic party, IV 29, *31*, 36
Anti-Saloon League, XI 30, 92; XII 120; XIII 23, 52
Anti-Semitism, X 72; XV *97*, 98; XVII 43, 50
Anti-slavery movement, see Abolition movement
Anti-trust movement, see Trusts
Anti-war movements, XII 55, 56–58, *56*, 114; Vietnam War, XIX 43, 46, 70–71, 100, 108, 110, 111, *127*; see also Isolationism; Pacifism
Anton Lizardo, Mexico, V 86
Antrim, William, IX 66
Antwerp, XVI 99
Anzio, Battle of (1944), XVI 88
ANZUS pact, XVIII 58
Apache, I 41, 45, 46; V 31; IX 16, 17, 101, *110*, 111, *116, 118*; see also Indians, American
Apache Canyon, V 81–82
Apollo, XIX 24, 84, 88, 89, *90*, 92
"Apostle of the Indians," see Eliot, John
Appalachians, I 16, 54–55, 107, *107*; III 48, 70; IV 49; VII 22
Appeal of the Independent Democrats, The, VI 101
"Appeasement" policy, XV 94, 95, 96, 112
Appert, Nicolas, X 32
Applegate, Jesse, V 59–60
Appomattox, Virginia, VII 128
Apportionment systems, VIII 42
April 6, 1830, Law of, V 40–41
April 9 draft (1941), XV 131
Arabic (ship), XII 42
Arab-Israeli war (1967), XVIII 138, 139
Arafat, Yassir, XVIII, 140, *140*

Arai, Shuri, XV *139*
Aranjuez, Convention of (1779), II 139
Arapaho, IX 17, 20, 22, *22*, 101, 102, 106, 108; see also Indians, American
Arawak, I 42; see also Indians, American
Arbella (ship), I 60
Arbenz, Jacobo, XVIII 70
Arbitration treaties, XII 129
Arcadia Conference (1941–42), XVI 14
Arcaro, Eddie, XVII *130*
Architecture, colonial, I 111, *111*, 113; early American, III 97, *98–101*, 100–101, 104; mid-19th century, IV 135; Gilded Age, X 92–93, *94*, 96, *96*; Progressive era, XI 116, 118–119; 1920s, XIII 101, *102–104*; Great Depression, XIV 105, *107*; the American influence, XVII 90; European influence, XVII 98; "modernism," XVII 98, *98*, 99–100
archy and mehitabel, XIII 95–96, *96*
Arc-lights, X 30
Arctic, XI 81
Arctic Ocean, XI 81
Ardennes, XVI 101, *101*, 102
Argentina, XV 43, 45
Argonne Forest, XVI 129
Arista, Mariano, V 72, 73–75, 76
Arizona, I 17, 41, 45; IX 15, 37; Spanish territory, V 31; Indians, IX 16, 17, 101; old age pensions, X 84; progressivism, XI 56; segregation, XVII 53; see also West, the
Ark (ship), I 73
Arkansas, IX 10; cotton, VI 44; secession, VII 18; Confederate state, VII 60; Southern Alliance, X 127; Ku Klux Klan, VIII 78; reconstruction politics, VIII 84; segregation, XVII 52; see also South, the
Arkansas Hot Springs, IX 124
Arkansas River, V 12, 13; IX 11, 96
Arkansas Valley Cattle Company, IX 56
Arkies, XIV 120
Armaments industry, IV 64; VIII 71; XII 58, 60, 105; XV 78; XVI 53–54
Armas, Castillo, XVIII 70
Armies of the Night, XIX 123
Armijo, Manuel, V 81, 82
Armistice Day (First World War), XII 98, *98*, 129
Armory Show (1913), XI 111, *111*, 113
Armour, Philip D., X 32
Armour Meat Company, X 19
"Arms and the Man," XV 78
Arms embargo, XV 72, 80, 83; see also Neutrality
Arms race, XV 71; Anglo-German naval rivalry, XII 16; US-Soviet nuclear, XVIII 130; see also Space program
Armstrong, John, III 127
Armstrong, Louis, XIII 87, *90*; XIV 100
Armstrong, Neil, XIX 95, *96*
Armstrong, Samuel Chapman, VIII 101
Army Aircraft Warning Service, XV 139
Army Distinguished Service Medal, XVI *79*
Army Group Command (Second World War), XVI 90
Army-Navy game (football), XI 136
Army of Northern Virginia (Civil War), VII 26, 28, 36, 37, 39, *74*, 117, 119, 128
Army of Tennessee (Civil War), VII 111, 115, 124
Army of the Cumberland (Civil War), VII 111, *110*, *136*
Army of the Potomac (Civil War), VII 21, 24, 29, 33, 36, 37, 41, *74*, 108, 115, 116, 137
Army of the West, V 81
Arnhem, Battle of (1944), XVI 98, *98, 99*
Arnim, Juergen von, XVI 80
Arno, Peter, XIII 96; XIV *134*
Arnold, Benedict, II 26, 40, 122; Green Mountain Boys, II 24, *25*; ability of, II 32; Quebec expedition, II 34; smallpox, II 43; treason, II 116, *117*
Arnold, Thurman, XIV 133
Around the World in 80 Days, XVII 132
"Arrastra," V *129*, 131; IX 83
Arrowsmith, XIII 95
Art, colonial, I 111, *115*, 116, *116*; early American, III 97, *97*, 104, *103–105*; mid-19th century, IV 127–128, 131, *131*, 132–133, *132*, *133*; in Gilded Age, X 98, *98–99*, 100; in Progressive era, XI 111; in 1920s, XIII 101, *103–104*; during Great Depression, XIV 32, 80, 82, 84, 88, *82–87*; dominance of American (1945–60), XVII 90;

abstract expressionism, XVII 91, 92, *92*, 94, *94*, 95–96, 97; sculpture in 1950s, XVII 96–97, *97*; pop, XVII 97; in 1960s, XIX 122
Art galleries, X 124
Arthur, Chester Alan (president), VIII 134; IX 35; X 30, 49–50, *50*
Arthur, Jean, XIV 96
Article Nineteen, Washington Naval Treaty, XV 53, 61
Articles of Confederation, II 47, 126; and Continental Congress, II 58, *58*; first draft, II 58; second draft, II 58, 60; ratification, II 133; defects of, III 11, 13, 16, 20; defenders of, III 18; and Constitution, III 10, 22, 30; state power, III 136
Article Ten (League of Nations Covenant), XV 58
Article 231 (Versailles Treaty), XII 137
Artillery, XII *80*, 82, 83, 93
Artist in his Museum, III *102*
Art of Thinking, The, XIII 77
A. S. Beck Shoe Corporation, XI 21
Asbury, Francis, IV 101
Ash, Roy, XIX *104*
Ashburton, Alexander Baring, 1st baron of, V 63, *64*
Ashcan School (art), XI 111
Ashley, James, VIII 35, *35*
Ashley, William, V 16, 20
Ask Me Another, XIII 77
Aslito Field, XVI 111
Aspen, Colorado, IX 38, 73
Asphalt, X 116
Assembly lines, XI *15*, 16; XIII 39
Assistance, writs of, I 120, 126; III 109
Assistant, The, XVII 103
Associated Press, X 124; XII 58
Association to Boycott, II 98
Astaire, Fred, XIV *94*, 95; XVI 60, 62
Astor, John Jacob, V 14–15, *15*; X 88; XI 27
Astoria, V 15, *16*, 51
Aswan High Dam, XVIII 72
Atcheson, George, XVIII 49
Atchison, David R., V 51
Atchison & Topeka Railroad, IX 36
Atchison, Topeka & Santa Fe Railroad, IX 36, 38, 63, 89; X 126; XI 53
Athapascan, see Na-Déné
Athenia (ship), XVI 70
Atherton, Gertrude, XIII 72
Atkin, Edmund, I 97, 99
Atkinson, Edward, VIII 121
Atlanta, Georgia, VII *61*, 113, 119, 120, *120*, 121, *121*, 124; VIII 121
Atlanta Compromise, VIII 100, 108
Atlanta *Constitution*, VIII 118, 139
Atlanta Cyclorama, VII *122*
Atlanta Exposition (1895), VIII 100; see also Fairs and expositions
Atlanta riot (1906), VIII 114–115, *114*
Atlanta University, VIII 66
Atlantic, Battle of the (Second World War), XVI 15, 52, 70–71, *70*, *71*, 73, 84, 85
Atlantic Charter, XV 122; XVI 12, 13; XVIII 13, 14
Atlantic Conference (1941), XV 122, 134; XVI 12, 13
Atlantic Monthly, IV 61; VII 80; X 22, 98, 102; XI 116, 124
Atlas Corporation, XVI 54
Atlas missile, XIX 86; see also Ballistic missiles
Atlas Shrugged, XVII 103
Atomic bomb, XVI 56, 126, 128–130, *129*, *130*, 134; XVIII 23, 34; see also Hydrogen bomb
Atomic power, XVIII 23–24
Attlee, Clement, XVIII 19, *21*
Atrocity stories (First World War), XII 58, 60, *110*
Atrocity trials, see War crimes' trials
Attu Island, XVI 27, 35
Atzerodt, George, VII *132, 134*
Auburn (automobile), XIII *42*
Auburn Penitentiary, IV 113
Auditorium, Chicago, X 96
Audubon, John James, III *106*
Augusta, Florida, VI 42
Aurora (ship), III 51, 56
Austin, Moses, V 39, *39*
Austin, Stephen F., V 39–40, *39*, 41, 48
Austin, Nevada, IX 77
Australia, X 58; XVI 25
Austria, XV *94*, 95; XVIII 21, 23; see also Austro-Hungarian Empire

Austrian Peace Treaty (1955), XVIII 68
Austrian Succession, War of (1741–48), II 62; see also King George's War
Austro-Hungarian Empire, X 58; First World War, XII 13–14, *14*, 16–18, 20, 21, 131, 136
Automatic car-coupler, X 28
Automobile racing, XI 140
Automobile industry, XI 12, 14–17, 18, 82, 120, 122, 129, 140; XIII 38–41, *39–42*, 44, 49, 58, 130;

XIV 73, 112, *115*; XVII 110, *111*; XIX 136–137; XX 44, 53
Avery, Henry, I 87
Aviation, XI 129; XII 84–85, 126; XIII 30; see also Aerospace industry; Aircraft industry
Aviles, Pedro Menendez de, see Menendez de Aviles, Pedro
Awake and Sing, XIV 91
Awakening, The, XI 107

Awful Disclosures of the Hôtel Dieu Nunnery at Montreal, IV 81
AWS, see Army Aircraft Warning Service
Axis powers (Second World War), XVI 10, 11, 13, 14, 15, 19, 60, 82; see also Second World War
Azores, I 33
Aztecs, I 15, 41, 43; see also Indians, American

B

Babbitt, XIII 66, 95
Babcock, Orville, X 42, 44
Babelthuap Island, XVI 113
Babes in Arms, XIV *100*
Babes in Toyland, XI 126
Babiche, I 38
Babson, Roger, XIII 140
"Babson break," XIII 140
Baby and Child Care, XVII 118
Bacall, Lauren, XVII *38*
Bachman, John, III *106*
Back country, definition of, I 101, 103, 104; life in, I 104; IV 10; community feeling in, I 105; grievances of, I 105–106; III 136; of Appalachians, I 106; evangelical pietism, I 110
"Backporch" campaigning, XIII 21
Backwoods, see Back country
Bacon's Rebellion (1676), I 77
Bacteriological laboratory, X 112
Badlands, South Dakota, IX *11*
Badoglio, Pietro, XVI 83, 84, 136
Baer, George F., X 85; XI 97
Baer, Max, XIV 75
Baffin Island, I 19
Baghdad Pact, XVIII 72, 77
Bahamas, I 11, 87; XIII 54
Bahia slave rebellion, VI 38
Bailey, Alonzo, VIII 108
Bailey, Josiah, XIV 132
Bailey, William, XIII 44
Bainbridge, William, III 123
Baird, James, V 34
Baker, Newton D., XII 66, 71, 76, 101, 102, 105, 106, 107, 108, 113; XIV 29
Baker, Ray Stannard, X 139; XI 31
Baker, Robert C. (Bobby), XIX 89
Baker v Carr (1962), XIX 35
Balboa, Vasco Nunez de, I 14, 15, 16, *43*
Bald eagle, III 108
Baldwin, James, XVII 66, 103
Baldwin Felts Agency, XIII 132
Baldwin Locomotive Works, XII 109
Balfour, Arthur James Balfour, 1st Earl of, XV 25, *22*
Balfour Declaration (1926), XV 46
Balkan League, XII 16
Balkans, XII 13, 16–17
Balkan Wars (1912–13), XII 16
Ballance of Power, II *62*
Ballinger, Richard A., XI 64
Ballistic missiles, XIX 83, 84, 86, 87, *87*
Ballot, secret, X 46
Baltic (ship), IV 57
Baltic states, XII 136; XVIII 13
Baltimore, George Calvert, 1st Baron of, I 72, 73
Baltimore, Maryland, IX 43; population growth, III 16, 65; IV 41; VI 42, 51
Baltimore and Ohio Railroad, IV 55; VII 84; X 75, 77; XI 118; XIII 73; see also Railroads
Baltimore clipper, IV 60
Baltimore *Sun*, XIII 107, 112, 113; XVII 48

Bambi, XVI 62
Bancroft, Edward, II 135, 137
Bancrofts of Lynn, II 92
Band (tribe), IX 20
"Bandit's Roost," X *66*
Bandung conference (1955), XVIII 69
Bangladesh, XVIII 134
Bankhead, William B., XV 94
Bankhead-Jones Act (1937), XIV 120
Banking, III 88; VIII 98; X 18; XI 68; XIII 46, 137; Great Depression, XIV *14*, 15–16, 30; Glass-Steagall Banking Act, XIV 34; see also Bank of the United States
Bank of America, XIII 46
Bank of North America, III 12
Bank of the United States, Alexander Hamilton's proposals, III 40, *40*, 45, 60, 137; Jefferson, III 78; Madison's Second Bank, III 88; charge of monopoly, IV 18; "Bank War," IV 34–35, *35*; see also Banking
Banks, Charles, VIII 100
Banks, Nathaniel P., VI 126, 128; VII 26, 115
"Bank War," IV 34–35, *35*; see also Bank of the United States
Banky, Vilma, XIII 85
Bannack, Montana, IX 73, 77
Bannock, IX 16; see also Indians, American
Banzai, XVI 35, 112
Baptism in Kansas, XIII 110
Baptists, education, IV 86, 101; state support for, IV 99; growth of church, IV 100, *100*; and Negroes, IV 108; and slavery, VI 74; in West, IX 99; see also Religion
Baptist Union, XI 47
Barabas, Al, XIV 75
Barbary shore, XVII 104
Barden, Graham, XVII 26
Barents Sea, XVI 73
Barkley, Alben William (vice president), XIV 133, 136; XVII 21
Barlow, Joel, III 91, 95
Barnard, Henry, IV 85, 86
"Barnburners," VI 88, 89, 90, 97, 104
Barnes, Harry Elmer, XV 78
Barnes, Jake, XIII 70
Barnett, Ross, XIX 21
Barnum & Bailey's Circus, XI *20*
Barré, Isaac, I 132
Barrie, J. M., XII 58
Barrington, Samuel, II 69, 72
Barrow, Clyde, XIV 77, 78
Barry, Philip, XIII 98
Bartlett, Josiah, II *13*
Barton, Bruce, XIII 32
Barton, Clara, VII 32
Bartram, John, I 114
Bartram, William, I *115*
Baruch, Bernard M., XII 67, 101, 102, 108, 109, 113; XIII 137, 140; XVIII 24
Baseball, X 119, *120*; XI 18, 134; XIII 77, *78*, *79*;

XIV *74*, 75–76; XVII *51*, 128–129, *128*; see also
   Sports
Basie, Count, XIV 100, *100*; see also Jazz
Basketball, XI 137; XIV 75; see also Sports
Bassett, Charlie, IX 64
Basso, Hamilton, XIV 42
Bastogne, XVI 101, *101*, 102
Bataan Peninsula, XVI 23, 25
Bates, Edward, VI 126, 128
Batista, Fulgencia, XV 39, *39*
Baton Rouge, Louisiana, III 130
''Battle Above the Clouds,'' VI *110*; VII 111
Battle Between Cheyennes and Soldiers, IX 104
Battle of Britain, see Britain, Battle of
Battle of Warbonnet Creek, IX 117
Battleships, XII 69; XV 24
Baugh, John, V 42
Bauhaus, XVII 98
Baylor University, XVII 14
Bay of Pigs, see Cuba
Bazelon, David, XIX 69, 80
Baziotes, William, XVII *96*
Bazooka, XVI 54
Beach Boys, XIX 76, *77*
Beach, Moses Yale, V 91–92
Beach, Sylvia, XIII 70
Beadle, Erastus, IX *134*, 136–137
''Beagle Street Blues,'' XIII 90
Bear, grizzly, V 19, 21, *22*; IX *14*
Beard, Charles A., VII 99; XI 115, 116; XV *78*, 79,
   122
Beard, James, III *16*
Bear Flag, V 118, *119*
Bear Flag Revolt, V 118, *119*
Bear River ''City,'' IX *30*
Beat Generation, XVII 101, 134, *134*, 136
Beatles, The, XIX 66–67, *67*, 76
Beatty, Sir David, XV 22
Beaufort, South Carolina, VII 22
Beau Geste, XIII 72
Beaujour, Felix de, IV 10
Beaulac, Willard L., XV 40
Beaumont, Pablo, I *45*
Beauregard, Pierre G. T., VII 19, 117, 125; VIII 20
Beau Sabreur, XIII 72
Beaver, V 21, *22*, 34; IX 13, 15
Bechet, Sidney, XIII 90
Beckett, Samuel, XVII 107
Beckley, John, III 52, 54, 61
Becknell, William, V 13, 33
''Bee'' (frontier), IV 40
Beecher, Henry Ward, IV 93, 108; X 97
Beecher, Lyman, IV 99, 102–103, 108, 116; VI 98
Beer, XIII 54, 56, 58, *58*, 65
Beery, Wallace, XIII 82
Begin, Menachem, XX 31
Behaviorism, XIII 49
Behrman, S. N., XIII 98
Beiderbecke, Bix, XIII 87, *88*
Belasco, David, XI 126
Belgium, XII 18, 46, 60; XV 103, *106*; XVIII 32
Belknap, Jeremy, III 97
Belknap, Reginald R., XII 69
Belknap, William W., X 42
Bell, Alexander Graham, X 26, *26*; XI 13
Bell, Daniel, XVII 107
Bell, David, XIX 19
Bell, John (biographer), II 111
Bell, John (politician), VI *128*, 129, 131
Bellamy, see XYZ affair
Bellamy, Edward, X 21, 102, 137, *137*
Belleau Wood, Battle of (1918), XII 89
Belleau Wood (carrier), XVI 118
Belle Isle Strait, I 22
Bell for Adano, A, XVI 62
Belloc, Hilaire, XII 58
Bellow, Saul, XVII 103, 104
Bellows, George, XI *20*, 89
Bell Telephone Company, X 26
Bemis, Samuel F., II 134
Benchley, Robert, XIII 96
Ben-Gurion, David, XVIII 73
Ben-Hur, XIII 81, *81*, 83
Benjamin, Judah P., VII 59
Bennett, Harry, XIII 61
Bennett, James Gordon, V 134
Bennett Law, X 53

Benny, Jack, XIV 102
Bent, Charles, V 82
Benton, Jessie, V 22, 24, *25*, 120
Benton, Thomas Hart (politician), and J. C. Frémont,
   V 22, 24, 116, 120; and 49th parallel, V 66;
   Mexican War, V 86; Pacific Railroad Bill, IX 28
Benton, Thomas Hart (painter), XIV 82, *82*, 84, *84*;
   XV *14*
Benton, William, XIV 19
Bentonville, Battle of (1865), VII 127
Bent's Fort, V 81
Bergan, Edgar, XIV 102, *103*
Bergen, Marten van, I *105*
Bergen, New Jersey, I 65
Bergen County, New Jersey, II 98
Berger, Victor, XII 114; XIII 13; XV 14
Bering Strait, I 35
Berkeley, Bishop, I 139
Berkeley, Busby, XIV 91, *92*
Berkeley, Lord John, I 65, 66, 74
Berkeley, University of California, XIX 70
Berkman, Alexander, XIII 13
Berle, Adolf, Jr., XIV 30, 31
Berlin, XII 10, 40, 43; XV 77, 91, 95, 97; XVI 10, 12,
   102, 103, 104, 106, 133; XVIII 32, 79, 83, 88, 93,
   94, 132
Berlin, Irving, XIII 92
Berlin, Treaty of (1920), XV 13–14
Berlin blockade, XVIII 32, *33*
Berlin Decree (1806), III 117
Berliner, Emile, X 26
Berlin Wall, XVIII 79, 88, *88*
Bermuda, I 72
Bernheisel, Ben, XII 76
Bernstein, Carl, XIX 112, *113*
Bernstorff, Johann Heinrich von, XII 42, 50, *50*
Berryman, Clifford, XIV *134*
Bethlehem, Pennsylvania, I *101*
Bethlehem-Fairfield Shipyard, XVI *49*
Bethlehem Steel Corporation, XI 16; XII 35; XIII 136
Bethmann-Hollweg, Theobald von, XII 43
Beveridge, Albert J., XI 45, 48, 61, 71
Beverley, Robert, I 77, 102, 111, 117, 139
Beverly Hills, Los Angeles, XIII 33
Bevin, Ernest, XVIII 30, *30*
Bewley, Marius, XVII 107
Biak Island, XVI 114
Biberman, Herbert, XVII 38, *38*, 39
Bible Argument, The, VI 72
Bible Belt, XIII 112, 113
Bickel, Alexander M., XVII 58
Bicycle, X 115, 119, *123*; XI 17–18, 120
Bidault, Georges, XVIII 30
Bienville, Celoron de, I 92
Bierstadt, Albert, IV 133; V *17, 47, 59*; IX *101*
''Big Apple'' (dance), XIV 72
Big bands, XIV 100, *100*; see also Swing
Big Black River, Battle of (1863), VII 36
''Big Bonanza'' (1873), IX 71
Big Foot (Chief), IX 112, *112*
''Big Four,'' IX 32, 36, 37
Big Money, The, XIV 88
Big stick diplomacy, XI 71, 82
''Bill Bailey, Won't You Please Come Home,'' XI 123
Billboards, XIII *41*, 44; see also Advertising
Bill Haley and the Comets, XVII 137, *138*
Bill of Rights, II 54–55; III 31, 33
Billy the Kid, see Bonney, William
Billy the Kid (music), XIV 100
''Billy Yank,'' VII 136, 137
Bimini, I 13
Bingham, George Caleb, IV *21, 27, 133*; V *18*;
   VII *47*
Bingham, John, VIII 27, *28*
Bingham, Utah, IX 74
Bingo, XIV 72; see also Games
Bintl brief, X 70
Biograph, XI 132
Birch, William, III *65*
Birds of America, The, III *106*
Birkbeck, Morris, IV 66, 74
Birmingham, Alabama, VIII 124, *124*; X 13
Birney, James G., VI 72, 77–78, *77*, 82
Birth of a Nation, VIII 116; XI 133
Bismarck, Otto von, XII 13, *16*
Bison, see Buffalo

Bissell, M. R., XIII 44
Black, Ian, XIV 136
Black Ball Line, IV 57
Blackbeard, see Teach, Edward
Blackboard Jungle, The, XVII 134, 137
Black Boy, XVII 103
Black Codes, VIII 15–16, 70
Blackfoot, I 40; IX 17; see also Indians, American
Black Hand (Italian), see Mafia
Black Hand (Serbian), XII 16, 17
Black Hawk War (1832), IV 67; VII 19
Black Hills, South Dakota, IX 11, 70, 73, 107
Black Kettle (Chief), IX 102, 106
Black Mountain College, XVII 101
Blackmun, Harry A., XIX 107
Black Muslims, XIV 68
Black Nationalism, XIX 56, 132
Black Oxen, XIII 72
Black Panther party, XIX 53, 57
''Black Power,'' XIX 42, 52, 57, *58*; see also
   Integration; Negroes
Blacks (race), first use of word, XVII 51; in 1970s and
   1980s, XX 56, 58–59, 66; see also Negroes
Blackstone, Sir William, I 135
Black Studies, XIX 57–58
Black Sun Press, XIII 70
Blackwell, Elizabeth, IV 123
Blackwood's Magazine, IV 127
Bladensburg, Battle of (1814), III 127
Blaine, James G., IX 37; X 47, 48, 49, 50, 51, 54
Blair, Henry W., VIII 129
Blair, James, I 77
Blair, Preston, Jr., V 82
Bland, Humphrey, I 97
Bland, Richard, I 126
Bland, Richard Parks, X 48
Bland-Allison Act (1878), X 48
Blease, Cole, VIII 135
Bledsoe, Albert Taylor, VI 57; VIII 140
Blimps, XII *70*; see also Airships
Blithedale Romance, The, IV 120, 139
Blitzkrieg (Second World War), XV 101, 103; XVI 10,
   11, 46
Block, Adriaen, I 51
Blockades, 1806, III 112, 116–117; 1812, III 124;
   Civil War, VII 21, *62*, 64, 66, 77, 101, 102, 107,
   108, 125; First World War, XII 38, 41, 44
Block Island, I 51
''Bloody Corps,'' II 120
Bloomer, Amelia, IV 123
Bloomers, IV 123–124, *124*
Blough, Roger, XIX 23
Blount, William, III 51
Blue-Backed Speller, III 94, *94*; IV 84
''Blue Danube Blues,'' XIII 92
Blue Eagle symbol (NRA), XIV 34
Blue Mountain, V 59
Blues (music), XIII 87, 90, 92; see also Jazz
Boardmans of Lynn, II 92
Board of Indian Commissioners, IX 114, 118
Board of Trade (Britain), I 122, 123, 124
Bobbed hairstyle, XIII 74, *74*; see also Fashions
Bocage, XVI 94
Boca Raton, Florida, XIII 38
Boer War (1899–1902), XII 14
Boggs, Hale, XIX 46
Bohemians, XIII 68, 70, 72
Boise Basin, Idaho, IX 73
Bok, Edward, XI 124
Bolivia, I 37; XV 40, *41*, 43; see also South America
Bolshevik Revolution, see Russian Revolution
Bomber Command (RAF), XVI 15, 74, 88, 102
Bombers, XII 85; see also Air power
Bombing, strategic, XVI 15, 74, 85, 88, 102, 133–134
Bond, Carrie, XI 123
''Bondocracy,'' X 82
Bonetta (ship), II 75–76
Bonhomme Richard (ship), II 113, *112–113*
Bonnet, Stede, I *87*
Bonneville Dam, XIV 35; see also Dams
Bonney, William (Billy the Kid), IX 61, 66, *66*, 67,
   133; see also West, the
''Bonnie Blue Flag, The,'' VII 80
Bonny, Anne, I *87*, *87*
Bonsack, James, VIII 122
Bonus Army Riot (1932), XIV 20, *20*
''Bonus Expeditionary Force,'' XIV 20, 21, *22*

Book of American Negro Poetry, XIII 99
Book-of-the-Month Club, XIII 73
''Boomers,'' IX 93, 119
Boone, Daniel, I 55, 107, *107;* IV 49; IX 133–134, *134*
Boone, Pat, XVII, 127, *138*
Boonesborough, Kentucky, I 107; IX 134
Boorstin, Daniel, I 137; XVII 104, 107, 108
Booth, Edwin, VII *80,* 82; IX 77
Booth, John Wilkes, VII *80,* 82, 130, *132,* 133, 134, 135
Booth, Junius Brutus, Jr., VII *80,* 82
Booth, William, X 119; XI 109; see also Salvation Army
Bootlegging, XIII 53, 54, 56, 58, *59,* 60, *60,* 61, 62; see also Prohibition
Borah, William E., XII 127, 140; XIV 133; XV *16,* 31, 61, 73, 98
Borden, Gail, IV 64; X 32–33, *33*
Borneo, XVI 20, 26
Bosnia, XII 16; see also Balkans
Boston, Massachusetts, relations with Indians, I 51; establishment of, I 60; growth of, I 62, 68; rebellion against James II, I 63, 69; early economic life, I 101, 112; culture, I 112; anti-British sentiment, I *129,* 130; Crown control of, II 14; siege of, II 24, 34; Crown closure of, II 86–87, 89; held by British, III 11; population, III 16; IV 41; first American railroad, IV 54; pauperism, IV 80; libraries, X 92; symphony orchestra, X 92; museums, X 92; cable-cars, X 109; fire, X 110; sewage, X 112; slums, X 113; parks, X 118; XI 118; urban landscaping, X *118;* police strike (1919), XIII 120–121, *121;* busing, XIX *52,* 53
Boston *Guardian,* VIII 109
Boston Indian Citizenship Committee, IX 118
Boston Massacre, I *130,* 132; II 85
Boston Port Act (1774), II 86–87
Boston *Post,* X 125
Boston Riot (1903), VIII 110, 111
''Boston Tea Party,'' I 133; II 16, 74, 84, 85
Boucher, Jonathan, III 90
Bougainville Island, XVI 36, 37, *39,* 41, *41*
Bouille, Marquis de, II 72
Boulder, Colorado, IX 74
Boulder Dam, XIII 46; see also Dams
Bounty jumping, VII 76
Bouquet, Henry, I 97
Bourbons (France), II 62, 67; VIII 129
Bourbons (the South), VIII 129, 132, 134, 135, 138, 141; see also South, the
''Bourbon Triumvirate,'' VIII 129
Bourget, Paul, XI 27
Bourne, Randolph, XI 115–116, 119
Boutwell, George, VIII 27, *28*
Bow, Clara, XIII *83*
Bowdoin, III *10*
Bowdoin College, IV 90; see also Education
Bowdre, Charlie, IX 67
Bowers, ''Sandy,'' V 82
Bowery, New York City, XI 29, *57;* XVII 116, *116;* see also Poverty
Bowery at Night, The, X *109*
Bowie, James, V 42
Bowl, The, XIV *87*
Bowles, Chester, XIV 19; XIX 19
Boxer Rising (1900), XI 46, *47*
Boxing, X *120;* XI 134, 136; XIII 77, *79;* see also Sports
Boycotts, II 87, 89, 98
Boy Friend, The, XIV 95
Boy Scout movement, XI 140
Bozeman Trail, IX 106
Bracebridge Hall, IV 131, 135
Brackenridge, Hugh Henry, III 95
Braddock, Edward, I *94,* 95, 96, 97
Bradley, Joseph P. VIII 87, *88*
Bradley, Omar Nelson, XVI 81, 90, *90,* 94, 96, 97, 98, 101, 102, 104, *104*
Bradstreet, John, I 97
Brady, ''Diamond Jim,'' XI 137
Brady, Mathew, X 33
Brady, William, IX 67
Bragg, Braxton, VII 33, 34–35, 63, 110–111
''Brahmin'' society, IV 138
Brain Trust (New Deal), XIV 30, 31
Brandebury, V 109

Brandeis, Louis D., XI 114; XIII 14; XIV 44, 46
Brando, Marlon, XVII 121, *134*
Brandt, Willy, XVIII *93,* 132
Brandy Station, Battle of (1863), VII 39
Brandywine Creek, Battle of (1777), II 107
Brannan, Charles F., XVII 25
Brannan, Sam, V 122, *122*
Brannan Plan, XVII 25, 26
Brant, Joseph, I 55, 97; II *43*
Bratton, Rufus S., XV 136
Bray, Thomas, I 77
Brazil, I 10, 12, 84; slavery, VI 10, 12, 24, *26,* 28, 30, 35, 38; Second World War, XV 46
Breakers, The, XI 27
Brebeuf, Jean de, I *80*
Brebner, John Bartlet, XV 46
Brecht, Bertholt, XVII 38
Breckinridge, John C., VI 125, *126,* 129, 131, 132; VII 117, 119, 134
Breda, Treaties of (1667), I 84
Breed's Hill, Battle of, see Bunker Hill, Battle of
Breeds of Lynn, II 92
Breezing Up, X 101
Brenner Pass, XVI 106
Brest-Litovsk, Treaty of (1918), XII 53, 136
Breton, André, XVII 90
Bretton Woods Conference (1944), XVI 136; XVIII 17, 137
Brever, Marcel, XVII 90, 98
Brewing industry, XIII 56, 58, 64
Briand, Aristide, XV 19–20, *22*
Bricker, John W., XIV 136; XVII 78, 86
Bricker amendment, XVII 78
Bridge (game), XIII 73; XIV 70; see also Games
Bridge on the River Kwai, XVII 132
Bridge, The, XIII 98
Bridgeman, Laura, IV 114
Bridger, Jim, V 20, 21
Bridges, Harry, XIV 111, 136
Bridges, X 29–30, *29*
Bright leaf tobacco, see Tobacco
Brisbane, Arthur, XI 124
Bristoe Station, Battle of (1862), VII 29
Bristol, England, I 21, 62, *121;* VII *105*
Bristow, Benjamin H., X 42
Britannia (ship), IV 57
British Columbia, I 39
British Empire, see Great Britain
Britton, Nan, XIII 30
Broadway Boogie-Woogie, XVII 90
Broadway Melody, XIII 85
Brocchus, Perry, V 109
Brock, Isaac, III 122
Bromfield, Louis, XIV 90
Bronx River Parkway, XIII 38
Bronze Star, XVI 79
Brook, Alexander, XIV 67
Brooke, Richard, VIII 60
Brook Farm, Massachusetts, IV 119–120, *120;* X 137
Brooklyn (ship), VI 136
Brooklyn Bridge, New York City, X 29–30, *29*
Brooklyn Bridge, XIII 101, *104*
Brooklyn Dodgers (baseball), XVII 129
Brooks, James, XVII 96
Brooks, Preston S., VI 107, *107*
Brooks, Van Wyck, XIII 66, 70; XIV 88; XVII 105
Broom, XIII 70
''Brother, Can You Spare A Dime,'' XIV 80
''Brother Jonathan,'' IV 10, *82*
Brown, Antoinette, IV 123
Brown, Claude, XIX 58
Brown, Henry Billings, VIII 138
Brown, James, XIX 58
Brown, John, VI 106, 107, 120, 122, *122,* 125, 132; see also Slavery
Brown, John C., VIII 82
Brown, Mrs Jonas, IX *80*
Brown, Joseph, VII 60, 63, 66; VIII 129
Brown, Juan Flaco (Lean John), V 119
Brown, Neil, IX 64
Brown v *Board of Education,* see *Oliver Brown et al* v *Board of Education of Topeka, Kansas* (1954)
''Brown Bess,'' II 31, *31,* 119
''Brown Bomber,'' see Louis, Joe
Brown Decades, The, X 87
Browne, Carl, X 141

Browne, Hugh M., VIII 111
Browne, J. Ross, IX 70–71, 77
Brownell, Herbert, XVII 43, 73, *77,* 78
Brownlow, William G., VIII 74, *74,* 78
Brownson, Orestes, IV 110
Brownsville, Texas, IX 45
Bruce, Blanche K., VIII 45, *47*
Bruce, Louis R., XIX 62
Brule Sioux, IX 102; see also Indians, American
Brunswick dragoons, II 31
Brush, Charles F., X 24, 32
Brush ''Everyman's Car,'' XI 140
Brusilov, Aleksei, XII 21
Brussels pact (1948), XVIII 32
Bry, Theodore de, I *26, 42*
Bryan, William Jennings, XV 22; ''Cross of Gold'' speech, X 134, *134;* Populist presidential candidate, X 141; presidential election, 1900, XI 13; anti-imperialist, XI 42; and Woodrow Wilson, XI 67; Wilson's secretary of state, XI 80; neutrality, XII 33, *34,* 37, 40, 43, 55; on munitions exports, XII 35; loans to First World War belligerents, XII 36; warning to Germans, XII 38; resignation, XII 41; American mediation in First World War, XII 44; Ford Peace Ship, XII 45; pro-war, XII 57; Florida land deals, XIII *36,* 38; Scopes trial, XIII 112–113, *112*
Bryant, Gridley, IV 54
Bryant, William Cullen, IV 133, 135
Bryce, James Bryce, 1st Viscount of, V 131; X 46–47; XI 18, 51; XII 60
Bryce Report, XII 60
Bryn Mawr College, X 92; see also Education
Brzezinski, Zbigniew, XX 27, 30–32
B-17, see ''Flying Fortress'' bombers
B-24, see Liberators
B-25, XVI 26
B-29, XVI 110, 112, 115, *115,* 126; see also Atomic bomb; Bombers
Buccaneers, I 25, 87, *87;* see also names of individual buccaneers
Buchanan, Franklin, VII 27
Buchanan, James (president), Oregon dispute, V 65; Mexican dispute, V 69, 91; ''Utah War,'' V 109, 112, 116; presidential candidate, VI 108; 1856 elections, VI 110; Dred Scott case, VI 112, *112,* 113, *113;* Kansas problem, VI 112; Lecompton constitution, VI 114, 116; Lincoln's challenge, VI 116, 117, 118, 120; VII 46; John Brown's Raid, VI 122; and Stephen Douglas, VI 125, *126;* 1860 presidential campaign, VI 129; secession, VI 132, 134, 136, 137; VII 12, 44; on Butterfield's stagecoach service, IX 26
Buchman, Frank, XIV 77
Buck, Paul, VIII 140
Buckley, William Lewis, XI 100
Buckner, Simon Bolivar, XVII 122, 124, 125
Buck's Stove and Range Company, XI 96, 97
Buddhist resistance (Vietnam), XVIII 108,
Budge, Hamer, XIX 106
Budget Bureau, XIII 24
Buell, Don Carlos, VII 24, 33
Buena Vista, Battle of (1847), V 80, *80,* 81
Buenos Aires Conference of American States (1936), XV 40
Buffalo (American bison), I 17; IX 12, *12,* 19, *19,* 20, 104, *111,* 122, *122*
Buffalo, New York, VI 51; X 116, 118; XI 128
''Buffalo Bill,'' see Cody, William Frederick
Buffalo grass, IX 11
Buick Motor Car Company, XIII 40; see also Automobile industry
Bulb (electric), see Incandescent bulb
Bulganin, Nikolai, XVIII 64, *68, 69*
Bulgaria, XII 16; see also Balkans
Bulge, Battle of the (1944), XVI *100,* 101–102
Bulkeley, Gershom, I 114
Bullard, Robert L., XII 79
Bull Durham tobacco, VIII 122, *122;* see also Tobacco
Bull market, XIII 137–138; see also Stock market
Bull Moose party, see Progressive party
Bulloch, James D., VII 108
Bullock, Rufus, VIII 82
Bull Run, First Battle of (1861), VII *18,* 19–20, *20,* 21, 60
Bull Run, Second Battle of (1862), VII *28,* 29, 72, 104

Bulova Watch Company, XVI 54
"Bummers," VIII 52
Bumppo, Natty, IV 136–137
Buna, New Guinea, XVI 32, 35
Bunau-Varilla, Philippe, XI 72
Bundy, McGeorge, XVIII 90, 110; XIX 19
Bunker Hill (Breed's Hill), Battle of (1775), II 18, *26*, 28, *28*, 29, 30, 92; effects on British, II 63, 64
Bunker Hill (carrier), XVI 125
Bunker Hill and Sullivan mine, IX 74
Bunny hug (dance), XI 126
Buntline, Ned, see Judson, Edward Zane Carroll
Buntline Specials, IX 64
Burchfield, Charles E., XIV 87
Bureau of Animal Industry, IX 56
Bureau of Corporations, XI 59
Bureau of Indian Affairs, IX 114; XIV 68; XIX 62; see also Indians, American
Bureau of Reclamation, IX 132
Bureau of Refugees, Freedmen and Abandoned Lands, see Freedmen's Bureau
Burger, Warren, XIX 107, 116
Burgoyne, General John, II 128; unfavorable terrain, II 30; soldiers' outfits, II 31; raising siege of Quebec, II 34; 1777 campaign, II 43–44, *43*; Saratoga, II 44, *44*, 106, 107, 116, 123, 136
Burke, Edmund, II 16, 83
Burke, E. A., VIII 129
Burke, Thomas, II 48, 58
Burleson, Albert S., XII 111

Burlesque, X *106*; XI 18, 126; see also Vaudeville
Burley tobacco, see Tobacco
Burlington, Vermont, I 67
Burlington and Union Pacific Railroad, IX 89; see also Railroads
Burma, XVI 20, 23, 120
Burma Road, XV 125, 127; XVI 23, *121*
Burnett, Frances Hodgson, X 104
Burnett, Peter H., V 59
Burnham, Daniel H., XI 118, 119
Burns, Anthony, VI 96
Burns, Arthur F., XVII 79; XIX 105
Burns, George, see Burns and Allen
Burns and Allen, XIV 102, *103*
Burns, Tommy, XI 136
Burnside, Ambrose E., VII 18, 32–33, 48
Burr, Aaron (vice president), and Washington, II 115; vice-presidential candidate, III 61–62, *80*; dreams of empire, III 80–81, *81*; V 12; duel with Hamilton, III 80, *80*
Burrills of Lynn, II 92
Burroughs, William S., X 26
Burwell, Carter, III *101*
Bush, Vannevar, XVI 56
Bushnell, David, II 35
Bushnell, Horace, IV 108
Business administration, XIII 41; see also Automobile industry; Industry
"Business Bourbons," VIII 129; see also Bourbons (the South)

Business ethic, XIII 31–32; see also Industry
"Businessmen's" revival, IV 108; see also Revivalism
Busing, XIX 36, *52*; see also Integration
Butler, Andrew, P., VI 107
Butler, Benjamin F., VII 91, 115, 117, 125
Butler, Frances, see Kemble, Fanny
Butler, Hugh A., XV 46
Butler, Nicholas Murray, XV 19
Butler, Pierce (politician), III 22
Butler, Pierce (plantation owner), VI 27
Butler, Pierce (judge), XIV 46
Butler case (1936), XIV 47
Butte, Montana, IX 70, 73, 77, 83, 84
Butterfield, Alexander, XIX 113
Butterfield, John, IX 26, 28
Butterfield Overland Mail, IX 26
"Butternuts," X 82
Butterworth, R. Walton, XVIII 48
Bwana Devil, XVII 132, *132*
"By Industry We Thrive," X *11*
By Love Possessed, XVII 103
Byng, John, I 96
Byrd, Harry, XIV 132
Byrd, William I, I 77, 102
Byrd, William II (of Westover), I 114, 117, 136, 138
Byrd, William III, I 97
Byrnes, James F., XVIII 17, 21, 23, 26
Byron, Admiral John, II 72

Cabeça de Vaca, Gaspar Núñez, I 16, 17
Cabell, James Branch, XIII 108
Cabinet of Dr Caligari, The, XIII 85
Cable, George Washington, VIII 132, 138, 140, *140*
Cable cars, X 109
Cabot, John, I 21, *21*, 23, 35
Cabot, Sebastian, I 23
Cache Valley, V *17*
Cadet Nursing Corps, XVI 58
Cadillac (automobile), XIII 41, *42*
Cadore, Duc de, III 119
Cadwalader, John, II 110
Caesar (slave), VI *11*
Caesar, Sid, XVII 125
Caesar's Column, X 72, 102
Caffery, Jefferson, XV 39
Cage, John, XVII 101
Cagney, James, XIV 91, *94*
Cahan, Abraham, X 69
Cahuenga, Capitulation of (1847), V 120
Caine Mutiny, The (book), XVII 103
Caine Mutiny, The (film), XVII 132
Cairo conferences, XVI 18, 19
Cajuns, VIII 140
Calamity Jane, see Cannaray, Martha Jane
Calaveras River, V *129*
Calder, Alexander, XVII 96–97, *97*
Caldwell, Erskine, XIV 56, 91
Caldwell, Tod R., VIII 82
Caldwell, Kansas, IX 45, 53, 55
Calhoun, John C. (vice-president), IV 96; VI 43; war hawk, III 121; public works, III 137; early career, IV 23–24; Jacksonian, IV 28; states' rights, IV 34; presidential aspirations, IV 36; on Texas, V 49, *86*; secretary of state, V 64; Oregon question, V 64, 65, 66; Mexican War, V 72–73, 91, 92; abolitionism, VI 76; slavery, VI *86*, 87, 88, 91, 93–94
California, I 17, 25, 39, 40, 45; IX 10, 15, 16; mining, IV 63; IX 38, 74, 77; settlement, V 21; infiltration, V 22; Spanish province, V 27–28, 30–31; conquest of, V 24, 69, 93, 116, 118–120; Kearny invasion, V 83; gold rush, V 101, 120, *121*, 122–125, *122–125*, 126, 127, *127*, 129, 130–131,

131–132, 134, 138–139; IX 24, 70; Compromise of 1850, V 109; VI 92; territorial government, V 138; constitution, V 139; state seal, V 139, *140*; statehood, V 139; VI 91; proslavery, VI 94; Workingmen's party, X 82; urbanization, X 106; corruption in, XI 53; reform, XI 55; population in 1920s, XIII 35
California, University of, IX 83, 128; X 88
California Crossing, IX *11*
California Institute of Technology, XVI 56
California News, V *133*
California Star, V 122
California Trail, V 55, 125; IX 26
Calles, Plutarco E., XV 44
"Call loans," XIII 137
Call of the Canyon, The, XIII 72
Call of the Wild, XI *109*, 124
Calvert, Cecilius, I *71*, 73, *75*
Calvert, Sir George, see Baltimore, George Calvert, 1st Baron of
Calvert, Leonard, I 73
Camargo, Mexico, V 76
Cambodia, XVIII 64, 96, 123
Cambrai, Battle of (1917), XII 74
Cambridge, Godfrey, XIX 58
Camden, Battle of (1780), II 78, 102
Camden and Amboy Railroad, X 28
Camel walk, XI 126
Cameron, Simon, VI 126, 128
Camino Real, XVII 106
Camotes Islands, XVI 118
Camp, Walter, XI 137
Camp David, XVII 86
Camp Floyd, V 112
Campbell, Douglas, XII 84, 85
Camp Fire Girls, XI 140
Camping, XI 140
Camp MacArthur, Texas, XII 67
Camp meeting, IV 101, *101*, 102–103, 108; see also Revivalism
Canada, and Cartier's expedition to, I 22; Indian tribes in, I 35, 38; French in, I 63, 91; French and Indian War, I 98; Quebec Act, II 14; American

invasion, II 33–34, *33*; plans for 1812 invasion, III 121, 124; wheat, X 58; effect of prohibition on, XIII 54; relations with US, XV 31, 46–47, 49; NATO, XVIII 34; see also New France
Canadian River, V 13; IX II
Canals, III 85, 137; IV 50–51, 52–53, *53*, 68; VI 48; XI 71
Canal Zone, XI 78, 82; see also Canals and Panama Canal
Canary Islands, I 11, 42
Canby, Edward R. S., IX 107
Cane, XIII 99
Cane Ridge, Kentucky, IV 102
Cannaray, Martha Jane (Calamity Jane), IX 61, 62–63, *63*, 133
Canned goods, XI 23; see also Canning
Canning, George, III 131; V 53, *53*
Canning, IV 64; X 32, *32*
"Can't Buy me Love," XIX 66
"Can't Help Lovin' That Man," XIII 92
Cantiguy, Battle of (1918), XII 88
Cantonment Adjustment Commission, XII 105
Cantor, Eddie, XIV 96
Cantos, XVII 101
CAP, see Community Action Program
Capa, Robert, XV *89*
Cape Breton Island, I 90
Cape Cod, I 59
Cape Engano, XVI 116
Cape Esperance, Battle of (1942), XVI 31
Cape Fear, I 22, 74
Cape Gloucester, New Britain, XVI 41
Cape Horn, V 124
Cape Kennedy, I 13; XIX *88*
Cape Sansapor, XVI 114
Cape Torokina, Bougainville, XVI 37, 39, 41
Cape Verde Islands, I 33
Capitalism, Black, VIII 92, 96–100, 101; corporate, XI 84; finance, XI 12, 13; industrial, IX 83; X 138; and New Deal, XIV 35, 37, 140; welfare, XI 57; XIII 49, 136; ecological side-effects of, XIX 137; see also Economy; Trade and industry
Capitol, III *42*, 46, 64, *65*, 127; VI 93; VII *15*, 16
Capone, Al, XIII 58, 60, 61, 62, *62*, 63
Caporetto, Battle of (1917), XII 74, *75*, 80, 105
Capote, Truman, XVII 103
Capper-Volstead Act (1922), XIII 26
Capra, Frank, XIV 95
Captain Jack (Chief), IX 107, *107*
Cárdenas, Lázaro, XV 43
Card games, XIII 73; XIV 70
Cardozo, Benjamin, XIV 46
Cardozo, Francis L., VIII 44, 46
Carey, Mathew, IV 14
Carib, I 14; see also Indians, American
Caribbean, I 23, 44, 84; II 67–69, *69*, 74; XI 72, 78; "American lake," XI 72, 78, 82; XV 31; and communism, XVII 86; see also Latin America
Caribou, Colorado, IX 73
Carleton, Sir Guy, II 33, 34, 43, 66, 106
Carlisle, Frederick Howard, 5th Earl of, II 106
Carlisle Commission, II 69, 106, 109, 138
Carlos, John, XIX *58*
Carmichael, Stokely, XIX 52, 57
Carnegie, Andrew, VIII 101, *105*, 107, 108, 111; X 13–14, *14*, 20, 88, 97, 125; XI 26
Carnegie Endowment for International Peace, XV 17, 19
Carnegie Homestead Plant, X 13, *14*, 139
Carnival, The, VIII *62*
Carolina, see North Carolina; South Carolina
Caroling Dusk, XIII 99
Carpenter, John Alden, XIII 93
Carpenter's Hall, II *52*
Carpetbaggers, VIII 39–40, *39*, *40*; see also Reconstruction
Carpet sweeper, XIII 44; see also Inventions
Carranza, Venustiano, XII 27, 29, 30
Carrillo, Jose Antonio, V 139
Carrizal incident, XII 30
Carroll, Charles, II *13*
Carson, Kit, V 24, 34, 120; IX 133, *134*, 136
Carson River, IX 15
Carson Valley, V 106
Carswell, G. Harrold, XIX 107
Cartagena, Colombia, I 90
Carter, Ann Hill, I *111*

Carter, Hodding, XVII 52
Carter, Jimmy (president), XX 15–18, 27–34
Carteret, Sir George, I 65, 66, 68, 74
Carteret, Philip, I 65, 66
Cartier, Jacques, I 22, 23, *26*
Cartoons, XIV 99–100, *99*; see also Comic strips; Movies
Cartwright, Peter, IV 101
Carver, George Washington, VIII *104*; XIII 32, *33*
Carver, John, I 59
Casablanca conference (1943), XVI 16–17, *16*, 81, 82, 85, 135
Casas, Bartolomé de las, I 42, *44*
Cascade Mountains, IX 10
Casement, Dan, IX 30, *30*, 31
Casement, Jack, IX 30, 31
Caserta Armistice, XVI 106
Casey, Pat, IX 82
"Cash-and-carry" clause (Neutrality Act), XV 90, 91, 98, 100, 114
Cash register, X 26; see also Inventions
Cass, Lewis, V 65; VI 88, *90*
Cassady, Neal, XVII 134
Cassatt, Mary, X 87
Cassino, Battle of (1943–44), XVI 88, *88*
Castle Garden, New York, IV 76; X 60, *61*
Castle Pinckney, South Carolina, VI 134
Castro, Fidel, XVII 86; XVIII 70, *70*; and Kennedy, XVIII 82; Bay of Pigs, XVIII 86, 88; see also Cuba
Castro, José, V 69, 116, 118, 119
Catawba-Wateree Valley, VIII 125
Catch 22, XVII 22
Catcher in the Rye, XVII 103, 104, 105, 127
Cather, Willa, X 92
Catherine II (Russia), II 78, 79, 135
Catholics, see Roman Catholics
Catlin, George, IX 19, *19*, 123, 137
"Cato," see Clinton, George
Cat on a Hot Tin Roof, XVII 106, *106*
Catron, Thomas, IX 66
Catskill Road, IV 67
Catt, Carrie Chapman, XV 17, 19
Cattle, I 104; V 30, 34; IX 43, *43*, 44, 96; trails, IX 44–46, 45, 59; cowboys, IX 46–49, *47*, *49*, *50*, *52*, 52–55; cattle town, IX 53, 54, *54*, 55; corporate enterprises, IX 56; settlers conflict, IX 49, 56, 66; end of open range, IX 59; beef trust, IX 97
Catton, Bruce, XVII 105
Caucus system, IV 26
Cavaliers, I 62
Cavell, Edith, XII 46, *46*, 60
Cayuga, I 53; see also Indians, American; Iroquois
Cazo, IX 83
CBS, see Columbia Broadcasting System
CCC, see Civilian Conservation Corps
Cebu Island, XVI 118
Cedar Creek, Battle of (1864), VII 119
Cedar Run, Battle of (1862), VII 29
Cempoala, I 15
Censors, Council of, II 55
Censorship, XII 110; XIII 81, 108–109, 111; XIX 111
CENTO, See Central Treaty Organization
Central America, XI 71, 72, 78, 80; XV 31
Central American Court of Justice, XI 80
Central City, Colorado, IX 82
Central conveyor belt, XI 16, 17; XIII 44
Central government, see Federal government
Central Intelligence Agency, Joseph McCarthy, XVII 36; Guatemala, XVIII 70; U-2 affair, XVIII 80; Bay of Pigs, XVIII 86; XIX 20; scandals, XIX 119
Central Labor Union, X 78
Centralia Massacre (1864), IX 67
Centralist faction (Mexico), V 40, 41, 69, 70, 76, 90, 91
Central Pacific Railroad, IX 28, 31–32, *32*, 35, 37; see also Railroads
Central Park, New York City, X 92, 118
Central Powers (First World War), XI 82; XII *14*, 21, 33, 37, 40, 44, 50
Central Treaty Organization, XVIII 72, 77
Century, IX 127; X 93, 103; XI 124
Century (club), XI 126
Century of Dishonor, A, IX 116
"Century of Progress" exposition (1933–34), XIV 78

Cerro, Sánchez, see Sánchez Cerro, Luis M.
Cerro Gordo, Battle of (1847), V 87, *87*
Cervera, Pascual, XI *40*
Céspedes, Carlos Manuel de, XV 38, 39
Ceylon, II 79
Cézanne, Paul, XI *113*
Chaco War (1933–35), XV 40, *42*
Chagres River, V 124
Chain gang, VIII *132*; see also Convict leasing system
Chain stores, XI 21
Chamberlain, Daniel H., VIII 44, 85, 86
Chamberlain, George, XII 106
Chamberlain, Neville, XV 91, 94, 95, 96, *96*, 112
Chambers, Thomas, II *92*
Chambers, Whittaker, XVII 40, *40*
Champion's Hill, Battle of (1863), VII 36
Champlain, Lake, III 121, 124, 126
Champlain, Samuel de, I *25*, *26*, 28, 79, *79*; see also Colonization; Exploration
Champoeg, Oregon, V 63
Chance, F. L., XI 134
Chancellorsville, Battle of (1863), VII 37
Chandler, Howard, XII 110
Chandler, Zachariah, VIII 27; X 36
Chandor, Douglas, XIV *26*
Chang Hsueh-Liang, XV 56, 59, 64
Chang Tso-lin, XV 55, 56
Channing, William Ellery, IV 115; VI 27
Chantilly, Battle of (1862), VII 29
Chaplin, Charlie, XI 133, *133*; XII 116, *117*; XIII 83, 85, *86*; XIV 97; see also Movies
Chappel, W. P., III *11*
Chapultepec, Battle of (1847), V 87, 90
Charbonneau, Toussaint, III 76–77
Charity organization societies, X 118, 119
Charity Organization Society (Buffalo), X 118
Charles I (England), I 60, 62
Charles II (England), I 62, 63, 65, 73
Charles VIII (France), I 10
Charles William, III *89*
Charlesbourg-Royal, I 23
Charles River Bridge case (1837), IV 16, 17–18
Charleston, South Carolina, I 74, *74*, 88, 101, 106, 112, 114, *133*; II 78, 102, 120; III 65, 136; VI 42, 51, *51*, 125; VII 125; VIII *11*
Charleston, the (dance), XIII *75*, 76
Charleston and Hamburg Railroad, IV 55; see also Railroads
Charleston Mercury, VI 129
Charleston *News and Courier*, VIII 119
Charlestown Neck, II 30
Charlotte *Observer*, VIII 119
Charmed Life, A, XVII 103
Charter of Privileges (1701), I 70
Charters, land, I 60, 63, 73
Chase, Richard, XVII 107
Chase, Salmon P., Liberty party, VI 89, 96; on Kansas-Nebraska Act, VI 101, 102; Republican candidate, VI 126, 128; secretary of the Treasury, VII *45*, 86–87; chief justice, VII 52; presidential nominee, VIII 35, 37
Chase, Samuel, II *13*; III 79, *79*
Chase, T. Frank, XIII 109, 111
Chase, National and Guaranty Trust Bank, XIII 44; see also Banking
Chasm of the Colorado, X 98
Chasseurs Alpin, XII 76
Chatauqua statement, XV 47
Chateau Thierry, XII 89, *91*
Chatham, 1st Earl of, see Pitt, William
Chattahoochee River, III 14
Chattanooga, Tennessee, VII 110–111; VIII 124
Chau, Phan Boi, XVIII 96
Chaudière, Quebec, II 34
Chauvin, Louis, XI 123
Chavez, Cesar, XIX 62, *63*
"Checkers" speech, XIX *101*, 103
Chemin des Dames offensive (1918), XII 89, *89*
Chennault, Claire, XVI 23
Cherbourg Peninsula, XVI 94
Cherokee, I 54–55, 107; II 120; III 44; IV 67; IX 15; XIX 62; see also Indians, American
Cherokee Outlet, IX 93
Cherry Valley Massacre, II *43*, 116
Chesapeake (ship), III 124
Chesapeake affair, III *116*, 117, 119, 120
Chesapeake and Ohio Canal, IV 51; see also Canals

Chesapeake and Ohio Railroad, VIII 125; see also
  Railroads
Chesapeake Bay, I 28, 77, 101, 102; III 124, 126
Chevrolet, Louis, XIII 40
Cheyenne, I 40; IX 17, 20, 22, 48, 101, 102, 106,
  108, 117; see also Indians, American
Chiang Kai-shek, XV 51, 53, 53, 56, 64, 64, 65; XVI
  10, 13, 18, 24, 120, 121; XVIII 40, 42, 44, 44, 45,
  53; see also China
Chiang Kai-shek, Madame, XVI 18; XVIII 46, 47
Chicago, Illinois, III 122; IV 56; VI 51, 125; IX 28,
  38; X 98; cattle, IX 44, 58; meat packing industry,
  X 18, 18; Haymarket riots, X 51, 78–79, 79;
  immigrants, X 63; libraries, X 92; symphony
  orchestra, X 92; Columbian Exposition, X 93, 96,
  118; XI 118; street cars, X 109; skyscrapers, X
  109–110; Great Fire, X 110, 110; sewage, X 112;
  slums, X 113; crime, X 113; politics, X 118;
  setting for novels, XI 107; Burnham, XI 119; black
  ghettoes, XII 122; suburbs, XIII 33; see also
  Cities
Chicago and Alton Railroad, X 28; see also Railroads
Chicago & North Western Railroad, IX 32, 38; see
  also Railroads
Chicago, Burlington & Quincy Railroad, IX 38; see
  also Railroads
Chicago Eight, XIX 122
Chicago Jockey and Trotting Club, X 120
Chicago, Milwaukee & St Paul Railroad, IX 38; see
  also Railroads
"Chicago Renaissance," XI 109
Chicago, Rock Island & Pacific Railroad, IX 29, 38;
  see also Railroads
Chicago Seven, XIX 122, 123
Chicago Tribune, X 80, 138; XV 115; see also
  Newspapers
Chicago White Sox, XI 134; XIII 77; see also Baseball
Chicago World's Fair, see World's Columbian
  Exposition
Chicanos, XIX 62
Chichimecas, I 43; see also Conquistadors; Indians,
  American; Mexico
Chickahominy River, VII 28
Chickamauga Creek, Battle of (1863), VII 111
Chickasaw, I 41, 54; IX 15; see also Indians,
  American
Chickasaw Bayou, VII 35
Chicken scratch, XI 126
"Chico and the Man," XIX 51
Chihuahua, Mexico, V 83
Child labor, X 63, 84, 84; XI 91, 92
Children's Bureau, XI 64
Chile, X 49; XV 40; XVIII 135, 136; see also Latin
  America
China, and American trade, III 18, 19, 112, 112; IV
  57; coolie labor, IX 32, 32; imperialist interest, XI
  43–44, 46, 74, 80; Shantung question, XII 135; XV
  23, 51; Open Door, XV 23, 51; Republican
  revolution, XV 51, 53; relations with Japan, XV 56;
  Manchurian invasion, XV 56, 58–59, 60, 61, 62;
  Sino-Japanese War, XV 62, 64–67, 65, 69; XVI 10,
  23; April 9 Japan-American draft, XV 131; United
  Nations, XVI 15, Second World War, XVI 18, 120;
  Hump airlift, XVI 24; "loss of," XVIII 36, 40, 42,
  44, 45, 46, 46, 47–48, 48; Korean War, XVIII 53,
  55; Middle East crisis 1958, XVIII 77; Sino-
  Soviet split, XVIII 77, 79, 131; Quemoy-Matsu
  crisis, XVIII 77; Indian border war, XVIII 89;
  opening of relations with US, XVIII 128, 131, 132,
  133; XX 24, 26, 30–32, 34, 39
China-Burma-India theater (Second World War), XVI
  23–25, 25, 120
China lobby, XVIII 46, 47, 48, 51, 53, 58
Chinese-Americans, X 82, 82
Chinese Nationalist government, see Kuomintang
Chinook, IX 11
Chippawa, Battle of (1814), III 126
Chiricahua, IX 111; see also Apache
Chisholm, Jesse, IX 45, 45, 47
Chisholm Trail, IX 45, 45, 47, 53
Chisum, John, IX 66, 67
Chisum, Melvin J., VIII 113–114
Chivington, John, IX 102, 102
Cho, General, XVI 125
Chocolate Soldier, The, XI 126
Choctaw, I 41, 54; III 44; IX 15; see also Indians,
  American

Choiseul, Etienne Francois, II 63
Choiseul Island, XVI 37
Cholera, IV 75; X 110
Chopin, Kate, XI 106–107
Chotiner, Murray, XIX 101
Chou En-lai, and Korean War, XVIII 55; détente,
  XVIII 133
Christensen, Axel, XI 123
Christianization, see Missionaries and mission work
Christian Philosopher, The, I 114
Christian Science, I 135
Christian Scientists, X 119
Christy, E. P., VI 47
Christy, George, VII 82
Chronicle of York, The, III 93
Chrysler Building, XIII 102; see also Architecture
Chrysler Corporation, XIII 40
Chungking, XV 65
Church, Frederick Edwin, IV 133
Church, Robert R. Sr, VIII 96
Church, IV 97–98, 97; see also Religion
Churchill, Winston (American author), XI 124
Churchill, Sir Winston Leonard Spencer, comes to
  power, XV 112–113; request for American aid, XV
  114–115; Atlantic charter XV 121–122, 121; XVI
  12, 13; Battle of Britain, XVI 10; and Roosevelt,
  XVI 13, 17, 136, 137, 140; Second Front, XVI 15,
  135; Operation Torch, XVI 16; Casablanca
  conference, XVI 16, 16; Teheran conference, XVI
  18, 18; Quebec conference, XVI 19; Anzio, XVI 88;
  and Alexander, XVI 90; "Mulberry" harbors, XVI
  92; American rift, XVI 102; line of advance of Allies,
  XVI 104; atomic bomb, XVI 128; and Russians,
  XVI 137, 138, 139; Yalta, XVI 19, 136; XVIII 10,
  15; Iron Curtain, XVIII 24–25, 25; summit
  conference, XVIII 68
Church of England, I 57, 70, 77, 120, 128; see also
  Religion
Church Supper, XIII, 110
Churubusco, Battle of (1847), V 90, 92
CIA, see Central Intelligence Agency
Cíbola, Seven Cities of, I 17
Cigarettes, VIII 122, 124; XIII 74; see also Tobacco
Cigarmakers' Union, X 81; see also Labor unions
Cimarron River, IX 11, 45
Cincinnati, Ohio, III 44; IV 48, 48, 51; XI 29, 51;
  XIII 60
Cincinnati, Society of the, IV 98
Cincinnati Bridge, X 30
Cincinnati Red Stockings, X 119; XI 134; see also
  Baseball
Cinema, see Movies
Cinque, Joseph, VI 35
CIO, see Congress of Industrial Organizations
Cipher machines, XV 131
Circuit rider, IV 101, 101; see also Revivalism
Circus, XI 20
Cities, X 106, 108–110; XI 10; municipal
  services, X 110, 110, 112–113, 115–116,
  115–116; education and politics in, X 116, 118;
  leisure activities, X 119, 120, 123, 124; civic
  reforms, XI 12, 51–53; city planning, XI 116;
  entertainment, XI 126; nativist fear of, XIII 11;
  see also Suburbs
Citizens' Industrial Association, XI 97
City Activities with Subway, XVI 82
City Lights, XIV 97
City-manager administration, XI 53
City of Memphis (ship), XII 53
City of Washington (ship), XI 35
City planning, X 118; XI 116, 118–119; see also
  Cities
Civil Disobedience, IV 16
Civilian Conservation Corps, XIV 32, 33, 65
Civilian Defense Volunteers, XVI 66
Civilization in the United States, XIII 70
Civil liberties, XIII 15; XVII 29; see also Civil rights
Civil Liberties Union, XIII 15
Civil rights, VII 89; VIII 42, 88, 108, 109, 116; XIX
  53; Freedmen's Bureau, VIII 25; Civil Rights
  Act (1866), VIII 25; Fourteenth Amendment,
  VIII 25; Civil Rights Act (1879), VIII 79;
  emancipated slaves, VIII 42, 50; W. E. B. Du Bois,
  VIII 111; Niagara movement, VIII 111, 113;
  NAACP, VIII 115; 1883 civil rights cases, VIII 138;
  W. Wilson, XI 68; First World War, XII 110–111;

Warren Harding, XIII 30; Truman, XVII 19, 20,
  21; post-Second World War, XVII 51; Civil Rights
  Act (1957), XVII 60; Civil Rights Act (1960), XVII
  60; civil rights movement, XVII 62; Civil Rights
  Act (1964), XVII 66; Kennedy, XIX 20–22, 22;
  Johnson, XIX 34, 36; Civil Rights Act (1968), XIX
  42; "Black Power," XIX 42, 43, 52, 57, 58;
  National Organization for Women, XIX 64; rock
  culture, XIX 69; see also Black Power; Integration;
  Negroes; Women's movements
Civil Rights Act (1866), VIII 25
Civil Rights Act (1875), VIII 79
Civil Rights Act (1957), XVII 60; XIX 20
Civil Rights Act (1960) XVII 60
Civil Rights Act (1964), XVII 66; XIX 36, 41, 52
Civil Rights Act (1968), XIX 42
Civil Rights cases (1883), VIII 138
Civil Rights Commission, XIX 20
Civil Service, VIII 81; X 39, 50; XI 53
Civil Service Commission, VIII 81; X 39
Civil War (1861–65), VII 10–141 passim; balance
  of forces at outset, VII 10–12; Union volunteers,
  VII 17; Confederate Soldier, VII 17; Fort Sumter,
  VII 15, 18; disposition of troops at outbreak, VII
  19; First Bull Run, VII 18, 19–20, 20; Union navy,
  VII 21–22, 123, 124–126; Western theater, VII 22,
  22, 24, 33–36, 119–120, 122, 124; "river war,"
  VII 22, 24; Shiloh VII 23, 24; Pea Ridge, VII 24;
  Ulysses S. Grant, VII 24, 112–113, 113; fall of
  New Orleans, VII 24; Merrimack v Monitor, VII
  24, 27, 27; Peninsula campaign, VII 25; eastern
  theater, VII 26, 26, 28–29, 32, 116; Valley
  campaigns, VII 26, 119; Robert E. Lee, VII 26, 28,
  112, 112; Seven days' campaign, VII 28; Second
  Bull Run, VII 28, 29; first invasion of North, VII
  29, 29, 32; Antietam, VII 29, 32; Fredericksburg,
  VII 33, 33; Perryville, VII 33; Vicksburg, VII 35–
  36, 35; Chancellorsville, VII 37; second invasion
  of North, VII 37, 39–40; Union politics, VII 44–46;
  Confederate army, VII 60, 62–63; armaments, VII
  72; conscription, VII 51, 60, 72, 76; prisoners of
  war, VII 73, 83, 83; logistics, VII 74; reportage,
  VII 78, 80; entertainment, VII 80, 80, 82; medical
  facilities, VII 82, 84–85; profiteering, VII 82, 85;
  Negro troops, VII 51, 67, 76, 94, 96, 97, 98–99,
  99; European reaction, VII 100–102, 100–101,
  104–105, 107–108; English cotton famine, VII
  101–102, 101; Chickamauga Creek, VII 111;
  Lookout Mountain-Missionary Ridge campaign,
  VII 110, 111; Cold Harbor, VII 117; Sherman's
  advance, VII 118, 119–120, 120, 122, 124;
  siege of Petersburg, VII 117, 128; Appomattox,
  VII 128; armies' size, VII 131; casualties, VII 131;
  cost, VII 131; cost VII 11, 12; conspiracy theory, VII
  134–135; strategy in, VII 139; war aims, VII 140;
  summary, VII 135–137, 139–141; effect on west,
  IX 101, 102; industrial growth, X 14; photography,
  X 33; Republican party, X 47
Civil War, English, I 62
Civil Works Administration, XIV 32, 47
Claiborne, Billy, IX 64
"Clampers, the," see E. Clampus Vitus, Ancient and
  Honorable Order of
Clansman, The, XI 126
Clanton, Billy, IX 64, 64
Clanton, Ike, IX 64
Clarendon, Edward Hyde, 1st Earl of, I 74
Clark, Abraham, I 13
Clark, Dick, XVII 124, 141
Clark, George Rogers, II 32, 116, 120
Clark, Joseph, XIX 14
Clark, Mark, XVI 76, 79, 86, 88, 106
Clark, William (explorer), III 73, 74, 74, 75, 76, 77;
  V 10, 24; see also Exploration; Lewis and Clark
  expedition
Clark, William A. (politician), IX 83
Clark University, X 92
Clarke, James C., IX 40
Class warfare, XIV 44, 44
Clausewitz, Karl von, XV 19–20
Clay, Cassius M., VI 48
"Clay-eaters," IV 10
Clay, Henry, IV 115; VI 43; war hawk III 120–121;
  "American system," IV 23, 23; secretary of state,
  IV 28; National Republicans, IV 29; presidential
  candidacy, IV 31, 36; VI 87; "bank war," IV
  34–35; on Texas, V 39, 49–50, 50; slavery, VI

92–93, *93*, 94, 96
Clayton, Powell, VIII 78, *78*
Clayton Antitrust Act (1913), XI 67, 68, 96–97; XVII 26
Clayton-Bulwer Treaty (1850), XI 71, 72
Clean Air Act (1963), XIX 42
Clean Water Restoration Act (1966), XIX 42
Clearwater, Idaho, IX 73
Cleaver, Eldridge, XIX 57, 58
Clemenceau, Georges, XII 130, 131, 134, *134*, 136, 137
Clemens, Samuel Langhorne, see Twain, Mark
Clergy, IV 87, 100; see also Religion
Clermont (ship), IV 50, *50*
Cleveland, Grover (president), VIII 91, 92; IX 130; X 46, 47, 50–52, *50–51*, 54, *54*, 72, 139, 141; XI 34
Cleveland, Ohio, X 113, 118; XI 51; XII 122; XIV 12; XIX 62
Cliff Dwellers, The, XI *89*
Clifford, Clark, XVIII 118; XIX 18
Clinton, De Witt, IV 52, 53
Clinton, George, II 13; III 30, 46, 48, 54, 88
Clinton, Henry II 30, 34, 43, 44, 68, 69, 74, 78, 106, 114, 115, 116, 120, 121, 128, 129
Clipper ships, IV 57, *60*
Clooney, Rosemary, XVII 137, *138*
Closed shop, XI 96; see also Labor unions
Clothing industry, IV 61–62; see also Industry
Clymer, George, II *13*
Coahuila-Texas, V 39, 40, 48
Coal industry, IV 63; VIII 124; XIII 130, 132–133, *133*; see also Industry
Coast Guard, XIII *55*, 56; see also US Navy
Coastwatchers, XVI 36
Cobb, Howell, VI 91
Cobb, T. R. R., VI 138
Cobb, "Ty," XI 134, *134*
Cobbett, Richard, IV 10
Cobbett, William, IV 39, 48
Cobden, Richard, IV 39, 48, 49, 56; XII 129
Cochise (Chief), IX 111
Cock-fighting, I 116
Cocktail, XIII 56
Code, see Cipher machines
Cody, William Frederick (Buffalo Bill), IX 27, 61, *62*, 67, 133, *134, 136*, 137, *137*; see also Cowboys
Coeducation, IV 89, *89–90*, 91; see also Education
Coercive Acts (1774), I 133; II 14
Coeur d'Alenes, Idaho, IX 73, 83
Coffin, Levi, VI 66, *67*
"Coffin Handbill," IV *28*
Cohan, George M, XII 13, *125*
Cohen, Ben, XIV 133
Cohen, Walter L., VIII 96
Cohn, Roy M., XVII 43, 44, *46*
Coinage Act (1873), X 134
Coin's Financial School, X 133
Cold Harbor, Battle of (1864), VII 113, 117
Cold war, XVII 25; Geneva summit (1955), XVII 47; XVIII 68, origins, XVIII, 10, *10*, 24–25; American defensive alliances, XVIII 26; Berlin blockade, XVIII 32; US aid programs, XVIII 36; U-2 affair, XVIII 81; J. F. Kennedy, XVIII 82; Cuban missile crisis, XVIII 91; nuclear test-ban treaty, XVIII 94; Vietnam, XVIII 131; détente, XVIII 132
Cole, Lester, XVII 38, *38*
Cole, Thomas, IV 133; IX 123
Coleman, Ornette, XIX 58
Coleman, Warren G., VIII 98, *98*
Colfax, Schuyler, IX 37; X 42
Collazzo, Oscar, XVII *28*
Collective bargaining, XI 97; XII 105; XIV 115; XIX 23; see also Labor unions
Colleton, Sir John, I 73, 74
Collier, Nat, XIV *134*
Collins Line, IV 57
Collins, J. Lawton, XVI 90
Collins, Michael, XIX *96*
Colmar Pocket, XVI 99, 102
Colombian Republic, XI 72; XV 40, 43; see also Latin America
Colombo, Ceylon, XVI 25
Colonel Dismounted, The, I *126*
Colonial agents, I 122, 123
Colonial wars, I 84, 85, 86, 88, 89, 90, 91, 92–99,

92–99; see also names of individual wars
Colonization, Spanish, I 10, 12, 13, 15, 16, 17, 44, 45, 46; Norse, I 20; French, I *26*, 79–83, *79, 80, 82*; English, I 28, 48–51, 53–55, 57–63, 65–77, 103, 129; colonial rivalry, I 84–91; American, V 39–41, 48, 53; Mormon, V 99, 101–106, *103–106*; black, VI 65, 70; VII 94–95; see also Imperialism and names of individual countries
Colorado, IX 15, 26, 38, 44, 56, 59; mining, IX 71, 73, 78; land, IX 92; statehood, IX 92; Indian warfare, IX 102; urbanization, X 106; Populists, X 133
Colorado Desert, IX *15*
Colorado River, V 34; IX 132; XIII 46
Colorado Volunteers, IX 102
Colored American, The, VI 82
Colosimo, Jim, XIII 58
Colquitt, Alfred H, VIII 121, 129
Colt, Samuel, IV 6; IX 82; X 24
Colt gun factory, VII *11*
Colton, Walter, V 122, 138
Colt revolver, IX 19–20, 64; X 24
Columbia, South Carolina, III 136; VII 127
Columbia (ship), X 30
Columbia Broadcasting System, XIII 44; XVII 124
Columbian Exposition, see World's Columbian Exposition
Columbia Plateau, IX 15
Columbia Records, XVII 137
Columbia River, I 17; III 75; V 14, 51, 52, 59, 63, 64, 69; IX 132
Columbia River Fishing and Trading Company, V 54
Columbia University, I 113; IX 83; X 92; XI 137; XVII 71; XIX 70–71, *71*; see also Universities and colleges
Columbia University Lions, XIV 75; see also Football
Columbus, Bartholomew, I 10, 12
Columbus, Christopher, I 10, *10*, 11, *11*, 12, *12*, 15, 18, 19, 21, 29, 33, 42; see also Exploration
Comanche, I 40, 45, 46; IX 16, 17, 19, 20, 101, 102, 106; see also Indians, American
Combined Chiefs of Staff (Second World War), XVI 14, 81, 85, 104, 108
Combined Food Board (Second World War), XVI 48
Combined Raw Materials Board (Second World War), XVI 48
Comer, Braxton B., XI 55
Comic strips, X 124; XI 124; XIV 102; XVII 124; see also Cartoons
Comintern, XVIII 10; see also Communism; Union of Soviet Socialist Republics
Comin' through the Rye, IX *138*
Commager, Henry Steele, XIX 125
Command of the Army Act (1868), VIII 33
Commentaries on the Laws of England, I 135
Commerce, see Trade and commerce
Commercial Club of Chicago, XI 119
Commission, the, XI 56
Commission administration, XI 53
Commission on training camp activities, XII 77
Committee for Improving the Industrial Condition of the Negro, XI 100
Committee for Industrial Organization, XIV 112
Committee of European Economic Cooperation, XVIII 30
Committee of Thirteen, VI 132, 135
Committee of Thirty-Three, VI 132, 135
Committee of Twelve for the advancement of the Negro Race, XI 100
Committee on displaced scholars, XIV 70
Committee on Equal Employment Opportunity, XIX 20
Committee on Government Operations, XVII 44
Committee on Public Information, XII 110, *110*, 111, 125
Committee on Urban Conditions among Negroes, XI 100
Committee to Defend America by Aiding the Allies, XV 109
Committee to Reelect the President, XIX 112, 113
"Common" school, IV 86, 92–93, 94; X 88; see also Education
Common Sense, I 139; II 19–20, 33, 47, *47*, 48
"Commonweal of Christ," X 139
Commonwealth Edison Company, XIII 46
Communications, X 26
Communist Manifesto, IV 125

Communist Party of America, XV 86; XVII 25, 35
Community Action programs, XIX 37
Commuting, X 108; XI *11*; XIII 33
Como, Perry, XVII 137
Compromise of 1850, V 109, VI 92, 94, 96, 97, 100, 101, 138
Compromise of 1877, VIII 88
Computer industries, XX 44–45, 49, 54
Comstock, Henry T. P., IX 70, 82
Comstock Lode, IX 71, 78, *78*, 83, 84, *84*; see also Mining
Concentrated foods, X 32–33, *33*
Concessions and Agreements (1665), I 65
Concord, Battle of (1775), II 22, 23, 24, *24*, 89
Concord, Massachusetts, I 134
Concorde (airplane), XIX 137
Condensed milk, X 32–33, *33*
Condon, Eddie, XIII 87
Conestoga wagon, IV 67
Coney Island, New York City, XI 128, *128, 140*
Confederate Army of Tennessee, VII 33
Confederate Brigadiers, VIII 129
Confederate Constitution, VII 56, 57
Confederate States of America, founding of, VI *139*, 140; VII 14; population, VII 10; Fort Sumter, VII *15*, 18; political conception, VII 55, 140; constitution, VII 56, 57; Great Seal, VII *57*; Jefferson Davis, VII 58–59; Davis administration, VII 59–60, 63; army, VII 60; conscription, VII 60, 62–63, 72; inflation, VII *61*, 64, 66, 78, 86; food shortage, VII 63–64; War Department, VII 64; impressment authority, VII 64; second Congress, VII 66; agriculture, VII 77; entertainment, VII 80, 82; black soldiers, VII 67, 99; European recognition, VII 11, 67, 100, *100*, 104–105, 107–108; navy, VII 125–126; cavalry, VII 137; strategy, VII 139; war aims, VII 140; defeat, VIII 10, 20–21; Black codes, VIII 15
Congo (Belgian), XVIII 69
Congregationalists, I 101, 128; IV 86, 95, 99, 100; V 91; IX 99; see also Religion
Congress, powers of, III 12, 13, 18, 26, 40–41; XVII 25; policy clashes, III 46; effects of Jay Treaty, III 53; birth of party politics, III 53; XYZ affair, III 56; abolition of foreign slave trade, III 82; action against British blockade, III 117, 120; War of 1812, III 121; early years, III 135; Oregon question, V 65; antibigamy laws, V 109; slavery issue, VI 91; 37th, VII 48, 58; Reconstruction, VIII 18, 24, 26, 27, 28, 33; 1866 election, VIII 26; Johnson impeachment, VIII 35–37; in Gilded age, X 46–47; and T. Roosevelt, XI 61–63; in early 1920s, XIII 23; 80th, XVII 18; 81st, XVII 25, 26; F. D. Roosevelt and Truman, XVII 78; Eisenhower, XVII 78, *79*; bipartisanship in foreign policy, XVIII 17–18, 28, 36, 37, 49; XIX 119; Tonkin Gulf incident, XVIII 110; in post-Nixon era, XIX 119, 136; XX 17, 22; seniority system, XIX 119; see also Constitution; Elections; Founding Fathers; Presidency; Representatives, House of; Senate
Congressional Government, X 46
Congressional Medal of Honor, XVI *79*
Congress of Industrial Organizations, formation of, XIV 112, 115; and F. D. Roosevelt, XIV 136; anti-Robert la Follette, Jr, XVII 37
Congress of Racial Equality, XIX 53, 57
Conjure woman, VI 31
Conkling, Roscoe, X 36, 48
Connally, John, XIX 29, 136
Connally, Tom, XVIII 18
Connally Resolution, XVIII 17
Connecticut, I 51, 106; colonial government, I 123; territorial claims, II 14, 86; navy in War of Independence, II 112; constitution, II 51; III 136; sectional interests, III 25; religion, III 110; education, IV 92, 93; abolition movement, VI 64
Connecticut code, I 62
Connecticut Compromise, see Great Compromise
Connecticut Valley, III 92; IV 68
"Connecticut Wits," III 95
Connecticut Yankee, A, XI 103
Connolly, Dick, X 43
Connolly, Joseph, XII 58
"Conscience Whigs," VI 88, 89, 104
Conscription, Civil War, VII 51, 60, 62–63, 72, 76, 81; First World War, XII *64*, 65–66, *65*, 125;

Second World War, XV 118, *119*; XVI 11, 46; see also Selective Service Acts
Conscription Act (Confederate), VII 60, 62, 64, 66, 72
Conscription Act (1863), VII 51, 72, 81
Conservation, IX 122–123; national parks, IX 123–128; forestry, IX 128–131, *129–131*; water, IX 132; XIX 42; T. Roosevelt, XI 61, 63, 140; progressives, XI 94; soil, XIV 123, 124, 126; see also Environment
Consolidated Tobacco, X 19; see also Tobacco
Constitution (ship), III 123, *123*
Constitution, III *27–29*, 133, 134, 135, 137, 138; IV 23; VI 92; VII 44, *44*; supreme law, III 26; democracy, III 26; balance of powers, III 26; XVII 25; ratification, III 30–31, *33*; civil rights, III 33; office of president, III 34; cabinet, III 39; powers of Congress, III 40–41; executive privilege, III 52; 1800 election, III 62; territorial expansion, III 68–69; treason, III 81; *Marbury v Madison*, III 82; see also Amendments, constitutional
Constitutional Convention (1787), II 47, 58; III 22, *23–25*, 24–26, *27–29*, 30–31; VI 85
Constitutional Courant, I 139
Constitutional Democratic party, VI 125
Constitutional Union party, VI 128–129, *128*; VII 12
Constitutionalist party (Mexico), XII 27, 29
Constitution league, VIII 115
Constitutions, state, II 51, 54–56; VIII 39, 40–42; federal, II 58, 60; of 1787, III 10, 18, 22
Construction industry, XIII 33, 35; see also Industry
Construction of the Dam, XIV *37*
"Consumer durables," XIII 44, 130
Containment policy, XVIII 26, 32, 37, 61, 62; see also Foreign policy
Continental Army (War of Independence), II 77, 90, *91*, 92–95, 98, 101, 104, 109, 114, 115, *118*, 127, 140; see also War of Independence; Washington, George
Continental Army (First World War), XII 24
Continental Congress, first (1774), I 133; II 10, 12, 13, *13*, 14, 15, *52*, 87, 89, 100; second (1775), II 14, 16, 19, 25, 26, 32, 33, 44, 58, 60, 109, 112, 127, 128, 132–133, 134
Continental currency, II 100, *100*
Continental Divide, III 76; V 10
Continental Land Office, III 16
Continuous strip mill, XIII 44; see also Mining
Contraband slaves, VII 91, 95; see also Slavery
Contract and Finance company, IX 37
Contract labor, X 72
"Control faction," see Tosei-ha
Controlled Materials Plan, XVI 48, 53
Convention for promoting the Abolition of Slavery, VI 68
Convention of 1818, V 51
Conveyor belt, see Central conveyor belt
Convict leasing system, VIII 40, 129, 132, *132*
Convoy system, First World War, XII *68*, 69; Second World War, XVI 70, 71, 73, 74, 84
Conway, Thomas, II 109, 110
Cook, Frederick A., XI 81
Cook, James, V 51
Cooke, Jacob E., VIII 138
Cooke, Jay, IX 35
Cooke, Philip St George, V 83
Coolidge, Calvin (president), VIII 135; XIII 31, 49; XV 19; becomes president, XIII 117–118, *117*; background, XIII 118, *118*, 119, 120, *120*; political philosophy, XIII 120, 123; Boston police strike, XIII 120–121; vice president, XIII 122; presidential qualities, XIII 123–124; Nicaragua, XV 31, 34
Coolie labor, IX 32, *32*; X 82
"Coon-song," XI 123
Cooper, Gary, XVII 38, *38*, 132, *132*
Cooper, James Fenimore, III 108; IV 10, 13, 131, 135, 136–138, *137*, 140; IX 134, *134*
Cooper, Peter (painter), I *105*
Cooper, Peter (industrialist), IV 87
Cooper-Front-Austin House, I *63*
"Cooperationists," VI 138
Cooperative ethic, XI 86
Cooperative movements, X 127, 131; XI 94, 96
Cooper Union, IV 87
Copeland, Royal, XIV 132
Copland, Aaron, XIII 92; XIV 100
Copley, John Singleton, I 116, *116*, II *48*, *132*; III

104, *104*; IV 132
Copper, V 33; IX 15, 73, 83; X 14; XI 62
"Copperheads," VII 46, 48, 52, 134, 135
Copyright, IV 130–131
Coral Gables, Florida, XIII *36*, 38
Coral Sea, Battle of (1942), XVI 26–27, *26*, *29*
Corbett, Jim, XI 136
Corcoran, Tommy, XIV 133
Córdoba, Francisco Hernández de, I 14
CORE, see Congress of Racial Equality
Corinth, Battle of (1862), VII 33
Corlett, Charles, XV 90
Corn, V 34, *35*; VI 40, 45–46, *46*; IX 43, 94, 95; XI 82
Cornell, Ezra, X 91, 92
Cornell University, X *91*, 92; XIX 58; see also Universities and colleges
Cornstalk (Chief), I 55
Cornwallis, Charles, II 39, 41, 78, 79, 81, 103, 120, 121–123, *121–122*, 124, *126*, 128, 129, *132*; see also War of Independence
Coronado, Francisco Vásquez de, I *16*, 17
Corporations, X 16; XI 51–56, 71, 74, 77, 80; XIII 26, 130, 134; XVI 26, 54; XVII 76, 77, 88, 114; XVIII 84; see also Industry
Corps of Discovery, III 74
Corpus Christi, Texas, IX 45
Corregidor Island, XVI 23, 25
Correll, Charles J., XIV 102, *103*
Corruption, Reconstruction, VIII 44, 81; Crédit Mobilier, X 40, 42; Tweed ring, X 42, 43, *43*, 44; political machines, XI 51–56 *passim*; Harding administration, XIII 24, 27, 28–30; Truman administration, XVII 30, *30*; Watergate, XIX 110–113, *111*, *112*
Corsairs, XVI 119
Corsicana oil field, Texas, VIII 125
Corso, Gregory, XVII 101
Cortés, Hernán, I 15, *15*, 16, 33, 43; see also Conquistadors; Exploration
Cosmopolitan, XI 27, 124
Cosmopolitan Club, VIII 116
Costa Rica, XI 82
Costello, Frank, XIII 60
Cota, Norman D., XVI 92
Cotton, III 65, *84*, 85, 140; IV 70; and slavery, VI 10–11, *20*; VIII 48; in South, VI 42; origins and growth of industry, VI 43–45, *44*, 46; strategic factor in Civil War, VII 11, *11*; during Civil War, VII 64, 85–86, 101–102, *101*; in new South, VIII 119, *119*, 120, 121–122, 126; liens, VIII 59; International cotton exposition, VIII 121; southern alliance, X 131; US production 1914, XI 82; in 1920s, XIII 130; and AAA, XIV 118
Cotton Centennial Exposition (New Orleans, 1885–86), VIII 116
Cotton gin, III 65, 140; VI 11, *11*, 43; X 24
Cotton States and International Exposition (1895), VIII 121
Cotton Textile National Industrial Relations Board, XIV 111
Coué, Emile, XIII 72
Coughlin, Charles E., XIV 41, *41*, 53, 131; XV 79; XVIII 47
Council Bluffs, Iowa, V 97; IX 30, 32; X 29
Council of Appointment, II 56
Council of Economic Advisers, XVII 15, 25; XIX 23
Council of Fifty, V 101
Council of Foreign Ministers, XVIII 23, 29, *30*, 32
Council of Four, XII 134, *134*
Council of National Defense, XII 102, 105
Council of Twelve, V 99, 101
Counter-culture, see Youth Culture
Counterinsurgency warfare, XVIII 106; see also Guerrilla warfare
"Counting coups," IX 22
Country School, X *88*
Coureurs de bois, I 80, 82, 86; V 14
Courier (ship), IV 57
Course of Empire, The, XVII 105
Coursey, O. W., IX 62
Courts, admiralty, I 124, 131; common law, I 131; circuit courts, III 38, 78; and slavery, VI 19; Reconstruction, VIII 25, 32, 33, 69; and Indian offences, IX 116; World Court, XI 77; and social reform, XI 91; and labor unions, XI 96, 97; see also Supreme Court
Cousin, Victor, IV 88

Couzens, James, XI 17
Cowboy Camp During the Roundup, IX *47*
Cowboys, IX 46–49, *49*, *50*, 52–55, *52*, 59; see also Cattle
Cowley, Malcolm, XIII 68, 70, 97
Cowpens, Battle of (1781), II 121
Cowperwood, Frank, XI 107
Cox, Archibald, XIX 19, 113, *114*
Cox, Jacob, X 37
Cox, James M., XIII 22, *22*; XIV 26; XV 11, *13*
Coxey, Jacob S., X 139, *139*, 141, *141*
Cozzens, James Gould, XVII 103
Cracker barrel, XI 23
"cradles" (mining), IX 77
Cradling Wheat, XIV *84*
Craft unionism, XIV 111, 112; see also American Federation of Labor; Labor unions
Crandall, Prudence, VI 74, *74*
Crane, Hart, XIII 98
Crane, Stephen, X *102*, 103; XI 106
Crater, The, IV 137
Craven, Earl of, I 74
Crawford, Joan, XIV 95
Crazy Horse (Chief), IX 108, *108*
Crédit Mobilier Company, IX 30, 37; X 40, 42
Creditanstalt bank, XIV 15
Credit system, reconstruction agriculture, VIII 59
Cree, IX *20*; see also Indians, American
Creede, Colorado, IX 73
Creek, I 41, 54; III 38–39, 44, 128; IV 67; IX 15, 93; see also Indians, American
Creel, George, XII 110, *110*, 111
Creel Committee, see Committee on Public Information
Creeley, Robert, XVII 101
CREEP, see Committee to Reelect the President
Creoles, VIII 140
Cresswell, Nicholas, II 41
Crèvecoeur, Hector St John de, I 137, 138, 140, 141; III 92, 110; XIX 50
Crime, IV 80, 112–114, *113*, *114*; X 113–114; XI 86; Prohibition, XIII 58, 60–64; Great Depression, XIV 77; labor unions, XIV 114; law and order, XIX 107, 127; gun lobby, XIX 127
Criminal syndacalism, XIII 13
Crimson, XIX 26
Cripple Creek, Colorado, IX 73, 74, 83, 84
Crisis, The, VIII 115, *115*
Crisis of Confidence, The, XIX 123
Crisis of the Old Order, The, XIV 56
Critical Period, III 10, 20
Crittenden, John J., VI 135, *135*, 140; VII 14
Croatan, I 48; see also Indians, American
Croats, XII 16
Crocker, Charley, IX 31, 32, 37
Crockett, Davy, IV 27; V 42, *43*
Croly, Herbert, XI 84, 116
Cromwell, Oliver, I 62
Cronica de Mechoadan, I *45*
Crook, George, IX 108
"Crooner," XIII 72; XIV 100
Crop lien system, VIII 59, 128; XIII 136
Crosby, Bing, XIV 100; XVI *67*
Crosby, Caresse, XIII 70
Crosby, Harry, XIII 70
Crossing, The, XI 124
Cross Keys, Battle of (1862), VII 26
"Cross of Gold" speech, X 134
Cross Word Puzzle Books, XIII 73
Crossword puzzles, XIII 72–73; *73*
Crow, Eyre, VII *90*
Crow, I 40; IX 15, 17, *18*; see also Indians, American
Crown Point, New York, II 15, 24, 33
Crucible, The, XVII 106
Cruddup, Arthur "Big Boy," XVII 137
Cruiser and Transport Force (First World War), XII 69
Cruisers, XII 69; XV 24
Crummell, Alexander, VIII 92
Crusade in Europe, XVII 71
"Crystall Night," XV 97
Cuba, I 11, 12, 13, 98; slavery, VI 10, 12, *25*, 30; US attempts to annex, VI 101, 120; rebellion, XI 34, 35; Spanish-American War, XI *39–40*, 42; American control of, XI 72, 78; XV 31; American

relations in 1920s, XV 37–40; Castro, XVIII 70, *70*; Kennedy, XVIII, 82; Bay of Pigs, XVIII 86, *87*, 88; missile crisis, XVIII 89–92, *91*
Cuban Missile Crisis, XVIII 89, 90–91, *91*, 92
Cuba-US Treaty (1903), XI 72
Cubism, XI 111; XVII 90–91; see also Art
Cudahy Meats, X 19
Culbertson, Ely, XIV 70; *71*
Cullen, Countee, XIII 99
Cullom, Shelby, XI 35
"Cultural Revolution," XVIII 132; see also China
Cumberland, Richard, II 74
Cumberland Gap, I 107, *107*; IV 49
Cumberland River, VII 24

Cumberland Road, see National Road
Cumming, Alfred, V 112, 113
Cummings, E. E., XIII 67, 98, *98*, 100; XVII 100, *100*
Cummins, Albert B., XI 64
Cunard Line, IV 57; X 57
Cundall, C., XV *107*
Curb Exchange, XIII 138
Currency system, X 54; greenbacks, VII 86–87; VIII 80; X 37, 38, 82; Hayes era, X 48; populist party, X 132; W. H. Harvey, X 133–134; free silverites, X134
Currier and Ives, II *96*; VI *44*; VIII *137*; IX 138, *138*
Curry, J. L. M., VIII 132
Curry, John Steuart, XIII *110*; XIV 82

Curtis, Charles, XIV 28
Curtis, George William, IV 120; X 39
Curtiss, Glenn H., XI 129
Cusabo, I 54; see also Indians, American
Cushing, Caleb, VI 125
Custer, George Armstrong, IX 73, 106, *106*, 107, 108–109, *108*, 133, *138*, 139
Custer City, South Dakota, IX 73
Custer's Last Rally, IX 139
Custis, Jack, II 126
Cycling, X 119, *123*; XIX *141*
Czech legion, XVIII 10
Czechoslovakia, XII 136; XV 96; XVIII 31, 37, *37*
Czolgosz, Leon, X 72

D

Dabney, Charles W., VIII 129
Dai, Bao, XVIII 99–100, *100*, 105
Dakota (tribe), IX 17; see also Indians, American
Dakota Farmer, IX 91
Dale, Sir Thomas, I 72
Daley, Richard, XIX 108, 110
Dali, Salvador, XVII 90
Dallas, George Mifflin, VI 88
Dallas, Texas, IX 44
Dames, XIV *92*
Dams, XIV 35, *37*; XVIII 72
Dana, Charles A., X 124
Dana, Richard Henry, V 21
Dangling Man, XVII 104
Daniels, Josephus, XII 54, 76; XV 20, 44
Danish West Indies, XI 78, 82
Dan Rogers case (1904), VIII 108
Dardanelles Campaign (First World War), XII 20
Dare, Virginia, I 48
Darien, see Santa Maria la Antigua
Darien, Gulf of, I 14
Darlan, Jean, XVI 79
Darrow, Clarence, XIII 64, 112–113, *112*
Dartmouth College, I 55; see also Universities and colleges
Darwin, Charles, X 96–97; XI 104; XIII 112
Darwin, Australia, XVI 25
Darwinism, X 96–97, 103; XI 71
Daugherty, Harry, XIII 21, *21*, 24, 29, 124
Daughters of Revolution, XIV 82, *82*
Daughters of the American Revolution, XIV 67, *82*
Dauphine (ship), I 22
Davenport, John, I 61
Davey, George, XI *36*, 42
David Copperfield (film), XIV 96
Davidson, Robert, II 120; III 91
Davie, William R., II 120; III 56
Davies, Arthur B., XI 111
Davies, John W., XIV *27*
Davies, Joseph E., XVII 38
Davis, Chester C., XIV 120
Davis, David, VI 128; VIII 87, 89
Davis, Henry Winter, VII 51; VIII 18
Davis, James, XIII 27
Davis, Jefferson, IV 71; Stephen Douglas, VI 120; Crittenden proposals, VI 135; president Confederate States, VI 140, *140*; VII 16, *57*; defense of territory, VII 22, 36; Robert E. Lee, VII 26; objective of Confederacy, VII 55; Confederate charter, VII 56; qualities, VII 58–59, 137; administration, VII 59–60; Confederate congress, VII 63; arming slaves, VII 66–67, 99; flight and capture, VII 67, *67*; VIII 16; foreign policy, VII 102; and Johnston, VII 120; strategy, VII 139
Davis, John, I 26, 28
Davis, John W., XIII 18, 124
Davis, Stuart, XIII 88, *88*, 101; XIV 84
Davis Cup, XI 137
Davro, Mindanao, XVI 120
Davy, Sir Humphrey, X 30, 32
Dawes, Charles G., XIII 24, 124; XIV 16; XV 26,

26, 59
Dawes, Henry L., IX 119
Dawes, William, I 133; II 22, 23
Dawes Act (1887), IX 119–120
Dawes Plan, XV 26
Dawson, Francis W., VIII 119
Day, Doris, XVII 121, *123*
Day, Henry, V 109
Day, J. Edward, XIX 19, *21*
Dayan, Moshe, XVIII *139*
Day at the Races, A, XIV 97
Day of Doom, The, I 117
Dayton, Jonathan, III 22
Day with the Cow Column, A, V 59
D-Day (Second World War), XVI 90, 92, *92*, 94, *94*
Dead River portages, II 34
Deadwood, South Dakota, IX 62, 73, *74*, 77
Deadwood Dick, IX 133, 137
Dean, Dizzy, XIV 76
Dean, James, XVII 121, 134, *134*
Dean, John, XIX 113, *114*
Deane, Silas, II 101, 135, 136–137
Dearborn, Henry, III 51, 122
"Dear John" letters, XVI 62
"Death march," XVI 23, *23*
Death of a President, The, XIX 31
Death of a Salesman, XVII 105–106, *105*
Death penalty, XIX 107
Death Valley, IX 15
De Bardeleben Coal and Iron Company, VIII 124
DeBow, J. D. B., VI 56, 57
Debs, Eugene V., X 139; XI 97; XII 57, 111, 114, *115*; XIII 13, 24
Debt Default Act, see Johnson Debt Default Act
Decatur, Stephen, III 114, *115*, 123
Decca Records, XVII 137
Decimal system, III 91
"Declaration and Resolves," II 15, 16
Declaration of Independence, II 28; Jefferson, II 10, *10*, 12, 20, 84; fundamental rights, II 12–13, 20; reaction to British laws, II 13–16; *Common Sense*, II 20, 33; Congress adopts, II 34; Virginia's constitution, II 54; congressional representation, II 60; racism, II 104; III 138; VI 71, 118; War of Independence aims, II 132; democratic impulse, II 20; III 10; nationalism, III 108; reform impulse, IV 109
Declaration of London (1909), XII 36–37
Declaration of Rights (Virginia), II 54–55; III 33
"Declaration of the Causes and Necessity of Taking Up Arms," II 15, 16, 18, 20, 28, 33
Declaration of the Immediate Causes of Secession, A, VI 134
Declaration of the United Nations (1942), XVIII 13
Declaration on Liberated Europe, XVIII 15
Declaratory Act (1766), I 132
Decline of the West, The, XIII 107
Deerfield, Massachusetts, I 88
Deering, James, XIII 38
Deer Park, The, XVII 104
Deerslayer, The, IV 137; IX *134*
Defeat of America, The, XIX 125

Defenders of the Christian Faith, XV 110
Deficit financing, XIV 31, 37, 140
De Forest, John, VIII 128, 129
Degas, Edgar, VIII *120*
De Gaulle, Charles, Second World War, XV 103;
    XVI 17, 76, 80, 81, 135, 136, 137, *139*; Algeria,
    XVIII 69; NATO, XVIII 92–93; Indochina, XVIII 97
Deguello, V 42
De Kooning, Willem, XVII 91, *96*
Delaware, origins, I 53, 65, 68, 70, 123; state
    constitution, II 56; boundaries, II 60; in War of
    Independence, II 103; population, III 24; party
    politics, III 54; secession, VII 16; industry, X 19;
    segregation, XVII 52
Delaware (tribe), I 53, *53*, 54, *54*, 92, 93; see also
    Indians, American
De La Warr, Lord, I 72
De Leon, Daniel, XI 97
D. E. Loewe Company, XI 96
Delta Democrat Times, XVII 52
De Mille, Cecil B., XIII 82
Democracy, II 16, 48, 51, 60, 87; Mayflower
    Compact, I 59; early stages of, III 10, 18, 20, 26,
    30, 134, 136, 138; as "anarchy," III 26, 40, 137;
    basis of American life, IV 13–14, 16–18; universal
    suffrage, IV 25; presidential elections, IV 26;
    national party conventions, IV 26; Lincoln's
    commitment to, VII 46; frontier hypothesis, IX 140;
    progressivism, XI 13, 54, 55, 86; Wilsonian
    idealism, XII 55; XVIII 133–134, 136; Mencken
    on, XIII 105, 113–114; effects of *Pax Americana*
    on, XIX 119; see also Constitution; Government
Democracy and Education, XI 115
Democracy in America, III 90
Democratic Advisory Council, XIX 15
Democratic party, IV 24, 29, 31, 34, 35, 110;
    annexation of Texas, V 48, 49, 50–51; Oregon,
    V 63, 65, 66; Mexican War, V 77, 91; VI 88; Van
    Buren, VI 86, 87; slavery, VI 88–89; 1848 election,
    VI 90–91; 1852 election, VI *94*, 97; Stephen
    Douglas, VI 100, 117; VI 118; Kansas-Nebraska
    Bill, VI 101; sectional pressures, VI 104; popular
    sovereignty, VI 100, 108; 1856 election, VI 110–
    112; Kansas elections 1857, VI 114; Lecompton
    constitution, VI 114; English Bill, VI 116; 1858
    elections, VI 120; southern dominance, VI 116;
    VIII 16; 1860 convention, VI 125, *126*; Civil War,
    VII 45, 92; 1864 election, VII 52; Military
    Reconstruction Act (1867), VIII 30; southern
    bitterness, VIII 44; resurgence of in South, VIII 46,
    82–87 *passim*; on tariff, VIII 80; 1874 election,
    VIII 84; 1876 election, VIII 87, 88; Bourbons,
    VIII 129, 132, 134, 135; splits in South, VIII 135;
    Democratic primaries, VIII 138; 1868 convention,
    X 36–37; money policy, X 36; elections 1872–96,
    X 45, 47, 48; in Cleveland era, X 47, 50–52,
    54; and labor, X 82; Farmer's Alliance, X 132;
    free-silver, X 141; 1910 election, XI 64; Wilson,
    XI 66–67; 1916 convention, XII 46–47; links with
    AFL, XII 116; 1918 election, XII 126–127; 1920
    election, XIII 18; 1924 convention, XIII 124;
    1928 election, XIII 126–127; 1932 election, XIV
    28; 1936 election, XIV 50–51; F. D. Roosevelt's
    recreation of, XIV 50–51; XVII 12; anti-New
    Dealers, XIV 132, 133; post-F. D. Roosevelt, XVII
    12–13; 1946 campaign, XVII 18; splits under
    Truman, XVII 21, *21*; 1948 convention, XVII 21;
    1952 convention, XVII 75; 1954 election, XVII
    79; 1956 election, XVII 80; 1958 election, XVII
    85; 1968 convention, XIX 44, 46, *46*, 47, 71–73,
    73, 75; anti Vietnamers, XIX 108; 1972 convention,
    XIX 108; in 1980s, XX 10; see also Party system
Democratic-Republican party (Jeffersonian), III 52,
    53, 54–55, 56, 58, 60; 1800 election, III 60–62,
    61; under Jefferson, III 65, 68, 73, 78–80; change
    after 1815, IV 25; War of 1812, III 88, 121;
    Tariff Act (1816), III 89; opposition to tax, III 21;
    criticism of Republican caucus, IV 26; "National
    Republicans," IV 29; slavery issue, VI 86
Demonstration Cities and Metropolitan Development
    Act (1966), XIX 41
Demonstration method (agriculture), VIII 126
Demorest's, IV 121
Demott, Benjamin, XIX 78
Dempsey, Jack, XII 126; XIII 77, *79*
Demuth, Charles, XIII *97*, 101
Denison, Edward F., XIX 93

Denman, William, XII 106
Dennies, Joseph, III 137
Denver, Colorado, V 12; IX 11, 73, 74, 77, 84;
    X *82*
Denver & Rio Grande Railroad, IX 36, 38; see also
    Railroads
Denver, South Park & Pacific Railroad, IX 38
Department of Commerce and Labor, XI 80; XIII 26
Department of Housing and Urban Development,
    XIX 41
Department of the Interior, IX 114; XIII 24, 29
Department stores, X 109; XI 21, *21*
Deportation, XIII 14, 15; see also Immigration
Deportation Act (1918), XIII 14
Depressions, 1873, VIII 43, 82; X 118, 119; XI 86;
    1890s, X 133, 139, 141; XI 12, 44; see also Great
    Depression
DePriest, Oscar, XIV 67
Depth Bomb, XVI 70
Derby, George Horatio ("John H. Phoenix"), IV 12,
    14, 18; V 87
Derevyanko, General, XVI 131
Desegregation, see Integration
Deseret, Provisional State of, V 109, 113
Desha, Joseph, III 120
Desire Under the Elms, XIII 98
d'Estaing, Admiral, see Estaing, Admiral Charles
    Hector d'
Destroyers, XII 69, *70*; XVI 44, 70
Destroyers-for-bases, XV 115–116, *115*; XVI 44, 70
Détente, XVIII 79, 128, 130, 132, 136, 137; XX 24–27;
    see also Foreign affairs
Deterrence, XVIII 61, 64, 65, 79, 84, 92
Detroit, Michigan, X 118; XI 16, 51; XIII 33, 60, 61;
    XIX 58, 61; see also Cities
Devaluation, XIV 34, 37, 116; XVIII 136–137
Devers, Jacob Loucks, XVI 90, 96, 104
Devil's Den, Gettysburg, VII 40
Devil Theory of War, The, XV 79
Devine, Edward T., XI 87
Devlin, Harry, XVII *48*
Devon Island, XI 81
DeVoto, Bernard, XIII 111; XVII 105
Dewey, John, X 115, *115*, 116, 119; XII 118; XIV 65
Dewey, Melvin, X 124
Dewey, Thomas E., XIV 114, 136; XVI 19;
    presidential candidate, XVII 22, 23–24, *23*, 71;
    XVIII 46
Dey, Peter A., IX 29–30
DH9 reconnaissance bombers. XII *86*
Dial, IV 119
Dial, The, XIII 68, 97
Diaz, Adolfo, XV 31
Diaz, Porfirio, XII 26
Dickens, Charles, IV 10, 12, 56, 62, 65; V 104
Dickinson, Emily, X 87
Dickinson, John, II *13*, 15, 19, 58, *58*; III 22
Dickson, William K., XI 132
Dictionary of American Biography, XIII 17
Die-casting, XIII 44
Dieckhoff, Hans Heinrich, XV 91, 95
Dicey, Edward, VII 82
Diegueño, I 40; see also Indians, American
Diem, Ngo Dinh, XVIII 104–109, *104*
Dien Bien Phu, Vietnam, XVIII 64, 100–101, *104*
Dieppe raid, XVI 16
Dies, Martin, XIV 115; XVII 35
Diet and Health, XIII 77
Dietrich, Marlene, XVI 62, *67*
"Diggers," IX 16
Dill, Augustus Granville, XI 32
Dillard University, VIII 66; see also Universities and
    colleges
Dillinger, John, XIV 78, *78*
Dillon, Douglas, XVIII 90; XIX 19, *21*, 23
Dillon, Sidney, IX 37
Dillon, Read and Company, XIII 138
Dilworth, Mary Jane, V 113
DiMaggio, Joe, XIV 75
Dime novel, XI 61, *134*, 136–137
Dimnet, Ernest, XIII 77
Dingley Tariff Act (1897), XI *13*
Dinner Party, The, XIX 78
Dinwiddie, Governor Robert, I 92, 93, *93*
Direct current, X 32
Directoire, III 55

Director of Purchases, XII 107, 108
Director of Storage and Traffic, XII 107, 108
Direct primary law, XI 54
Disarmament, XV 17, 20, 71–72; atomic, XVIII 24,
    88; SALT, XVIII 132, *136*, 137
Disarmament and Arms Control Agency, XVIII 137;
    XIX 20
Discourse Concerning the Plague, I 114
Discovery (ship), I 28, 71
Disfranchisement, Confederates, VIII 30, 32, 42;
    black, VIII 82, 91, 107, 108, 114, 134, 135, 138;
    see also Suffrage
Disney, Walt, XIV 99–100, *99*; XVI *67*; XVII 38
Dissent, XVII 108
Distillers' and Cattle Feeders' Trust, X 19
Distilling Company of America, X 16
Distilling industry, XIII 58, 64
Distinguished Flying Cross, XVI *79*
District of Columbia, VI 91, 92, 104; VII 92; XI 118;
    XVII 52
District (electoral) system, IV 25–26
Divine, Father, XIV 76
Dix, Dorothea, IV 114–115, *115*; VII 82
Dix, John A., V 66; IX 29
"Dixie," VII 82
"Dixiecrat" party, see States' Rights party
Dixon, Thomas, Jr., XI 126
Dmytryk, Edward, XVII 38, *38*, 39
Dobrynin, Anatoly, XVIII 91
Dock Street Theater, I 114
Dr Sevier, VIII 140
Dodd, William E., XV 94
Dodds, "Baby," XIII 90
Dodds, Johnny, XIII 87
Dodge, Grenville M., IX 30, 31
Dodge City, Kansas, IX 36, 44, 45, 53, 54, 55, 56, 59,
    63, *65*, *122*
Dodge Motor Company, XIII 40
Dodsworth, XIII 95
Doenitz, Karl, XVI 70, *71*, 73, 84, 85, 88, 106;
    XVIII 22, *22*
Doheny, Edward, XIII 29, 30
Dolan, J. J., IX 66, 67
Dollar diplomacy, XI 71, 78, 82
Dominica, I 12; II 69
Dominican Republic, XI 78; XV 31; see also Latin
    America
Domino Theory, XVIII 84, 88, 100
Donald, David, VI 51
Donald Duck, XIV 99; XVI *67*
Donnelly, Ignatius, X 72, 102, 132, 136
Donner, George, V 63
Donner party, V 63
"Don't Sit Under The Apple Tree With Anyone Else
    But Me," XVI 62
"Dooley, Mr.," XI 31, 42
Doolittle, Hilda, XI 109
Doolittle, James Harold, XVI 24, 26, *27*
Dooman, Eugene, XV 130
Dorchester Heights, II 30, 34
Dorsey, Tommy, XIV 100
Dos Passos, John, XIII 66, 67, 109; XIV 82, 88, 89,
    89; XVI 66; XVII 105
Dos Passos, John R., X 21, 23
Doughboys, XII *76*, *91*, 92, 95, *95*
Douglas, Helen Gahagan, XVII 29; XIX 101
Douglas, Stephen Arnold, territorial expansion, V 48;
    Mormon state, V 109; compromise of 1850, VI 94,
    96; Kansas–Nebraska Act (1854), VI 100–101, *101*,
    108; IX 28; Lecompton constitution, VI 114, 116;
    Lincoln's challenge, VI 116–118, *118*–*119*, 120;
    1860 convention, VI 125, *126*; presidential
    campaign, VI 129, 131; attempts to calm the
    South, VI 132; and Lincoln, VII 46
Douglas, William O., XIV 133; XVII 117
Douglass, Frederick, VI 24, 25, 38, 83, *83*; VII 91,
    96, *97*; VIII 91
Douhet, Giulio, XVI 74, 85
Dove, Arthur, XIII 101
Dove (ship), I 73
Dover, New Hampshire, I 61
Downing, Andrew Jackson, IV 134
Doyle, Arthur Conan, XII 58
Draft (military), see Conscription
Drake, Francis, I 23, *24*, 25, 48
Drake (ship), II 113

Drama, see Literature
Dreadnought (ship), XII 16
Dred Scott case (1857), VI 112, 113, *113*, 114, 116, 117
Dredge mining, IX 80, 83
Dreikaiserbund, see League of the Three Emperors
Dreiser, Theodore, X 97, 103; XI 107, *107*; XIII 72
Dresden raid, XVI 102–103
Drewry, William S., VI 37
Drewry's Bluff, VII 25
Drift and Mastery, XI 84, 116
Drought, James M., XV 131
Drought, IX 95, 96
Drugs, Youth Culture, XIX 78; addiction, XIX 127
Drum, Hugh A., XII 79, 92
Drums Along the Mohawk, XIV 90
"Dry farming," XIII 135
Dry plates, X 33
Dual Alliance (1879), XII 13
Dual Monarchy (Austria-Hungary), XII 16
Dubinsky, David, XIII 136; XIV 52, 111, 114
Du Bois, William Edward Burghardt, VIII 111, 113, 115, *115*, 116; XI 31
Duchamp, Marcel, XI 111, *113*
Duchess County, New York, II 98

"Duck" (military), see DUKW
Duck Soup, XIV 97
Dudley, N. A. M., IX 96
Dudley, Thomas, I 60
Duke, James Buchanan, VIII 122, *122*, 124, 125; XI 11
Duke University, XIX 100
Duke, Washington, VIII 122
DUKW ("Duck"), XVI 56, 82, 108
Dulles, Allen, XIX 29
Dulles, John Foster, XII 33; and Alger Hiss, XVII 40; and Eisenhower candidacy, XVII 73; corporate interests, XVII 76, 77; "massive retaliation," XVII 76–77; XVIII 67; and Eisenhower, XVII 79; XVIII 61, *61*; death, XVII 86, *86*; Japanese treaty, XVIII 49; J. McCarthy, XVIII 64; SEATO, XVIII 64–65; German rearmament, XVIII 68; summit conferences, XVIII 68; on nonalignment, XVIII 69; Latin American policy, XVIII 70; Suez crisis, XVIII 71, 72, 73; East European risings, XVIII 75; Sino-Soviet split, XVIII 79; Berlin crisis, XVIII 79; appraisal of, XVIII 79; Domino Theory, XVIII 100
Dumbarton Oaks Conference (1944), XVI 136; XVIII 17, *18*
Duncan, Robert, XVII 101

Dunkirk, Battle of (1940), XV *107*, 113; XVI 10, 70
Dunlop, John T., XIX *104*
Dunmore, John Murray, 4th Earl of, II *18*, 24, 85, *85*
Dunne, Finley Peter, XI 31
Dunning motion, II 74
Duplex machine, X 26
DuPont, Samuel, VII 125
Du Pont Corporation, XI 60; XVI 54, 129
Durand, Asher, IV 133, *135*
Durand, Peter, X 32
Durango, Colorado, IX 38
Durant, Thomas C., IX 29, 32, 37
Durant, W. C., XIII 38, 40; XIV 28
Durant, Will, XIII 77
Durante, Jimmy, XIV 96
Dust Bowl, XIV 120, 122–123, *123*
Dutch, see Netherlands
Duyckinck family, I 116
Dwight, Timothy, III 95
Dye, John Smith, VII 135
Dyer, Eliphalet, II 26
Dykeman, Wilma, XVII 66
Dylan, Bob, XIX 76, *77*
Dynamic Sociology, X 98; XI 84
Dynamo, X 24, 32

E

Eads, James B., X 29
Eagle (ship), II 35, *35*
Eaker, Ira, XVI 90
Eakins, Thomas, X 98, *98*, 100, 102
Early, Jubal A., VII 37, 119
Early Sunday Morning, XIV 82
Earney, Henry, IX *105*
Earp, Jim, IX 64
Earp, Morgan, IX 64, 66
Earp, Virgil, IX 64, 66
Earp, Wyatt, IX 63–64, *65*, 66, 67
Earthquake, San Francisco, XI 90
Eastern Europe, XII 136, 139, *139*; XVI 138; XVIII 15, 23, *23*, 62, 75, 84
Eastern Frontier Command, XVI 73
Eastern Solomons, Battle of the (1942), XVI 30
Eastern State Penitentiary, Pennsylvania, IV 113
Eastern Trail, IX 46
Easter Rising (1916), XII 46
East Germany, 1953 uprising, XVIII 62, *62*; Berlin Wall, XVIII 88, *88*; see also Germany
East Hopei autonomous region, XV 64
East India Company (Dutch), I 28
East India Company (English), I 28, 87, 133; II 14
East India Docks, II *64*
Eastland, James O., XVIII 47
Eastman, George, X 33, *34*; XI 132; XIII 32
Eastman, Seth, V *59*
East River, X 29, 30
Easy Rider, XIX 76
Eaton, Theophilus, I 61
E-boat, XVI 88
E. Clampus Vitus, Ancient and Honorable Order of, V 138
Eccles, Marriner, XIV 44
Ecclesiastical History of New England, see *Magnalia Christi Americana*
Eckener, Hugo, XV 93
Eckford, Elizabeth Ann, XVII 56, *56*
Ecology, see Conservation; Environment
Economic Bill of Rights, XVI 140
Economic Cooperation Act (1948), XVIII 31
Economic Defense Board, XVI 45
Economic Interpretation of the Constitution, A, XI 115
Economic Opportunity Act (1964), XIX 37
Economy, American view early 19th century, IV 14, 16; "Bank War," IV 34–35; southern, VI 46, 48, 116; panic of 1857, VI 114, 116; IX 28; panic of 1873, IX 35, 37, 40, 83; panic of 1893, IX 37, 83; growth of industry, X 10, 12, 13–16, *17*, 18–20,

18–20; imperialism, XI 71, 80; effect of First World War on, XII 114–115; wartime, XII 115–116, *115*; 1927 recession, XIII 128; in 1920s, XIII 129–130; New Deal, XIV 34–35; post-war years, XVII 14, 17; Council of Economic Advisers, XVII 15; under Eisenhower, XVII 79, 81–82; under Kennedy, XIX 23, 92–93; under Johnson, XIX 35; technological spin-offs, XIX 93–94; new criteria of 1970s, XIX 98; "stagflation," XIX 105; and Nixon, XIX 106–107; lack of growth in 1970s, XIX 137; 1976–86, XX 44–54; see also Devaluation; Industry; Trade and commerce
Ecuador, XV 43
Eden, Anthony, XV 94, 95; XVIII 68, *69*, 72, 73
Eden, William, II 106
Edinburgh Review, IV 127
Edison, Thomas Alva, X 26, 30, *31*, 32, 109; XI 13, 132; XII 45; XIII 46
Edison Electric Light Company, X 30
Edmonds, Richard Hathaway, VIII 119
Edmonds, Walter, XIV 90
Education, pre-Revolution, I 55, 62, 77, 113; III 110; mid-19th century, IV 18, 84–90, *84–85*, 92–96, *87–93*, *95–96*; "spellers and readers," IV 84–85; academies, IV 86; colleges, IV 86; lyceums, IV 86–87; universities, IV 89–90, *89–90*; X 88, 92, *91*, 94–95; common school, IV 92–93; professional training, IV 95–96; Mormon, V 113, *113*; in the South, VI 56; VII 96; VIII 40, 64, 129, 132; Negro, VIII 64–67, 69, 132; Peabody Fund, VIII 132; Bennett Law, X 53; philanthropy, X 88, *91*; growth of public, X 88, *88*; XVII 113; in cities, X 116, 118; J. Dewey, XI 115; in 1920s, XIII 49; during Great Depression, XIV 65; federal aid to, XVII 19, 26; XIX 25; segregation in, XVII 52–53, *53*, 60; *Brown* v *Board of Education*, XVII 53–54, *54*; Little Rock, XVII 55–56, *56*, 58; integration, XVII 60; Elementary and Secondary Education Act (1965), XIX 41; Black Power, XIX 57; effect of Sputnik, XIX 92, *92*
Education of Henry Adams, The, XI 105
Edwards, Clarence, XII 79
Edwards, Frederick Trevenen, XII 68
Edwards, Hayden, V 40
Edwards, Jonathan, I 109, *110*; IV 100
Efficiency, industrial, XIII 32
Effingham, Earl of, II 29
Egypt, XVIII 71–73, *71*, *73*, 138, *139*
Ehninger, J. W., IV 65
Ehrlichman, John, XIX *112*
Eichelberger, Robert, XVI 35
Eight, the, XI 111; see also Ashcan School

Eighteenth Amendment, XII 120; XIII 52, 53, 64, 65; XIV 29; see also Amendments, constitutional; Prohibition
Eighth Army (Second World War), XVI 76, *77*, 86, 88
Eight-hour day, X 75, 81, 84, 85, *85*; XI 68, 91; XII 105; XIII 49
Eighty-second Airborne Division (Second World War), XVI 101
Einstein, Albert, XVI 128, *128*
Einstein, Izzy, XIII *59*
Eirik the Red, I 19, 20
Eiriks saga rauoa, see Vinland Sagas
Eiriksson, Leif, I 20
Eisenhower, Dwight D. (president), Bonus Army riot, XIV 20, *22*; assistant chief of staff, XVI 14, 15; Operation Torch, XVI 16, 76, 78, 79, 80; XVII 69; Overlord, XVI 19; ETOUSA, XVI 74; XVII 69; Husky, XVI 82; Italy, XVI 83, 86; Supreme Commander, XVI 88, 90, *90*, 134, 136; XVII 69; D-Day, XVI 92; Paris, XVI 97; field command, XVI 98; Battle of Bulge, XVI 101; final push, XVI 102–104, *104*; V-E day, XVI 106; 22nd amendment, XVII 18; Democratic presidential nomination, XVII 21; Republican presidential candidate, XVII 31–32, 68, 73, *73*; J. McCarthy, XVII 36, 78; Earl Warren, XVII 53; integration, XVII 54, 58; Little Rock, XVII 56, 58; conception of presidency, XVII 58, 78, 84–85; racial issues, XVII 58, 59, 60; Civil Rights Act (1957), XVII 60; early career, XVII 68–71, *68–71*; Columbia University, XVII 71; NATO, XVII 71; XVIII 36; inauguration, XVII 76; Cabinet, XVII 75–76, *77*; 1954 elections, XVII 77, 79; Bricker amendment, XVII 78; 1956 elections, XVII 79, 80, *82*; "open skies" scheme, XVII 79; and public, XVII 80–81, *81*; illness, XVII *84*, 85; Adams scandal, XVII 85; 1958 elections, XVII 85; loss of aides, XVII 86, *87*; Hawaii, XVII *86*; on Nixon, XVII 88; farewell address, XVII 88; XVIII 84; summit conferences, XVII 68, *69*, 79; Suez crisis, XVIII 73; Eisenhower Doctrine, XVIII 75; U-2 affair, XVIII 81; Geneva Conference (1954), XVIII 101; Vietnam, XVIII 105
Eisenhower, Milton, XVIII 70
Eisenhower Doctrine, XVIII 75
El Alamein, Battle of (1942), XVI 16, 79
Elbe, XVI 104
El Brazito, Battle of (1846), V 83
El Caney, Battle of (1898), XI *39*
Eldorado, Kansas, X 126
Eldorado *Republican*, X 126
"Eleanor Clubs," XVI 62
"Eleanor Rigby," XIX 76
Elections, midterm, 1866, VIII 26, *26*; 1874, VIII 84; 1918, XII 115–127; 1922, XIII 27; 1934, XIV 38, 44, 49; 1938, XIV 126, 134, 136; XVII 12; 1946, XVII 181; 1950, XVII 29; 1954, XVII 77, 79; 1958, XVII 85; 1966, XIX 43; 1974, XIX 118
Elections, presidential, IV 20, 25–26, 36; 1789, III 34–35; 1793, III 46; 1796, III 54–55; 1800, III 60–62; 1824, IV 21; 1828, IV 28; 1840, IV 31; 1844, VI 87; 1848, 91–91, *89*, *90*; 1852; VI *94*, 96, *96*, 97; 1856, VI 102, *102*, 110; 1860, VI 129, 131; 1864, VII 51–52, *52*; 1868, VIII 35; 1872, X 40; 1876, VIII *86*, 87, *87*, 89; 1888, X 52; 1892, X 54; 1896, X 141; 1900, XI 13; 1904, XI 60; 1908, XI 63–64; 1912, XI 64–67, *65*, *66*, *67*; 1916, XII 47, *47*; 1920, XIII 10; 1924, XIII 124; 1928, XIII, 125–127, *125–127*; XIV 10; 1932, XIV 24, 28–29, *29*; 1936, XIV, 50–52; 1940, XVI 10; 1944, XVI 19; 1948, XVII 22–23, *23*, *24*; 1952, XVII 31, *75*, *76*; 1956, XVII 80, *82*; 1960, XVII 86, 88; XIX 15, *17*, 18; 1964, XIX 38, *38*, 40; 1968, XIX 103, *103*, 104, 105, 123; 1972, XIX 110; 1976, XX 10, 13, 15–16; 1980, XX 10, 17–19; 1984, XX 20–21
Electoral college, III 26, 34; IV 25–26
Electoral Commission, VIII 87, *88*, 89
Electricity industry, III 125; X 30, 32; XI 13, 14; XIII 44; TVA, XIV 35, 49; see also Industry
Electric motors, see Motors, electric
Electronic industry, XIX 93
Elementary and Secondary Education Act (1965), XIX 41
Elevated railways, X 109, *109*
Elevator, X 96, 109
Eliot, Charles W., X 92
Eliot, John, I 52, *52*

Eliot, Thomas Stearns, XI 109; XIII 18, 97, *97*; XVII 100, *100*
Elitism, VIII 113; XI 86, 94; XIII 114, 115
Elizabeth I (England), I *24*, 25, 27, 48, 62
Elizabethan strike (1929), XIII 132
Elizabethtown, New Jersey, I 66
Elk Hills, California, XIII 29
Elkhorn Tavern, Battle of, see Pea Ridge, Battle of
Ellery, William, II *13*
Ellesmere Island, XI 81
Ellington, Duke, XIII 92, *93*; XIV 100
Ellis, Edward S., IX 137
Ellis Island, New York, X 60, *63*
Ellison, Ralph, XVII 103
Ellsberg, Daniel, XIX 111
Ellsworth, Oliver, III 22, *23*, 56
Ellsworth, Kansas, IX 46, 55, 63
Ellsworth Trail, IX 46
Elmer Gantry, XIII 68
Elmwood Park, Chicago, XIII 33
El Salvador, XX 33, 37
Ely, Richard T., X 139
Emancipation, IV 34, 35, 65; VII 46, 51, 67, 87, 89, 90–92, 96, 99, 140; VIII 48
Emancipation in the West Indies, VI 72
Emancipation Proclamation, VII 32, 51, 92, 94, *94*, 99, 102, 104, 140; VIII *17*
Emancipator, VI 72
Embargo of 1807, III 85, *85*, 117, *118*, 119
Emergency Fleet Corporation, XII 106, *107*
Emergency Peace Federation, XII 55
Emergency Relief and Construction Act (1932), XIV 19–20
Emerging Republican Majority, The, XIX 135
Emerson, John, VI 113
Emerson, Ralph Waldo, II 20; III 108; IV 14, 67, 82, 86, 87, 89, 118, 119, 128, *128*, 140–141; VI 43, 88; IX 106, 126
Emirau Island, XVI 41
Emma, Utah, IX 73
Emmett, Dan, III 82
Emperor Jones, The, XIII 98
Empire State Building, XIII 33, 101
Empiricism, XI 114
Employers' Associations, XI 97
Employment Act (1946), XVII 15
Empresarios, V 40, 48
Empress of China (ship), III 18
Enciso, Martin Fernandez de, I 14
Encomienda, I 42, 43
Encyclopaedia Britannica, IV 84
Endicott, John, I 59, 60
End of the American Era, The, XIX 123, 141
"End Poverty in California," XIV 41
Enforcement Act (1870), VIII 79
Engelbrecht, H. C., XV 78
Engineering, training, IV 95, 96
England, see Great Britain
English, William, VI 116
English bill, VI 116
English language, as unifier, I 127–128; growth of American dialect, I 137; in the United States, III 92, 94–95; IV 129–130
"Enola Gay," XVI 126
Enormous Room, The, XIII 67
Enright, Don, XVII 120
Entente Cordiale (1904), XI 82; XII 14
Enterprise (carrier), XVI 28, 30, 31, 110
Enumerated commodities, I 122, 124
Environment, XIX 42, 136–137, *139*; see also Conservation
EPIC, see "End Poverty in California"
Episcopalians, IV 86, 95, 99, 100; IX 114; see also Religion
E Pluribus Unum, III 108
Epstein, Brian, XIX 66
Equal opportunity, IV 16–18; VII 89; income inequality, XIII 129–130, *129*; Truman, XVII 21; Johnson, XIX 36
Equal Opportunity Employment Commission, XIX 36
Equal rights, VII 89, 98; VIII 69, 87; see also Civil rights
Equal Rights Amendment, XX 61–62
Ericsson, John, VII 27
Erie, Lake, I 81, 92; III 124
Erie Canal, IV 50–51, 52–53, *52–53*, 68, 70; VII 84;
Erie Railroad, VII 84; see also Railroads

Ernst, Jimmy, XVII *96*
Ernst, Max, XVII 90, *91*
Ersatz, XVI 140
Ervin, Sam J., XIX 113
Esch-Cummins Act (1920), XII 113
Eskaleut, I 37; see also Indians, American
Espionage Act (1917), XII 110–111
Esquire, XIV 62, 105
Esquirel, Juande, I 13
Essanay Film Company, XI 133
Essex, class carriers, XVI 108, 110, 118
Essex decision (1805), III 116
Essex result, II 56
Estaing, Admiral Charles Hector d', II 68, 69, *69*, 72, 74, 114
Estonia, XII 136; XV 101; XVI 138; XVIII 13
Estridsson, Svein, I 19
Ethiopia, XV *49*, 74, 80, *81*, *82*, 83, 84
Etiquette, XIII 77
Ettor, Joseph J., XI 98, *98*
Eugenics, XIII 52
Eureka, IV 135
Europe, conception of New World, I 18, 29, *29*, 33, 139, 140; and colonial wars, I 85, 86, 96; II 62, 67, 78; influence on colonial culture and art, I 111, 116; and American non-involvement, III 134, 135, 139, 140; III 44, 65, 85, 112, 119; XI 33, 77; XII 23, 32, 48, 56, 62, 140; XV 78, 80; and American trade, III 18, 85, 116, 119; and American nationalism, III 108, 110; and American culture and art, IV 127, 128, 132, 136, 137, 138; X 87; XI 106, 111, 114, 132; XIII 66, 70, 71, 99; XVII 90, 91, 107; and the South, VII 44, 52, 54; and US Civil War, VII 100–102, 105, 107, 108; competition for markets, XI 43, 44; First World War, XII 10, 11, 13, 17; first US troops, XII 74, 76, 106; and Wilson, XII 129, 132, *133*; and Fourteen Points, XII 131; and American policy between the world wars, XV 11, 19, 20, 23, 28, 29, 98; and war debts, XV 24–27; rise of fascism in, XV 71, 74, 77, 84; Second World War, XV 100–103; XVI 10, 133, 134, 139; post-war reconstruction, XVIII 28–29; NATO, XVIII 32, 34; American troops, XVIII 53; see also names of individual countries
Europe After the Rain, XVII *91*
European Advisory Commission, XVI 102
European Defense Community, XVIII 68
European Recovery Program, XVIII 32
European Theater of Operations, US Army (ETOUSA), XVI 74
Eutaw Springs, Battle of (1781), II 121
Evangelicalism, VI 68, 70, 71; see also Religion
Evans, John, IX 38
Evans, Oliver, X 24; XI 16
Evans, Walker, XIV 56, 81
Everest, Wesley, XIII 12, *12*
Everett, Edward, IV 110, *110*; V 64; VI *128*, 129
Evergood, Philip, XIV 84
Ever-Normal Granary, XIV 126
Evers, J. J., XI 134
Everybody's, XI 31, 124
Evolution, X 96–97
Ewell, Richard S., VII 39, 40
Executive Committee of National Security Council, XVIII 90
Executive office, III 52; VII 51; X 37, 46
Exeter, New Hampshire, I 61
Exhuming the First American Mastodon, III *102*
Exile's Return, XIII 68
"Exodusters," VIII 98–99
Expansionists, V 22, 24, 48, 49–50; VI 120; X 44; XI 70; economic, X 36; XI 45, 80; Far East, XI 71–72
Experiments and Observations on Electricity, I 114
Exploration, Columbus, I 10, 11, 12, 14, *14*, 15; Spanish, I 16; Norse, I 19, 20; English, I 21, 25, 27; French, I 22, 23, *27*, 28, 80, 81, *81*; Dutch, I *27*; traumatic effects of, I 29–30; Lewis and Clark, III 74–77, *74–77*; Zebulon Pike, V 10, *11*, 12–14, 22; Pacific coast, V 51–52; see also Westward movements
Export-Import Bank, XV 43, 44
Expositions, see Fairs and expositions

Fables in Slang, XI 124
Factory system, IV 61–63, 66, 68, 112; VI 68
Fadiman, Clifton, XIV 80, 102
Fads, XIII 74, 77
Fair, James, IX 83
Fairbanks, Douglas, Sr, XII 116; XIII *81*, 82
Fair Deal, Leon Keyserling, XVII 25; major proposals of, XVII 26; opposition to, XVII *26*; Truman's defense of, XVII 31; Adlai Stevenson, XVII 75
Fair Employment Practices Committee, XVII 15, 26
Fairfax Militia Company, II 25
Fairfield, John, VI 66
Fair Labor Standards Act (1938), XIV 115, 128
Fairs and expositions, Great Exhibition, London (1851), IV 63, 132–133; X 24, 33; cotton (1881), VIII 121; Chicago (1893), X 93, *94*, 118; XI 109, 118, 128; Omaha (1898), XI 128; Buffalo (1901), XI 128; St Louis (1904), XI 128; San Francisco (1915), XI 128; San Diego (1915), XI 128; Chicago (1933–34), XIV 78; San Francisco (1935), XIV 78; New York (1939), XIV 78
Falaise Pocket, XVI *94, 95*, 96
Falklands War, XX 36
Fall, Albert B., XIII 24, *24*, 30
Fallen Timbers, Battle of (1794), III 139, *139*
Fall Line Road, IV 67
Falter, John, XVII *124*
Family, slaves, VI 35; VIII 60; immigrants, X 69; in Progressive era, XI 21, 25, 28–29; during Great Depression, XIV 60
Family Assistance Program, XIX 107
Family Compact, II 135
Fandango, V 36, *37*
Fannin, James W., V 41
FAO, see Food and Agriculture Organization
FAP, see Family Assistance Program
Faraday, Michael, X 24
Farewell to Arms, A, XIII 67; XIV 88
Farley, James, XIV 28, 29, 30, 133
Farm Bureau Federation, XIII 136; XVII 10
Farm Credit Administration, XIV 34
Farmer, James, XIX 57
Farmer-Labor party, XIII 136
Farmer's Alliance, VIII 128; X 126–127, 131–132
Farmers' National Council, XIII 136
Farmers' Non-Partisan Political League, XIII 136
Farmers' Union, XIII 136
Farm Holiday Association, XIV 117
Farming, see Agriculture
Farm Security Administration, XIV 65, 120, 124, *124*, 128
Farnham, Thomas J., V 52; IX 12
Faroe Islands, I 19
Farragut, David Glasgow, VII 22, 24, *25, 31, 123*, 125
Farrand, Max, III 22
Farrell, James T., XIV 56, 89
Fashions, XI 137, 140; XII *33*; XIII 74, *74–76*; XIV 56, *56*, 59
Fashions of 1934, XIV 92
Fast Carrier Task Force (Second World War), XVI 110, 116, 118, 119, 122, 125, 126
"Father Knows Best," XVII 128, *129*
"Fat Man," XVI *129*
Faubus, Orval, XVII 55, 56, *56*, 58
Faulkner, William, XIII 71, 98; XIV 88, *89*, 91; XVII 100
Fay, Larry, XIII 60
FBI, see Federal Bureau of Investigation
FCA, see Farm Credit Administration
FDIC, see Federal Deposit Insurance Corporation
Federal Bureau of Investigation, XIII 14; XIX 119
Federal Commodities Corporation, XIV 34
Federal Council of the Churches of Christ, XV 31
Federal Deposit Insurance Corporation, XIV 34
Federal Elections Bill, VIII 89, 135; X 53
Federal Emergency Relief Administration, XIV 31, 120
Federal Farm Board, XIII 127; XIV 116
Federal government, III 134; 135–137; powers of, III 12–13, 20, 26; X 36, 47; administration, III 18; public works, III 85, 137; IV 49–50; control of commerce, IV 50; control of Indians, IV 67; secession, VI 132; VII 12, 13, 44; confederate conception of, VII 55; extension of powers, VIII

79; XII 113; First World War, XII 101; see also Constitution; Government; Presidency
Federal Highway Act (1916), XII 114
Federalist faction (Mexico), V 41, 69, 91
Federalist Papers, The, III 30, *32*, 95; V 14
Federalists, III 30, 40, 46, 48, 52, 53, 54, 55, 56, 58; 1800 elections, III 60–62, *60*; under Jefferson, III 65, 68, 73, 78; Marshall, III 80; opposition to War of 1812, III 88, 121; on 1807 Embargo, III 117; defeat, III 137–138; IV 25; Hartford Convention, III 88; IV 24; on slavery, VI 86
Federal Music Project, XIV *33*
Federal Power Commission, XIII 46
Federal Reserve Act (1913), XI 67, 68, 80
Federal Reserve Board, XIII 26; XIV 10
Federal Road, IV 67
Federal Steel, X 18; see also Iron and steel industry
Federal Theater Project, XIV 81, 91
Federal Trade Commission Act (1914), XI 67, 68
Federal Writers Project, XIV 32, 34
Feininger, Lyonel, XVII 90
Feke, Robert, I 116
Fellowship of Reconciliation, XV 17
Felton, Rebecca Latimer, VIII 132
Feminine Mystique, The, XIX 64
Fenian Brotherhood, IV 80
Fenway Park System, X 118
FEPC, see Fair Employment Practices Committee
FERA, see Federal Emergency Relief Administration
Ferber, Edna, XIII 72
Ferdinand II (Spain), I 10, 11
Ferguson, Patrick, II 31
Ferlinghetti, Lawrence, XVII 101, 134
Fermi, Enrico, XVI 128, *128*
Fernow, Bernhard E., IX 129, 130
Ferran, Augusto, V *131, 134*
Ferraro, Geraldine, XX 63
Fetterman Massacre (1866), IX 113, 114
Fibber McGee and Molly, XIV *103*
Fiedler, Leslie, XVII 107; XIX 75
Field, Cyrus W., X 26
Field, Marshall, IX 83; X 109
Fielden, Samuel, X 78
Fields, W. C., XIV 96
Fifteenth Amendment, VII 89, 99; VIII 33, *34*, 39, 79, 88; see also Amendments, constitutional
Fifteenth Army Group (Second World War), XVI 86, 102
Fifth Army (Second World War), XVI 86, 88
Fifth Corps (Second World War), XVI 90, 92
Fifth Fleet (Second World War), XVI 110
Fifth Panzer Army (Second World War), XVI 101
"Fifty-Four Forty," V 63, 64, 65, 66, *66*, 71
Fifty-Fourth Massachusetts Regiment (Civil War), VII 98, 125
"Fifty-Niners," IX 71
"Fighting 69th," see Rainbow Division
Figueroa, José, V 30
Fiji Islands, XVI 25
Filibuster (Congress), XII 51; XIV 67
Filibustering expeditions, VI 101, 135
Fillmore, Millard (president), IV 82; V 109; VI 89, 94, *94*, 110, *111*
Film, X 33; XI 132; see also Movies
Filson, John, I 107
Financier, The, XI 107
Finland, XII 136; XV 28, 101, 103; XVIII 12, *12, 13*
Finney, Charles Grandison, IV 102–103, *102*
Finnigan, Jack, XI 136
Finny Fish, XVII 97
Fire Departments, X 113, *115*; XI *91*
Fire Island National Seashore, XIX 38
Fires, X 110, *110*, 113; XI 91
"Fireside chats" (F. D. Roosevelt), XIV 30
First Army, AEF (First World War), XII 92, 95, 96, 98
First Army (Second World War), XVI 90, 94–95, 96, 98, 99, 100, 101, 102, 103
First Battalion Light Infantry (War of Independence), II 31
First Canadian Army (Second World War), XVI 99
First Division, AEF (First World War), XII 76, 79, 88, 91, 92
First Marine Division, Tenth Army (Second World War), XVI 125
First Marine Regiment (Second World War), XVI 113
First National Film Company, XI 133

First Presidency (Mormons), V 99, 101
First South Carolina Volunteers (Civil War), VII 96, 98
First Tennessee (Colored) Battery, VII *94*
First Virginia Regiment, VII *12*
First World War, devastating effects, XII 10–11, 98, *98*; colonials in, XII *12*, 13; alliance system, XII 13–14, *14*; naval arms race, XII 14, 16; Balkan unrest, XII 16–17; declaration of war, XII 17–18; Schlieffen Plan, XII 18; Marne and Ypres, XII 19, *19*; Eastern front 1914, XII 20; Verdun and Somme, XII *20*, 21; Eastern Front 1916, XII 21; US neutrality, XII 22, 32–37, *36*, *37*; submarine warfare, XII 37–38, *37–39*; 42, 43, 50, 51–52, 53, 61, 62, 68–69, *68*, 70; House-Grey memorandum, XII 44, 46; Wilson's mediation attempts, XII 48–50; Zimmermann Note, XII 52–53, *52*; US enters war, XII 54–55, *54*, 62; Allied position in April 1917, XII 61; convoy system, XII *68*, 69; French mutiny, XII 73, *73*; Passchendaele and Cambrai, XII 74; Operation Michael, XII 80, *80*, 84; air war, XII 84–85, *84, 85, 86*, 87, *87*; Chemin des Dames offensive, XII 89, *89*; ''Peace Offensive,'' XII 91; Aisne-Marne counteroffensive, XII 91–92; St Mihiel, XII *93*, 95, *95*; Meuse-Argonne offensive, XII 95–96, *95*, 98; Armistice, XII 98; American industrial war effort, XII 102–113, *103, 105, 108, 110, 111*; opposition to, XII 55, 56–58, *56*, 114; economic effects on US, XII 114–115; XIV 10; social impact, XII 118–120, 122–125, 127; peace negotiations, XII 130–131, 134–137, *138*, 139; intellectual reaction to, XIII 107; XV 78–79
Fish, Hamilton, X 37, 44
Fisher, Irving, XIII 140
Fisher, Kate, IX 64
Fisher's Hill, Battle of (1864), VII 119
Fishing industry, I 21, 23, 62, 98, 106
Fishing Lady, The, I 115
Fisk, C. B., VIII 22
Fisk, ''Jubilee Jim,'' X 39
Fisk University, VIII 66
Fitch, John, IV 50; X 24
Fitzgerald, F. Scott, XIII 66, 70–71, *71*, 90, 97; XIV 91
Fitzhugh, George, VI 57, 58
Fitzpatrick, Benjamin, VI 125
Fitzsimmons, Bob, XI 136
Fiume, Yugoslavia, XII 136
Five Civilized Tribes, I 54; IX 15, 119; see also Creeks; Choctaws; Chickasaws; Cherokees; Seminoles; Indians, American
Five dollar day, XI 14, 16, 17
Five Forks, Battle of (1865), VII 128
Five Nations' League, I 53; see also Iroquois
Five Points, Manhattan, IV 79, *79*
Five-Power Treaty (1922), XV 23
Flagg, James Montgomery, XII *23*
Flaherty, Robert, XIII 83
Flanagan, Hallie, XIV 91
Flandin, Pierre-Etienne, XV 84
Flannagan, John B., XIV 84, *84*
Flathead, V 54; XIV *68*; see also Indians, American
''Fleapits,'' XI 133
Fletcher, Martin, XIV *111*
Fletcher, XVI 26, 27
Fletcher v *Peck* (1810), III 82
''Flip Wilson Show,'' XIX 58
Floradora, XI 123
Floradora Sextette, XI *123*
Florence, Nebraska, V 98
Florida, origins of, I 13–14, 16–17, 23, *26*, 44, 46, *47*, 54; struggle for, I 85, 90; II 63–64; III 130–131; secession convention, VI 132, 134; Black Codes, VIII 15; apportionment of representatives, VIII 42; reconstruction politics, VIII 85, 86; convict leasing, VIII 132; land boom, XIII 35, *36–37*, 38, 128, *128*, segregation in schools, XVIII 52; see also South, the
Florida (ship), VII 108, 125
Flower, Benjamin O., XI 86
Flowering of New England, The, XIV 88
Floyd, John, V 53
Floyd, William, II *13*
Fluoroscope, X 30
''Flying Fortress'' bombers, XVI *72*, 74, *75*, 85
Foch, Ferdinand, XII *72*, 84, 91, 92, 95, 137

Fokker, Anthony, XII *86*
Fokker D7s, XII *86*
Folksong, XIV 100; see also Music
Folsom, Abby, IV 109, 125
Folsom, William, V *107*
Folsom, California, IX 28
Food Administration, XII 103, *105*
Food and Agriculture Organization, XVIII 17
Food for Peace program, XVIII 85
Food Ministers' Conference (1959), XVII 86
Foote, Andrew H., VII 24, 72
Forand Bill, XVII 84
Forbes, Charles, XIII 28
Forbes, John, I 97
Force Act, IV 34
''Force Bill,'' see Federal Elections Bill
Ford, Bob, IX 67, 68, *68*
Ford, Gerald (president), Vietnam, XVIII 126; SALT, XVIII 137; as president, XIX 116, *121*, 125; XX 13–15, 25; unpopularity, XIX 116, 136; and Congress, XIX 119
Ford, Henry, XI 14–16, *15*, 140; XII 44, 45, *45*, 114; XIII 31, *31*, 39, 40, 130; XVII 119
Ford, John, XIV *90*
Fordham University, IV 86; see also Universities and colleges
Ford Motor Company, XI 16; XIII 31, 49; XIV 11
''Ford Service Department,'' XIII 61
Ford's Theater, VII 130, 133, *133*
Foreign affairs, in 1780s, III 14, 16; Jay Treaty, III 51; XYZ affair, III 55, 56; Louisiana Purchase, III 68–70, *70*; Tripolitan War, III 114, 115; relations with Britain in early 19th century, III 48, 49, 85, 116–117, 119–121; War of 1812, III 121–124, 126–128; Monroe Doctrine, III 131; influence of commercial interests on, IV 57; XI 71, 74, 77, 80; XVIII 128; Manifest Destiny, V 50–51; VI 43; IX 133; XI 33; Mexican War, V 68–77; during Civil War, VII 100–102, *100, 101, 103*, 104, 107; Treaty of Washington, X 44; imperialism, XI 33–34, 43–48; Spanish-American War, XI 34, *36*, *39–40*; Theodore Roosevelt, XI 70, 71, 74, 77, *82*; XII 22–23; ''Big Stick'' diplomacy, XI 71, 82; ''Dollar diplomacy,'' XI 71, 78, 82; Punitive Expedition, XII 27, *27*, 29, *30*; isolationism, XII 23, 56, 140; Wilsonian neutrality, XII 32, 34–37; Wilson's mediation efforts in First World War, XII 54–55, *54*; League of Nations, XIII 129, 130, 139–141, *141*; intervention in Latin America, XV 31–38, *32, 34, 35*; renewed isolationism, XV 14, 74, 77, 78–79, 90, 91, 109, *109*, 113, 115, 116; Spanish Civil War, XV 90; Czech crisis, XV 95–98; Proclamation of Neutrality, XV 100; relations with Japan, XV 132, 134; Pearl Harbor, XV 127, 129, 130, 131, 136; XVI 12, 13, 20, *20, 22*; Roosevelt and Second World War, XVI 135–140; cold war, XVII 25; XVIII 10, 24–25; containment, XVIII 26, 32, 37, 61, 62; Dulles and ''massive retaliation,'' XVII 76–77; NATO, XVIII 34–36; summit conferences, XVII 79; XVIII 64, 79, 81; Berlin blockade, XVIII 32, *33*; Korean War, XVIII 50, 51, 53, *55, 56*; U-2 affair, XVIII 80–81, *81*; Berlin wall, XVIII 88; Cuban missile crisis, XVIII 90–91, *91*; Vietnam, XVIII 58, 61, 79, 99, 100, 105, 131; Middle East crisis, XVIII 137, 138; détente XVIII 79, 128, 130, 132, 134, 137; *Pax Americana,* XIX 110, 119; 1976–86, XX 24–42; see also US–Soviet relations; also see individual countries
Foreign Affairs, XVIII 26, 84
Foreign Affairs, Committee for, II 133
Foreign aid, XVIII 28–29, 36, 85, 135
Foreign Ministers' Conference (1959), XVII 86
Foreign conspiracy against the Liberties of the United States, A, IV 81
Foreign Relations Committee (Senate), X 44; XII 42, 140; XV 79; XVIII 28
Foreman, Carl, XVII 132
Foresters, The, III *92*
Forest Management Act (1897), IX 130
Forest Reserve Act (1891), IX 129
Forestry, VIII 125; IX 128–131, *129, 130, 131*
Forever Amber, XVI 62; XVII 103
Forging the Shaft, X *13*
''Forgotten Man,'' X 97
Formosa, XVI 116; XVIII 48
Forrest, Edwin, VII 82

Forrest, Nathan Bedford, VII 33, 99; VIII 74, *74*, 76, 78
Forrestal, James, XVI 138; XVIII 17, 49, *49*
Fortas, Abe, XIX 35, *35*, 107
Fort Boise, V 59, 63
Fort Bridger, V 20, *20*, 63, 98, 106
Fort Brown, V 72, 76
Fort Buford, North Dakota, IX 45
Fort Chambly, II 33
Fort Churchill, Nevada, IX 27
Fort Clark, North Carolina, VII 22
Fort Dearborn, III 122
Fort Detroit, I 54; III 14, *14*, 122, *122*, 124
Fort Donelson, VII 24, 72, 112
Fort Duquesne, I 93, *94*, 95, 97; see also Pittsburgh
Fort Fisher, VII *62*, 125
Fort Frontenac, I 97
Fort Hall, V 44, 54, *54*, 63
Fort Harker, Kansas, IX 85
Fort Harmer, III *45*
Fort Hatteras, North Carolina, VII 22
Fort Henry, Tennessee, VII 24, 72, 112
Fort Jackson, VII *25*
Fort Kearny, Nebraska, V 63, 98; IX 27
Fort Lapwai, Idaho, IX 107
Fort Laramie, V *62*, 63
Fort Leavenworth, Kansas, V 63, 81
Fort Le Boeuf, I 92, 93
Fort Lyon, Colorado, IX 102
Fort Malden, III 122, 124
Fort Mandan, III 75
Fort Moultrie, VI 134
Fort Necessity, I 94
Fort Niagra, I 97, 98
Fort Oswego, I 89
Fort Pierre, South Dakota, IX 123
Fort Pillow massacre, VII 99
Fort Pitt, I 54
Fort Pontchartrain, I 98
Fort Presque-Isle, I 92
Fort Pulaski, Georgia, VII 22
Fortress Europe, see *Festung Europe*
Fortress Monroe, VI 136; VIII 16
Fort Ross, V 21
Fort Rouillé, I 92
Fort St Philip, VII *25*
Fort Stanwix, siege of, II 43
Fort Stanwix, Treaty of, I 55
Fort Stedman, Battle of (1865), VII 128
Fort Sumter, VI 134, 136, *136*; VII *15*, 18, *55*
Fort Supply, V 106
Fortune, T. Thomas, VIII 106, 110
Fortune, XIV 105
Fort Vancouver, V 52, 54, 64
Fort Venango, I 92, 93
Fort Wagner, Battle of (1863), VII 98, 125
Fort Washington, II 37, 94
Fort Washington, Battle of (1776), II *37*, 39
Fort Wayne, III 44
Fort William Henry, I 96
Fort Worth, Texas, IX 85
Forty-Niners, V 124; *126, 129*, 130, 139; VI 47
Forty-Ninth parallel, III 130; V 51, *51*, 53, 64, 65
Forty-Second Division, AEF (First World War), XII 79–80
42nd Parallel, The, XIV 88
Forum, VIII 140; X 137
For Whom the Bell Tolls, XIII 71; XIV 88
Fosdick, Raymond, B., XII 76, 77
Foster, John W., XII 33
Foster, Murphy J., VIII 135
Foster, Stephen, VI 47, *47*
Foulois, Benjamin D., XII 85
Founding Fathers, III 33, 109, 138; IV 21, 26, 84; VI 85, 92, 118; XI 12, 115; XVII 25; XIX 136
Fountainhead, The, XVII 103
Four Freedoms speech (F. D. Roosevelt), XIV 139, *139*
Four Horsemen of the Apocalypse, The, XIII 83, 84
Fourier, Charles, IV 120
Four Power Treaty (1922), XV 23
Fourteen Points (Wilson), XII 130–132, 134, 137; XV 20
Fourteenth Amendment, VI 113; VII 89, 99; VIII 25, 27, 30, 88, 138; X 85; XVII 52; see also Amendments, constitutional
Fourth Marine Division (Second World War), XVI 108, 111

Fourth of July, IV 13, *14*, 98; see also Independence Day
Fourth Reconstruction Act (1868), VIII 33
Fowey, II 24
Fox, Charles James, II 16
Fox, George, I *68*; see also Society of Friends
Fox, Richard K., IX 66
Fox, I 41, 92; see also Indians, American
Foxtrot, XI 126
Frampton, John, I 113
France, exploration and colonization activities, I 10, 21–23, 28, 33, 44–45, 53–54, 63, 80–83; colonial rivalry, I 84–86, 88–89, *98*, *99*; II 66–69, *70–71*; aid to War of Independence, II 28, 44–45, 66–67; threat to Britain, II 62, 73–74; war with Britain, II 66–69, 70–*71*, *77*, *78*, 79, 135–140; Treaty of Paris, II 130; slave rebellion in West Indies, III 41; relations with US, III 55–56, *58*, *112*, 116–117, 119; Louisiana purchase, III 70; Civil War, VII 102, 104, 107; Morocco crisis, XI 77; influence on art, XI 111; alliance system, XII 13–14, *14*; First World War, XII 17, 18; Marne, XII 19; Verdun, XII *20*, 21; army mutinies, XII 73, *73*; Chemin des Dames offensive, XII 89, *89*; "Peace Offensive," XII 91; Aisne-Marne counteroffensive, XII 91–92; Meuse-Argonne offensive, XII 95–96, *95*, 98; peace conference, XII 130, 136; Geneva Disarmament conference, XV 71–72; war reparations, XV 24–25; Second World War, XV 103; XVI 10, 13, 17, 76, 78, 80–81, 92, *92*, 94–96, *94–95*, 97, 136; Marshall plan, XVIII 30; Brussels pact, XVIII 32; German rearmament, XVIII 35–36, 67, 68; Southeast Asia, XVIII 40; SEATO, XVIII 64; Algeria, XVIII 69; Suez crisis, XVIII 71–73; Kennedy's attack on, XVIII 84; Vietnam, XVIII 96, 98, 99, 100, 101, *101*, *103*; Geneva Conference (1954), XVIII 101, 104; Diem, XVIII 105
Francis I (France), I 22
Franciscans, I 44; V 27
Franco, Francisco, XV 84, 86, *86*, 90; XVI 76, 110
Franco-American Treaty (1778), II 67, 69, *70*, 74, 133, 137
Franco-Russian Alliance (1894), XII 13
Frank, Hans, XVIII 22
Frank, Jerome N., XIII 107; XIV 44, 120
Frankfurter, Felix, XIII 14, 133
Franklin, Aretha, XIX 58
Franklin, Benjamin, and Braddock, I 95; and backwoods rioters, I 105; moralist, I 110; scientific and cultural contributions, I 114, 117, *136*; X 24; humiliation by Privy Council, I *119*; colonial agent, I 123; education of, I 135; style, I 136; Anglo-American, I 136, *136*, 139; deputy post master, I 138; union of colonies, I 139; Declaration of Independence, II *10*, 12, *13*; ambassador to France, II 44, *132*, 134, 136, 1̣38,

139; radical, II 48, 55, 60; III 20; on price of liberty, II 101; on B. Arnold, II 116; Treaty of Paris, II 130, *130*, 135; on government, III 13; constitutional convention, III 24, 26, 30; *Autobiography,* III 97; on bald eagle, III 108; legacy, III 109; on education, IV 86; work ethic, X *11*
Franklin, John Hope, VI 55, 58
Franklin, William Temple, II *130*
.Franklin, Pennsylvania, I 93
Franklin, Battle of (1864), VII 122
Franklin (carrier), XVI 118, 124
Franklin Institute, IV 87
Franks, Bobby, XIII *115*
Franny and Zooey, XVII 103
Franz Ferdinand (Austria), XII 17, *17*
Franz Joseph I (Austria), XII *16*
Fraser, Sir Bruce, XVI 131
Fraser River, British Columbia, V 52; IX 73
Frayser's Farm, Battle of (1862), VII 28
Frederick Douglass' Paper, VI 82
Frederick Road, IV *68*
Fredericksburg, Battle of (1862), VII 32–33, *33*, *34*
Frederick the Great (Prussia), I 96
Fredonia, Republic of, V 40
Fredonian Rebellion, V 40
Freedmen, see Negroes
Freedmen's Bureau, VI 35; VIII 25, 32, 39, 43, 51, 53–55, *53*, *54*, 64, 65, 99
"Freedom Rides," XVII 64; XIX 52; see also Integration
Freedom's Journal, VI 82
Free enterprise, IX 129, 132; X 36, 37, 87; see also Capitalism; Corporations; Industry
Free French, XVI 17
"Free labor," VI 103, 104
Free Lands of Dakota, The, IX 89
Free Speech movement, XIX 70
Freeman, Orville, XIX 19, *21*
Freemasons, IV 29, *31*; XI 126
Free silver coinage, X 133–134, 141; XI 13
"Free-soil" issue, VI 87, 89, *89*, 90, *90*, 91, 94, 97, 106
Free-soil party, VI 87, 89, *89*, 90, *90*, 91, 94, 97, 106
Free territory convention, VI 89
Frémont, John Charles, V 22, 24, *24–25*, 69, 71, 109, 116, *116*, 118–119, 120, 138, 139; VI 107, 111; IX 28
Frémont Peak, Wyoming, V 116, *116*
French and Indian War, I 54, 94–99, *94–99*, 105 106; II 63; Washington's attack on Jumoville, I 94–95; Braddock's fiasco, I *94*, 95–96; Pitt's strategy, I 97; Rogers' Rangers, I *97*, 98; fall of Quebec, I 98; peace, I 99; colonial disregard of Navigation Acts, I 125
French Canadians, I 83; immigrants, X 63
French Committee of National Liberation, XVI 81

French North Africa, XVI 15, 74, 76, 78
French Resistance (Second World War), XVI 95
French Revolution, II 83–84; III 48, 90, 138
Freneau, Philip, III 95
Freshman, The, XIII 85
Freud, Sigmund, XI 114; XIII 17, 68, 114
Freydis, I 20
Frick, Henry Clay, X 125
Frick, Wilhelm, XVIII 22
Friedan, Betty, XIX 64; XX 63
Friedenberg, Edgar Z., XIX 70
Friedman, Milton, XIX 132; XX 45–46, 70
Friedman, William F., XV 131
Friends, Society of (Quakers), I 53, *53*, 66, *68*, 69, *69*, 70, 105, 113; II 96; IV 100; V 91; VI 62–63; Indian agencies, IX 114; see also Religion
Friends of the American Indian, IX 118
Frobisher, Martin, I 27, 28
Fritsche, Hans, XVIII 22
From Here to Eternity (book), XVIII 103; (film), XVII 132, 132
"From the Depths," XI *84*
Frontenac, Louis de Buade, Comte de, I *80*, 82, 86
Frontier, IX 122, 123, 133–141; X 15; XI 10, 80; XIX 50; see also Westward movement
Frontier hypothesis, IX 140, 141
Frontiersmen, III 48; IV 71
Frontier society, VI 55
Front Royal, Battle of (1862), VII 26
Frost, Robert, XI 109, *111*; XIII 98; XVII 100; XIX 19, *20*
Fruitlands, Massachusetts, IV 119, 120
Fry, James B., VII 51
Fry, Joshua, I 93
FSA, see Farm Security Administration
Fuel Administration, XII 105, *105*
Fugitive, XIII 71
Fugitives, the, XIII 71–72, 98
Fugitive Slave Laws, VI 92, 94, 96, 118, 135; VII 91
Fulbright, J. William, anti-McCarthy, XVII 44; Bay of Pigs, XVIII 86; on foreign policy, XVIII 130, *130*; possible secretary of state, XIX 19; antiwar movement, XIX 43
Fulbright Resolution (1943), XVIII 17
Fuller, Margaret, IV 121, *121*
Fulton, Robert, III 109, *109*; IV 50, *50*
Fundamental Constitutions of Carolina, I 74
Fundamentalism, XIII 113
"Fundamental Orders of Connecticut," I 61
Fundy, Bay of, I 95
Funk, Walter, XVIII 22
Furniture, colonial, I 112, *112*, 117, 137
Fur trade, I 51, 53, 68, 79, 81, *82*, 83, 95, *123*; III 14, 18, 48, *50*; V 14–16, *17*, 18–19, *18*, 21, 22, 34, 51; IX 13
Furutaka (ship), XVI 31

Gable, Clark, XIV 95, *96*; XVI 62
Gabor, Naum, XVII 90
Gadsden, Christopher, II 121
Gadsden purchase (1853), V 93; IX 28, 36
Gagarin, Yuri, XIX 84, *84*, 86
Gage, General Thomas, II 14, 15, 16, 22, 23, 28, 29, 30, *87*, 96, 128, 129
"Gag rule," VI 76, 87
Gaines's Mill, Battle of (1862), VII 28
Galbraith, John Kenneth, XVII 107; XIX 19, 23

Gall (Chief), IX 107, 108
Gallatin, Albert, III 51, 52, 78, 79, *79*, 85, 88; V 53
Gallaudet, Thomas, IV 114
Gallipoli (campaign, First World War), XII 20
Gallo, V 36
Galloway, Joseph, II 51, 87
Gallup, George, XV 79
"Galvanized yank," IX 31
Galveston, Texas, XI 53
Galvez, Bernardo de, II 139

Gambling, XI 134
Games, XI 123; XIV 70, 71
Gang-i-sawai, I 87
Gang warfare, XIII 58, 60, 61, 62, 63; see also Crime
Garbage collection, X 115, *115*
Garbo, Greta, XIII 85, *119*; XIV 95
Garden grove, V 97
Gardoqui, Drego de, III 14
Garfield, Harry, XII 103, 105
Garfield, James A. (president), VIII 81, 134; IX 37, 82; X 42, 45, 49, *49*
Garland, Hamlin, X 103
Garment industry, X 63, *64*, 66
Garner, John Nance (vice president), XIII 122; XIV *28*, 29, 132, 137
Garret, Pat, IX 66, *66*, 67
Garret, Thomas, VI 66
Garrison, William Lloyd, VI 61, *61*, 62, 63, 68, 70–71, 75, 78, *79*, 81, 82, 83, 98; VIII 114; IX 116; see also Abolition movement
Garroway, Dave, XVII 120
Garvey, Marcus, XIII 35
"Gas and water socialism," XI 53
Gasoline, XI 13, 14; XIII 41
Gaspee (ship), III 14, 16
Gass, Patrick, III 74
Gas Station, The, XIX 122
Gas stations, XIII *41*, 44
Gaston, Paul M., VIII 140, 141
Gas warfare, XII *98*
Gates, "Bet-a-million," XI 137
Gates, Horatio, II 26, 40, 44, 78, 106, 109, 121
Gates, Paul, VI 45
Gates, Sir Thomas, I 72
Gatling, Richard Jordan, VII *121*
Gatling gun, VII *121*
Gato (submarine), XVI *51*
Gear, Joseph W., IV 77
Geary, John, VI 107
Geddes, John, IV 52
Gehrig, Lou, XIV *74*, 75
Gemini spacecraft, XIX 89, *90*
General Allotment Act, see Dawes Act
General Amnesty Act (1872), VIII 46
General Board of the navy, XI 82
General Electric, IX; XIII 141
General Motors, XI 16, 140; XIII 40–41; XVII 114; see also Automobile industry
General staff (First World War), XII 107, 108
General ticket system, IV 25–26
"General William Booth enters into Heaven," XI 109
Genesis of the World War, The, XV 78
Genêt, Edmond Charles, III 48
Geneva Conference (1927), XV 24
Geneva Conference (1954), XVII 79; XVIII 101, 104, 123
Geneva Disarmament Conference (1933), XV 71
Geneva Summit (1955), XVII 79; XVIII 68, *69*
Genius of American Politics, The, XVII 107
Genius of Universal Emancipation, The, VI 68, 70
Genna, Angelo, XVIII *62*
Gentlemen's Agreement, XVII 50
Gentz, Friedrich, III 138
Geography Epitomized, III 91
Geological and Geographical Survey of the Territories, IX 125
George II (England), I 126
George III (England), I 70, 120, 126, 127, 134; II 15, 16, 64, 136; attacks on, II 20, 83, *83*; on American war, II 74, 79; rejects mediation, II 140
George V (England), XV 24
George VI (England), XV *49*
George, Henry, X 136, 137, *137*
George, James Z., VIII 129
George, Milton, X 131
George, Lake, II 24, *25*
George Peabody College for Teachers, VIII 132
Georgetown, Colorado, IX 73
George Washington Battalion (Spanish Civil War), XV 86
Georgia, origins of, I 44, 54, 67, 89, *102*, 103; in colonial wars, I 90; absence at continental congress, II 14; state constitution, II 56–58; III 136; VIII 40–41; in War of Independence, II 72, 103, 120; Indian treaties, III 38; expulsion of Cherokees, IV 67; education, IV 92; slavery, VI 21; plantation owners, VI 40; cotton, VI 43; rice,

VI 44; anti-abolition acts, VI 75; secession convention, VI 137–138, *137*; secession ordinance, VI 138; reconstruction politics, VIII 73, 82–83; Bourbon triumvirate, VIII 134; Negro politicians, VIII 134; "grandfather clause," VIII 135; progressivism, XI 55; representatives, XIII 42; segregation, XVII 52; see also South, the
Georgia Jungle, XIV 67
Gerard, Conrad, II 138, 139, 140
Germain, Lord George, II 41, 64–65, *67*, 72, 73, 74, 77, 81, 106, 115
German-American Bund, XV 109, 110, *110*
German-Americans, in War of Independence, II 98; in mid-19th century, IV 73–74, *74*, 78; VI 110; Civil War, VII 108; 1890s, XI 29, *29*; First World War, XII 32, 35–36, 113, 123, *122–123*; see also Immigration
German Federal Republic (West Germany), formation, XVIII 32; NATO, XVIII 36, 68; rearmament, XVIII 35–36, 53, 65, 67, 68; see also Germany
German Information Service, XII 60
Germantown, Battle of (1777), II 107, *107*
Germany, X 58; imperial power, XI 74; Morocco crisis, XI 77; relations with US to 1914, XI 82; alliance system, XII 13–14, *14*; naval arms race, XII 14, 16; First World War, XII 17; Schlieffen plan, XII 18; Marne and Ypres (1914), XII 19; Eastern front, XII 20, 21, 74, *75*; Verdun and Somme, XII *20*, 21; Jutland, XII 21–22, *22*; submarine warfare, XII 22, 37–38, *37*, 38, *39*, 42, 43, 50, 61, 62, 68–69, *68*, *70*; *Lusitania* crisis, XII 38, 40–41; war aims, XII 49; propaganda, XII 60; Passchendaele and Cambrai, XII 74; Operation Michael, XII 80, *80*, 84; Chemin des Dames offensive, XII 89, *89*; "Peace Offensive," XII 91; Aisne-Marne counteroffensive, XII 91–92; St Mihiel, XII 95, *95*; Meuse-Argonne Offensive, XII 95–96, *96*, 98; scuttling of fleet, XII *131*; peace conference, XII 131, 136, 137, *138*, 139; war debts and reparations, XV 26–27, *26*; Geneva Disarmament Conference, XV 71–72; Weimar, XV 74; remilitarized Rhineland, XV 84, *84*; Spanish Civil War, XV 86, 90; pact with Italy, XV 90; Anti-comintern pact, XV 91; annexation of Austria, XV 94, 95; Czech crisis, XV 96; "Crystal Night," XV 97; Non-Aggression pact, XV 100; Tripartite pact, XV 127, *127*; Second World War, XV 103, *103*, *106*; *Blitzkrieg,* XVI 10, *11*, *13*; invasion of Russia, XVI 10–11, 13; Stalingrad, XVI 16; Torch, XVI 16; Battle of the Atlantic, XVI 70–71, *70*, *71*, 73; North African defeat, XVI 79–80; Sicilian campaign, XVI 82–84, *82*, *83*; bomber offensive, XVI 85; Italian campaign, XVI 86, *88*, *89*; D-Day, XVI 92, *92*, 94–96, *94–95*; Market Garden, XVI 98–99, *98*; Battle of Bulge, XVI 101–102; V-E day, XVI 106; indemnity, XVI 138; Potsdam Agreement, XVIII 21; West German integration, XVIII 31–32; rearmament, XVIII 35–36, 53, 65; see also Berlin; East Germany; German Federal Republic
Geronimo, IX 110, 111, 120
Gerow, Leonard T., XV 141; XVI 90, 102
Gerry, Elbridge, II *13*; III 22, 23, 26, *55*, 56
Gershwin, George, XIII 92, *93*; XIV 100
Gershwin, Ira, XIII 92
Gettysburg, Battle of (1863), VII 40–41, *38–41*, 54, 64, 104
Ghent, Peace of (1814), III 128, 130, 134
Ghettos, X 66, *66*, 68–69, *68*; XVII 111; XIX 58, *61*, 62
Ghormley, Robert L., XVI 70
Ghost dance, cult of the, IX 111–112, *111–112*
Giannini, Amadeo P., XVIII 46
Giants in the Earth, X 69
Giap, Vo Nguyen, XVIII *103*
Gibbon, John, IX 108
Gibbons v *Ogden,* IV 50
Gibbs, Willard, X 92
"GI Bill of Rights," XVII 116
Gibraltar, II *72*, 73, 74, 75, 77, 78, 81, *81*, 139
Gibson, Charles Dana, XI *138*
Gibson, Hoot, XIII 82
"Gibson Girl," XI *138*, 140
Giddings, Joshua, VI 91
Gideon v *Wainwright* (1963), XIX 35
Gila Desert, IX 15
Gila River, V 22; IX 101

Gilbert, Sir Humphrey, I 25, 28
Gilbert, John, XIII 82, 85
Gilbert, Prentiss, XV 59
Gilbert Islands, XVI 20, 108, *108*
Gilbreth, Frank B., XIII 32
Gilded Age, X 45, 46, 87; XI 28
Gilder, George, XX 71
Giles, William Branch, III 51
Giles v *Harris* (1903), VIII 108
Giles v *Teasley* (1904), VIII 108
Gili Gili Field, XVI 32
Gillespie, Archibald, V 116, 118, 119
Gillett, Frederick, XII 126
Gilman, Daniel Coit, X 88
Gimbel's, XI 21
Gin, XIII 56, 57
Ginsberg, Allen, XVII 101, 134, *134*; XIX 78
Ginseng, III 18
Giovanni, Nikki, XIX 58
Giovannitti, Arturo, XI 98, *98*
Girard, Stephen, X 88
Giraud, Henri, XVI 17, 76, 79, 80
Girdler, Tom, XIV 112
Girl of the Golden West, The, V 138; XI 126
Girl of the Limberlost, A, XI 126
Girl scouts, XI 140; XII *112*
Gist, Christopher, I 93
Giving the Butt, X 138
Glacken, William J., XI 111, *126*
Gladstone, William, III 31
Glass, Carter, XIV 132
Glass Menagerie, The, XVII 106
Glass-Steagall Banking Act (1933), XIV 34
Glazer, Nathan, XIX 50
Glazier, Willard, X 106
Gleason, Jackie, XVII 128
Gleason and Ballou publishing company, IX 136
Glorious Revolution (1689), I 62
Gloucester, Massachusetts, I 59, 60
Glover, John, II 32
Godey's Lady's Book, IV 44, 121, *121*
Godspeed (ship), I 71
Goering, Hermann, XVI 71; XVIII 22, *22*
Goethals, George W., XVII 106, 107, 108, 109, 113
Gold, I 11, 16, 17, *42*, 48; gold rush, V 105, 107, 120, *121*, 122–125, *122–129*, 127, 130–131, *130–132*, 134, *134–138*, 138–139; IX 15, 70; mining, V 127, *127–129*, 130–131, *131*; IX 77; 1869 scandal, X 39; see also California; Mining
Gold, Mike, XIV 80
Gold beach, XVI 92
Goldberg, Arthur, XIX 19, *21*, 23, *35*
Gold Diggers of 1933, XIV 91, *92*
Golden Castile, see Panama, Isthmus of
Golden Day, The, XIII 101
Golden Gate, V 118
Golden Gate International Exposition (1935), XIV 78
Golden West, IV 60
Goldfine, Bernard, XVII 85
Gold Hill, Colorado, IX 73
Goldman, Emma, XIII 13
Goldrick, O. J., IX 77
Gold Rush, The, XIII 85
Goldsboro, North Carolina, VII 127
Gold standard, X 37, 38, 48, 134, 141; XIV 15, 34; XV 73
Goldwater, Barry, XIX 36, 38, *38*, 40, 103, 136
Goldwyn, Sam, XIV 91
Golf, X 119; XI 18, 137; XIII 77, *78*; see also Sports
Goliad, Texas, V 41
Gomara, Lopez de, I 33
Gompers, Samuel, X 74, 81, *81*, 82, 83; XI 12, 68, 96, 97, 98; XIII 105, 113, 116, 118; XIII 27, 136
Gona, New Guinea, XVI 32
Gone with the wind (book), XIV 90; (film), XIII 82; XIV 90, 96
Gonzales, Texas, V 41
Goodbye, Mr Chips, XIV 99
Good-bye Wisconsin, XIII 68
Goodell, Charles, XIX 118
Good Government conferences, X 118
Good Hope, Cape of, II 79, 81
Goodhue, Grace, XIII 118, *120*
Goodman, Benny, XIV 72, 100, *100*
Goodman, Paul, XVII 107; XIX 70
Good Neighbor Policy, XV 31, 37, 38, 40, 43, 46, 47;

XVIII 85
Goodnight, Charles, IX 45, 46–47, 49
Goodnight-Loving Trail, IX 45
Goodwin, William J., XVIII 47
Goodyear, Charles, IV 64, *64*; X 24
"Goon squads," XIV 112, 114
Goose-step, The, XIII 67
"Gopher Prairie," XIII 66, 95
Gorbachev, Mikhail, XX 39
Gordon, John B., VIII 129
Gore, Albert, XVII 55
Gore, Thomas P., XII 42
Gore-McLemore resolutions, XII 42, 46
Gorges, Sir Ferdinando, I 72
Gorky, Arshile, XVII 91, *92*, 97
Gosden, Treeman F., XIV 101, *103*
Goss, A. H., XIII 44
Go Tell It On the Mountain, XVII 103
Gothic style, X 93
Gottlieb, Adolph, XVII 94, *96*
Gottwald, Klement, XVIII *37*
Gough, John B., IV 116
Gould, George Jay, XI *122*
Gould, Jay, X 39
Gould Railroad, X 77; see also Railroads
Government, in English colonies, I 59, 60, 63, 65,
66, 67, 69, 70, 72, 73, 86, 123, 124, 133; in New
France, I 80, 82, 83, 86; theories of, II 12, 13, 20;
popular, II 47–48; Hogarth on British
electioneering, II *50*; formation of state, II 51,
54–56; federal, II 58, 60; III 26; problems in
creating, II 132–133; Jeffersonian and Jacksonian
concept of, IV 16–17, 20; Henry Clay's view of,
IV 23; Van Buren's concept of, IV 24; progressive
theory of, XI 86; growth of big, XIV 139; see also
Constitution; Federal government; Presidency;
States' rights
Grable, Betty, XVI *67*
"Grade" school, IV 86; see also "Common" school
"Gradualism" (slavery), VI 65, 68, 71
Grady, Henry Woodfin, VIII 118, 119, 139
Graf Zeppelin, XV 93
Graham, Billy, XVII 119, *119*
Graham, Isaac, V 22
Grama grass, IX 11
Gramophone, XI 140
Granada (fall of), I 10
"Grand Alliance, the," XVIII 13, 24
Grand Canyon, I *16*, 17; IX 132
Grand Coulee Dam, XIV 35, *37*
Grand Cyclops (Ku Klux Klan), VIII 74
"Grand Fantastical Parade," IV *21*
"Grandfather" clause, VIII 108, 115, 135
Grandissimes, the, VIII 140
Grand Island, V 55
Grand Magi (Ku Klux Klan), VIII 74
Grand Old Party, X 45, 47; see also Republican party
Grand Ronde, V 59
Grand Tour, XI 25
Grand Turk (Ku Klux Klan), VIII 74
Grange, "Red," XIII *79*.
Grange, the, VIII 128; IX 41; X 21, 126–127, *129*,
131, 131
"Granger" laws, X 127, 131
"Granger" railroads, IX 37–38, *37*
"Granite railroad," IV 54–55
Grant, General James, II 74
Grant, Ulysses Simpson (president), Civil War, VII 24,
33, 35–36, *35*, 72, 83, 98, 111, 112–113, *113*, 115,
115, 116–117, *127*, 128, 137, 139; VIII 10;
reconstruction, VIII 33; suspension of *habeas
corpus* in South, VIII 79; southern violence, VIII
83–84, 85; Custer, IX 108; Indian peace policy,
IX 114; national parks, IX 124; president, VIII 81;
X *36*, 37, *38*, 46; civil service commission, X 39;
gold scandal, X 39; Liberal Republicans, X 39–40;
reelection, VIII 87; X 40; scandals, X 41, 42, 44;
foreign policy, X 44
Grant (M3) tank, XVI 54
Grapes of Wrath, The (book), XIV 56, 89, *89*;
(film) X *90*
Grasse, Comte Francois de, II 79, 81, 122, 123, 126,
129
Grasshopper Creek, Idaho, IX 73
Grasso, Ella, XIX 64
Grateful Dead, The, XIX *77*, 78
Grattan, C. Hartley, XV 78

Grau san Martín, Ramón, XV 38, 39
Graves, Admiral, II 75, 81, 123
Gray, Asa, X 96
Gray, Gilda, XIII 38
Gray, Jesse, XIX 63
Gray, Robert (soldier), II 103
Gray, Robert (explorer), V 51
Gray, Thomas R., VI 36, 37
Gray's Inn Creek, Maryland, I *103*
Grayson, William J., VI 57
"Greaser," V 68
Greasy Grass River; see Little Big Horn
"Great American Desert," V 24; IX 11, 12, 24,
132, 133
Great Awakening, I 108, 109, 110, 135; IV 100;
see also Religion
Great Basin, V 63, 97, 103, 106; IX 15, 132
Great Britain, colonies, I 10, 13, 21, 22, 33, 48–49,
51, 53, 54, 55, 57–63, 65–77; colonial rivalry,
I 84–86, 88, 89, 90, 91, 92–99, *92–99*; supports
German migration to America, I 103;
administration of colonies, I 122–125; attitude
toward American rebels, II 10, 13, 16; War of
Independence, II 28–30; tactics in War of
Independence, II 31, *128–129*; loss of allies,
II 62; Treaty of Paris, II 130; relations with new
republic, III 44, 48–49, 51, 85, 112, 114, 116–117,
119–121; War of 1812, III 121–124, 126–128,
130; Convention of 1818, V 51; Oregon question,
V 63–64; US Civil War, VII 100–102, *100–101*,
103, 104; Treaty of Washington, X 44; agricultural
depression, X 58; Clayton-Bulwer Treaty, XI 71;
Hay-Pauncefote Treaty, XI 72; interests in
China, XI 74, 80; Caribbean interests, XI 82;
alliance system, XII 14, *14*, naval arms race, XII
14, 16; First World War, XII 18, *18*; Ypres 1914,
XII 19, *19*; Somme 1916, XII *20*, 21; Jutland,
XII 21–22, *22*; Declaration of London, XII 36–37;
House-Grey plan, XII 44, 46; war propaganda,
XII 58, 60; Passchendaele and Cambrai, XII 74;
operation Michael, XII 80, *80*, 84; peace, XII 130;
Washington Naval Conference, XV 20, 22–23;
Geneva Disarmament conference, XV 71–72;
appeasement, XV 94, 95; Churchill, XV 112–113;
Lend-lease, XV 116; XVI 44; Japanese demands,
XV 125, 136, 138; "ABC-1" plan, XV 129;
XVI 12, 13; Second World War, XVI 10, *10*, 11;
Atlantic Charter, XV 122; XVI 12; United Nations,
XVI 15; Torch, XVI 16; Casablanca conference,
XVI 16–17, *16*; war supplies to, XVI 43–44, 48,
73; relations with US, XVI 137; Greek Civil War,
XVIII 26–27; decline as great power, XVIII 29;
Marshall plan, XVIII 30; Brussels pact, XVIII 32;
Southeast Asia, XVIII 40; SEATO, XVIII 64; Suez
crisis, XVIII 71–73; CENTO, XVIII 72; Skybolt,
XVIII 92; Indochina, XVIII 98; 1954 Geneva
conference, XVIII 101, 104; see also War of
Independence; War of 1812
Great Britain (ship), IV 57
"Great Commitment," XVI 43, 44
Great Compromise, III 24, 25, *25*
Great Conspiracy, The, VII 135
Great Depression, XIII 64; XIV 10, 11, *11*, 16;
unemployment, XIV 11, *11*, *12*; Hoover, XIV 14;
relief, XIV 12; banks, XIV *14*, 15–16; advertising,
XIV *18*, 19; sales tax, XIV 19; Bonus Army riot,
XIV 20–21, *20*, 22; Roosevelt's election, XIV 24;
Roosevelt's bank policy, XIV 30; welfare state,
XIV 47; life during, XIV 56, 71; the rich, XIV 56,
59; social life, XIV 60, *60*, *62*, *64*; migratory
workers, XIV 65; sports, XIV 71–76; religion,
XIV 76–77; crime, XIV 77–78, *77*; fairs, XIV
78–79; cultural life, XIV 80–92, *81–90*, *92*, *94*,
95–100, *96*, *99*, *100*, *103*, 104, *104*, 105, *107*;
labor, XIV *109*; agriculture, XIV 116, *117*; AAA,
XIV 117–120; effects on foreign policy, XV 27–29,
56, 74, 90, 98; see also New Deal; Roosevelt,
Franklin Delano
Great Dictator, The, XIV 97
Greater Antilles, XI 70, 78
Greater East Asia Co-Prosperity Sphere, XV 65, 69;
XVI 10, *30*
Great Exhibition (London, 1851), IV 63, 132–133;
X 24, 33
Great Gatsby, The, XIII 71, 90
Great God Brown, The, XIII 98
Great Illusion, The, XII 13

Great Lakes, I 85; III 18, 124, 130; see also names
of individual lakes
"Great Migration" (Blacks), XIII 133
"Great Migration," I 60
Great Northern Railway, IX 35–36; see also Railroads
Great Plains, V 13, 14, *14*, 39; IX 10–13, *11*, *12*,
104; settlement, IX 15, 17, 40, 85, 86, *90*, 92
133; agriculture, IX 94–97, *95*, 99, *99*
Great Powers, XII 13, 14, 24
Great Salt Lake, V 20, 97, *100*
Great Seal of the Confederacy, VII *57*
Great Society, XIX 35, 38, 41, 43, 132
Great South, The, VIII 139
Great Spirit, I 41; IX 41
Great Strike (1877), X 75, *76*, 77
Great Train Robbery, The, XI 132, *132*
Great Valley Road, IV 67
Great Wagon Road, I 104
Great War, The, see First World War
Great Western (ship), IV 57
"Great White Fleet," XI 77, 78; XII 24
Greece, Balkan wars, XII 16; Communist threat,
XVIII 26–27; American aid, XVIII 28, *29*; NATO,
XVIII 36
Greed, XIII 82–83
"Greek slave," IV 132, *132*
Greek-Turkish Aid Bill (1947), XVIII 28
Greeley, Horace, VII *49*; VIII 81; IX 74, 123; on
work, IV 38; railroads, IV 57; *New York Tribune,*
IV 61; on Oregon, V 60; antislavery, VI 89;
Republican party, VI 102; Stephen Douglas,
VI 117; peace convention 1860, VI 140; on
secession, VII 14; war fever, VII 19; on first battle
of Bull Run, VII 20; Liberal Republican, X 40, *40*
Green, John Ruffin, VIII 122
Green, Thomas Jefferson, V 139
Green, William, XIII 136
Greenbackers, VIII 80, 128
Greenback-Labor party, VIII 128; X 82
"Greenbacks," VII 86–87; VIII 80, *80*; X 37, 38, 48,
82, 134; XI 84
Greene, Nathanael, II 32, 39, 121, 128, 129
Greener, Richard T., VIII 113
Greenfield, Jeff, XIX 75–76, 78
Greenfield quilt, I *115*
Greenfield Village museum, XI 14; XVII 119
Greening of America, The, XIX 123
Green Island, XVI 41
Greenland, I 19, 20, 37; XV 119
Green Mountain Boys, II 24, *25*, 43, 86
Greenough, Horatio, IV 127–128, *127*, 129, 131,
131, 132, 133–134
Green River, V 17, 54, 55
Greenville, South Carolina, VI *49*
Greenville, Treaty of (1795), III 139
Greenwich village, XIII 66, 68, 70
Greer (ship), XV 122; XVI 71
Gregory, Dick, XIX 51
Grenada, XX 33, 38
Grenadiers, II 31
Grenville, George, I 130
Grew, Joseph C., XV 69, 127, *127*, 130, 134;
XVIII *18*
Grey, Major General Charles, II 30
Grey, Sir Edward, XII 13, 44, 46
Grey, Zane, IX 133; XI 126; XIII 72
Grid system, XIII 44
Grierson, Benjamin H., VII 36
Griffith, David Wark, XI 133
Griffith, Raymond, XIII 85
Grimke, Angela, IV 123
Grimke, Sara, IV 123
Groce, Jared, V 40
Groenlendings saga, see Vinland sagas
Gropius, Walter, XIV 105; XVII 90, 98
Gropper, William, XIV *37*, 84
Grosch brothers, IX 70
Groseilliers, Medart Chouart, Sieur de, I 80, 81
Gross Clinic, The, X *98*, 100
Grosse Pointe, Detroit, XIII 33
Grosz, George, XIV *60*; XV *71*
Groton, XI 120
Ground We Stand On, The, XIV 89
"Group economy," VIII 96
Group Theater, XIV 91
Groves, Leslie R., XVI 129, 130
Groves of Academe, The, XVII 103

Growing Up Absurd, XVII 107; XIX 70
Grund, Francis, IV 13, 39
Grundy, Felix, III 120
Guadalcanal, XVI 29, 30, 31, 32, 36
Guadalcanal, Battle of (1942–43), XVI 29–32, *31, 34*
Guadalupe Hidalgo, Treaty of (1848), V 93, 120, 138, 139
Guadeloupe, I 98
Guam, XI 42, 44, 71; XVI 20, 22, *22,* 110, 112
Guaranty Building, Buffalo, X 96; see also

Architecture
Guatemala, XVIII 70; see also Latin America
Guaymas, Mexico, V 83
Guerrero, Vicente, V 40
Guerrière (ship), III 123, *123*
Guerrilla warfare, Vietnam, XVIII 97, 106
Guggenheim, Peggy, XVII 91
Guggenheim fellowships, XIII 101
Guggenheim museum, XVII 99, *99*
Guichen, Admiral, II 75, 77

Guilford, Battle of (1781), II 121
Guinea, I 10
Guiteau, Charles J., X *49*
Gun Control Act (1968), XIX 127
Gun lobby, XIX 127
Gustav line, XVI *89*
Guthrie, Woody, XIV 56
Guthrie, Oklahoma, IX 93, *93*
Gwin, William M., V 139, *140*
Gymnasium (German), IV 89

Habeas corpus, VII 48, 60, 62; VIII 79
Habeas corpus act (Confederate), VII 60, 62
Habitant, I 83, 86
Habitants, company of the, I 79
Hacendados, V 32, *32,* 33
Hacienda, see *Hacendados*
Hacker, Andrew, XIX 123, 141
Haeberle, Ronald, XVIII 123
Hagerty, James C., XVII 75, 81, 86
Haggin, James Ben Ali, IX 74
Hague peace conferences, XI 77; XII 23; XIV 14
Haig, Alexander, XX 35–37, 40
Haig, Douglas Haig, 1st Earl of, XII 74, 84
"Hail, Columbia," III 97
Haile Selassie, XV 80, *81*
Hairy Ape, The, XIII 98
Haiti, I 11, *11,* 12, 13, 42; VI 38; XI 82; XV 31
Hakluyt, Richard, I 121
Haldeman, H. R., XIX 112, *112*
Hale, Nathan, II 39; III 109
Haley, Bill, XVII 137, *139*
Halfa man, XI 100
Halibut Treaty (1923), XV 46
Hall, A. Oakley, X 43
Hall, Edward, XIII 72
Hall, John H., IV 64
Hall, Samuel, IV 88
Hallam, Lewis, I 114
Halleck, Henry W., VII 28
Halpine, Charles G., VII 80
Halsey, William Frederick, XVI 26, 31, 32, 36, 37, 39, 41, 113, 114, 116, 118, 119, 120
Halstead, Murat, VI 128
Hamaguchi, Yuro, XV 55
Hamakaze (ship), XVI 126
Hamburg-Amerika line, X 57
Hamburg, South Carolina, VIII 46, 85
Hamilton, Alexander, II 104, 115; III 13;
    Constitutional convention, III 22, 24, 26, 30, 31;
    Federalist, III 30–31, 53, *53;* on Washington, III 35; on Constitution, III 38; secretary of Treasury, III 39–41, *39,* 60; political clashes, III 45; on Washington's retirement, III 46; charges against, III 46; Whiskey Rebellion, III 48; pro-British, III 49; and John Adams, III 54; elections, III 55; inspector-general, III 56; duel and death, III 80, *80;* on America, III 91; southern opposition to, III 137
Hamilton, Charles V., XIX 57
Hamilton, Henry, II 116
Hamilton, James, V 44
Hamilton, Paul, III 120
Hamilton, Thomas, IV 12
Hamlin, Hannibal, VI 128, *128*
Hammann (ship), XVI 28
Hammerstein, Oscar, XVI *64*
Hammerstein Roof Garden, XI *126*
Hammond, George, III 44
Hammond, James H., VI 24, 53
Hampton, Wade, VIII 85, 86, 129

Hampton Institute, VIII 66, 101, *107*
Hampton Roads, Virginia, VI 136; VII 24
Hancock, John, I 132; II *13, 14,* 18, 22, 23, 25; III 30, 39
Hancock, Winfield Scott, X 48
Handicapped persons, IV 114
Handlin, Oscar, XVII 107
Handy, W. C., XIII 87, *88*
Hanging Rock, Battle of (1780), II 121
Hanighen, F. C., XV 78
Hanna, Mark, XI 12, 58, 64
Hannibal & St Joseph railroad, IX 28, 39
Hapgood, Hutchins, X 68
Happy Hooligan, XI 124
Happy hunting ground, I 41; see also Indians, American
Hara, Rear-Admiral, XVI 26
Harbord, James G., XII 71, 91
Hard Day's Night, A, XIX 76
Hardin, Lil, XIII 90
Hardin, Wes, IX 64, 67
Harding, Chester, III 119
Harding, Florence Kling DeWolfe, XIII 20, 27; XV 13
Harding, Warren Gamaliel (president), XIII 10, *10,* 15, *20, 46;* 1920 convention, XIII 20; *Marion Star,* XIII 20; senator, XIII 21; presidential election, XIII 21–22; XV 11, 13, *13;* presidential qualities, XIII 22–23, *24;* cabinet, XIII 24, 26–27; death, XIII 27–28, *28, 29;* scandals, XIII 28–30; Washington Naval Conference, XV 22
Hard Labor Creek, Treaty of (1768), I 54
Hard Times, XIV 105
Hardy, Admiral, II 74
Hardy, Oliver, XIV *96,* 97
Hare, I 39; see also Indians, American
Hare, Nathan, XIX 58
Harlan, Marshall, VIII 138
Harlem, New York City, X *112;* XIII 87, 98, *98;* XIX 58, 61
Harlow, Jean, XIV 95
Harmar, General Josiah, III 44
Harmonium, XIII 98
Harold, David, VII *132, 134*
Harpers Ferry, Virginia, VI 120, 122, *122,* 125; VII 28, 29, 32
Harper's, X 102, 103; XI 124; XVII 48
Harper's New Monthly Magazine, VII 80; X 124
Harper's Weekly, IV 61; VII 78; X 43, 124
Harriman, Averell, XVI 135, 138; XVIII 17, 123
Harriman, E. H., XI 60, 80
Harrington, James, II 48
Harris, Sir Arthur Travers, XVI 88
Harris, David Golightly, VIII 55
Harris, Joel Chandler, VIII 139, *139*
Harrisburg, Pennsylvania, III 136
Harrison, Benjamin (Declaration of Independence), II *13*
Harrison, Benjamin (president), IX 93, 128, 129; X 46, 47, 51, 52–54, *52, 53*
Harrison, George, XIX 66–67, *67*
Harrison, William Henry (president), III 120, *120,*

124, *124*; IV 24, 31, *33*; V 91; VI 87
Hart, Lorenz, XIV *100*
Hart, Thomas, XVI 22
Hart, William S., XI 132
Harte, Francis Bret, V 138; IX 74, *74*
Hartford, Connecticut, I 51, 61; VII 80
Hartford convention (1814), III 88; IV 24
Hartz, Louis, XVII 108
Harvard, John, I 62
Harvard University, I 62, 113, 135, *137*; IV 89, 90, 95, 96; X 92; XI 120, 137; XIII 66; and F. D. Roosevelt, XIV 26; see also Universities and colleges
Harvest of Shame, XVII 116
Harvey, Frederick H., IX 36
Harvey, William Hope, X 133–134
Harvey Birch (ship), VII *107*
Hassam, Childe, XI *116*
Hastings Cutoff, V 63
Hat Act (1732), I 122, 125, *125*
Hatfield, Massachusetts, II 85
Hatfield-McCoy feud, XIII 132
"Hat-in-the-ring" squadron, see Ninety-fourth Squadron
"Hatrack" case, XIII 109, *109*, 111
Hats, silk, V 21; beaver, V 21, *22*, 34
Hatsukaze (ship), XVI 39
Haugen, Nils P., XI 54
Haunting of Hill House, The, XVII 103
Hauser, Sam, IX 83
Hauteval, III 56
Havana conference (1940), XV 45
Haverly, Jack, IX 82
Haverly's Mastadon minstrels, IX 82
Hawaiian islands, XI 42, 44, 71, 72, 74; XVI 20; state, XVII 86, *86*
"Hawkeye," IV 136
Hawkins, John, I *22*, 25
Hawley-Smoot Tariff Act (1930), XV 47
Hawthorne, Nathaniel, III 95, 108; IV 119, 120, 138–139, *139*, 140
Hay, John, XI 46, 71, 72, 80; XV 20
Hayate (ship), XVI 22
Hayden, Ferdinand V., IX 125, *126*
Hayden, Tom, XIX 78
Hayes, Isaac, XIX 58
Hayes, Rutherford Birchard (president), VIII 87, *87*, 88, 134; IX 31, 37; X 26, 48
Haymarket riot, X 51, 72, 77, 78–79, *79*, 80, 102
Hayne, Robert, VI *85*
Haynes, John James, IX 54
Haynesworth, Clement F., XIX 107
Hay-Pauncefote Treaty (1901), XI 72
Hays, Arthur Garfield, XIII 109
Hays, Jack, V 87
Hays, Will H., XIII 21, 81
Hays office, XIII 81
Hayward, Shephard, VI 122
Haywood, William, XI 97; XIII 12, 13
Hayworth, Rita, XVI 60, 62, *67*
Hazen, W. B., IX 85
"HD," see Doolittle, Hilda
Health insurance, XI 92
Healy, G. P. A., VI *85*, *94*
Hearst, George, IX 74
Hearst, William Randolph, X 124, *124*; XI 35, 124; XIV 29; XV 79, *79*
Heath, Sir Richard, I 73
"Heathen Chinee, The," IX 74, *74*
Hecht, Ben, XIII 109
Hecker, Isaac, IV 108, 119
Hedges, Cornelius, IX 124–125
Heenan, John C., VII 69
Heffernan, Joanna, X *98*
Heinz, Henry John, X 32
Heinze, "Fritz," IX 84
Held, John, Jr., XIII *73*, 94, *95*
Helena, Montana, IX *72*, 73, 84
Helgi, I 20
Hellcats, XVI 119
Heller, Joseph, XVII 90
Heller, Walter W., XIX 23
"Hell on wheels," IX *30*, 31
Hell Roaring Creek, IX 48
Helluland, I 19, 20
Helm, Benjamin, VII 131, 134
Helper, Hinton Rowan, V 131

Hemmingway, Eliza, IV 110
Hemingway, Ernest, XIII 67, 70–71, *70*, 95, 97; XIV 88, *88*; XV *89*; XVI 60; XVII 100
Hemphill, Robert N., VIII 55
Hendrick, I *95*
Henderson, James Pinckney, V 44, 76
Henderson, Richard, I 107
Henderson Field, Guadalcanal, XVI 31, 32
Henderson the Rain King, XVII 104
Hendrix, Jimi, XIX *77*, 78
Henie, Sonja, XIV 73
"Hennessy, Mr.," XI 31
Henri, Robert, XI 111
Henry VII (England), I 10, 21
Henry, Andrew, V 16
Henry, O. (W. S. Porter), XI 116
Henry, Patrick, I 126, 141; II 18, 24, 58; III 24, 109; VII 25
Henry, Robert Selph, VII 36
Henry Street settlement, New York City, XI 56, 100
Hepburn, Katharine, XIV 95
Hepburn Act (1906), XI 61
Herberg, Will, XVII 103
Herbert, Victor, XI 126
Hercules Corporation, XVI 54
Herd, The, IX 43
Herjolfsson, Bjarni, I 19
Herkimer, General Nicholas, II 43
Herning, James, III *94*
Herrera, Alberto, XV 38
Herrera, José de, V 69, 70
Herrick, Robert, XI 107
Herrin strike (1922), XIII 133
Herriot, Edouard, XV *29*, 72
Hersey, John, XVI 62
Herter, Christian, XVIII 79, 81; XIX 103
Herzegovina, III 18
Hesselius, Gustavus, I 116
Hessian troops, II-40, *40*, 64, *119*, 121, 128
Heston, Charlton, XVII 121
Hewes, Joseph, II 13
Heyward, Thomas, Jr., II 13
Hiawatha, IV 138
Hickok, James Butler ("Wild Bill"), IX 62, *62*, 63, 66, 67, 133
Hickory Point, Battle of (1856), VI *108*
Hicks, David, II *54*; III *92*
Hidalgo, I 42
Hidden persuaders, The, XVII 107
Hiei (ship), XVI 32
Higginson, Thomas Wentworth, VI 37; VII 96, 98
"Highbrow" culture, XIII 66, 93, 101
Higher Education Act (1965), XIX 41
Higher Learning in America, The, XI 106; XIII 67
Highland Park Plant, XI 14, 16, 17
High Noon, XVII 132, *132*
High School, IV 89; X 88; see also Education
Highway construction programs, XIII 30, 38, *39*; see also Public works; Roads
Highway Safety Act (1966), XIX 137
Hiking, XI 140
Hill, A. P., VII 32
Hill, James Jerome, IX 35, 36; XI 60
Hill, Nathaniel, IX 78
Hillers, John, IX *17*, *132*
Hillman, Sidney, XIII 136; XIV 52, 112; XVI 45
Hindenburg, Paul von, XII 21; XV 74, *76*
Hindenburg disaster, XV 93, *93*
Hindenburg line, XII 95, 96
Hine, Lewis, X *84*
Hines, John L., XII 96
Hippies, XIX 73, 74, 123
Hireling and the Slave, The, VI 57
Hirohito, Emperor, XV 55, 135, 138; XVI 131
Hiroshima, Japan, XVI 112, 126, 130, *130*
Hirota, Koki, XV 64
Hirschfield, Al, XVII *35*
Hiryu (carrier), XVI 28
Hispanicization, I 43, 44, 45, 46; see also Colonization; Conquistadores; Missionaries; Spain
Hispaniola, see Haiti
Hiss, Alger, XVII 25, 40, *40*; XVIII 47; XIX 101
Historical Reader, III 133, 134
Historiography, XI 104, 115
History and Present State of Virginia, The, I 111, 117, 139
History of New Hampshire, III 97

History of South Carolina, III 97
History of the Archbishops of Hamburg-Bremen, I 19; see also Adam of Bremen
History of the dividing line betwixt Virginia and North Carolina, I 117
History of the United States during the administrations of Jefferson and Madison, XI 104
History of Women's Suffrage, IV 125
Hitchings of Lynn, II 92
Hitler, Adolf, XII 137; XV 74, *76*, 77, *84*, 94, 95, 96, 97, 98; XVI 10, *12*, 13, 82, 101, 106, 131; see also Germany; Second World War
Hiye (carrier), XVI 111
H. L. Hunley (submarine), VII 125
Hoar, Ebenezer R., X 37, *37*, 39
Hoar, George Frisbie, X 46
Hobart, Garret, IX 82
Hobbs, Abigail, I *64*
Hobkirks Hill, Battle of (1781), II 121
Hobson, Laura L., XVII 50
Ho Chi Minh, XVIII 40, 49, 96; and Vietminh, XVIII 96–97, *98*; capture of Hanoi, XVIII 99; and Bao Dai, XVIII 99, 100; fight against French, XVIII 100, *103*; division of Vietnam, XVIII 104
Ho Chi Minh trail, XVIII *115*
Hocknell, John, IV 106
Hodges, Courtney, XVI 90, 94, 98, *104*
Hodges, Luther, XIX 19, *21*
Hoe, Richard M., X 24
Hoff, Maxie, XIII 60
Hoffman, Abbie, XIX 122, 123
Hofstadter, Richard, XIII 18; XIV 34; XVII 107; XIX 75
Hogan, Ben, XVII *130*
Hogan, Frank, XVII 120
Hogarth, William, II *50*
Hog Island, Pennsylvania, XII 106, *108*
Hokan-Siouan, I 37; see also Indians, American
Holbrook, Josiah, IV 86
HOLC, see Home Owners Loan Corporation
Holden, William W., VIII 79, 82
Holderness, Earl of, I 92
Holding companies, XI'12
Holladay, Ben, IX 28
Holland, Ben, IX 28
Hollandia, XVI 114, *114*
Holliday, Cyrus K., IX 36
Holliday, "Doc," IX 64, 66, 67
Hollister, S. E., V *21*
Holly Springs, Mississippi, VII 35
Hollywood, California, XIII 81, 82, 83, 84, 85; XIV 91, 95, *92–99*, 100; XVI 62, *67*; Hollywood Ten, XVII 38, *38*, 39; in the 1950s, XVII 132
Hollywood Ten, XVII 38, *38*, 39
Holmes, Oliver Wendell (author), IV 96, 138; VII 82
Holmes, Oliver Wendell (jurist), VII 82; XI 114, *115*; XII 111
Holtzendorft, Admiral Henning von, XII 50
Home Found, IV 137
"Home on the range," IX 133
Home Owners Loan Corporation, XIV 34, 65
Home Relief Station, XIV *59*
Homer, Winslow, IV *43*; VII *130*; VIII *62*, *68*; IX *85*; X 98, 100, *101*
Homestake Mining Company, IX 74
Homestead Act (1862), IX *85*, 86, 87, 89, 93, 94, 128; X 14
Homesteading, IV 70; VI 128; IX 56, *57*, 59, 61, 66, 87, 89, 91; XIII 135
Home to Harlem, XIII 99
Homeward Bound, IV 137
Honduras, XV 31; see also Latin America
"Honeymooners, The," XVII 128, *129*
Hong Kong, XI 71; XVI 23
Honolulu (ship), XVI *50*
Hood, John B., VII 120, *120*, 122, 124
Hooker, Joseph, VII 33, 36–37, 39, 111
Hooker, Thomas, I 61
Hooper, William, II 13
Hoover, Herbert Clark (president), education, X 92; Belgium food relief, XII 46; US food administration, XII 101, 102–103; XIII 113; secretary of commerce, XIII 26, 123; Russian food relief, XVIII 10; presidential candidate, XIII 18, 50; prohibition, XIII 53; 1928 campaign, XIII 125–127, *125*, *126*; XIV 10; president, XIII 127; XV 37; German reparations, XV 27; Manchuria question, XV 60; Great Depression, XIV 10, 11, 12,

14, 16, 19; Bonus Army, XIV 20–21; appraisal of role, XIV 22; 1932 campaign, XIV 24, 28, 30; and Negro, XIV 67; and Indians, XIV 68; and labor, XIV 109
Hoover, J. Edgar, XIII 14
Hoover commission (1946–47), XIV 128
Hoover Company, XIII 44
Hoover Dam, see Boulder Dam
"Hoover village," New York City, XIV 12
"Hoovervilles" (Great Depression), XIV 12, *12*, 14, 56
Hope, Bob, XVI *67*
"Hope, party of," II 20
Hopi, I 40, 41; IX 16; see also Indians, American
Hopkins, Esek, II 111
Hopkins, Harry, XIV 26, 32, 37, 44, 47, 120; XVI 15, 18, 44
Hopkins, Mark, IX 31, 37
Hopkins, Stephen, II *13*
Hopkinson, Francis, II *13*
Hopper, Edward, XIV 82, *82*, 84, *87*
Hopper, Hedda, XIV 91
Hopper, Isaac, VI 66
Horii, Tomitaro, XVI 32
Hornaday, William T., IX 12
Hornet (carrier), XVI 26, 31
Horse racing, X 119, *120*; XI 134, 137
Horseshoe Bend, Battle of (1814), III 128; IV 67
Hosogaya, Admiral, XVI 35
Hotham, Commodore, II 69
Hot Mikado, The, XIV 91
Hottingeur, III 56; see also XYZ affair
Hough, Franklin B., IX 129
Housatonic (ship), VII 125
House, Edward M., XII 17, 34, 35, *35*, 36, 37, 38, 40, 42, 43, 44, 48, 132
House Appropriations Committee, XVI 43
House Committee on Un-American Activities, XIX 65; formation, XIV 115; XVII 35; Alger Hiss, XVII *40*; Hollywood, XVII 38, *38*; heyday of, XVII 119; and Nixon, XIX 101; young radicals, XIX 122
"House Divided" Speech (Abraham Lincoln), VI 117, 118
House-Grey memorandum, XII 44, 46
Household appliances, XIII 44, *44*
House of the Seven Gables, The, IV 139
Housing, X 108; XI 89; XIII 33; XVI 58; Great Depression, XIV 34; US Housing Administration, XIV 128; Truman, XVII 19, *19*; Housing Act (1949), XVII 26; Kennedy, XIX 20; Civil Rights Act (1968), XIX 42
Housing Act (1949), XVII 26
Housing Act (1965), XIX 41
Houston, Sam, V 41, 42, 44, *44*, 139; VI 132, 139
Houston, Texas, IX 45; XX 49–51

Howard, Oliver Otis, VIII *53*
Howard, Sidney, XIII 98
Howard University, VIII 66; XIV 67; see also Negroes; Universities and colleges
Howe, Frederic, XI 86
Howe, Louis, XIV 26, 30
Howe, Richard, II 68, 72, *78*, 81, 106
Howe, Samuel Gridley, IV 114
Howe, Sir William, II 28, 29, 30, 32, 34, 38, 39, 40, 41, 43, *43*, 66, *78*, 95, 96, 98, 106–108, 128, 129
Howe sewing machine, IV 64
Howells, William Dean, VII 137; X 87, 100–101, 102–103, *103*; XI 106, 119
Howitzers (First World War), XII 83
Howl, XVII 101
How the Other Half Lives, X 66, 118; XI 89
"How to Make Our Ideas Clear," XI 114
"How 'Ya Gonna Keep 'Em Down On The Farm," XII *125*
Hoxie, Herbert M., IX 30
Hsuan-tsung, Emperor, XV 60
Huakutake, General, XVI 31
HUD, see Department of Housing and Urban Development
Hudson, Henry, I 28, *28*, 51
Hudson, Rock, XVII 121, *123*
Hudson Motor Company, XIII 40; see also Automobile industry
Hudson Bay, I 28
Hudson River, I 28, *28*, 65, 69
Hudson River Bracketed, XIII 72
Hudson River Landscape, XVII 97
"Hudson river school," IV 133
Hudson's Bay Company, I 81, *86*; V 14, 21, 51, 52, 53, 54, 60, 64
Hue, Vietnam, XVIII 115
Huerta, Victoriana, XII 27, 29
Huertegen, Battle of (1944), XVI 99–100
Hughes, Charles Evans, XII 46, *46*, 47; XIII 24, 123; XIV 46, 54, 109; XV 17, 20, 22, *22*, 37, 54–55
Hughes, Sir Edward, II 81
Hughes, Ensign, II 30
Hughes, James, XV 66
Hughes, John, IV 81; V 91
Hughes, Langston, XIII 99
Hughes, Rupert, XVII 38
Huguenots, I 74, 103, 113
Hull, Cordell, secretary of state, XIV 31; Lima conference, XV 37; nonintervention, XV 37; Cuba crisis, XV 38–39; Good Neighbor policy, XV 40; Chaco War, XV 43; Mexico, XV 44; Manchukuo, XV 62; on Japan in China, XV 69; on embargo, XV 72; London Economic conference, XV 73; Neutrality, XV 79, 95; Neutrality Act, XV 80;

Spanish Civil War, XV 90; Japanese-American treaty of commerce, XV 125; April 9 draft, XV 131–132; warning to Japanese, XV 134; Plan A, XV 135–136; ten point program, XV 136; Japanese declaration of war, XV 138; Roosevelt's disregard of, XVI 18; Conference of Foreign Ministers, XVI 136
Hull, Edith M., XIII 72
Hull, Isaac, III 123
Hull, William, III 122, *122*
Hull House, Chicago, XI 56
Humanism, XIII 107
Humboldt River, V 63; IX 15
Humboldt-Truckee route, V 63
Hump airlift, XVI 15, 24
Humphrey, George M., XVII 76, *77*, 86
Humphrey, Hubert (vice president), 1948 democratic convention, XVII 21; presidential candidacy, XIX 14, 44, 46, *46*, 47; vice president, XIX *38*, 40; 1968 election, XIX 72, 104–105; 1972 campaign, XIX 108
Hundred Days legislation (F. D. Roosevelt), XIV 30, 31
Hungary, XVIII 15, 23, *23*, 75, *75*
Hunkpapa Sioux, IX *109*; see also Sioux; Indians, American
Hunt, E. Howard, XIX 111, 112, 113
Hunt, Gilbert J., III 133, 134
Hunt, Richard Morris, XI 27
Hunt, Thomas, I 50, 51
Hunt, Wilson Price, V 15
Hunter, David, VII 119
Hunter, Robert, XI 86–87
Huntington, Collis P., VIII 101, 125; IX 31, 37
Huntington, Samuel, II *13*
Huon Peninsula, XVI 35
Hupmobile, XIII *42*
Hurly, Edward M., XII 106
Huron, I 53, 79, *79*; see also Indians, American
Huron, Lake, I 28
Hurst-Miller draft, XII 130
Hussey, Thomas, II 74
Hutcheson, William, XIV 112, 136
Hutchins, Robert, XIV 65
Hutchinson, Thomas, I 126; II 85
Huxley, Aldous, XIII 109
Hyakutake, General, XVI 31, 39
Hyde Park, New York, XIV 26
Hydraulic mining, V 131; IX 80, *80*; see also Mining
Hydrocarbon fuels, XI 82
Hydroelectric power, VIII 125; XIII 44, 46; XIV 35
Hydrogen bomb, XVIII 34, 53; see also Atomic bomb

I

ICBM, see Intercontinental ballistic missile
Ice Age, I 35
Iceland, I 19; XV 119; XVI 70
Iceman Cometh, The, XVII 106, *106*
Ickes, Harold, XIV 31, *31*, 32, 42, 133; XV 95; XVII 17, 22
Idaho, IX 15, 17, 73
Idaho Springs, Colorado, IX 73
"Idle Curiosity," XI 106
"If You Talk in Your Sleep, Don't Mention My Name," XI 126
"I have a Dream" (Martin Luther King), XIX 55
Illinois, origins of, I 81; statehood, III 131; industry,

IV 63; pioneering in, IV 70; 1858 election, VI 116–118, *118–119*; the Grange, IX 41; cattle, IX 43, 59; railroads, X 22, 131
Illinois (ship), XII 53
Illinois Central Railroad, IV 56; IX *24*; X 16
Illinois Crime Survey, XIII 60
Illiteracy, VIII 129; XI 120, 140; see also Education
I'll Take My Stand, XIII 72
"I love Lucy," XVII 128, *129*
Image, or what happened to the American Dream, The, XVII 104, 107
Imagism, XI 109
Imamura, General, XVI 32

Immigration Act (1920), XIII 15
Immigration Act (1924), XIII 16
Immigration Act (1965), XIX 25
Immigration and immigrants, German settlements in colonial America, I 103, 104, 105; III 93; Scotch-Irish settlements, I 104, 105; Dutch settlements, I 105; constraints on English, I 121; definition of settler, I 134–135; during War of Independence, III 16, 65; on eve of Civil War, IV 65; European, IV 72–76, 72–74, 77, 78–82, 78–79, 81–82; American fear of, VII 110; during Civil War, VII 108; between Civil War and First World War, X 56–58, 56, 58, 60, 61, 63, 64, 67, 68–72, 68, 70, 73, 74, 74; liners, X 57–58; economic pressures on, X 58; political/religious pressures on, X 58; work for immigrants, X 63; ghettos, X 66, 68–69, 66, 68; family life of, X 69; religion of, X 70, 70; culture of, X 70; mutual aid society, X 70–71; restrictions on, X 72, 74, 77; XIII 15, 16, 128; First World War, XII 123, 125; XIII 11; nativist fear of, XIII 11–12; Great Depression, XIV, 16, 70; Japanese, XV 54, 54; Kennedy, XIX 25; melting pot theory, XIX 50–51; in the 1960s, XIX 51; ethnic communities, XIX 51; 1970–80, XX 57–58, 66
Immigration Restriction League, X 74
Impeachment, VIII 35–37, 36, 79, 82; XIX 116
Impending Crisis of the South, The, VI 131
Imperial Germany and the Industrial Revolution, XI 106
Imperialism, V 22, 24, 44; IX 122; X 33–34, 70; McKinley, XI 13; Spanish-American War, XI 34, 42; social reformers, XI 43, 43; in Far East, XI 43–48, 45, 80; economic justification for, XI 71, 80, 82; in Caribbean and Central America, XI 72, 74, 78, 80; decline of, XIX 100; see also Pax Americana
Imperial Presidency, The, XIX 119, 125, 133
Imperial War Conference, XV 46
"Imperial Way faction," see Kodo-ha
Imperial Wizard, VIII 74; see also Ku Klux Klan
Impressionism, XI 111
Impressment, III 51, 112, 114, 116, 117, 120
Incandescent bulb, X 30
Ince, Thomas, XI 132
Incendiary bombs, XVI 102–103, 115
Inchon, Korea, XVIII 53, 55
Income distribution, XIII 129–130
Income tax, X 39, 132; XI 27, 28, 55, 64, 68; XII 105
Indentured labor, I 77, 102, 103
Independence, Missouri, V 55; IX 26
Independence Day, III 140; IV 13; see also Fourth of July
Independence Hall, II 57
Independence Rock, Wyoming, V 59, 60
Independent Company, I 93
Index of American Design, XIV 81, 81
India, II 79; XVI 23, 137; XVIII 65, 89, 134, 135
Indiana, Battle of Tippecanoe, III 120; statehood, III 133; Improvement Bill (1836), IV 51; early industry, IV 63; education, IV 92; IV 95
Indian Bureau, see Bureau of Indian Affairs
Indian Peace Commission, IX 114, 116
Indian Reorganization Bill, see Wheeler Act
Indian Rights Committee, IX 118
Indians, American, relations with Spaniards, I 11, 13, 14, 15, 16, 20, 26; origins of, I 33, 35, 35, 36; religion of, I 36, 39, 40, 41; pre-Columbian culture, I 37, 38, 38, 39, 39, 40, 41; language I 37, 38; relations with white settlers, I 42, 43, 44, 45, 45, 46, 47, 48, 49, 49, 50–54, 54, 55, 55, 59, 61, 62, 140; trade with whites, I 74, 77; war allies of whites, I 86, 92, 93, 94, 95, 96, 97; Pontiac's Conspiracy, I 99, 115; treaty of Sycamore Shoals, I 107; in War of Independence, II 43, 95, 120; relations with US, III 38–39, 44; war with US, III 44–45; in collusion with British, III 48, 51, 120; Louisiana Purchase, III 73; Lewis and Clark Expedition, III 74–77; in US society, III 138–139; cession treaties, III 139; cession of their lands, IV 67; Black Hawk and Seminole Wars, IV 67; slavery, VI 10; in Civil War, VIII 24; in West, IX 15–23; and cattle drives, IX 48–49; conflict with settlers, IX 101–103, 102; Indian Wars, IX 103–109, 104–110, 111–112, 111–112; federal policy, IX 112–116, 115, 116; reform movement,

IX 115–120, 115; under Hoover, XIV 68, 68; under F. D. Roosevelt, XIV 70; protest movement, XIX 62, 63
Indian Territory, IX 15, 39, 44, 45, 48, 53, 56, 92, 93, 106, 119; see also Oklahoma
Indian Warfare, IX 105
Individualism, III 134; IV 12–13, 140; IX 116, 140; X 87; XI 84; XII 113; XIII 105, 114
Indochina, XV 125, 127, 132, 134; XVI 10; XVIII 40, 96, 97; origins of US committments, XVIII 58; trusteeship, XVIII 98–99; post-war American policy towards, XVIII 99; see also Vietnam
Indo-Pakistan War (1971), XVIII 134, 135, 134
In Dubious Battle, XIV 89
Industrial alcohol, XIII 54, 56, 57
Industrial Commission, X 23
Industrial relations, XIII 136
Industrial Revolution, IV 73, 118–119; VI 43
Industrial towns, XI 12; XIII 131–132
Industrial Unions, XIV 111, 112
Industrial Valley, XIV 56
Industrial war effort, First World War, XII 67, 102, 103–109, 103, 105, 108; Second World War, XVI 44–45, 47, 48, 52–56, 49, 56
Industrial Workers of the World (IWW), XI 97–99, 98; XII 111, 118, 123; XIII 12–15, 12, 14
Industry, development in back country, I 104; early iron, I 106; regulations on colonial, I 122, 125; III 84, 85; government aid to, IV 61; labor force, IV 61–63, 62; child labor, IV 112; largest producer in world, X 10, 12; iron and steel, X 13–14, 13–14; growth of, X 14–16; organization of big business, X 16, 17, 18–20, 18–20; trusts, X 19; public reaction to, X 21–23; antitrust movement, X 22; technology, X 24–34; XIX 88, 93; immigrant labor, X 63, 64, 66; construction, XIII 35; electrification, XIII 44; crime XIII 61; in 1920s, XIII 32, 130–133, 131, 133; big corporations, XVII 114; Nixon, XIX 105; 1976–86, XX 47–51, 54; see also Corporatism; Economy
Inflation, X 134; Civil War, VII 61, 64, 66, 78, 86–87; VIII 80; post Second World War, XVII 14, 17, 19; and Korean War, XVII 29, 30; in late 1960s, XIX 105; 1976–86, XX 45–46, 51, 54
Inflationist movement, X 38, 48, 134; XIV 116
Influenza, XII 96, 121, 121
"Information Please," XIV 102
Ingalls of Lynn, II 92
I-19 (submarine), XVI 31
Inman, Henry, VI 27
Inness, George, IV 133; X 98
In Ole Virginia, VIII 140; X 104
Inönü, Ismet, XVI 19
Inouye, Daniel K., XVI 25; XVII 86
"Inquiry" group (First World War), XII 130
Installment credit, XIII 39, 41, 49, 130
Instinct of Workmanship, The, XI 106
Institute for Pacific Relations, XVII 44
Instruction Book No. 1 for Rag-Time, XI 123
Instrumentalism, XI 115
Insull, Samuel, XIII 46, 46
Insurance Companies, VIII 96
Integration, Brown v Board of Education, XVII 54; Massive Resistance, XVII 54; "Southern Manifesto," XVII 54–55; Little Rock, XVII 55–56, 56, 58; in armed forces, XVII 58; under Eisenhower, XVII 59, 60; Montgomery bus boycott, XVII 62, 63; University of Alabama, XVII 60; and Black Power, XIX 57
Intendant (New France), I 82, 83
Intercolonial congress, I 131–132
Intercontinental ballistic missile, XIX 84, 86
"Interest, party of," III 40
Interlocking system, X 28
"Interloper," I 25
Intermediate region, IX 10, 15
International Apple Shipper Association, XIV 12
International Brotherhood of Teamsters, XIV 119
International Cotton Exposition (Atlanta, 1881), VIII 121
International Harvester, X 16, 18; XIII 49, 141
International Joint Commission, XV 46
International Ladies Garment Workers Union, X 66
International law, XII 37, 38, 43, 62; XV 14, 17, 115
International Longshoremen's Association, XIV 111
International Mercantile Marine, X 18, 19
International Monetary Fund, XVIII 17, 73

International Non-Intervention Committee, XV 90
International Securities Corporation, XIII 138
Interstate Commerce, IV 50; X 22
Interstate Commerce Act (1887), X 22, 52
Interstate Commerce Commission, IX 40; X 22, 52; XI 64; XIX 52
Interstate highways, XIII 38
In the American Grain, XIII 97
In the Land of Promise, X 61
Intolerable Acts, see Coercive Acts
Intrepid (ship), III 115
Intrepid (carrier), XVI 118
Inventions, X 24–34 passim; XIII 32, 44
Investment trusts, XIII 138, 141; see also Trusts
Invisible Man, XVII 103
Invisible World, The, XIII 44
"Invitation to Learning," XIV 102
I-168 (submarine), XVI 28
Iowa, IX 10, 28, 41, 43; X 22; XI 55
"Iowa Ideal," XI 64
Iran, XVIII 26, 72; XX 31, 33–34
Iraq, XVIII 77
"Irascible Eighteen, The," XVII 94, 96
Irish Americans, emigration to US, I 104; IV 73, 73, 76, 78–79, 78; VI 110; VII 108; X 57, 63; religion, X70; in 1890s, XI 29–30; First World War, XII 32, 35–36, 46; J. F. Kennedy, XIX 13; see also Immigration
"Irish Mafia," XIX 13, 18
Iron Act (1750), I 122, 125
Iron Age, The, X 21
Iron and steel industry, IV 61; VI 120; X 13–14, 13, 14, 20, 20; XI 12, 65, 82; XIII 46; XVII 31; XIX 23; XX 44, 47–48
Iron, Blood and Profits, XV 78
"Ironbottom Sound," XVI 29, 30
Ironclads, VII 22, 24, 27, 27, 125
Iron Curtain, XVIII 24
Iron Heel, The, XI 107
Iron Molders, International Union, X 75
Iroquois, I 28, 41, 53, 54, 55, 79, 79, 80, 85; war against French, I 86, 92, 96, 97; see also Indians, American; Five nation's league
Irreconcilables, XII 140, 141
Irrigation, IX 96, 132
Irving, Washington, III 95, 96; IV 131, 135–136, 135, 137, 138, 140
Isabella (Spain), I 10, 11, 42
Isely Field, XVI III
Island Number Ten, VII 24; VII 25
Isokaze (ship), XVI 126
Isolationism, First World War, XII 23, 56, 140; XIII 107; Second World War, XV 14, 74, 77, 78–79, 90, 91, 109, 109, 112, 113, 115, 116, 122; XVI 11, 22; rejection of, XVIII 18, 32; post Vietnam, XVIII 132–133; see also Neutrality
Israel, Suez Crisis, XVIII 73; Yom Kippur War, XVIII 137, 140, 140; Six Day War, XVIII 138, 139; American support, XVIII 138–139; 1976–86, XX 27, 29, 31, 33–34, 39–40
Isthmian canal, XI 72, 74, 80
It, XIII 83
Italian-Americans, X 58, 63; XIII 10; padrone, X 63; ghettos; X 66, 66; religion, X 70; Mafia, X 72; see also Immigration and immigrants
Italy, X 58; alliance systems, XII 14, 14; First World War, XII 20, 74, 75, 130, 135–136; Ethiopian campaign, XV 80, 81, 82, 83, 84; Spanish Civil War, XV 86, 90; pact with Germany, XV 90; Tripartite pact, XV 127, 127; Second World War, XV 103; XVI 10, 17, 82–84, 82, 84, 106; peace treaty, XVIII 23
It Can't Happen Here, XIV 91
It Happened One Night, XIV 95
I Thought of Daisy, XIII 68, 92
It's a Great Life, XIII 85
Iuka, Battle of (1862), VII 33
Ivory soap, XI 23
Ivy League colleges, XI 120, 137; XIV 70
Iwabuchi, Rear-Admiral Sanji, XVI 120
"I Want to Hold your Hand," XIX 66
Iwo Jima, XVI 120, 122, 122
IWW, see Industrial Workers of the World

J

Jacales, V 30
Jackass Brandy, XIII 56
Jackson, Andrew (president), national hero III 109; war against Creeks, III 128; Battle of New Orleans, III 128, *128*, 130, 133; IV 24; Florida campaign, III 130; political philosophy, IV 16, 110; on "rotation," IV 17; bank of US, IV 18; on American destiny, IV 20; V 48; presidential candidate and president, IV *17*, 21–22, *22*, 24, 27, 28; VI 43, 86; background, IV *17*, 24, 29; "spoils system," IV 17, 27; VIII 81; "Coffin Handbill," IV *28*; action against South Carolina, IV 34; "Bank War," IV 34–35, *35*; Indian policy, IV 67; recognition of Texas, V 44; relations with Mexico, V 68
Jackson, George, XIX 58
Jackson, Helen Hunt, IX 116
Jackson, Henry, XVIII 134
Jackson, Robert, XIV 133
Jackson, Robert, XVIII 22
Jackson, Shirley, XVII 103
Jackson, Thomas J. "Stonewall," VII 10, 26, 28–29, 37, 112, *112*, 137
Jackson, William, III 22
Jackson, William Henry, V *17*; IX *11*, 125
Jacobite risings, II 10
Jacobs, George, I *64*
Jacobson, Eddie, XV 14; XVII 11
Jacoby, Oswald, XIV 70, *71*
Jagger, Mick, XIX 77
Jamaica, I 12–13, 84; II 73, 74, 77; slavery, VI 12, 22, 28, 30, 38
Jamaica Race-Track, Long Island, XI 134, 137
James I (England), I 58, 62, 72, 104, 121
James II (England), I 62, 63, 65, 66, 68, 69, 70
James, Dingus, see James, Jesse
James, Frank, VII 79; IX 67, *67*, *68*
James, Henry, III 108, *108*; VII 137; X 87, 92, 100–101, 102, *102*; XI 27, 106; XIII 66
James, Jesse, VII 79; IX 61, 67, *67*, *68*
James, William, X 92; XI 114, 119, *115*
James Monroe (ship), IV 57
James River, VII 28, 117
Jamestown, Virginia, I 49, 72, 111
Jane's Fighting ships, XII 24
Janney, Eli, X 28
Japan, I 11; and Perry, IV 57; Sino-Japanese War (1895), XI 43, 74; Russo-Japanese War, XI 48, 74, *75*, 77, *77*; imperial power, XI 74, 77, 80; threat to US, XII 24; Versaille peace conference, XII 135; Washington Naval Conference, XV 20, 22–23, 51, 53; London Naval Conference, XV 24; First World War gains, XV 51; attitude to US, XV 53–54, *54*; military clique, XV 55–56; Manchuria, XV 56, *56*, 58–60, *58*; Manchukuo, XV 60, 62, *62*; Sino-Japanese War, (1937–45), XV 64–67, *69*, 125; Anti-Comintern Pact, XV 91; abrogation of Japanese-American treaty, XV 125; swing toward extremism, XV 125; invasion of Indochina, XV 127, 132; Tripartite pact, XV 127, *127*; Dooman-Ohashi conversation, XV 130; Soviet Neutrality pact, XV 130; Pearl Harbor plan, XV 130–131, 136, 139; April 9 US-Japanese draft, XV 131; oil embargo, XV 134; September 6 Imperial conference, XV 135; "Plans A & B," XV 135–136; preparation for war, XV 138; martial spirit, XV *136*, *141*; Axis power, XVI 10; US embargoes, XVI 11; preparation for war, XVI 12; Pearl Harbor attack, XVI 12, *13*, 20, *20*, 22; Pacific strategy, XVI 20; Philippine and Malaya invasion, XVI 23; Southeast Asian advance, XVI 23, 25; Battle of Coral Sea, XVI 26–27, *26*; Midway, XVI 28, 32, *32*; Guadalcanal, XVI 29–32, *31*, *32*, *34*; Papua campaign, XVI 32, 35; Aleutian campaign, XVI 36–37, 39, *39*; Rabaul defense, XVI 41; Makin and Tarawa, XVI 108, *108*; Marianas, XVI 110–112, *110–111*; Palaus campaign, XVI 113; New Guinea, XVI 114; Tokyo fire raids, XVI 115, *115*; Leyte Gulf, XVI 116, *116*, 118–119; China Expeditionary Army, XVI 120; Iwo Jima, XVI 120, 122, *122*; Okinawa, XVI 122, 124–126, *127*; atomic bomb, XVI 126, 130, *130*; defeat, XVI 131, *131*; American occupation of, XVIII 39, 40, *40*; stabilizing anti-Soviet force, XVIII 49, 58; US-Japan Security treaty, XVIII 79
Japanese-Americans, immigrants, X 82; XI 77; evacuation, XVI 59, *59*
Japanese-American Treaty (1911), XV 125
Jarama, Battle of, (1937), XV 86
Jardine, William, XIII 123
Jarrell, Randall, XVII 107
Java, XVI 25
Java (ship), III 123
Java Sea, Battle of the (1942), XVI 25
Jay, John, II 55, 56, 130, *130*, 133, 139, 140; III 14, 16, 30, 38, *50*, 51, 52; IV 84
Jay Cooke and Company, VIII 82; X 75
Jay Treaty (1794), III *50*, 51–53, 54, 55, 112
Jazz, VI 30; XI 126; XIII 87, *88*, 90, *90*, 92–93, *92–93*; see also Music
Jazz Age, XI 14
Jazz Singer, The, XIII 85, *86*
J. C. Penney, XI 21
Jeeps, XVI 133
Jefferson Airplane, XIX 78
Jefferson, Thomas (president), III *101*; on William Penn, I 68; on rights of colonies, I 131, 139; during War of Independence, II 122; education of, I 136; Declaration of Independence, II 10, *10*, 12, 13, *13*, 14, 15, 16, 19, 20, 84, *84*; Virginia's constitution, II 20; political theorist, II 48; IV 16; on independence, II 134; Treaty of Paris, II 140; on Constitutional Convention, III 22, 24; on Constitution, III 31, 33, 41; at state department, III 39, *39*; on Indians, III 44; political clashes, III, 45; Washington's retirement, III 46; and Hamilton, III 46; pro-French, III 49, *52*; Democratic-Republican party, III 53; presidential candidate, III 54–55; vice president, III 55; Alien and Sedition Acts, III 58; 1800 election, III 60–62; president, III 64–69, *64*, 135; Louisiana Purchase, III 68–73, 74, 77; V 10, 51; party politics, III 78–80; Aaron Burr, III 80–81; slavery, III 82, 85; VI 65; protectionism, III 85; effectiveness as president, III 85; Monticello, III 87, 104; decimal system, III 91; on America, III 92; "Notes on Virginia," III 97; architect, III 101, 104; war with Tripoli, III 114, *115*; foreign policy, III 114, 117, 119; Embargo of 1807, III 117, *118*, 119; southern support, III 137; IV 16–17, 110; on extent of government, III 137; IV 16–17, 110; on land policy, IV 70; on rights of man, IV 109, 125; on Missouri Compromise, VI 86; advocate of neutrality, XII 32; on potential of America, XVII 88
Jeffries, James J., XI 134, 136
Jehovah's Witnesses, XIV 76
Jellicoe, John Rushworth Jellicoe, 1st Earl of, XII *22*
Jenkins' Ear, War of (1739), I *89*, 90
Jenkins, Robert, I 89
Jenner, William, XVII 73
Jenney, William, X 109
Jennie Gerharett, XI 107
Jersey Lightning, XIII 56
Jet fighter, XVI 101, 133
Jewel (ship), I 60
Jewish Daily Forward, X 70
Jews, immigration, X 57, 58, 63, XIII 16; Lower East side, X 68–69; anti-semitism, X 72; XIV 76; synagogues, X 119; First World War, XII 32, 58; American reaction to Hitler, XIV 70; in Soviet Union XVIII 134
Jigsaws, XIV 71
Jim Crow, VII 98; VIII 116, 138; XI 10; XVII 52; see also Negroes; Racism
Jiménez, Cha Cha, XIX 63
Jintsu (ship), XVI 31
Jitterbug, XVI *65*
Joan of Arc, X 104, *104*
Jocelyn, Simeon, VI 74
Jodi, Alfred, XVI 106; XVIII 22, *22*
Joffre, Jacques, XII 19, *19*, 71
John II (Portugal), I 10
John B. Rich Institute for Physical Education, IV *43*
"John Bull," III 108
John F. Slater Fund, VIII 132
"Johnny Reb," VII 136, 137; VIII 10
Johns Hopkins University, X 92; see also Universities and colleges
Johnson, Andrew (president), X 46; Reconstruction, VIII 18–19, *19*, 22; Freedmen's Bureau, VIII 25; 1866 elections, VIII 26, *26*; opposition to Military Reconstruction Act, VIII 30, 32–33, *31*, *32*; impeachment, VIII 35–37, *36*, *37*; see also Reconstruction

Johnson, Eastman, VI *22, 33, 46, 67*; VIII *51*; X *45*
Johnson, Henrietta, I 116
Johnson, Herschel V., VI 125, 137, 138
Johnson, Hiram W., XI 57; XII 140; XIV 30, 133; XV 16, *16*, 80
Johnson, Hugh, XIV 34, 42, 132
Johnson, Jack, XI 134, 136, *136*
Johnson, James Weldon, XIII 99
Johnson, Sir John, II 116
Johnson, "Lady Bird," XIX 137
Johnson, Louis, XV 114
Johnson, Lyndon Baines (president), Medicare, XVII 32; XIX 25, 40–41; "Southern Manifesto," XVII 55; civil rights, XVII 60, 66; Vietnam, XVIII 106, 109–110, 112, 113–114; search for peace, XVIII 115, 121, 123; Dominican Republic, XVIII 135, *135*; Six day war, XVIII 138; Senate leadership, XIX 14; vice president, XIX 15, *21*, 34; Committee on Equal Employment Opportunity, XIX 20, 34; Immigration Act, (1965), XIX 25; and Senate, XIX 27, 34; president, XIX *33*, 34; early career, XIX 33–34; Great Society, XIX 35; Supreme Court, XIX 35; tax reduction, XIX 35; poverty action, XIX 36–38, *38*; 1964 election, XIX 38, *38*, 40; federal aid to education, XIX 41; Voting Rights Act, XIX 41; environmental policy, XIX 42; Civil Rights Act, (1968), XIX 42; loss of consensus, XIX 42; Democratic dissent, XIX 43–44; appraisal of, XIX 47–48, *48*; space program, XIX 86; Baker scandal; XIX 89; alarm at power of, XIX 133

Johnson, Nelson T., XV 53
Johnson, Philip, XVII 99
Johnson, Richard M., III 120; IV 24
Johnson, Robert Underwood, IX 127, 128
Johnson, Tom, X 118
Johnson, Sir William, I 96, 97, 98, 99
Johnson Act, see Johnson Debt Default Act
Johnson Debt Default Act (1934), XV 78, 118
Johnson Space Center, XIX *88*, 89
Johnston, Albert Sidney, V 112; VII 22, 24
Johnston, Joseph Eggleston, VII 19, 24–25, 36, 66, 111, 115, 119–120, 127, 128; VIII 20
Johnstown flood, X 125, *125*
Joint Committee on Reconstruction, VIII 24, 25
Jolliet, Louis, I 81
Jolson, Al, XI 126; XIII 85, *85*
Jones, Bobby, XIII 77, *77*
Jones, Buck, XIII 82
Jones, James, XVII 103
Jones, Joe, XIV *111*
Jones, John B., VII 78
Jones, John Paul, II 79, 112–113, *112–113*, 114; III 109
Jones, Leroi, XIX 58
Jones, Samuel M., XI 52–53, *52*
Jones, Thomas ap Catesby, V 69, 118
Jones, W. E., VII 119
Jones Act (1929), XIII 53
Jonesboro, Battle of (1864), VII 120, 121
Joplin, Janis, XIX 77, 78

Joplin, Scott, XI 123; XIII 87
Jordan, XVIII 77
Jordan, David Starr, XI 45; XII 57
Joseph (Chief), IX 107, *107*, 111
Journalism, X 124; see also Newspapers
Journal of a Residence on a Georgian Plantation, VI 27
Journal of Major George Washington, The, I 93
Journal of the Times, VI 70
Joyful News Out of the New Found World, I 113
J. P. Morgan and Company, X 18; XII 36; XIV 16
Juan de Fuca Strait, V 51, 52, 53, 64, 65, 69
Judah, Theodore Dehone, IX 31, 32
Judd, Walter, XVIII 45
Judicial review, III 82
Judiciary, III 26, 38, 78–79, 81–82
Judiciary Act (1789), III 38, 79–80, 82
Judiciary Act (1801), III 78, 80
Judson, Edward Zane Carroll (Ned Buntline), IX 61, 64, 137
Juin, Alphonse, XVI 76, 88
Julesburg, Colorado, V 55
Julian, George, VIII 27, *28*
Jumonville, Sieur de, I 94, 95
June Beach, XVI 92
Junto, I 114
Jurgen, XIII 108
"Just before the Battle Mother," VII 82
Jutland, Battle of (1916), XII 21–22, *22*

K

Kaga (carrier), XVI 28
Kaiser, Edgar, XIX 23
Kajioka, Admiral, XVI 22
Kalb, Johann, Baron de, II 45
Kalinin, Mikhail, XV 73
Kalm, Peter, I 138
Kaltenborn, H. V., XIV 102
Kaltenbrunner, Ernst, XVIII 22
Kamikaze, XVI 118, 119, 125, 126
Kanagawa, Treaty of (1854), IV 57
Kane, Helen, XIII 92
Kane, Paul, IX *20*
Kane, Thomas L., V 112, *112*
Kanesville, see Council Bluffs
Kangaroo dip, XI 126
Kansas, I 17; IX 10, 92; Platte territory VI 100; Kansas-Nebraska Act, VI 100–102; Settlers, VI 105; free versus slave state, VI 105–108, *105–108*; Robert J. Walker, VI 112, 114, *114*; Lecompton constitution, VI 114; Osage, IX 17; Grange, IX 41; cattle, IX 44, 55, 56, *56*, 59; land, IX 86, 87, 89, 90, 91; agriculture, IX 94, 95, 96, 97, 99, *99*; Indian warfare, IX 102; Farmer's Alliance, X 126–127, 131; Populist party, X 136; segregation, XVII 53
Kansas Alliance, X 127, 131
Kansas City, Missouri, IX 44; X 106, 118; XIII 60
Kansas Farmer, X 85; X 136
Kansas-Nebraska Act (1854), VI 100–102, *101*, 108, 116; IX 28
Kansas Pacific Railroad, IX 39, 44, 63
Karlsefni, Thorfinn, I 20
Karras, Alex, XIX 132
Kassem, Abdul, XVIII 77, *77*
Kasserine Pass, Battle of (1943), XVI 80
Kasumi (ship), XVI 126
Kathai, Company of, I 27
Katnip Blues, XIII 93
Katyn Massacre, XVI 139
Katzenjammer Kids, XI 124

Kaufman, Irving, XVII 43
Kavanaugh, Hugh, X 132
Kavieng, XVI 41
Kazin, Alfred, XVII 108
KDKA radio station, XIII 44
Kean, Thomas, I 114
Kearney, Denis, X 82
Kearny, Stephen Watts, V 81, *81*, 82, 120, 138
Kearny (ship), XV 122, *123*; XVI 71
Kearsarge (ship), VII *107*, 126
Keaton, Buster, XIII 83, 85, *86*; XIV 96
Kee-a-kee-ka-sa-coo-way, IX *20*
Kefauver, Estes, XVII 55, 80; XIX 13
Keitel, Wilhelm, XVI *71*; XVIII 22, *22*
Keller, K. T., XVI 54
Kelley, Hall Jackson, V 53, 54
Kelley, Oliver Hudson, IX 41; X 127
Kellogg, Clara Louise, VII 82
Kellogg, Frank B., XIII 123; XV 20, *21*, 31
Kellogg, William, P., VIII 83
Kellogg-Briand Pact (1928), XV 19–20, *21*, 43, 58
Kelly, Abby, IV 122, 123
Kelly, William D., VIII 119
Kelvinator, XIII 44
Kemble, Fanny, VI 26, 27, *27*
Kennan, George F., XVIII 26
Kennebec River, II 34
Kennedy, Edward, XIX 44
Kennedy, Jacqueline Lee, XIX 12, 29, *29*, 33
Kennedy, John Fitzgerald (president), integration, XVII 60; Civil Rights Act, XVII 66; race issue, XVII 66; presidential candidate, XVII 86; oath of office, XVIII 82; foreign policy, XVIII 82–85; armaments, XVIII 84; Bay of Pigs, XVIII 86, *87*, 88; and Khrushchev, XVIII 88, *88*; Berlin wall, XVIII 88; Cuban Missile Crisis, XVIII 90–91, *91*, 92; Nassau conference, XVIII 92, *92*; European tour, XVIII 93, *93*, 94; nuclear test ban treaty, XVIII 94, *94*; and Ngo Dinh Diem, XVIII 105; Vietnam inheritance, XVIII 106, 107; popularity,

XIX 10, *10*; early career, XIX 10, 12, *12*;
McCarthyism, XIX 12, 13; Stevenson, XIX 13; bid
for presidency, XIX 13–15, *17*; 1960 election, XIX
15, *17*; cabinet, XIX 19, *21*; inauguration, XIX 19,
20, *20*; civil rights, XIX 20–22, *22*; US steel, XIX
23; space age, XIX 23–25, *24*, 86; medicare, XIX
25; immigration, XIX 25; education, XIX 25;
difficulties with Congress, XIX 25, 27; personal
style, XIX 27, *27*, 29, *29*; press relations, XIX 29;
assassination, XIX 29–31, *30, 31*; "missile gap,"
XIX 84; economy, XIX 92–93
Kennedy, Joseph P., XIII 140, XV 112, *112*; XIX 10
Kennedy, Robert, Cuban Missile Crisis, XVIII 90, 91;
Vietnam, XVIII 130; adviser to J. F. Kennedy, XIX
10, 13; attorney general, XIX 19, *21*; civil rights,
XIX 21; antiwar movement, XIX 43; campaign for
presidency, XIX 44, *44*; assassination, XIX 44, *45*
Kennedy Space Center, XIX 88–89, *88*
Kennesaw Mountain, Battle of (1864), VII 120
Kenney, George Churchill, XVI 35, 41, 119
Kensington Stone, I 20
Kent State University, XIX 65, *78*
Kentucke, I 107
Kentucky, origins of, I 55, 107, *107*; III 70;
Transylvania Company, I 106; population, III 16;
Indian attacks, III 44; presidential election, III 54;
statehood, III 133; V 139; tobacco, VI 44;
secession, VII 16; cattle, IX 43; school segregation,
XVII 52
Kentucky Derby, XI 137
Kentucky Resolution, III 58
Kentucky rifle, I 104, 113; II *31*
Keppel, Admiral, II 29
Keppler, Joseph, X *83*
Ker, William Balfour, XI *84*
Kern, Jerome, XIII 92
Kernstown, Battle of (1862), VII 26
Kerouse, Jack, XVII 134, *134*, 136
Kettle Hill, Battle of, see San Juan Hill
Key, David, X 48
Key, Francis Scott, III 128; VI 75
Keyes, Sir Roger, XV 20
Keynes, John Maynard, XIV 37; XV 29, 73; XIX 93
Keyserling, Leon, XVII 25
"Keystone Cops," XI *133*
Key to Uncle Tom's Cabin, A, VI 98
Khomeini, Ayatollah, XX 31
Khrushchev, Nikita, visit to US, XVII 86; XVIII 79,
79; accession to power, XVIII 62; 1958 Middle
East crisis, XVIII 77; U-2 affair, XVIII 80–81; and
Kennedy, XVIII 88, *88*; Cuban Missile Crisis, XVIII
91, 92; on wars of national liberation, XVIII 130
Kicking Bear (Chief), IX *108, 112*
Kicking Bird, IX *16*
Kidd, William, I 87

Kidder, Peabody, X 18
Kieft, Willem, I 51
Kikusui (ship), XVI 125
Killens, John O., XIX 58
"Kill the Bone," IX *17*
Kilrain, Jake, X *120*
Kimball, Heber C., V 99
Kim Il Sung, XVIII 50
Kimmel, Husband E., XV 138
Kindergarten, IV 88–89; see also Education
Kindred Spirits, IV 133, *135*
Kinetoscope, XI 132; see also Movies
King, Billie Jean, XIX *130*
King, Clarence, XI 104
King, Edward, VIII 139, 140
King, Ernest J., XVI 14, 52, 108, 113, 120; XVIII 39
King, Martin Luther, Jr , XVII *61*; XIX 52; on
antiracial laws, XVII 61–62; Montgomery bus
boycott, XVII 62, *63*, 64; and John F. Kennedy,
XIX 21; march on Washington, XIX 36, 55, *55*; and
northern racism, XIX 43; "I Have a Dream," XIX
55; assassination, XIX 56; see also Negroes
King, Rufus, III 22, *23*
King, William Lyon Mackenzie, XV 47, 49, *49*
King George's War (1744), I 90, 91
King of Kings, The, XIII 82
"King" Oliver's Creole Jazz band, XIII 87, *90*
King Philip's War (1675–76), I 52, 61
King's College, see Columbia University
King's Mountain, Battle of (1780), II 103, 121
King William's War (1689), I 86
Kinkaid, Thomas Cassin, XVI 31, *36*, 116
Kinnersley, Ebenezer, I 114
Kinugasa (ship), XVI 32
Kiowa, IX 15, *16*, 20, 101, 102, 106, *119*; see also
Indians, American
Kipling, Rudyard, XII 58
Kirishima (ship), XVI 32
Kirk, Russell, XVII 108
Kisaragi (ship), XVI 22
Kishi, Nobusuke, XVIII 79
Kiska Island, XVI 27, 35
Kissinger, Henry, and Vietnam, XVIII 123, 124;
XIX 119; China, XVIII 132, *133*; secretary of state,
XVIII 132, 140; foreign policy philosophy, XVIII
134; Indo-Pakistan War, XVIII 134; Chile, XVIII
136; Middle East, XVIII 137, *139*, 140; XX 24–27
Kitchen at Mount Vernon, VI *22*
Kitchin, Claude, XII 114, 116
Kivas, I 41
"K-K-K-Katy," XII *125*
Klamaths, IX 107; see also Indians, American
Klamath Tribal Incorporation Bill, XIV 68
Kleindienst, Richard, XIX 125
Kline, Franz, XVII 94, 97

Kluge, Guenther von, XVI 95
Knapp, Seaman A., VIII 126
Knarr, I *19*
Knights of Labor, X 72, 77, 80, 81, 82, 84; XI 94; see
also Labor unions
Knights of Pythias, VIII 98
Knights of the White Camellia, VIII 74; XV 110
Knopf, Alfred A., XIII 109
Knowland, William F., XVII 75, 78, 86; XVIII 47, 48,
58
Know-Nothing party, IV 81–82, *81*; VI 97, 102, 104,
110, *111*, 128; IX 61
Knox, Frank, XV 114, *114*; XVI 14
Knox, Henry, II 32, 128; III 39, *39*, 46
Knox, Philander Chase, XI 60, 80
Knudsen, William, XVI 45, 54
Kochertal, Joseph, I 103
Kodak camera, X 33, *34*; XI 23, 140
Kodo-ha, XV 126
Koga, Admiral Mineichi, XVI 39
Kohlberg, Alfred, XVIII 47
Kolombangara, XVI 36
Kondo, Vice-Admiral, XVI 31
Konoye, Fumimaro, XV 125, 132, 134, 135
Korea, XI 74, 77; XVIII 49, 50, 112; see also Korean
War
Korean War (1950–53), XVII 29, 30, 31, 32, 44, 71,
75, 79, 90; XVIII 34, 36, 37, *53*; origins of, XVIII
49–50; outbreak of, XVIII 50; and Truman, XVIII
51; American offensive, XVIII 53, *55, 56*; and
Chinese, XVIII 53, 55; MacArthur dismissed,
XVIII 58; armistice, XVIII 64
Koror Island, XVI 113
Kosciusko, Tadeusz Andrzej, II 45, *84*
Kramer, Alvin D., XV 132
Krazy Kat Ballet, XIII 93
Kriemhilde Stelling, see Hindenburg line
Krimmel, John Lewis, III 104
Kuhn, Fritz, XV 110, *110*
Kühn, Justus Englehardt, I 116
Kuhn, Loeb & Co., X 18
Ku Klux Act, VIII 79
Ku Klux Klan, VIII 74, *74*, 76, *76*, 78–79, 82, 83; XII
122; XIII 11, 16–17, *17*, 111, 124; XVII 11
Kundt, Hans, XV 40; 41, *41*
Kuomintang, XV 51, 53; XVI 10, 15, 18; XVIII 42,
44; see also China
Kuribayashi, Lieutenant-General Tadamichi, XVI 120
Kurita, Vice-Admiral Takeo, XVI 116, 118
Kursk, Battle of (1943), XVI 84
Kurusu, Saburo, XV 136
Kwajalein Atoll, XVI 22, 108
Kwakiutl Indians, I 40; see also Indians, American
Kwantung Army, XV 55, 56, 60
Ky, Nguyen Cao, XVIII 109

La Bajada Hill, V 31
Laboratory school, XI 115
Labor day, XI 126
Labor force, shortage in early nineteenth century, IV
39, 62; industrial work force, IV 61–63;
workingmen's movement, IV 110–112; immigrant,
X 63, *64*, 66; tenement work, XI 91–92;
unorganized, XI 99; women and blacks, XI 100;
see also Labor unions
Labor legislation, XI 91–92, 120; XII 105; XIV 49;
XVII 18–19
Labor movement, see Labor unions
Labor standards board, XII 105
Labor unions, origins, IV 110–112, *111, 112*; in
mining, IX 83; immigrants, X 66, 72, 74, 82;
W. H. Sylvis, X 75; Knights of Labor, X 72, 77; AFL,

X 74, 80–81, 94, 96; and politics, X 81–82;
pensions, X 84; social legislation, X 83–85; trusts,
XI 12–13, 68; goal of, XI 94, 96; hostility to, XI
96–97; IWW, XI 97–99; women and blacks, XI
100; First World War, XII 105; crime, XIII 61; in
1920s, XIII 136–137; Wagner Act, XIV 49; and
F. D. Roosevelt, XIV 51–52; and New Deal, XIV
109; strike, XIV 111; craft versus industrial, XIV
111–112; corruption, XIV 114; communism in,
XIV 115; and Truman, XVII 15, 17; Taft-Hartley
Bill, XVII 18–19; farm labor conferences, XVII 25;
steel strikes (1952), XVII 31; and John F.
Kennedy, XIX 23; see also Strikes
Labrador, I 18, 19, 20
Lachine, I 22, 86
La Cañada, Battle of (1847), V 83

Lachaise, Gaston, XIV 88
Laconia, (ship), XII 51–52, *52*
Lacrosse, I 41; IX 22
Ladies Home Journal, XI 23, 31, 124
Lady Be Good, XIII 92
Lae, New Guinea, XVI 35
La Farge, John, XI 104
Lafayette, Marie Joseph Paul, Marquis de, II 45, 108, *110*, 122, 128, 138; III 44; IV *31*
Lafayette Escadrille, XII 85
Laffer, Arthur, XX 46
La Follette, Robert, XI 48, 54–55, *55*, 57, 61, 65; XII 56, *56*, 57, 113, 114, 115, 116, 127; XIII 18, 23, 29, 124; XIV 30
La Follette, Robert, Jr, XVII 37
La Follette Eight Hour Act (1915), XI 68
La Follette Seaman's Act (1915), XI 68
Laton, Thomy, VIII 96
La Guardia, Fiorello H., XIV 72–73; XV 94
Laird Brothers, VII 107, 108
Laissez-faire, VIII 129; X 87, 98; XI 84
Lake, Agnes Thatcher, IX 62
Lake George, Battle of (1757), I *96*
Lake Mohonk conferences, IX 118
Lalemant, Gabriel, I *80*
Lamar, Lucius Quintus Cincinnatus, VIII 45, 129
LaMare, Chester, XIII 61
Lamb, A. A., VIII *17*; XI *58*
"Lambeth Walk," XIV 72
Lame-duck amendment, see Twentieth amendment
Lamson, Edward Henry, X *88*
"Lancasterian" method, see "Monitorial" method
Land Act (1785), IV 92
Land Act (1796), IV 70
Land-grant colleges, IV 94, 96; X 92
Land-grants, IX 29, 32, 35, 36, 38–40
Landis, Kenesaw Mountain, XIII 77
Land monopoly, X 136–137
Land of Gold: Reality versus Fiction, The, V 131
Landon, Alfred, XIV 52
Land redistribution, VIII 51–52
Lane, Charles, IV 119
Lane, Frankie, XVII 137
Lane, Jim, VII 79
Lane, Joseph, VI 125
Lane, Lunsford, VI 24
Lane, Ralph, I 48
Lane Theological School, VI 75
Langdon, Harry, XIII 83, 85
Lange, Dorothea, XIV 56, *129, 131*
Langford, Nathaniel P., IX 124–125
Lanier, Sidney, VII 128; VIII 126
L'Anse-aux-Meadows, New Foundland, I 20, *20*
Lansing, John, III 22, 30
Lansing, Robert, XII 33–34, *34*, 35, 36, 37, 38, 40, 41, 42, 43
Laos, XVIII 64, 88, 96, 106, 110
La Paz, Mexico, V 83
La Plata, Colorado, IX 73
Lapointe, Ernest, XV 46
Lapowinsa (Chief), I *54*
"La Raza," XIX 62
Lardner, Ring, XIII 94–95
Lardner, Ring, Jr, XVII 38, *38*
Larkin, Thomas O., V 21, 116, 118
La Salle, René, Sieur de, I 81, *81*, 93
Last Chance Gulch, IX *72*, 73
Last of the Mohicans, The, IV 137
Las Vegas, V 106
Latin America, liberation from Spanish, III 131; trade expansion, XI 46; US policy between wars, XII 26; XV 31–44; US policy post Second World War, XVIII 69–70; Alliance for Progress, XVIII 85; Dominican Republic, XVIII 135, *135*
Latter-day Saints, Church of Jesus Christ of (Mormons), I 135; III 109; IV 105; V 81, 95, *95*, 97–99, *98*, *100–101*, 101–111; IX 26; see also Religion
Lattimore, Owen, XVII 44, *44*
Lattre de Tassigny, Jean de, XVI 95, *95*
Latvia, XII 136; XV 101, 138; XVIII 13
Laud, Archbishop William, I 60, 61, 62, 63
Laudonnière, René de, I 23
"Laugh In," XIX 76
Laughton, Charles, XIV 95
Laurel, José, XVI 23
Laurel, Stan, XIV *96*, 97

Laurens, Henry, I 104, 132; II 130, *130, 132*, 140
Lausanne conference (1932), XV 27, *29*
Laval, François de Montmorency, I 82
Laval, Pierre, XV 83
Lavery, Emmet, XVII 38
Law, James, X *91*
Law, I 126, 127, 135; training, IV 95, 96; slavery, VI 18–19, 21, 92, 94; legal philosophy, XI 114; and moralism, XIII 52; see also Courts
"Law of the jungle," see Darwinism and Social Darwinism
Lawrence, Kansas, VI 105, 106; VII 79, *79*
Lawrence, Massachusetts, X 112; XI 98
Lawson, Ernest, XI 111
Lawson, John Howard, XIII 98; XVII 38, *38*
Lazarus, Emma, X 74
Lazarus Laughed, XIII 98
LCI (landing craft-industry), XVI *80*, 82
LCT (landing craft-tanks), XVI 82
Lead, S. D., IX 74
Leadville, Colorado, IX 38, 73, 77, 83
League of Armed Neutrality, II 78, 79
League of Nations, III 129, 134, 135, 136, 139–141; XIII 21, 22; XV 11, 13, 14, 16, 17, 43, *49*, 58, 59, 62, 69, 72, 80, 83, 84
League of Nations Convenant, XV 54, 58
League of Nations Non-Partisan Association, XV 17
League of the Three Emperors (*Dreikaiserbund*), XII 13
League of Women Voters, XV 19
Leahy, William Daniel, XV 129, *130*; XVI 17; XVIII 39
Lease, Mary, X 136
Leatherstocking, IX 133, 134–135, *134*
"Leatherstocking" novels, IV 136, 137, 138; IX 134
"Leave it to Beaver," XVII 178
Leaves of Grass, IV 131, 140
Leaving the Manor House, VIII *141*
Lebanon, XVIII 75, 77, *77*; XX 33, 40; see also Middle East
Leclerc, General Jacques, XVI 97
Lecompton constitution, VI 114, 116, 117
Le Corbusier, XVII *98*
Ledyard, John, V 10
Lee, Ann, I 135; IV 104, 106–107
Lee, Arthur, II 135
Lee, Charles, II 26, 33, 38, 39, 98, 114
Lee, Daniel, V 54
Lee, Don E., XIX 58
Lee, Ezra, II 35
Lee, "Light-Horse Harry," II 32, 114, 121; VII 26
Lee, Jason, V 54, *55*, 55
Lee, Peggy, XVII 137
Lee, Richard Henry, II 12, *13, 14*, 40, 109; III 33
Lee, Robert Edward, I *111*; V 87; VI 122; VII 10, 26, 63, 66, 99, 110, 112, *112*, 113, *127*, 137; VIII 10, 20, *20*; Seven Day's campaign, VII 28; Second Bull Run, VII *28*, 29, invasion of North, VII 29; Antietam, VII 32; Fredericksburg, VII 33, *33*; Chancellorsville, VIII 36–37; second invasion of North, VII 37, 39–40; Gettysburg, VII 40–41; Wilderness, VII 116–117; Petersburg, VII 117, 128; Appomattox, VII 128; see also Civil War; Confederate States of America
Leese, Sir Oliver, XVI 86
Leete, Doctor, X 137
Leeward Islands, II 73, 74, 77
Left-all-alone again blues, XIII 92
Left Hand (Chief), IX 102
Legal Defense and Educational Fund (NAACP), XVII 53
"Legend of the Sleepy Hollow," III 95, *96*
Leger, Fernand, XVII 90
Leggett, William, IV 110
Legion of Merit, XVI *79*
Legislative Reference and Research Group, XI 55
Legislatures, state, II 51, 54–56; III 13; federal, II 58, 60; X 37, 46
Legree, Simon, VI 98
Lehar, Franz, XI 126
Lehman, Herbert, XIV 136
Leif (son of Eirik the red), I 19
Leigh, Janet, XVII 121, *123*
Leigh, Vivien, XIV *96*
Leigh-Mallory, Sir Trafford, XVI *90*
Leister, Jacob, I 70
Leisure, XI 18, 122, 123; Progressive era, XI 126–140

passim; new era, XIII 49; 1950s, XVII 127, 128
Lemay, Curtis, XVI 115; XIX 47
Lemhi Pass, III 76
Lemley, Harry J., XVII 58
Le Moyne, Jacques, I *26*
Lend-Lease, XVI 11, *14*, 44, 135, 140; XVIII 14
Lend-Lease Act (1941), XV *116*, 118–119, 121; XVI 44, 70
L'Enfant, Pierre Charles, III 41, *42*, 135; XI 118; see also Washington, DC
Lennon, John, XIX 66–67, *67*, 69
Lenz, Sidney, XIV 70, *71*
Leo XIII, X *83*
León, Juan Ponce de, see Ponce de León
Leopard, III 117
Leopold, Nathan, XIII 72, 114, *115*
Lerner, Max, XVII 108
Leslie's Illustrated Weekly, IV 121
Lesser Antilles, XI 78
Lester, Julius, XIX 57
Let 'em eat cake, XIII 92
Leticia, Colombia, XV 40, *42*, 43
Letters from an American Farmer, I 137, 140; III 110
Letters from Illinois, IV 74
Letters-patent, I 21, 28, 48
"Letter to American teachers of History," XI 105
Let Us Now Praise Famous Men, XIV 56
Leuchtenberg, William, XIV 34
Leutze, Emanuel, V *11*
Lever Act (1917), XII 102
Leviathan (ship), XII 68
Levin, Harry, XVII 107
Levinson, Salmon D., XV 17
"Levittowns," XVII 110–111
Lewelling, L. D., IX 96
Lewis, Dixon H., V 50
Lewis, Francis, II *13*
Lewis, John L., United Mineworkers, XIII 132, 133, 136; XIV 109; CIO, XIV 111–112, 114, 136; and Truman, XVII 17, *17*
Lewis, Meriwether, III 73, 74, *74*, 75, 77; see also Lewis and Clark expedition
Lewis, R. H., XII 88
Lewis, Ross, XVII *84*
Lewis, R. W. B., XVII 107
Lewis, Sinclair, XIII 66, *66*, 68, 71, 74, 95, 108; XIV 91
Lewis, William H., VIII 107, 113
Lewis and Clark expedition, III 73, 74–77, *74–77*; V 10, 51, 53
Lexington, Battle of (1775), II 18, 22, 24, *28*, 89, 92
Lexington, Kentucky, II 92
Lexington, Massachusetts, I 133, 134
Lexington (carrier), XVI 27, *29*, 118
Leyte Gulf, Battle of (1944), XVI *116*, *116*, 118–119
"Liaison conference" (Japan), XV 126, 132, 135
Libby, Frederick J., XV 17
Liberal Republican party, VIII 81; X 21, 39–40
Liberal Tradition in America, The, XVII 108
Liberator, VI 61, 71, 72
Liberators (B-24s), XVI 85
Liberia, VI 65
Liberty Bell, II *57*; III 108
"Liberty Bands," XII 105, 116, *116–117*, 125; XV 28
Liberty League, XIV 40, 52
Liberty party, IV 31; VI 82, 87, 89, *89*; XIV 53
Liberty ships, XVI 48, *49*, 52
Libraries, IV 87; X 92, 124; XIII 49
Library of Congress, X 92
Liddy, G. Gordon, XIX 111
Liebling, A. J., XVIII 81
Lie Down in Darkness, XVII 103
Lien system, see Crop lien system
Life, XI 126; XII *127*; XIII 96
Life (post-1935), XIV 105
"Life in America" series, XIV 34
Life of Emile Zola, The, XIV 95
Liggett, Hunter, XII 92, 96, 98
Lighting, street, X 106, 108, 110
Lights of New York, The, XIII 85
Lily, IV 123
Lima Conference of American States (1938), XV 37, 40
Limericks, XI 126
Linares, Mexico, V 75
Lincoln, Abraham (president), pioneer family, IV 71; on Mexican War, V 72; admired by

Negroes, VI 38; abolition of slavery in DC, VI 91; VII 92; and H. B. Stowe, VI 98; Whig leader, VI 102, 104; 1858 election, VI 116–118, *118–119*; "House Divided" speech, VI 117, 118; presidential candidate, VI *126*, 128, 129, *129*, 131; Crittenden proposals, VI 135; VII 14; president-elect, VII 12; on secession, VII 14; first inauguration, VII *15*, 16; Fort Sumter, VII 18; Black Hawk war, VII 19; Seven Day's campaign, VII 28; call for volunteers, VII *17*, 18, 70; emancipation, VI 117–118; VII 46, 90–92; Emancipation Proclamation, VII 32, 51, 92, 94, *94*; and McClellan, VII 32, *32*; qualities as president, VII 46; X 46; on Constitution, VI 118; VII 46, 89; politician, VII 46, 48; legislative activity, VII 51; reelected, VII 51–52, *52*; second inauguration, VII 130; Gettysburg address, VII 54; war aims, VII 89–90, 140–141; black colonization, VII 94–95; black enlistment, VII 96, 98; foreign policy, VII 100; and Grant, VII 113, 115; military leadership, VII 136–137; assassination, VII 130, 133, *133*; X 28–29; and reconstruction, VIII 16, 18

Lincoln, Benjamin, II 78, 120, 126, *126*
Lincoln, Robert Todd, VIII 108
Lincoln, Thomas, IV 71
Lincoln County war, IX 66–67
Lincoln highway, XIII *39*
Lindbergh, Charles A., XIII 77, 80, *80*; XV 109, *119 t*
Lindeman, F. A., XVI 128
Lindsay, John, XIX 136
Lindsay, Nicholas Vachel, XI 109, *111*; XIII 98
"Liners," IV 57; X 57–58
Lingayen Gulf, XVI 120
Lingg, Louis, X 78
Linn, Lewis F., V 63
Lion, XII 22
Lippmann, Walter, XI 84, 116; XIII 18, 114; XIV 102; XVI 59; XVIII 135; XIX 10, 110
Lippold, Richard, XVII 97
Lipset, Seymour Martin, XVII 107–108
Lipton, Seymour, XVII 97
Lisbon, Portugal, I 10
Literacy tests, VIII 135; X 74; XII 125
Literary Digest, XIV 105
Literacy guild, XIII 73
Literature, colonial, I 117, *117*, 136, 137; early republic, III 95, *96*; mid-nineteenth century, IV 129–131, *129*, 130, 135–141, *135–137*, *139–141*; Progressive era, XI 106–109; 1920s, XIII 66–68, *66–67*, *69*, 70–73, 108–109; Great Depression, XIV 80, 81, 88–91, *88–90*; 1950s, XVII 100; Black Mountain, XVII, 101; popular fiction, XVII 103; novelists' dilemma, XVII 104; tradition, XVII 105; and theater, XVII 105–107; sociological, XVII 107–108; black confessional, XIX 58; effect of rock culture on, XIX 78; in 1980s, XX 75–78, 80
Lithuania, XII 136; XV 101; XVI 138; XVIII 13
Lithuanian-Americans, X 63
Little, A. D., XIII 130
Little, Frank, XIII 12, *12*
Little, Lou, XIV 75
Little Belt, III 120
Little Big Horn, Battle of (1876), IX 107, 108–109, *108–109*
Little Big Man, XIX 128, *128*
"Little Boy," XVI *129*, 130
Little Caesar, XIV 91, *94*
"Little Egypt," XIII 133
Little Entente, XV 19
Little Orphan Annie, XVI 62
Little Lord Fauntleroy, X 104
Little Richard, XVII 137
Little Rock, Arkansas, XVII 55–56, *56*, 58
Little Round Top, Gettysburg, VII 40
"Little steel" dispute (1937), XIV 112, *112*
Little White Girl: Symphony in White No. 2, X *98*
Little Women, IV 88
Litvinov, Maksim, XV 72, 73–74
Lively Arts, The, XIII 100
Liver is the Cock's Comb, The, XVII *92*
Liverpool, England, VII 107; VIII 48
"Living Newspaper, The," XIV 91
Livingston, Philip, II *13*
Livingston, Robert H., III 51, 52, 70
Livingston, Robert L., I 101, 104; II 12, *13*
Livingston, Robert R., II 55, 98, 108, 133, 140; III

35; IV 50
Lloyd, Harold, XIII 83, 85, *86*
Lloyd, Henry Demarest, X 21, 22, 77, 137–138, *137*, 141
Lloyd George, David, XII 49, *49*, 130, 131, 134, *134*, 136
Lobbying, AFL, X 81; rules, XI 56; XIII 23
"Lobsters," II 32
Locarno pact (1925), XV 84
Locke, Alain, XIII 99
Locke, John, I 74, *75*; II 12, 48, 84; XI 84
Lockport, New York, IV 52, *53*
Locomotive, electric, X 30
Lodge, Henry Cabot, VIII 135; XI 71; XII 55, 114, 126, 135, *135*, 140, 141; XIII 121
Lodge, Henry Cabot, Jr, Eisenhower man, XVII 73; Vietnam, XVIII 108, 123; and John F. Kennedy, XIX 12
Lodge Bill, see Federal Elections Bill
Loeb, Richard, XIII 72, 114, *115*
Loewe, D. E., XI 97
Logan, James, I 117
Log Cabin campaign (1840), IV 31, *33*, 34
"Log college," I 113
Logstown, I 92
Loks Land, I 27
Lombard, Carole, XIV 95
London, Jack, X 97, 103; XI 106, 107, *109*, 124; XIII 52
London, Meyer, XII 56
London, Treaty of (1915), XII 136
London Company, I 49, 71
London Economic conference (1933), XV 71, 72–73
London Naval conference (1930), XV 24, *24*
London Naval conference (1935), XV 84
Lonely Crowd, The, XVII 107, 117
"Lone Ranger, The," XIV 102
Lone Star republic, V 44
Long, Huey, XIV 41, 42–43, *43*, 53
Long, Stephen H., V 13–14, *14*; IX 11
Long day's Journey into Night, XVII 106
Longfellow, Henry Wadsworth, IV 129, *129*, 138; XI 106
Longhorns, V 34; IX 43, *43*, 44, 46–47; see also Cattle
Long Island, I 65
Long Island, Battle of (1776), II 34, *36*, 98
Long Island Sound, I 51
"Long lance" torpedoes, XVI 36
Long Land Pattern musket, II *31*, *119*
Long March (China), XVII 103
Longstreet, James, VII 36, 40, 111; VIII 20, *20*
"Long terms," XVI 82
"Long tom," V 127, *127*
Look Homeward, Angel, XIII 98; XIV 89
Look Out Whitey! Black Power's Gon' Get Your Momma, XIX 57
Looking Backward, X 21, 102, 137
Lookout Mountain-Missionary Ridge campaign, VII *110*, 111
"Loran" (long range aid to navigation), XVI 57
Loray Mill strike (1929), XIII 132
Lord Baltimore shilling, I *75*
Lord Dunmore's war (1774), 155
Lorentz, Pare, XIV 91
Lorimer, George Horace, XI 124
Los Angeles, California, V 30, 119–120; IX 26; XIII 33
Lost Cause, VIII 129, 140
Lost Cause, The, VIII 140
"Lost generation," XIII 18, 71
Lothian, Philip Henry Kerr, 11th Marquess of, XV 125
Lottery, The, XVII 103
Louis XIV (France), I 79, 80, 86, 88, 103
Louis XV (France), II 62
Louis, Joe, XIV 73, *74*, 75; XVI 45, 62
Louisbourg, Nova Scotia, I 90, *90*, 91, 97
Louisiana, I 46; II 139; III 39; Louisiana Purchase, III 68–73; statehood, III 133; settlement of, V 48; slavery, VI 11, 22; plantation owners, VI 40; cotton, VI 44; sugar, VI *52*; VIII 126; anti-abolition acts, VI 75; secession convention, VI 139; secession ordinance, VI *138*, 139; black codes, VIII 15; racial discrimination, VIII 40; and Reconstruction, VIII 83–84, 85, 86; "grandfather" clause, VIII 108, 135; lottery, VIII 129; segregation, VIII 138; XVII 52; G. W. Cable,

VIII 140; southern alliance, X 127; Huey Long, XIV 42–43; see also South, the
"Louisianna Belle," VI 47
Louisiana lottery, VIII 129
Louisiana Purchase, III 68–73, *70*, 114, 117, 130, 134; V 48, 51; VI 86, 100
Louisiana Purchase Centennial Exposition (1904), XI 128, *128*
Louisville, Kentucky, VI 42, 51, *58*; VII 33
Louisville and Nashville Railroad, VIII 42; see also Railroads
Louvain, burning of, XII 46
Lovejoy, Elijah, VI 78, *79*
Lovell, James, II 133
Love Parade, The, XIII 85
Lovett, Robert, XIX 19
Loving, Oliver, IX 45
Low, Seth, XI 52, *52*
"Lowbrow" culture, XIII 66, 93
Lowden, Frank O., XIII 18
Lowell, A. L., XIII *18*
Lowell, Amy, XI 109, *111*
Lowell, Charles Russell, IX 39
Lowell, Francis, III 85
Lowell, James Russell, IV 129, *129*, 138
Lowell, Robert, XVII 100, 107
Lowell, Massachusetts, X 63
Lowell Institute, IV 87
Lowell Offering, IV 62, *62*
Lowenstein, Allard, XIX 43
Lower classes, XI 29–30
Lower Falls on the Yellowstone, IX *125*
Lowndes, William, III 121
Loy, Myrna, XIV 95
Loyalists (War of Independence), II 34, 64, 78; 87, 90, 95, 98, 101, 102, 103, 112, 115, 128, 130, 140; III 12, 14, 90; see also "Tories"
LST (landing ship-tanks), XVI 82, *86*
Lucas, A. F., VIII 125
Lucas, John P., XVI 88
Luce, Clare Boothe, XVIII 45
Luce, Henry, XIV 105; XVIII 42, 45
"Luck and Pluck," X 97
Lucy, Autherine, XVII 59, *59*, 60
"Lucy in the Sky with Diamonds," XIX 78
Luden, W. J., XIII 38
Ludendorff, Erich von, XII 49, 98
Ludendorff Bridge, XVI 103
Ludlow, Louis, XV 94
Lufbery, Raoul, XII 85
Luftwaffe, XV *103*; XVI 10, 85, 90
Luke, Frank, XII 85
Luks, George, XI 111
Lumbering, VIII 124–125; IX 83, 84; X *15*
Lumber shovers union, X 78
Lundy, Benjamin, VI 68, *70*
Lundy's Lane, Battle of (1813), III 126
Lusitania (ship), XII 38, *39*, 40, *40*, 41, *124*
Luxembourg, XII 18; XV 103; XVIII 32
Luzerne, Chevalier de la, II 140
Luzon, XVI 119, 120, 122
Lycée (French), IV 89
"Lyceum" movement, IV 86–87, *87*, 88
Lynch, John Roy, VIII 45, 46
Lynch, Thomas, Jr, II *13*
Lynchings, VIII 138; XII 122
Lynd, Robert S., XIII 49
Lynn, Massachusetts, II 90, 92–95, 104

Mabley, Moms, XIX 58
Macadam roads, X 115, 116
McAdoo, William G., IX 126; XII 101, *101*, 102, 106, 108, 113, 116; XIII 30
McAlexander, Ulysses Grant, XII 91
McAllister, Ward, XI 26–27
MacArthur, Douglas, Rainbow Division, XII 80, *80*; Bonus Army Riot, XIV 20, *22*; on Arcadia strategy, XVI 14, 22, 23; Philippines, XVI 29, 32, 35, 36, 41, 136; Tarawa, XVI 108; recapture of Philippines, XVI 113, 114, *118*, 120, 122; New Guinea campaign, XVI 114; Leyte Gulf, XVI 116, *116*, 118, 119; V-J Day, XVI 131; as Republican, XVII 73; occupation of Japan, XVIII 40, *40*, 49; Korean War, XVII 29, 71; XVIII 51, 53, 55, 58
McAuliffe, Anthony, XVI 102
McCabe, E. P., VIII 99
McCall, Jack, IX 62
McCall, Samuel, XII 126
McCall's, XIV *56*
McCanles affair, IX 62
McCarran, Patrick, XVII 43, *43*, 44
McCarran Internal Security Act (1950), XVII 29
McCarthy, Eugene, XVIII 130; XIX 43, *43*, 44, 46, 71–72, 133
McCarthy, Joe (baseball), XIV 75
McCarthy, Joseph Raymond, XVII 25, 26, *35*, *44*; defeat of Tydings, XVII 29; character, XVII 36; early career, XVII 36, 37, *37*; Red scare, XVII 40; Korean War, XVII 44; XVIII 53, 58; Committee on Government Operations, XVII 44; Schine affair, XVII 44, 46, *46*; televised hearings, XVII 46, 47; Senate condemnation, XVII 46; and Murrow, XVII *47*, 48; decline, XVII 46, 47, *48*; assessment of, XVII 48; pro-Taft, XVII 73; China lobby, XVIII 47; foreign policy, XVIII 62, 64
McCarthy, Mary, XVII 103
McCarthyism, Korean War, XVII 29, 44; Republican party, XVII 77; see also McCarthy, Joseph Raymond
McCartney, Paul, XIX 66–67, *67*
McCarty, Catherine, IX 66
McClellan, George B., VII, 19, 21, *21*, 24–26, 28–29, 32, *32*, 45, 52, *52*, 63, 72, 139
McLemore, Jeff, XII 42
McClintock, Mary Ann, IV 123
McClure, S. S., XI 31
McClure's Magazine, XI 31, 124
McCone, John, XVIII 90
McCord, James, XIX 113, *114*
McCormack, John, XIX 25
McCormick, Cyrus Hall, IX 82; X 24
McCormick, Vance, XII 105
McCormick factory, X 78
McCormick reaper, IV 63, *63*; X 24
McCosh, James, X 97
McCoy, Bill, XIII 56
McCoy, Joseph G., IX 44, 45, 46, 53, 63
McCrea, Jane, II 116, *117*
McCrady, John, XIV *42*
McCullers, Carson, XVII 103
MacDonald, Ramsay, XV *29*, 72
Macdonald, Dwight, XVII 124
Macdonough, Thomas, III 126, *126*
McDowell, Irvin, VII 19, 20, 26
McDowell, John, XVII 38
McDowell, Battle of (1862), VII 26
Macedonian (ship), III 123
McGee, William John, IX 132
McGiffin, Norton, XIV 43
McGillicuddy, Cornelius, see Mack, Connie
McGillivray, Alexander, III 44
McGinnity, Joseph, XI 134
McGovern, George, XIX 108, *109*, 110
McGranery, James, XVII 30
McGrath, J. Howard, XVII 30, *30*
McGregor, John, V 42
McGuffey, Alexander Hamilton, IV 85
McGuffey, William Holmes, IV 85
Machado, Gerardo, XV 38
McHenry, James, III 22, 58
Machine age, XI 12, 13
"Machine process," XI 10
Mack, Connie (McGillicuddy, Cornelius), XI 134, *134*
McKay, Claude, XIII 99
McKean, Thomas, II *13*
McKees Rocks, Pennsylvania, XI 98

McKenney, Ruth, XIV 56
Mackenzie, Alexander, III 74; V 52
Mackenzie, Colonel, II 29
Mackenzie King, W. L., see King, William Lyon Mackenzie
Mackenzie-Papineau Battalion, XV 86, 88
Mackenzie River, V 52
McKim, Charles Follen, X 93
McKinley, William (president), X 19, 45, 47, 72, 124, 141; XI 13, *13*, 64, 128; Spanish-American War, XI 34, 35, *40*
McKinley Tariff, X 53
McKissick, Floyd, XIX 57
McLane, Louis, V 66
Maclay, William, III 39, 40, 41
MacLeish, Archibald, XIV 26, 80
McLoughlin, John, V 14, *15*
McLowry, Frank, IX 64, *64*
McLowry, Tom, IX 64, *64*
Macmillan, Harold, XVIII 73, 92, *92*
MacMurray, John V. A., XV 51, 53
McNamara, Robert, XVIII 84, 85, *85*; Cuban missile crisis, XVIII 90; Skybolt, XVIII 92; Vietnam, XVIII 109; secretary of defense, XIX 19, *21*; "missile gap," XIX 86
McNary, Charles, XIV 68
McNary-Haugen Bill, XIII 124, 136; XIV 116
McNeill, Joseph, XVII 64
Macon's Bill, Number 2, III 119
McParlan, James, X 75
McPherson, Aimee Semple, XIII *111*
McRea, James, VIII *55*
McReynolds, James C., XIV 46
McSorley's Back Room, XI *120*
McSween, Alexander, IX 66
McTeague, X 103; XIII 82
Macune, C. W., X 131
Macy's, XI 21
Mad, XVII 125
Madden, Owney, XIII 60
Maddox (destroyer), XVIII 110, *111*
Madeira Islands, I 10, 22, 33
Madero, Francisco, XII 26–27
Madison, Dolley, III 127
Madison, James (president), II 54, 133; III 12, 13, 20; Constitutional Convention, III 22, 24, 25, 26; VI 85; Federalist, III 30, 31; V 14; Bill of Rights, III 33; on selection of vice president, III 35; on Constitution, III 41; on Bank of United States, III 45; on Washington's retirement, III 46; on Jay Treaty, III 51; Alien and Sedition Acts, III 58; 1800 election, III *62*; *Marbury v Madison*, III 81; southern support, III 137; on limits of government, III 137; protection for industry, III 85; president, III 85, 88–89, 119, 133, 135; Second Bank of the United States, III 88; foreign relations, III 119–121; War of 1812, III 121; Florida question, III 130; on education, IV 84
Madoc, Prince, I 19
Madrid, Treaty of (1670), I 84
"Mae West" life jacket, XVI *75*
Mafia, X 72
Maffitt, John N., VII 125
Magazines, IV 61; X 124; XI 124, *125*; XIII 73; XIV 105
Magellan, Ferdinand, I 15, 22
Maggie, X 103
Magic Barrel, The, XVII 103
Magic lanterns, XI 18
Maginot Line (France), XV 101
Magnalia Christi Americana, I 117
Magoffin, James W., V 82
Magruder, Jeb Stuart, XIX 113, *114*
Magruder, John Bankhead, VIII 20
Maguire, Molly, X 75
Mahan, Alfred Thayer, XI 44, 71; XV 20
Mah Jong, XIII 74, *74*
Mahone, William E., VIII 134
Mailer, Norman, XVII 90, 103, 104; XIX 78, 123
Mail order service, XI 21
Maine, I 61, 65, 106; statehood, V 139; VI 86
Maine (ship), XI 35, *35*
"Main Principles of Japan's Policy for Coping with the situation in Accordance with World Developments," XV 126–127
Main Street, XIII 66, *66*, 95, 108
Makers and Finders, XVII 105

Makin, Battle of (1943), XVI 108
Malamud, Bernard, XVII 103
Malaria, XI 77
Malaya, XVI 20, 23
Malcolm X, XIX 56, 58
Mallison, W. L., XIII 44
Mallory, Stephen R., VII 59, 124
Malmédy Massacre, XVI *100*, 102
Malthus, Thomas, IV 75
Maltz, Albert, XVII 38, *38*
Malvern Hill, Battle of (1862), VII 28
Management, and F. W. Taylor, XI 16; XIII 32
Managua, XV *32, 34*
Man and Nature: or Physical Geography as Modified by Human Action, IX 128
Manassas Junction, Virginia, VII 19, *20*, 21
Manchester, William, XIX 31
Manchild in the Promised Land, XIX 58
Manchukuo, XV 60, 62, *62*, 69; see also Manchuria
Manchuria, XI 74, 80; XV 53, 56, *56*, 58–60, *58*, 62; XVI 10; XVIII 42, 45
Mandalay, Burma, XVII 23
Mandan, I 40; III 75; IX 15, 17; see also Indians, American
Mandate system, XII 135
Manet, Edouard, VII *107*
Mangin, Charles, XII 91
Manhasset, I 51; see also Indians, American
Manhattan Engineer District, XVI 129
Manhattan Island, I 51
Manhattan Project, XVI 130
Manhattan Transfer, XIII 66
Manhattes, I 51; see also Indians, American
Manifest Destiny, V *25*, 48, 50–51, 65; VI 43; IX 133; XI 33
Manila, XVII 118, 120
Manila Bay, Battle of (1898), XI *36*
Manila Conference (1954), XVIII 64, *65*
Manila Conference (1965), XVIII 114–115
Mann, Dudley, VII 100
Mann, Horace, IV 18, 85–86, *85*, 88, 93, 94
Mann-Elkins Act (1910), XI 64
Man Nobody knows: A Discovery of the Real Jesus, The, XIII 32
Mansfield, Colonel, II 92
Mansfields of Lynn, II 92
Manteo, I 48
Man that Corrupted Hadleyburg, The, X 103; XI 103
Manufacturers Record, VIII 119
Manufacturing industry, X 10, 16; tariffs, X 39; US largest in world, XI 82; black, VIII 98
Manumission, VI 11, 21, 28
"Man who never was, The" (Second World War), XVI 82
Manypenny, George W., IX 116
Mao Tse-tung, winning of China, XVI 113; XVIII 42, *42*, 47, 48, *48*; Middle East crisis 1958, XVIII 77; Cultural Revolution, XVIII 132
Maple Leaf Rag, XIII 87
Marache's boarding house, Philadelphia, III 60
Marble House, Newport, XI 27, *27*
Marbury, William, III 81–82; see also *Marbury v Madison*
Marbury v Madison (1803), III 81–82; XVII 58
Marcantonio, Vito, XIX 101
March, Peyton C., XII 67, 107–108
"March of Time" newsreels, XIV 98–99
"March on Washington," XIX 55, *55*
Marco Polo bridge incident, XV 64
March, William Learned, VI 101
Margin sales, XIII 138, 140, 141
Marianas, Battle of the (1944), XVI 110–112, *110, 113*
Marin, John, XI 111; XIII 101
Marine Shipbuilding Workers' Convention (1942), XVI *47*
Marion, Francis, II 120
Marion, Ohio, XIII 20–21
Marion County, Kansas, IX 92
Marion Star, XIII 20
Marion strike (1929), XIII 132
Mariposa, California, V 127
Marjorie Morningstar, XVII 103
Markland, X 19, 20
Marks, Percy, XIII 66, 74
Marne, Battle of the (1914), XII 19
Marquand, John P., XVII 103

Marquette, Jacques, I 81
Marquis, Don, XI 124; XIII 95–96
Married Lady's Companion, IV 121–122
Marryat, Frederick, IV 131
Marsh, George Perkins, IX 128
Marsh, Reginald, XIV *11, 44,* 84, *87*
Marshall, Alfred, X 16
Marshall, Burke, XIX 21
Marshall, Christopher, II 101
Marshall, George C., XII 64, 95; XV 113–114, 131; XVI 14, 15, 16, 17, 19, 45, 74, 76, 81, 90, 99, 102, 104, 106, 136; and McCarthy, XVII 36; and Eisenhower, XVII 69; on Soviet relations, XVII 17; secretary of state, XVIII 28, *28*; Marshall Plan, XVIII 16, 28–31, *30, 31*; and China, XVIII 44–45, *44*
Marshall, James Wilson, V 120, *121*, 122
Marshall, John, III 55–56, *55*, 58, 81–82, *81*, 97, 137; IV 16
Marshall, Thurgood, XVII 53; XIX 35, *35*
Marshall Field building, X 93
Marshall Plan, XVIII 16, 28–31, *30, 31*
Martin, Bradley, XI 28
Martin, Josiah, I 106
Martin, Luther, III 22, *23*
Martin, Joe, XVII 18
Martin, Joseph W., XVIII 47, 58
Martin Chuzzlewit, IV 10
Martineau, Harriet, IV 12, 62
Martin Eden, XI 107
Martínez, Antonio María, V 39
Martinique, II 72, 75
Martin Road Race, X *123*
Martin v Hunter's Lessee (1816), III 82
Martin v Mott (1827), III 137
Marty, XVII 134
Marx, Karl, IV 125
Marx Brothers, XIV 96, *96,* 97
Marxism, XI 94
Mary, Queen of England, see William and Mary
Maryland, origins of, I 53, 65, 73, *73*, 75, 77; slavery, I 103; VI 18; shipbuilding, I 103; colonial architecture, I 111; "transportation," I 121; Crown control, I 123; boundaries, II 60; in War of Independence, II 103; sectional interests, III 25; party politics, III 54; agriculture, III 65; VI 44; secession, VII 16; school segregation, XVII 52
Masefield, John, XII 58
Mason, A. E. W., XII 58
Mason, George, II 54, *55*; III 22, 26, 33
Mason, James Murray, VII 102, *103*, 104
Mason, Richard B., V 122, 138; VI 93
Mason-Dixon line, II 115; VII 140
Massachusetts, origins of, I 50, 51, 57, 63; in colonial wars, I 91; charter of 1691, I 108; religion, I *109*; political maturity, I 119; defense of British rights, I 126; under Crown control, II 13, 14; territorial claims, II 14; defeat of British, II 24; constitution, II 51, 56; IV 25; provincial congress, II *93*; population, III 24; party politics, III 54; religion, III 110; industry, IV 61, 62; education, IV 92; and slavery, VI 10, 64; Know-Nothings, VI 102; and Civil War, VII 70; labor laws, X 84; 1918 elections, XII 127
Massachusetts Bay Colony, I 51, 60, 61, 63
Massachusetts Bay Company, I 60, 63
Massachusetts Centinel, III *31*
Massachusetts Women's Political Club, XV *116*
Massasoit, I 50, 51, 52; see also Indians, American
Mass consumption, XIII 32, 49, 130
Mass entertainment, X 100–101
Massive Resistance, XVII 54
"Massive retaliation," XVII 77; XVIII 65, 67
Mass media, XIX 69, 80
Masson, André, XVII 90
Mass production, X 24, 32; XI 16–17; XIII 32
Masters, Edgar Lee, XI 109; XIII 98
Masterson, "Bat," IX 63–64, *65,* 66, 67
Masurian Lakes, Battle of (1914), XII 20
Matagalpa, XV *32*
Matamoros, V 72, 75, 76
Matewan strike, XIII 132
Mather, Cotton, I 64, 108, 109, 110, 114, 117
Mather, Increase, I 108
Mathewson, "Christy," XI 134
Matisse, Henri, XI *113*
Matoaka (Pocahontas), I 49, *49*; III 109

Matsu, XVIII 77
Matsuoka, Yosuke, XV 125, 130, 132, 134
Mauldin, Bill, XVI 60; XVII *76*
Maurer, Louis, IX 138
Mauritius, II 79
Maury, Matthew Fontaine, VII 124–125
Maximilian (Austrian archduke and emperor of Mexico), VII 104–105; VIII 20
Mayas, I 41; see also Indians, American
Mayer, Louis, XVII 38
Mayflower (ship), I 50, 57, *57*, 58, 60
Mayflower Compact, I 59
Mayor, alderman system, XI 53
Mays, Willie, XVII 129, *130*
Meacham, Joseph, IV 106
Mead, Lake, XIII 46
Meade, David, VII *64*
Meade, George G., VII 39–40, 41, 110, 115, *115*, 116, *127*, 134
Meaning of Truth, The, XI 114
Meany, George, XV 94
Meatpacking industry, X 19; XIII 46
Mechanics Savings Bank, VIII 98
Mechanic's Union of Trade Association, IV 110
Mechanicsville, Battle of (1862), VII 28
Mechanization, X 34, 66; XI 15–16; XIII 32, 133
Medals (Second World War), XVI *79*
Medicare, XVII 32; XIX 25
Medicare Act (1965), XVII 32
Medicine, training, IV 95, 96; Second World War, XVI 57; national health service, XVII 26, 32, 84; XIX 25
Medicine Lodge Creek, Treaty of (1867), IX 106, 114
Medicine Man, IX 22
Medows, General, II 72
Mejía, Francisco, V 72, 76
Méliès, George, XI 132
Mellon, Andrew William, X 125; XIII 24, 26, *26*, 31, 123, 132, 137; XIV 16; XV 29
Melodrama, X *106*; XI 18, 126
Melonsville, Pennsylvania, X 69
Melting Pot, The, XIX 50
Melting pot theory, XIX 50–51
Melville, Herman, IV 82, 131, 139–140, *139*; X 87; XI 106
Melville Goodwin, U.S.A., XVII 103
Member of the Wedding, XVII 103
Memminger, Christopher G., VII 59
Memoirs of an American Citizen, The, XI 107
Memorable Providences Relating to Witchcrafts and Possessions, I 64
Memphis, Tennessee, I 16; VI 42; VIII 24, *25*, 84; X 110, 112
Memphis Blues, XIII 87
Men and Manners in America, IV 12
Mencken, Henry Louis, VII 137; XIII 65, 66, 68, 70, 96, 105, *105*, *106*, 107–109, *108, 109,* 111–112, 113–115
Mendieta, Carlos, XV 39
Mendelsohn, Eric, XVII 90
Mendès-France, Pierre, XVIII 68
Menéndez de Avilés, I 23, 44
Menjou, Adolph, XVII 38
Menlo Park, X 30
Mennonites, I 103; IX 92; X 57
Mental illness, IV 114–115; VIII *45*
Mercantilism, I *120*, 121–122, 125; II 63; IV 75
Mercenaries, in British Army (War of Independence), II 30, 33, 64
Merchant marine, III 112, 114, 117; XI 44, 71
Merchant Marine Act (1920), XII 113
Merchant Marine Act (1936), XVI 48
Merchants of Death, XV 78
Mercury, V 130; X 77, 83–87
Mercury spacecraft, XIX 86, 89
Meredith, James, XIX 21, 52, *52*
Mergenthaler-Linotype Company, XVI 54
Mergers, X 18, 19–20, *20*, 23; XIII 46, 114; XX 52; see also Trusts; Monopolies
Merrett, Susan, IV *14*
Merit system, VIII 81
Merrick, George E., XIII 38
Merrick, John, VIII 96
Merrill, Admiral "Tip," XVI 39
Merrimack (ship), VII 24, 27, *27*
Merritt, Ezekial, V 118
Merry, Anthony, III 80

Merry Widow, The, XI 126
Mescal, V *36*
Messina, Sicily, XVI 82, *84*
Mestizos, I 47; V 31, 39
Metacom, I 52, *52*
Metate, V 34
Methodism, IV 86, 99, 100–102, *101*, 108; VI *62*, 63, 74; IX 99; see also Religion
Metropolitan Association, XIV 114
Metropolitan Museum of Art, New York City, X 92, *93*
Metropolitan Opera, New York City, X 92
Meuse-Argonne Offensive (First World War), XII 78, 85, 95–98, *95*
Mexican-Americans, XIX 62
Mexican Cession, V 93, 138; VI 91
Mexican War (1846–48), V 68, 69, 70–77, *72, 75, 76, 77, 79*, 80–83, *80, 81, 82, 85*, 86–87, *87–89*, 90–93; *90, 93*, 118; VI 87–88, 120; VII 112, 131; IX 24, 136
Mexico, I 15, 16, 17, 43, 45, 46; V 13, 27, *27*, 30, 31, 33–34, 40–41, 42, 44, *44*, 68, 69, 70–77, 80–83, 86–87, 90–93, 116, 118, 119, 138; VII 104–105; punitive expedition, XII 25, 26–27, 27, 29–30, *29, 30*; Zimmermann Note, XII 52–53, *52*; effect of Prohibition, XIII 54; Nicaragua, XV 31; oil expropriation, XV 43–44; protest at Dominican invasion, XVIII 135
Mexico, Gulf of, I 85; VI 42
Mexico City, I 15; V 27, *27*
Mexico City, Battle of (1847), V *89*, 90
Meyenberg, Julius, VII *59*
Meyer, Ferdinand, XV 53
Meyerson, Bess, XVI *65*
Mézières, Athanase de, I 46
M'Fingal, II *90*; III 95
Miami, Florida, XIII 35, *36*
Miami, I 41, 92; II 44; see also Indians, American
Miami and the Siege of Chicago, XIX 123
Miami *Daily News*, XIII 49
Michigan, Scandinavian settlements, IV 76, *78*; education, IV 92, 95; H. Pingree, XI 55
Michigan Sugar Company, XIII 123
Michilimackinac, Michigan, III 122
Mickey Mouse, XIV *67*, 99, *99*
Microchronometer, XIII 32
Microwave radar, XVI 84
Middlebrow culture, XIII 72–74, 77, 93
Middle classes, and progressivism, XI 10, 18, 21, 25, 28–29; reformers, XI 84, 86; Coral Gables, Florida, XIII 38; social life in 1950s, XVII 127, 128
Middle East, Suez crisis, XVIII 71–73, *71, 73*; 1958 crisis, XVIII 77, *77*; Six Day War (1967), XVIII 138, 139, *139*; Yom Kippur War (1973), XVIII 137, 140, *140*; American policy, XVIII 138–140; XX 26–27, 29, 31, 33–34, 39–40
Middleton, Arthur, II *13*
Middletown, New Jersey, I 66
"Midnight appointments," III 78
Midway Island, XI 44; XVI 22, 25, 28
Midway, Battle of (1942), XVI 28, 32, *32*
Mifflin, Thomas, II 109
Migratory workers, XIV 65
Mikawa, Vice-Admiral Gunichi, XVI 30
Mikolajczyk, Stanislaus, XVIII 15
Mikuma (ship), XVI 28
Milan Decree, III 117
Miles, Nelson, XI *40*
Miles, Sherman, XV 141
Milholland, John E., VIII 115
Military Reconstruction Act (1867), VIII 30
Militia, VIII 39, 46, 78, 79, 85; XII 23
Militia Act (1862), VII 98
Millay, Edna St Vincent, XIII 68, 69
Milledgeville, Georgia, III 136
Miller, A. J., V *62*
Miller, Elizabeth Smith, IV 123
Miller, Henry, XVII 104
Miller, Arthur, XVII 105, *105*, 106, 107
Miller, Lewis, III *93*; IV *97*; VII *17*
Miller, William, XIX 38
Mills, C. Wright, XVII 107
Mills, Wilbur, XIX 105, 136
Millis, Walter, XII 58; XV 78
Mills Act (1888), X 52
"Mill village" system, XIII 131, 132
Milne Bay, Papua, XVI 32, 36

Milwaukee, Wisconsin, IX 28; XI 29, 54
Mindanao Island, XVI 23, 114, 116, *118*, 120
Mindoro, XVI 119
"Miners Ten Commandments," V *130*
Mines (military), XII 69; see also Torpedoes
"Minimum standards" legislation, XI 89, 91, 92
Minimum wage rates, XI 91
Minimum working-age laws, XI 91
Mining, IV 63; copper, V 33; gold, V 127; *127–129*, 130–131, *130*; quartz, V 131; and the West, IX 15, 70–71, *70–72*, 73–84, *74–76*, 78–82, *84*; immigrant labor, X 63, *64*; strikes, X 75
Mining Company Nederland, IX 80
Minneapolis, Minnesota, X 106; XIV 109, 111
Minnesota, IX 10, 17, 41, 87, 89; Indian warfare, IX 101, *102*; forestry, X *15*; railroads, X 22; the Grange, X 127; reform, XI 55
Minorca, I 96; II 73, 81, *81*
Minow, Newton, XIX 19
Minstrel shows, VI 47; XI 18, 126
Minuteman missile, XIX 86; see also Intercontinental ballistic missile
Minutemen, II 22, 23, *23*, 24; III 109
Miquelon, I 98
"Miracle of the Seagulls," V *101*
Miranda v Arizona (1966), XIX 35
Miruelo, Diego, I 14
MIRV, see Multiple Independently-Targetted Reentry Vehicles
Miscegenation, see Amalgamation
Mrs Wiggs of the Cabbage Patch, XI 124
"Missile gap," XVII 84; XVIII 67, 79, 83, 84; XIX 84, 86
Missionaries and mission work, Spanish, I 15, 33, 42, 43, 44, *44*, 45, *45*, 46, *47*; V 28, *29*; English, I 52, 55; French, I 80, *80*, 82; American, V 54–55; *55*; Mormons, V 102–103; in China, XI 47, 48; in Vietnam, XVIII 96
Missionary diplomacy, XII 26, 30
Mission establishments, I 45, 46, *47*; V 27–28, *28, 29*, 30
Mission to Moscow, XVII 38
Mississippi, statehood, III 133; V 48; slavery, VI 18; plantation owners, VI 40; cotton, VI 43; secession convention, VI 132, 134; secession ordinance, VI 134; black codes, VII 30; readmission, VIII 30; defeat of Confederate disfranchisement, VIII 42; and Reconstruction, VIII 42; James Alcorn, VIII 44–45; Reconstruction politics, VIII 84–85; and A. Ames, VIII 85; and Bourbons, VIII 129; pig law, VIII 132; convict leasing, VIII 132; Negro disfranchisement VIII 135; segregation, VIII 138; XVII 52; progressivism, XI 55; see also South, the
Mississippi, & Missouri Railroad, IX 29; see also Railroads
"Mississippi Plan," VIII 85
Mississippi River, I 16–17, *17*, 53–54, 81, 85; II 139; III 14, 16, 18, 48, 65; V 10; VI 42, 45; VII 22, *22*, 24, *25*; VII 36, 84; VIII *130*; IX 10; X 29
Mississippi Valley, III 14, 70, 88, 120; IV 71, 72, 79; V 24; IX 11, 13
Missouri, V 16; IX 10; debates on admission to Union, VI 65, 85; slave question, VI 85; influx of Missourians into Kansas, VI 105; railroad, IX 28, 41; cattle, IX 43, 44; reform, XI 55; school segregation, XVII 52
Missouri (ship), XVI 131, *131*
Missouri Compromise (1820), VI 78, 85, 100, 101, 112, 113, 116; VII 89
Missouri debates, VI 65, 85–86, *85*, 91, 121
Missouri Mounted Volunteers, V 83
Missouri River, III 76; VI 42; IX 11; X 29
Mr Deeds Goes to Town, XIV 95
Mr Smith Goes to Washington, XIV 95, *96*
Mitchell, Billy, XII 72, 85; XVI 35, 74
Mitchell, John, XIX 111, *112*
Mitchell, John F., X 66; XI 60, 99
Mitchell, Margaret, XIV 90
Mitchell, Wesley, XIII 130
Mitscher, Marc Andrew, XVI 110, 111, 125
Mix, Tom, XIII 82
Mizner, Wilson, XIII 38, 128
Moana, XIII 83
Mobile, I 16; see also Indians, American
Mobile, Alabama, VI 42, 51; VII *123*, 125; XVI 66
"Mobiles" (sculpture), XVII 96, *97*
Mobilization, economic, XII 114–116; XVI 43, 48,

47; see also Industrial war effort
Moby-Dick, IV 140
Model, Walter, XVI 95, 96
Model A Ford, XIII 40, *42*
Model T Ford, XI 14, 15, *15*, 16, 17, 140; XIII 31, 39, 40, *40*, 41
Model Tenement House Law, XI 89
Modern Chivalry, III 95
Modern City and its Problems, The, XI 86
Modern Distance, A, X 101
Modernity, XIII 17–18
Modern Times, XIV 97
Modoc (tribe), IX 107, *107*
Mogami (ship), XVI 28
Mohawk and Genesee Turnpike, IV 67
Mohawk, I 53, 55, *95*, 97; see also Indians, American; Iroquois
Mohawk Trail, XIII 38
Mohawk Valley, II 43, 98
Mohegan, I 51, 55; see also Indians, American
Mohican, see Mohegan
Moholy-Nagy, Laszlo, XVII 90, 98
Mojave Desert, IX 15
Moley, Raymond, XIV 30, 31
Molino del Rey, Battle of (1847), V 90
Molotov, Vyacheslav M., XV *101*; XVI 15, *17*, 18, *139*; XVIII 14, 30, *30*
Moncada, José, XV 31, 34
Mondale, Walter, **XX 13, 21**
Monday Night at the Metropolitan, XIV 44
Mondrian, Piet, XVII 90, *90*
"Money Power," IV 36
Monitor (ship), VII 24, 27, *27*
"Monitorial" method, IV 88
Monk, Maria, IV 81
Monmouth, Battle of (1778), II 114, *114*
Monongahela River, I 95
Monopolies, IV 17–18; X 19, 22, 23; XIV 128; see also Trusts
Monopoly (game), XIV 71
Monroe, Harriet, XI 107, 109, *111*
Monroe, James (president), at battle of Trenton, II 41; minister to France, III 70; president, III 89; IV 25, *25*; Florida question, III 130; Monroe Doctrine, III 131; "amalgamation" policy, IV 25; slavery issue, VI 86
Monroe Doctrine (1823), III 131; VII 104; XI 33, 46, 70, 74, 77; XII 23, 53, 135; XV 31; XVIII 135
Monschau, XVI 100, 101
Montana, IX 17; cattle, IX 44, 56, *58*; mining IX 73; statehood IX 92; Indian warfare, IX 106, 107; Populists, X 133; corruption, XI 53
Montcalm, Marquis Louis Joseph de, successes in North America, I 96; difficulties of, I 97; defeat and death, I 98, 99, *99*
Monterey, California, V 30, 122
Monterey convention (1849), V 139
Monterrey, Battle of (1846), V 77, *79*
Montevideo Conference of American States, XV 40
Montezuma, I 15, *15*
Montgomery, Isaiah T., VIII 99, *100*
Montgomery, Richard, II 32, 33, 34
Montgomery, Robert, XVII 38
Montgomery of Alamein, Bernard Law Montgomery, 1st Viscount of, XVI 16, 76, *77*, 78, 79, 80, 82, 86, 90, 94, 97, 98, 101, 102, 103, 104, 134
Montgomery, Alabama, VI 140; VII 19, 55, 56, *57*; desegregation, XVII 62
Montgomery bus boycott, XVII 62, *63*, 64
Montgomery Convention, VI 140; VII 56, 58, 59
Montgomery Ward and Company, X 131
Monticello, Virginia, III *87*
Montreal, Canada, I 22, *82*, 83, 88; II 33, 34; III 122, 124, 126
Mont Saint Michel and Chartres, XI 105
Moody, Dwight L., X 119
Moody, John, X 16
Moon brothers, I 106
Moon landing, XIX 95, *96*
Moonshine liquor, XIII 53, 54, 56, 57
Moore, Aaron M., VIII 96
Moore, Marianne, XVII 100
Moore, Ridgeway, XI *28*
Moralism, I 109, 110
Moral Majority, XX 71
Moral Re-Armament, XIV *76*, 77
Moran, Bugs, XIII 63

Moran, Thomas, VI *20*; IX 125, *125*; X 98
Moravian Brethren, I *101*, 103; encouragement of music, I 113, 138
Mordido, V 30
Morgan, Daniel, II 31, 32, 34, 44, 115, 121, *121*
Morgan, Sir Frederick, XVI 19
Morgan, Hank, XI 103
Morgan, John Hunt, VII 33
Morgan, John Pierpont, X 18, 20; XI 12, 60, 120; XIII 140; see also J. P. Morgan and Company
Morgan, Louis Henry, X 98
Morgan, William, IV 29
Morgenthau, Henry J., secretary of Treasury, XIV 31, *31*, 133; XV 113, 115, 127; XVI 138
Mori, Admiral, XVI 35
Morison, Samuel Eliot, IV 95; X 87
Mormon, Book of, IV 105
Mormon Battalion, V 81, 101
Mormon Corridor, V 106
Mormonism, see Latter-day Saints, Church of Jesus Christ of
Mormon Trail, IX 26
Morocco, XI 77; XVI 15, 76
Morotai Island, XVI 114
Morrill Act (1862), IV 94, 96; V 113; X 92
Morris, George P., VI 47
Morris, Gouverneur, II 55, 97–98; III 22, *24*, 24
Morris, Lewis, II *13*
Morris, Newbold, XVII 30, *30*
Morris, Robert, II *13*, 41, 101, 123; III 12, 13, 18, 22, 41
Morris Meats, X 19
Morrison, Herb, XV 93
Morristown, New Jersey, II 43, 90, *136*
Morristown mutinies, II 81
Morse, Samuel F. B., IV 57, *61*, 81, 132; X 24
Morton, Fred ("Jelly Roll"), XIII 88, 90, *90*
Morton, William, IV 96
Moscow protocol (1941), XVI 44
Moses, Franklin J., VIII 44, *44*
Moses, Robert, XIV 73
Mosler, Henry, IV *69*
Mother Lode, V 127; IX 70
Motherwell, Robert, XVII 91, *96*
Motion picture industry, see Movies
Motion Picture Patents Company, XI 133

Motion Picture Producers and Distributors of America (MPPOA), XIII 81
Motion-study, see Time-and-motion study
Motley, John L., IV 138
Motor Vehicle Safety Act (1966), XIX 41
Motors, electric, X 32
Mott, Lucretia C., IV 122–123, *122*; IX 116
Moulmein, Burma, XVI 23
Moultrie, William, II 34
Mound Bayou, Mississippi, VIII 99–100, *100*
Mount, William Sydney, IV 133; V *123*
Mountain Meadows massacre, V 110, *110*
Mountain men, V 14, 15–16, *17*, 18–19, 20, *20*, 21, *21*, 34; IX 13, 136
Mountbatten of Burma, Louis Mountbatten, 1st Earl of, XVI 41, 108
Mount Davidson, Nevada, IX 70, 71, 74, 84
Mount Holyoke College, IV 90
Mount Pisgah, Iowa, V 97
Mount Suribachi, Iow Jima, XVI 122, *122*
Mount Vernon, Virginia, I *89*; III *46–47*
Mouton, Alexander, VI 139
Moveable Feast, A, XIII 71
Movement, the (race relations), XVII 62
Movies, XI 18, 129, 132–133, 140; XIII 77, 81–85, *81–84, 86*; XIV 91, 95–100, *97–99*; crisis of 1950s, XVII 132, *132*, portrayal of youth, XVII 134, *134*; XIX 76; XX 75
Moynihan, Daniel P., XVIII 134; XIX 29, 50
Muckrakers, X 21, 23; XI 30, 31, 82
Mugwumps, X 48
Muhammad, Elijah, XIV 68; XIX 56
Muir, John, IX 126–128, *127*
Mulattoes, VI 19, 26
Mulberry Bend, New York City, X *66*, 68, *113*
"Mulberry" harbors, XVI 92, *92, 93*, 94, 95
Muller v Oregon (1908), XI 114
Multinational society, XIX 50–51; see also Immigration and immigrants
Multiple Independently-Targetted Reentry Vehicles, XVIII 137
Mulvany, John, IX 139
Mumford, Lewis, X 87; XIII 70, 101; XIV 90
Munda, New Georgia, XVI 36, 37
Mundelein, George William, XV 94
Mundt, Karl, XVII *40*

Munich agreement, XV 96
Municipal Voters' League, X 118
Munitions Assignment Board, XVI 48
Munitions Standards Board, XII 102
Munroe, Jack, XI 136
Munsey's, XI 124
Münsterberg, Hugo, XI 122
Murdock, Thomas Benton, X 126
Murfreesboro, Battle of, see Stone's River, Battle of
Murmansk, USSR, XVI 73
Murphy, Edgar Gardner, VIII 138
Murphy, Frank, XIV 115, 136
Murphy, L. G., IX 66
Murray, Walter, I 114
Murray, William Vans, III 56
Murrow, Edward R., XIV 102; anti-McCarthy XVII *47*, 48; *Harvest of Shame*, XVII 116; on television, XVII 124, *125*
Masashi (ship), XVI 110, 116
Muscle Shoals Act (1933), XIV 35
Muscle Shoals power plant, XIII 46, 123
Muscovy Company, I 23, 25, 28
Museums, X 92
Music, Moravian encouragement of, I 113; early concerts, I 114, 116; rag time, XI 123, 126; jazz, XIII 87, *88*, 90, *90*, 92–93, *92–93*; swing, XIV 100, *100*; rock 'n' roll, XVII 137, 141, *141*; XIX 65, 66–67, 75, 76, *77*, 78
Muskie, Edmund, XIX 42, *46*, 47, 108, 110
Muslim Mosque, Inc, XIX 56
Mussolini, Benito, XV 74, *74*, 80, 84, 97, 98, 103; XVI 13, *15*, 17, 82, 83, 106, 131
Mutiny on the Bounty, The, XIV 95
Mutsuki (ship), XVI 32
Mutt and Jeff, XI 124
Mutual aid societies, X 70–71
Mutual Defense Assistance Act (1949), XVIII 34, 36
Mutual Security Act (1951), XVIII 36
Muybridge, Eadweard, X 100
"My Day," XIV 102
My Egypt, XIII 101
Myers, Myrl S., XV 56
My Lai Massacre, XVIII *123*, 126
Myrdal, Gunnar, XVII 52, 66
Mysterious Rider, The, XIII 72
Mysterious Stranger, The, XI 104, *104*

NAACP, see National Association for the Advancement of Colored People
Nacogdoches, Texas, V 40
Na-Déné, I 37; see also Indians, American
Nader, Ralph, XVII 125; XIX 42, 105, 136–137
Nadzab, New Guinea, XVI 35
Nagano, Osami, XV 134
Nagab, Kita, XV 136
Nagasaki, Japan, XVI 112, 126, *130*
Nagumo, Vice-Admiral Chuichi, XV 138; XVI 28
Nahl, Charles, V *132*
Nájera, Francisco Castillo, XV 43
Nakano, Lieutenant-General, XVI 35
Naked and the Dead, The, XVII 90, 103
Nanking, China, XV 51, 53, 65, 66
Nanook of the North, XIII 83
Nantes, Revocation of the Edict of (1685), I 103
Nanticoke, I 53; see also Indians, American
Nantucket, Massachusetts, III 12; V 21; X *45*
Napalm bombs, XVI 112
Napier, James C., VIII 98
Napoleon I (Napoleon Bonaparte), I 47, 98; III 69, 70, *70*, 117, 119, 121, 124, 131, 138
Napoleon III, VII 37, 102, 104, *104*, 108
Napoleonic Wars, III 88; XI 33
Narragansett Bay, I 50, 51, 61

Narragansett Indians, I 52
Narrative of Arthur Gordon Pym, The, IV 135
Narváez, Panfilo de, I 13, 16
NASA, see National Aeronautics and Space Administration
Nash, William Beverly, VIII 70, 71
Nash (motor company), XIII 40
Nashville, Tennessee, VII 24, 122, 124
Nashville (ship), VII *107*
Nashville (cruiser), XVI 119
Nashville, Battle of (1864), VII 124
Nashville and Chattanooga Railroad, VIII 42, 43
Nashville Convention (1850), VI 94
Nassau Conference (1962), XVIII, 92, *92*
Nassau Hall, II *53*
Nasser, Gamal Abdel, XVIII 71, *71*, 72, 138
Nast, Thomas, VIII *23, 40, 84*; X *19*, 43, *43*
Natchez, I 41; see also Indians, American
Natchez, Mississippi, VI 41, *49*
Nathan, George Jean, XIII 107; XV 14
Nation, Carry, XIII *53*
National Academy, XI 111
National Advisory Commission on Civil Disorders, XIX 62
National Aeronautics and Space Administration, XIX 88, 93, 94, 95, 98; see also Space program

National Aeronautics and Space Council, XIX 34

National Anti-Slavery Standard, VI 72

National Association for the Advancement of
Colored People (NAACP), founding, VIII 115, 116;
XI 100; fight against school segregation, XVII 53;
XIX 53

National Association of Manufacturers, X 85; XI 97

National Banking Act (1863), VII 87

National Biscuit Company, XI 12, 23

National Board of Farm Organizations, XIII 136

National Broadcasting Company (NBC), XIII 44;
XVII 124

National Child Labor Committee, XI 91

National City Bank, XIII 46

National Civic Federation, XI 12

National Collegiate Athletic Association, XI 137

National Conference for the Cause and Cure of War,
XV 19

National Conference on the Negro, VIII 115

National Consumers' League, XI 91, 92, 100

National Council for the Prevention of War, XV 17,
31, 79

National Council for Limitation of Armaments, XV 19

National Credit Corporation, XIV 16

National Defense Advisory Commission, XVI 44, 45

National Defense Education Act (1958), XVII 84; XIX
24, 41

National Defense Research Council, XVI 56, 128

National Defense Training Act (1916), XII 126

National Era, VI 96

National Farmers' Union, XIV 116

National Freedmen's Convention (1867), VIII 70

National Gazette, III 45, 46

National Grange of the Patrons of Husbandry, see
Grange, the

National Guard, XI 126; XII 24, 68, 79–80; XVI 46

National health insurance, XVII 19, 26, 32; XIX 25

National Housing Agency, XVI 48

National Housing Association, XI 89

National Humiliation Day (Japan), XV 54

National Industrial Recovery Act (1933), XIV 34, 44,
47, 109

National Invitational Tournaments (basketball), XIV
75

Nationalism, American, I 134–141; III 90–92, 94,
108–110; IV 23; V 48, 63; VI 43, 78; IX 140, 141;
X 36; XV 14; see also Pax Americana

Nationalist Government (China), XV 51, 53, 56, 64;
see also China

"Nationalist" movement, X 137

National Labor Board, XIV 109

National Labor Relations Act, see Wagner Labor
Relations Act

National Labor Relations Board, XIV 50

National Labor Union, X 75; XI 94

National Lead Trust, X 19

National League of Professional Baseball Clubs, X
119; XI 134; XVII 129

National League for Protection of Colored Women,
XI 100

National League on Urban Conditions Among
Negroes, XI 100

National Liberation Front (Vietnam), XVIII 112, 123

National Line, X 58

National Linseed Oil Trust, X 19

National Negro Business League, VIII 96, 106, 106,
108, 110

National Negro Committee, VIII 116

National Negro Conference (1909), XI 100

National Organization for Women, XIX 64; XX 61–62

National Parks, IX 123–128, 130; XI 63; XIX 48

National Peace Conference, XV 79

National Police Gazette, IX 66

National Progressive Republican League, XI 50, 64

National Recovery Administration, XIV 33, 34, 47,
67, 109, 111, 139

National Recovery Administration Codes, XIV 109,
111

National Republicans, IV 29, 31

National Resources Committee, XIV 133

National Road, IV 50, 66, 67

National Security League, XII 111

National Socialist German Workers' party, see
Nazism

National Union Convention, VIII 26

National Urban League, XIX 53

National War Labor Board, XVI 48

Nation of Immigrants, A, XIX 25

Nation of Islam, XIX 56

Nation of Sheep, A, XVII 117

Native American party, IV 81

Native Son, XVII 103

Nativism, IV 80–82; VI 97, 110; X 70, 72; XI 29, 30;
XII 119, 127; XIII 11, 12–13, 15–16

NATO, see North Atlantic Treaty Organization

Naturalization, III 58; IV 17, 80, 81

"Natural rights," II 12; IV 110; VIII 69; XI 94

Natural selection, X 36

Nauvoo (Mormon settlement), V 95, 97, 97

Navajo, I 41, 45, 46; V 31, 32, 83; IX 17, 17, 111; see
also Indians, American

Navigation Acts, see Trade and Navigation, Acts of

Navy, see United States Navy

Navy and Marine Corps Medal, XVI 79

Navy Cross, XVI 79

Navy Distinguished Service Medal, XVI 79

Navy League, XV 23

Nazism, XV 71, 74, 97, 110

Nazi-Soviet Non-Aggression Pact (1939), XIV 81; XV
100, 101, 120, 125; XVI 10; XVIII 12

NBC, see National Broadcasting Company

Nebraska, IX 10, 39; Platte territory, VI 100;
Kansas-Nebraska Act (1854), VI 100–102; Pawnee,
IX 17; the Grange, IX 41; land, IX 86, 87, 89, 90,
90, 91; statehood, IX 92; agriculture, IX 94, 95,
95, 96, 97, 98

Negapatam, Battle of (1782), II 78

Negri, Pola, XIII 84, 84

Negro Convention Movement, VI 68

Negroes, I 13, 77, 102; II 15; in War of
Independence, II 90, 94; in early American society,
III 138, 140; stereotype of, IV 10; VIII 51;
education of in nineteenth century, IV 92, 93, 94;
VIII 64; religion, IV 108; exclusion from
California, V 139; slavery, VI 10, 13–38 passim;
American Colonization Society, VI 65, 68; Negro
Convention Movement, VI 68; in Union Army, VII
51, 76, 94, 96, 97, 98, 99, 99; VIII 50; in Confederate
Army, VII 67, 99; civil rights, VII 89; VIII 42, 50;
XI 68; XVII 60; Northern hostility to, VII 94;
nationalism of, VII 94; racial attitudes in South,
VIII 14–16, 18; Reconstruction, VIII 18–19, 22,
27, 28; race riots, VIII 24; 14th amendment, VIII
25, 27; suffrage, VIII 27, 28, 30, 33, 70–71,
70–71, 73, 79; radical rule in South, VIII 39;
militia, VIII 39, 46, 78; state schooling in South,
VIII 40; Alcorn's Mississippi, VIII 45; and
Republican party, VIII 50, 83; land redistribution,
VIII 48, 51–52, 52; land owners, VIII 53, 57;
Freedmen's Bureau, VIII 53–55, 53; contract
labor, VIII 54, 55; farm rentals, VIII 55, 57–59;
sharecropping, VIII 59; credit, VIII 59; post Civil
War society, VIII 60–61, 60; education, VIII
64–65, 65, 66, 69; religion, VIII 68, 69; Ku Klux
Klan, VIII 74, 76, 78–79; intimidation at polls, VIII
82–87; compromise of 1877, VIII 88; Booker T
Washington, VIII 91, 100–101, 105–109;
disfranchisement, VIII 91, 107, 108, 114, 134,
135; black capitalism, VIII 92, 96, 96, 98, 106;
all-black communities, VIII 98–100, 100; W. M.
Trotter, VIII 109–110, 111; W. E. B. Du Bois, VIII
111; Niagara Movement, VIII 111, 113, 113;
NAACP, VIII 115–116; John F. Slater Fund, VIII
132; penal servitude, VIII 132; segregation, VIII
138; XI 10; XVII 52–53, 53; Kansas, IX 92;
Republican party in Gilded Age, X 47; labor
movement, XI 100; in sport, XI 136; in AEF, XII
78, 78; effects of First World War on, XII 120,
122–123; separatist movement, XIII 35; jazz,
XIII 87; 1920s renaissance, XIII 99–100, 99;
work in 1930s for, XIII 133–134; and F. D.
Roosevelt, XIV 51, 67; unemployment in
Depression, XIV 68; "Buy Black" campaign, XIV
68; Second World War service, XVI 45, 53, 62;
Brown v Board of Education, XVII 53–54, 54; Little
Rock, XVII 55–56, 56, 58; Civil Rights Acts 1957,
1960, XVII 60; Montgomery bus boycott, XVII 62,
63; northern migration, XVII 66; and Truman,
XVII 19, 20, 21; conditions in 1945, XVII 50; use of
word "blacks," XVII 51; effect of Second World
War on, XVII 52; black power, XIX 42, 57;
integration, XIX 51–52; new mood of, XIX 52–53;
unemployment, XIX 52; income of, XIX 53;
organizations, XIX 53; Martin Luther King, XIX
55; Malcolm X, XIX 56; Black Studies, XIX
57–58; "civil disorders," XIX 58, 61, 62; see also
Black Power; Integration; Racism; Race riots;
Segregation; Slavery

Negro Labor Committee, XVII 20

"Negro Soldier Law," VII 99

Neighborhood Job Corps, XIX 37

Nelson, Donald M., XVI 48

Nelson, Thomas, Jr, II 13

Neshaminy, Pennsylvania, I 113

Nester, Agnes, XI 100

Netherlands, American exploration and the colonies,
I 10, 22, 51, 53, 54, 65, 69, 70, 84; colonial
rivalry, II 45, 64, 67, 74; war with British, II
78–79, 139; Nazi conquest, XV 103, 104; Brussels
Pact, XVIII 32

Neurath, Konstantin von, XV 29, 94; XVIII 22

Neustadt, Richard, XIX 18

Neutral Conference for Continuous Mediation, XII 45

Neutrality, XII 32–37, 36, 37, 42, 43, 44, 48, 55, 56,
58, 61; XV 90, 91, 94, 100, 119; XVI 11; see also
Isolationism

Neutrality Act (1935), XV 80

Neutrality Act (1936), XV 83, 90

Neutrality Act (1937), XV 90, 98

Neutrality Act (1939), XV 100

Neutrality laws, XV 69, 78, 80, 83, 91, 100, 113, 115,
122

Nevada, IX 15, 26, 38; silver mines, IX 70–71, 78

Nevada City, California, V 132; IX 76

Nevelson, Louise, XVII 97

New Albion, see California

New Almaden, California, V 130

New American Poetry, 1945–1960, The, XVII 101

New Amsterdam, I 51, 65, 67, 84, 112; see also New
York City

Newark, New Jersey, I 66; XIX 58, 61

New Bedford, Massachusetts, V 21

New Britain Island, XVI 41

Newburgh, New York, I 104

Newburgh Addresses, II 127

New Caledonia, XVI 25

New Century Cotton Mill, VIII 98

New Deal, XV 74; and Herbert Hoover, XIV 24;
relief, XIV 31, 47; CCC, XIV 32; Civil Works
Administration, XIV 32; support for Arts, XIV 32,
34; first New Deal, XIV 34; appraisal early years,
XIV 37; challenges to, XIV 38, 40–41; Liberty
League, XIV 40; Supreme Court, XIV 46–47,
53–54, 126; agriculture, XIV 49; labor relations,
XIV 49–50, 109; 1936 elections, XIV 50–52;
migratory workers, XIV 65; racism, XIV 67;
second New Deal platform, XIV 128; opposition,
XIV 128, 132–133; failures, XIV 133; assessment,
XIV 137, 139–140; end of, XVII 12; and Truman,
XVII 13

New Democracy, The (1912), XI 116

New-Departure Democrats, VIII 129

Newell, Frederick H., IX 132

New England, origins of, I 50–51, 53, 58, 59, 61–66,
63; in colonial wars, I 86, 88, 91, 96; effects of
war, I 101; economic life as colony, I 102, 106; II
63; population pressures, I 106; colonial culture, I
112–113; mercantilist system, I 122; reaction to
writs of assistance, I 126; influence of
Protestantism, I 128; in War of Independence, II
43, 66, 77, 89, 90, 92–93, 95, 95; on treaty
conditions, II 139; trade, III 25, 65; criticism of
Washington, III 39; War of 1812, III 88, 121–122,
124, 137; IV 24; in literature, III 95; opposition to
Embargo of 1807, III 117; character of New
Englander, IV 10; support for John Quincy Adams,
IV 28; industry, IV 62; VI 48; VII 85; agricultural
upheaval, IV 68, 69, 70; education, IV 92; against
Texas annexation, V 44; desegregation, VI 83;
population 1880s, XI 10

New England, Council for, I 72, 73

New England, Dominion of, I 63, 68

New England Anti-Slavery Society, VI 71

New England Confederation, I 61

New England Emigrant Aid Society, VI 105

New England Offering, IV 62

New England Society, VIII 118

New England Suffrage League, VIII 113

Newfoundland, I 18, 19, 20, 23, 28

New France, I 79–83 passim, 85, 86, 88, 90, 92, 97

New Frontier, XVIII 82, 84, 85, 88

Newgate prison, Connecticut, II *97*
New Georgia, XVI 36
New Guinea, XVI 25, 32, 35, 114
Newhalls of Lynn, II 92
New Hampshire, origins of, I 61, 106; first state
  government, II 51; slavery, VI 63
New Harmony, Indiana, IV 118–119, *118*
New Haven, Connecticut, I 61
New History, The, XI 115
New Humanism, see Humanism
New Immigration Act (1966), XIX 41
New Jersey, origins of, I 65, 66, 69, 70; constitution,
  II 51; boundaries, II 60; in War of Independence,
  II 95; at Constitutional Convention, III 25; party
  politics, III 54; slavery, VI 48; Whig V 10, 64; reform, XI 55, 67
  X 19; reform, XI 55, 67
New Jersey, College of, II *53*
New Lebanon, New York, IV 106, *106*
New Left, XVIII 130
New Madrid, Mississippi, VII 24
Newman, Barnett, XVII 94, *96*
New Market, Battle of (1864), VII 119
New Masses, XIV *44,* 80
New Mexico, IX 15, 36, 37, 56; Spanish territory, I
  17, 45, 46; V 31–34, *31, 32, 33,* 69; conquest, V
  82; Compromise of 1850, V 109; VI 92; territorial
  government, V 138; Indians, IX 16, 17;
  segregation, XVII 53; see also South, the
"New Nationalism," XI 64, 66, 116
New Orleans, Louisiana, II 74; III 69, 70, *70,* 73, *73,*
  114, 119, 128; VI 42, *42,* 43, 51; VII 43; VIII 20,
  24, 83, 84, *120, 130;* IX 43; XIII 68, 87
New Orleans (ship), IV 50
New Orleans, Battle of (1815), III 128, *128,* 129,
  129, 130, 133; IV 22, 24
New Orleans Daily True Delta, VI 129
New Panama Canal Company, XI 72
New Populist party, X 126
Newport, Christopher, I 72
Newport, Rhode Island, XI 26–27, *27*
Newport News, Virginia, VIII 125
New Republic, The, XI 116, 119
New South, VIII 118–119, 121–122, 124, 126, 129,
  138–141; see also South, the
New South Creed, The, VIII 140
Newspapers, I 117, 140; II 16; IV 61, 87; VII 69, *69,*
  78, 80; X 24, 124; XI 124, 140; foreign language,
  X 70; First World War, XII 110; Great Depression,
  XIV 102; censorship, XIX 111
Newsreel, XIV 98
Newsweek, XIV 105; XVII 48
Newton, Huey P., XIX 57
New World, I *29,* 33, 35
New York, origins of, I 63, 65, 66, 69, 70; in colonial
  wars, I 84, 86, 89, 92; state constitution, II 55–56;
  IV 25; territorial claims, II 86; in War of
  Independence, III 95, 96, 98; on Constitution, III
  30–31; Republican party, III 54; political style in
  early nineteenth century, IV 24; industry, IV 63;
  VI 48; controlled immigration, VI 76; slavery, VI
  10, 64; Know-Nothings, VI 102; Civil War, VII 70;
  anti-trust laws, X 19; reform XI 55; Tenement
  House Law (1901), XI 89; 1918 elections, XII 127
New York Aeronautical Society, XI 129
New York *Age,* VIII 106
New York *American,* VIII 116
New York Association for Improving the Condition
  of the Poor, IV 80
New York Bay, I 22
New York Central Railroad, VII 84; X 16; XI 118; see
  also Railroads
New York Charity Organization Society, XI 87, 89
New York City, I 54, 65, 66, 68, 69, *84;* colonial
  commerce in, I 101, 103, 112; in War of
  Independence, II 34, 38–39, 92–93, 98; III 11,
  11; population, III 16; IV 41; politics, III 30;
  capital city, III 41; trade, III 65; VI 51; public
  water supply, III 66; civic amenities, III 67, *67;*
  benefit of Erie Canal, IV 51, 53, *53;* shipbuilding
  center, IV 57; crime, IV 80; school controversy of
  1840s, IV 81; Civil War, VII 69, *70, 71,* 82; draft
  riot, VII 76, 77, 81, *81,* 94; cattle, IX 43; Tweed
  Ring, X 42–44; immigrants, X 63; Lower East Side,
  X 66, *66,* 68; symphony orchestra, X 92; streetcars,
  X 108, *108;* skyscrapers, X 110; health
  board, X 110; slums, X 112; XI *30, 56;* sanitation,
  X 115–116, *115, 116;* Central Park, X 118; relief

agencies, X 118; saloons, XI 30; reform, XI 51;
  black ghettoes, XII 122; construction, XIII 33, *35;*
  artists' haven, XIII 68, 96; XVII 97; Great
  Depression, XIV 12, 16; Chinatown, XIX *50;* see
  also Cities
New York *Critic,* VIII 140
New York draft riot, VII 76, 77, 81, *81,* 94
New Yorker, XIII 85, 96; XIV 105; XVII 48; XIX 121
New York Hat, The, XI *133*
New York *Herald,* V 123; VII 12, *47,* 78
New York *Journal,* XI 124
New York Mechanick Society, III *17*
New York *Morning Journal,* X 124
New York Morning News, V 65
New York Movie, X 87
New York Public Library, X 92
"New York Realists," XI 111
New York School (art), XVII 91
New York's Seventh Regiment (Civil War), VII 70, *70*
New York State Barge Canal, X *64*
New York State Bureau of Labor Statistics, X 66
New York Stock Exchange, XIII 138, *138*
New York *Sun,* V 92; X 48, 124
New York Times, X 43; XI 111; XV 34; XVII 48; XIX
  111
New York Times v Sullivan (1964), XIX 35
New York *Tribune,* IV 61; VII *49,* 76, 80, 96, 98
New York Weekly, IX 61
New York *World,* X 124, 125; XI 60, 124; XII 41;
  XIII 125
New York Yankees, XIV 75; XVII 129, *130;* see also
  Baseball
New York World's Fair (1939), XIV 78; see also Fairs
  and expositions
New Zealand, XVIII 58, 64, 112
Nez Percé, V 54; XI 17, *18,* 107, *107,* 111; see also
  Indians, American
Nguyen Ai Quoc, see Ho Chi Minh
Niagara Bridge, X 30
Niagara Movement, VIII 111, 113, *113,* 115
Niagara River, III 122
Ni-aung-pi-kai (Indian game), IX *17*
Nicaragua, II 74, 77; XI 72, 80; XV 31–38, *32, 34,*
  35; XX 33, 37–38; see also Latin America
Nicaragua Canal Survey, XI 81
Nichols, George Ward, IX 61, 62
Nicholls, Richard, I 65, 66
Nicholson, Harold, XII 130
Nickelodeons, XI 14, 18, *19,* 30, 129, 132
Nicola, Lewis, II 126
Nicolan, Valeriano Weyler Y., XI 35
Nicuesa, Diego de, I 14
Niebuhr, Rheinhold, XIV 76
Nigger Heaven, XIII 99
"Night and Day," XIV 100
Night area bombing, XVI 74
Night at the Opera, A, XIV *96,* 97
Nimitz, Chester William, XVI 28, 32, 41, 108, 110,
  113, 114, 116, 122, 131, 136
Niña (ship), I 11, *12*
"999" (racing car), XI 15–16
Nine-Power Conference, XV 94
Nine-Power Treaty, XV 23, 58, 60, 61
Nine Stories, XVII 103
1919, XIV 88
Nineteenth Amendment, XII 119; see also
  Amendments, constitutional
Ninety-fourth Squadron (First World War), XII 85
Ninety-second division, AEF (First World War), XII 78
Ninety-Six, Battle of (1781), II 121
Ninth Army (Second World War), XVI 101, 104
Nipissing, Lake, I 28
Nipmucs (tribe), I 52
Nisbet, Eugenius, VI 138
Nishimura, Admiral, XVI 24, 116
Nivelle, Robert George, XII 49
Nixon, Richard Milhous (president),
  anticommunism, XVII 29, 78, 85; XIX 101, *101;*
  vice-presidential candidate, XVII 73, *73,* 75, 80;
  XIX *101, 102,* 103; presidential candidate, XVII
  86, 88; XIX *102,* 103, *103,* 104, 105; Korean War,
  XVIII 58; massive retaliation, XVIII 67; 1960
  election, XVIII 82, 106; XIX 15; on Manila
  conference, XVIII 115; Vietnam, XVIII 123, 124;
  invasion of Cambodia, XVIII 128; review of
  foreign policy, XVIII 128; China, XVIII 132, *133;*
  Bangladesh, XVIII 134; devaluation of dollar,

XVIII 136–137; XIX 93; 1968 election, XIX 46,
  103, *103,* 104, 105; "Red power," XIX 62; trade
  deficit, XIX 93; space program, XIX 95, 98; nature
  of his presidency, XIX 100; on anti-Vietnam
  protests, XIX 100, 110; early career, XIX 100–101,
  103; "Checkers" speech, XIX *101,* 103; "Southern
  strategy," XIX 104, 135–136; economic policy,
  XIX 105–106; advisers, XIX 106, 135; on social
  spending, XIX 106–107; on Supreme Court, XIX
  107; law and order, XIX 107, 126–127; 1972
  campaign, XIX *109,* 110; foreign policy, XIX 110;
  and Vietnam War, XIX 110; Watergate, XIX
  110–113, *111,* 116, *116,* 118, *118; Pax Americana,*
  XIX 119; assessment of, XIX 125–126, 135;
  isolation of, XIX 135, *135*
Nixon Agonistes, XIX 125
NLRA, see Wagner Labor Relations Act
Nobel Peace Prize, T. Roosevelt, XI 77; XV 20;
  Martin Luther King, XIX 55
Noble, John W., IX 129
Nobody Knows You When You're Down and Out,
  XIII *92*
Noemfoor Island, XVI 114
Nomura, Kichisaburo, XV 131, 132, 134, 135, 136,
  138, *130*
Non-Aggression Pact, see Nazi-Soviet Non-
  Aggression Pact
Nonimportation Act (1806), III 117
Nonintercourse Act (1809), III 119
Non-Intervention Protocol (1936), XV 43
Nootka, I 40; see also Indians, American
Norfolk, Virginia, VII 22
Norfolk, Burning of, II 33
"Normal School," IV 88, *88;* see also Education
Normandy invasion (1944), XVI 19, 92, *92,* 94–96,
  94–95
Norris, Frank, X 69, 103; XI 53, 106, 107, *107*
Norris, George W., XII 56, 57, 114, 127; XIII 46; XIV
  30, 133; XV 31
Norris, Kathleen, XV *119*
Norris-La Guardia Act (1932), XIV 109
Norsemen, I 18, *18,* 19, *19,* 20, *20;* see also
  individual names
North, Frederick North, Lord, I *131,* 132, 133; II 13,
  16, 18, 63, 64, 68, 74, 79, 87, 106, 136–137, 140
North, Simon, IV 64
North, the, hostility to the South, VI 86, 88, 91, 101,
  116, 120; Republican strength, VI 103;
  expansionists, VI 120; Civil War industrial might,
  VII 10, 76; economic boom, VII 82, 84–87; Civil
  War aims, VII 140; cost of Civil War, VIII 11; on
  secession, VIII 16; 1866 elections, VIII 26, 27,
  39; free labor economy, VIII 28; universal
  suffrage, VIII 30, 33, 70; tired of "Southern
  question," VIII 79
North African campaign (Second World War), XVI 10,
  15–16, 74, 76, *76,* 77, 78–80, *78*
North American Review, VII 80
North Atlantic Treaty (1949), XVIII 32, 34, *35*
North Atlantic Treaty Organization, origins, XVIII
  32, 34, *35;* Eisenhower, XVII 71; Truman, XVIII
  16; Germany, XVIII 36; Greece and Turkey, XVIII
  36; reduction in conventional forces, XVIII 67;
  Skybolt, XVIII 92, *92;* frictions within, XVIII
  92–93; and US, XX 27–29, 33, 38, 40–42
North Carolina, origins of, I 48, 54, 73–75;
  backwoods, I 104; II 86; War of Regulation, I 106;
  state constitution, II 56; in War of Independence,
  II 103; on Constitution, III 31; not in Union, III 38;
  tobacco, VI 44; VIII 126; secession, VII 18;
  Confederate state, VII 60, 76; Ku Klux Klan, VIII
  79; redemption, VIII 82; Negro disfranchisement,
  VIII 135; segregation, XVII 52; see also South, the
North Carolina (ship), XVI *50*
North Carolina Mutual Life Insurance Company, VIII
  96
North Dakota, IX 44, 86, 87, 91, 92; statehood, IX
  92; agriculture, IX 94, 95, 97, 99; Northern
  Alliance, X 127
North Dakota (ship), XII *70*
Northern Alliance, X 127, 131–132
Northern Expedition (China), XV 51, 55
Northern Pacific Railroad, IX 35, 36, *36,* 38, 89, *89,*
  128; see also Railroads
Northern Securities Company, XI 60
North German Lloyd Line, X 57
North Korea, XVIII 50, 53, 55, 64; see also Korean War

North Platte, Nebraska, IX 31
North Pole, XI 81
North Star (abolitionist paper), VI *83*
North Star (film), XVII 38
North Vietnam, see Vietnam
North West Company, V 14, 52
Northwest Ordinance (1787), III 139, 140; IV 18; VI 65, 113, 118
Northwest Passage, I 22, 23, 25, *25, 86*
Northwest Territory (US), III *14–15,* 44–45, 48, 76, 85, 122, 139; IV 70, 92, 93; V 53–55, *54, 55,* 63; VI 105

Norway, emigrants to US, IV 76; conquest by Germany, XV *104*
Notes on Virginia, III 97
Notions of the Americans, III 108; IV 136
Noumea, XVI 31
Novarro, Ramon, XIII 82
Nova Scotia, I 90, 91
November Evening, XIV *87*
NOW, see National Organization for Women
Noyes, John Humphrey, IV 104–105, *104*
Nozick, Robert, XIX 140
NRA, see National Recovery Administration

Nuclear chain reaction, XVI 128, *129*
Nuclear test-ban treaty, XVIII 94, *94;* XIX 25
Nuclear weapons, XVII 77; XVIII 67, *67,* 68, 94; XX 25–26, 28–29, 32–34, 40–42
Nude Descending a Staircase, XI 111, *113*
Nueces River, V 69, 72
Nugget, The, IX 64
Nullification, doctrine of, VI 132
No. 29 (Pollock), XVII 94, *94*
Nuremberg trials, XVIII 21, 22, *22*
Nye, Gerald P., XII 58; XV 78, *78;* XVII 40
Nye Committee, XII 60, 61; XV 78, 80; XVII 40

Oakies, XIV 120
Oakland House, Louisville, VI *58*
Oakley, Annie, IX 133, *137*
Oberlin College, IV 89, 123; X 92
Occom, Samson, I 55
O'Connor, John, XIV 136
Octopus, The, X 103; XI 53, 107
Odd Fellows, VIII 108
Odets, Clifford, XIV 91
ODM, see Office of Defense Mobilization
OES, see Office of Economic Stabilization
Of Civil Government, II 12
Office of Defense Mobilization, XVII 30
Office of Defense Transportation, XVI 48
Office of Economic Stabilization, XVII 30
Office of Price Administration and Civilian Supply, XVI 45, 48, 66; XVII 17
Office of Price Stabilization, XVII 30, 31
Office of Production Management, XVI 45
Office of Scientific Research and Development, XVI 56
Office of Strategic Services, XVIII 97
Office of the Chief of Engineers, XII 66, 102
Office of the Chief of Signals, XII 102
Office of the Chief of Staff, XII 102, 107
Of Mice and Men, XIV 89
O'Folliard, Tom, IX 67
Of Time and the River, XIV 89
Ogallala, Nebraska, IX 45
Ogden, Peter Skene, V 14, *15*
Ogdensburg meeting (1940), XV 49
Oglala Sioux, IX 102, 106, *106;* see also Sioux
Oglethorpe, James, I 54, 90, *91, 102,* 103
O'Hara, John, XVII 103
Ohashi, Chuichi, XV 130
Ohio, Indian attacks, III 44, 70; building of forts, III *45;* statehood, III 133; industry, IV 63; education, IV 92, 94; cattle, IX 43; antitrust laws, X 19; Northern Alliance, X 127; reform, XI 55
Ohio Company, I 92, 93, 99
"Ohio idea," X 36–37, 38
Ohio River, III 48; VI 42, 45; X 29
Ohio Valley, I 55, 92, 99, 133; III *16;* IV 68, *69*
"Oh! Susanna," VI 47
Oikawa, Koshiro, XV 135
Oil crisis, 1970s, XX 45, 51, 53
Oil embargo, US, XV 134; Arabs, XVIII 137, 140
Oil leasing, XIII 29–30; XV 43
Ojeda, Alonso de, I 12, 14
Ojibwa, I 41, 54, 92; see also Indians, American
Okanagan, I 40; see also Indians, American
OK Corral, gunfight at, IX 64
O'Keeffe, Georgia, XI III; XIII *35,* 101
Okinawa, Japan, XVI 119, 122, 124–126, *127*

Oklahoma, IX 15, 37, 56; land rush, IX 92, 93, *93;* agriculture, IX 96, 99; black migration, VIII 99; Negro disfranchisement, VIII 135; segregation, XVII 52; see also Indian Territory
Oklahoma! (musical), XVI *64*
Oklahoma (film), XVII 132
Oklahoma City, Oklahoma, IX 93
Old-age pensions, X 84; XI 92; XIV 47
Old Art Museum, Boston, X 92
Old Creole Days, VIII 140
Old Dominion (ship), VII *105*
Oldendorf, Vice-Admiral Jesse, XVI 116
Oldfield, Barney, XI 16, *16*
"Old Folks at Home," VI 47
Oldham, John, I 51
Old Howard, Boston, XI 126
Old Kentucky Home, The, VI *33*
Old Mill, The, XIV 99
Old Plantation, The, VI *31*
Olds, Ransom E., XI 16; XIII 39, 40
Oldsmobile, XI 16
"Old Uncle Ned," VI 47
"Olive Branch" petition (1775), II 15, 16
Oliver, "King," XIII 87, *90*
Oliver Brown et al v Board of Education of Topeka, Kansas (1954), XVII 53, 54, 59, 62, 79
Olmsted, Frederick Law, VI 24; VII 82; X 118; XI 118
Olsen, Charles, XVII 101
Olson, Floyd B., XIV 111
Olympic Games, XI 137; XIV 73, 75; XIX *58;* XX 33, 39, *81*
Omaha, I 40; IX 17; see also Indians, American
Omaha, Nebraska, IX 29; X 29; XI 128
Omaha Beach, XVI 92, *92,* 94
Omerhausse, John, VII *73*
Ommaney Bay (carrier), XVI 119
Omnibus Bill (1889), IX 92
Omnibus Crime Control and Safe Streets Act (1968), XIX 43
Omoo, IV 140
One Cent Savings Bank, VIII 98
101st Airborne Division (Second World War), XVI 101, 102
One Hundred Associates, Company of, I 79
165th Infantry, see Rainbow Division
Onida community, IV 105, *105*
Oneida, I 53; see also Indians, American; Iroquois
O'Neill, Eugene, XIII 66, 98; XIV 91; XVII 106, *106*
One Man's Initiation, XIII 67
One-Third of a Nation, XIV 91
Onis, Luis de, III 130
Only Yesterday, XIII 74
Onondaga, I 53; see also Indians, American; Iroquois

Ontario, Lake, I 28, 81, 92; III 124; see also Great Lakes
Ontario, Utah, IX 73
On the road (painting), IX *40*
On the road (book), XVII 134, 136
OPA, see Office of Price Administration
Opata, I 46; see also Indians, American
OPEC; see Organization of Petroleum Exporting Countries
Opechancanough (Chief), I 49, 51
Open door policy, XI 46–47, 48, 78, 80; XII 22, 23; XV 23, 51, 61; see also China
Open Housing Act (1968), XIX 48
"Open-range," IX 56, 59
Open shop, XI 97; XIII 136
"Open Thy Lattice, Love," VI 47
Opequon Creek, Battle of (1864), VII 119
Opera, X 92; XI 126
Operation A-Go, XVI 111
Operation Anvil, see Operation Dragoon
Operation Avalanche, XVI 86
Operation Bolero, XVI 74
Operation Cherry Blossom, XVI 37
Operation Cobra, XVI 94
Operation Dragoon, XVI 17, 95–96
Operation Forager, XVI 110–111, *110–111*
Operation Husky, XVI 82
Operation Ka, XVI 30
Operation Magic, XV 131, 132, 136
Operation Market Garden, XVI 98–99, *98*
Operation Michael, XII 80, *80*, 84
Operation Overlord, XVI 15, 17, 18–19
Operation Roundup, see Operation Overlord
Operation Sea Lion, XV 115
Operation Sho, XVI 116
Operation Torch, XVI 15–16, 74, 76, *76*, *77*, 78–81
Opinion polls, XV 79, 97; XVII 29; XIX 10, 126
Oppenheim, Germany, XVI 103
Oppenheimer, J. Robert, XVI 130

OPS, see Office of Price Stabilization
Oran, XVI 78
Orange county, New York, II 98
Orchestras, symphony, X 92
Order of St Luke, VIII 96
Order of Sons of Italy, X 71
Order of the Star-Spangled Banner, IV 81
Orders in Council (1807), III 116, 119, 121
Ordnance Bureau (First World War), XII 66, 102
Ordnance Department (Second World War), XVI 54
Ordnance manufacturers, see Armaments industry
Oregon, III 131; IX 10, 15, 24; American expansion into, V 46–47, 53–55, *54*, *55*, *56*, 59–60, 63; VI 87; annexation of, V 63–66, *65–66*, 69; Anglo-American occupancy, V 51–53, *51*; territorial government, V 138; and Progressivism, XI 55, 56
Oregon (ship), XI 71
Oregon City, Oregon, V 60, *60*
Oregon system, XI 56
Oregon Trail, V 20, *47*, 55, *56*, 59–60, *59*; IX 12, 26
Oregon Treaty (1846), V 69
Organization Man, The, XVII 107, 117
Organization of Afro-American Unity, XIX 56
Organization of American States, XV 40; XVIII 86, 92, 135
Organization of Petroleum Exporting Countries, XVIII 140
Orgen, Augie, XIII 61
Origin of species, X 96
Orinoco, I 12
Orkney Islands, I 19
Orlando, Vittorio Emanuele, XII 134, *134*
Ormoc, Philippines, XVI 118, 119
Ornitz, Samuel, XVII 38, *38*
Oro Bay, New Guinea, XVI 36
Oro Fino, Idaho, IX 73
"Orphan Brigade," VII 34
Orr, James, VII 102
Osage, IX 17; see also Indians, American

Osawotomie raid, VI 107, 122
Oshima, Hiroshi, XV 130
Oshkosh, Wisconsin, X 63
Osliaba (ship), VII *108*
OSS, see Office of Strategic Services
Ostend manifesto (1854), VI 101–102
Ostpolitik, XVIII 132
O'Sullivan, John L., V 65
O'Sullivan, T. H., VII *115*
Oswald, Richard, II 130, 132
Oswald, Lee Harvey, XIX 29, *30*
Other Voices, Other Rooms, XVII 103
Otis, James, I 126, *126*; III 109
Otoe, III 74; see also Indians, American
Ottawa, I 54; see also Indians, American; Pontiac
Ottawa River, I 28
Otter, Thomas, IX *40*
Otto, Louis-Guillaume, III 20
Ottoman Empire, XI 77; XII 16
*Ouachita River, I 17
Our American Cousin, VII 133
Ouray, Colorado, IX 73
Our Indian Wards, IX 116
"Outdoor Girl," XI 140
Outlook, XI 31, 111, 133
Ovando, Nicolás de, I 42
Overland journey, An, IV 38
Overland Telegraph Company, IX 26
Overman Act (1918), XII 109
"Over There," XII *125*
Ovington, Mary White, VIII 116; XI 100
Owen, Robert, IV 118–119, *118*
Owen-Keatings Act (1916), XI 91
Owens, Jesse, XIV *74*, 75
Owen Stanley mountains, XVI 32
Oxford Group, XIV 77
Ozark mountains, I 17
Ozawa, Admiral Jisaburo, XVI 111, 116
"Ozzie and Harriet," XVII 128, *129*

P

Paca, William, II 13
Pachebel, Karl Theodor, I 114
Pacific Fleet, XV 129
Pacific Ocean, I 15, 48; III 74–75, 76; XI 71, 82; XV 53, 55
Pacific Railroad Act (1862), IX 13, 28; see also Railroads
Pacific Railroad Survey Act (1853), IX 28; see also Railroads
Pacific Telegraph Company, IX 26
Pacific trade, V 21; XI 71
Pacific Wooden Mills, IX 83
Pacifism, XII 56, 114, 118; XV 19
Packard, Vance, XVII 107
Packard (motor company), XIII 40, 42
Paderewski, Ignacy Jan, XII 136
Page, Thomas Nelson, VIII 140; X 104
Page, Walter, Hines, VIII 119, 140; XI 80; XII 34, 37
Paine, Lewis, VII 132, 134
Paine, Robert, Treat, II *13*
Paine, Tom, I 135; *Common Sense*, I 138; II 19–20, 33, 47, *47*; *The Crisis*, II 40; III 109; and Pennsylvania constitution, II 55; land, II 60; foreign entanglement, II 134; democratic impulse, III 20; absent from Constitution debate, III 24; nationalism, III 91, 92; contribution to philosophy of government, III 97; on past, III 108; fate of, III 138
Paiute, IX 16, *17*, 101; see also Indians, American
Pakenham, Edward, III 128
Pakenham, Richard, V 64, 69, 70
Pakistan, SEATO, XVIII 64; CENTO, XVIII 72;

Indo-Pakistan War, XVIII 134, *134*
Palau Islands, XVI 113, 116
Palestine Liberation Army, XVIII 138
Palestine Liberation Organization, XVIII 140
Palisades, storming of (1776), II *38*, 39
Palmares, Brazil, VI 38
Palm Beach, Florida, XIII 38
Palmer, A. Mitchell, XIII 13–14, *14*, 15
Palmer, Fanny, IX 138, *138*
Palmer, Frederick, XII 65
Palmer, John McAuley, XII 74
Palmer, Joseph, IV 119
Palmer, William Jackson, IX 36, 38
Palmer Raids, XIII 14–15, *15*
Palmerston, Henry John Temple, 3rd Viscount, VII 100, *100*
Palo Alto, Battle of (1846), V 73, *75*
Panama, Isthmus of, I 12, 14; V 124, *125*; XI 71, 72
Panama, Republic of, XI 72, 78
Panama Canal, XI 44, 72, 73, 77, 82; XII 22, 24, 26; XX 29–30
Pan American Conference (1889), X 53
Panama Conference (1939), XV 45
Pan-American Exposition (1901), XI 128
Pan-American Security Zone, XVI 70
Pan-American Union, XV 31
Panay incident, XV 66–67, *66–67*, 67, 94
Panhandle (Alaska), XI 74
Pan Hellenic Union, X 71
Panics, 1857, VI *114*, 116; IX 28; 1873, VIII 43, 82; IX 35, 37, 40, 83; X 38, 42, 75, 127, 134; 1893, IX 37, 83; 1907, XI 63; 1929, XIII

137–138, *138*, 140–141, *140*; see also Economy; Great Depression
Panning, V 127; IX 77, *78*; see also Mining
Pantelleria Island, XVI 82
Panther Whiskey, XIII 56
Paoli Massacre, II *106*, 107, *107*
Papacy, I 11; see also Roman Catholics
Papago, I 41; IX 16
Papen, Franz von, XV 29; XVIII 22
Papua, XVI 32
Paraguay, XV 40, *42*
Paredes, Mariano, V 70, *70*, 71, 72, 76, 90, 91
"Parental Bent," XI 106
Paris, liberation of (1945), XVI 97, *97*
Paris, Peace of (1763), I 98; II 62
Paris, Treaty of (1783), II 130, *130*, 132, 133, 139; III 14, 48; V 10
Paris, Treaty of (1898), XI 42, 70
Park Bench, The, XIV 11
Parke, John, III 91, *91*
Parker, Alton B., XI 60
Parker, Bonnie, XIV *77*, 78
Parker, Dorothy, XIII 96
Parker, Sir Gilbert, XII 58
Parker, Captain John, II *23*; III 109
Parker, Sir Peter, II 120
Parker, Samuel, V 54
Parker, Theodore, IV 82, 87, 108
Parker, Tom, XVII 141
Parkman, Francis, I 95, 99; IV 138; IX 12
Park Ridge, Chicago, XIII 33
Parks, Rosa, IV 125; XVII 62, *63*
Parks, Bill, IX 83
Parks, see Public parks
Parliament (British), II 14, 15, 18
Parliamentarians, see Roundheads
Parmenter, James P., XIII 111
"Parochial" school system, IV 94; see also Education
Parry, David M., XI 97
Parsons, Albert, X 80
Parsons, Louella, XIV 91
Parsons, Theophilus, III 97
Parsons, Kansas, IX *99*
Partridge, Alden, IV 86
"Party of memory," II 20
"Party of principle," III 40
Party system, III 46, 53, 78, 133; birth of, III 53–56, 67–68; national conventions, IV 21, 26; Van Buren's advocacy of, IV 24; after 1815, IV 25–26; general ticket system, IV 26; in Jacksonian era, IV 26, 29; party manager, IV 26–27; "second American party system" (1820–50), IV 27–28; two party system, IV 28, 31; X 54; XIV 137; 1870–90 stalemate, X 45; public involvement in, X 46; federal nature of, XVII 25–26; instability of, XIX 121–122; see also Democratic party; Government; Political machines; Republican party, and names of other parties
Passaic, New Jersey, X 63
Passaic River, I 65
Passchendaele, Battle of (1917), XII 74
Passenger Acts, IV 75; X 60
Pasteur, Louis, X 33
Pastoral Visit, The, VIII *60*
Patch, Alexander, XVI 90, *95*
Patents, X 24
Paterson, William, III 22, 25
Paterson, New Jersey, X 106; XI 97
Paterson, XVII 101
Pathet Lao (Laos), XVIII 88
Pathfinder, The, IV 137
Patio, IX 83
Patrick, Mason M., XII 85
Patriots (War of Independence), II *18*, 20, *20*, 22, 38, 51, 120, 121; see also Whigs
Patronage, see "Spoils system"
Patrons of Husbandry, see Grange, the
Patterson, General, VII 19
Patti, Adelina, VII 82
Pattie, James Ohio, V 22
Pattie, Sylvester, V 22, *23*
Patten, Simon Nelson, XI 116
Patton, George S., Jr, XII 71; Bonus Army Riot, XIV 20; Second World War, XVI 76, 78, 81, 82, 83, 90, 94, 95, 97, 98, 99, 101, 102, 103, 104, *104*, 134
Pauley, Edwin, XVII 17

Pauncefote, Julian Pauncefote, 1st Baron of, XI 72
Pauperism, IV 80, 112; X 118; XI 86; see also Poverty
Pawnee, IX 17; see also Indians, American
Pax Americana, XIX 100, 110, 119; see also Imperialism
Paxton Boys, I 105
Payne-Aldrich Tariff Act (1909), XI 64
Peabody, George, VIII 132
Peabody, Elizabeth, IV 89
Peabody Fund for Education, VIII 132
Peabody Insitute, IV 87
"Peace Act of 1939," XV 98
Peace Convention (1860), VI 140
Peace Corps, XVIII *83*, 85; XIX 20
Peace movement, XV 17, 19, *19*
"Peace Offensive" (First World War), XII 91
"Peace Ship" (First World War), XII 44, 45, *45*
Peach Orchard, Gettysburg, VII 40
Peach Tree Creek, Battle of (1864), VII 120
Peale, Charles Wilson, III *102*, 104
Peale, Norman Vincent, XVII 119
Peale, Titian, V *14*
Pea Ridge, Battle of (1862), VII 24
Pearl Harbor, Hawaii, XV 127, 129, *129*, 130–131, 136, 139; XI 82; XVI 12, 13, 20, *20*, 22
Pearl River, I 17
Pearson, Drew, XIV 102
Peary, Robert Edwin, XI 81, *81*
Pecos River, I 17
Peel, Sir Robert, V 64
Peffer, William A., X 136
Pegler, Westbrook, XIV 102
Peirce, Charles, XI 114
Peleliu, XVI 113
Pemberton, John C., VII 36
Penal System, VIII 132
Peña y Peña, Manuel de la, V 91
Pendergast, Tom, XIV 52; XVII 11, 12, *12*
Pendergast machine (Kansas City), XIV 52; XVII 11; see also Political machines; Truman, Harry S.
Pendleton, William Nelson, VII 110
Pendleton Act (1883), X 50
Peninsula campaign (1862), VII 25, 28
Penn, Richard, II 16
Penn, William, I 53, *53*, 67–68, *68*, 70; III 66, 109
Pennsylvania, origins of, I 53–54, *53–54*, 65, 67, 70, 92; in colonial wars, I 95; colonial commerce, I *105*; Moravian settlement, I *101*; German immigration, I 104; backwoods, I 104; colonial politics, I 105; colonial culture, I 112–113; colonial education, I 113; Crown control, I 123; state constitution, II 55, 58; III 136; boundaries, II 60; views on War of Independence, II 85, 96, 98; in War of Independence, II 95; state powers, III 13; immigration, III 16; Whiskey Rebellion, III 48; party politics, III 54; industry, IV 63, 48; education, IV 92; slavery, VI 10, 64; Know-Nothings, VI 102; iron and steel, X 13; petroleum, X 14
Pennsylvania, University of, I 113
Pennsylvania Central Railroad, XIX 105; see also Railroads
Pennsylvania Frame of Government, I 67
Pennsylvania Gazette, I 117
Pennsylvania Journal, The, I *127*
Pennsylvania Railroad, VII 84; IX 37; X 16; XI 118
Pennsylvania Station, New York City, XI *119*
Penobscot Bay (Maine) raid on, II 112
Penrose, Boies, XV 11
Pensacola, Florida, III 130
Pensacola Bay, I 13
Pentagon Papers, XIX 110, 111
Peonage, VIII 108, 126
People's Benevolent Industrial Life Insurance Company, VIII 96, 97
People's Drug Stores, XI 21
People's party, see Populist party
Pepperrell, William, I 91
Peguot, I 51; see also Indians, American
Perceval, Spencer, III 121
Percy, Lord Hugh, 2nd Duke of Northumberland, II 24
Perdido River, III 130
Perelman, S. J., XIV 81
Peress, Irving, XVII 46
Perestrello, Felipa Monez, I 10
"Perfect Way, A," XI 123

Perkins, Frances, XIV 31, *31*, 44, 47, 133
Perkins, James A., XIX 58
Perkins, T. H., IV 54
Perkins Institute for the Blind, IV 114
Permanent Court of International Arbitration, XI 77
Permanent Joint Board on Defense, XV 49
Perpetual Immigrating Fund, V 102, 103, 105
Perry, M. C., IV 57, *59*
Perry, Oliver Hazard, III 124
Perryville, Battle of (1862), VII 33
Pershing, John J., punitive expedition (Mexico), XII 30, *30*; commander AEF, XII 71, *71*, *72*; strategy, XII 73–74; independent force, XII 74; anti-VD campaign, XII 78; Belleau Wood, XII 89; friction with French, XII 91; Battle of St Mihiel, XII 92, *93*, 95, *95*; First Army, XII 95, 96; Meuse-Argonne offensive, XII 95, 96, 98
Pershing tank, XVI 54
Persons, Wilton B. ("Jerry"), XVII 76
Perth Amboy, New Jersey, I 68
Peru, I 16, 37; XV 40, 43
Pestalozzi, Heinrich, IV 88
Pétain, Henri Philippe, XII 73, *73*, 74, 84, 89, 91, 95; XV 103; XVI 16, 79
Peterborough, New Hampshire, II 92–95, 104
Peters, Lulu Hunt, XIII 77
Petersburg, Siege of (1864–65), VII 117, *117*, 118, 128, *128*
Peterson's, IV 121
Petroleum industry, VIII 125, *125*; X 14, 22; XIII 41, *41*; see also Oil leasing
Pettiford, William Rueben, VIII 98
Pewterers, Society of, III 33
Phelan, James D., XI 52
Philadelphia, Pennsylvania, IX 43; origins, I 68, 70; colonial commercial life, I 101, *105*; backwoods grievances, I 105; colonial culture, I 105; Continental Congress, II 14, 87, *88*; carpenter's hall, II *52*; Independence Hall and Liberty Bell, II 57; British occupation, II 98, 107; population, III 16; IV 41; capital city, III 40; commercial center, III 65, 66; VI 51; civic improvements, III 66–67; Fourth of July celebration, III *140*; school controversy in 1840, IV 81; commuters, X 108; slums, X 113; relief agencies, X 118; gangsterism, XIII 60
Philadelphia (ship), III *115*
Philadelphia, College of, see Pennsylvania, University of
Philadelphia Centennial Exposition (1876), X 93, 110, 124
Philanthropist, VI 72, 77
Philanthropy, VIII 132; X 88, *91*, 92
Philip (King of the Wampanoag), see Metacom
Philippines, I 15, 98; XI 13, 71, 74; XII 22; Spanish-American War, XI *36*, 42, 44, 70; Taft-Katsura agreement, XI 77; strategic importance, XI 71, 74, 82; Pacific Fleet, XV 129; Japanese threat to, XVI 12, 20, 22; Japanese invasion, XVI 22–23, *23*, 25; recapture, XVI 113, 114, 118, 120; Leyte Gulf, XVI 116, *116*, 118–119; SEATO, XVIII 64, 112
Phillips, Kevin, XIX 104, 135
Phillips, Sam, XVII 137
Phillips, Wendell, IV 87, 109, 116; VI 81; IX 116
Phillips, Andover, IV 86
Phillips County, Kansas, IX 99
Phillips, Exeter, IV 86
Phipps, Benjamin, VI 37
Phips, Sir William, I 64, 86, 87, 89
"Phoenix, John H.," see Derby, George Horatio
Phoenix, II 37
Phonograph, X 30, *31*; XI 14, 140
"Phony War," XV 101
Photography, X 33, *34*; XI 140
Photoplay, XIII 85
Phouma, Souvanna, XVIII 88
"Pianola," XI 140
Picasso, Pablo, XIII *71*
Pickawillany, I 92
Pickens, Andrew, II 120
Pickens, Francis, VI 137
Pickering, Timothy, III 56, 58
Pickett, George E., VII *39*, 40–41
Pickford, Mary, XI 133, *133*; XII 116; XIII 85
Picnic Scene-Fourth of July, IV *14*
Pico, Andres, V 119, 120
Pico, Pio, V 69, 119

"Picture Palaces," XI 133
Piedmont, Battle of (1864), VII 119
Pierce, Abel H., IX 47
Pierce, Franklin (president), VI 96, 97, 100, 101, 107, 108, 118
Pierce, William, III 22, 24
Pierce-Arrow (automobile), XIII 42
Pierce City, Idaho, IX 73
Pierre's Hole, V 17, 53
Pietism, I 108, 109, 110
"Pig Law," VIII 132
Pike, Nicholas, III 91
Pike, Zebulon Montgomery, III 127; V 10, 12–13, 12, 13; IX 11
Pike's Peak, IX 15, 71
Pilgrim Fathers, I 50, 50, 51, 57, 57–58, 59; III 109
Pima, I 41, 46; see also Indians, American
Pinchot, Gifford, IX 123, 130–131, 132; XI 63, 64
Pinckney, Charles, III 22, 23
Pinckney, Charles Cotesworth, III 22, 23, 55, 55–56, 61–62
Pinckney, Thomas, III 54, 55, 61
Piñeda, Alonso Alvarez de, I 14
Pine Mountain, Battle of (1864), VII 120
Pine Ridge Reservation, IX 112
Pine Top's Boogie-Woogie, XIII 90
"Pine Tree" shilling, I 60
Pingree, Hazen S., XI 52, 55
Pinkerton Agency, X 75
Pins and Needles, XIV 91
Pinta (ship), I 11, 12
Pinzón Brothers, I 10, 11, 12
Pinzón, Vincente Yañez, I 12
"Pioneer" (railway), X 28–29
Pioneers, The, IV 137
"Pioneer Village," Salem, I 59
Piscataway, New Jersey, I 66
Pit, The, XI 107
Pitcher, Molly, II 114
Pitt, William, I 97, 99, 134; II 63, 106
Pittman, Key, XV 78, 79, 80, 97
Pittsburgh, Pennsylvania, I 93; X 106; XI 99–100; XIV 68
Pizarro, Francisco, I 16
Plain Language from Truthful James, IX 74
Plain Talk, XVIII 47
Plains Indians, I 37, 40; IX 16, 17, 18, 19, 19–20, 22–23, 22; see also Indians, American
"Plan A," XV 135
"Plan B," XV 135, 136
Planet, IV 55
"Plan of 1776," II 135
"Plan Orange," XV 55
Plantations, VI 12, 12, 13, 13, 21–22, 27–38 passim; VI 40, 40–59 passim; VIII 55, 57, 59
Plantation society, I 77, 102, 111, 111, 112
Planter, III 56
Plastic Age, The, XIII 66, 74
Platt Amendment (1902), XI 72; XV 38
Platte River, V 13, 55; IX 11, 17, 96, 106
Platte, Territory of, VI 100
Plattsburg Bay, Battle of (1814), III 126, 126, 130
Pleasant Hill, Battle of (1864), VII 115
Pleasonton, Alfred, VII 39
Plessy, Homer, VIII 138
Plessy v Ferguson (1896), VIII 138; XVII 52, 53, 61
Pleven, René, XVIII 36, 36
Plow that Broke the Plains, The, XIV 91
Plummer, Clifford H., VIII 113
Plummer, Henry, IX 77
Plutocracy, see Upper classes
Plutonium, XVI 128, 129, 129
Plymouth, Massachusetts, I 50, 51, 59
Plymouth Company, I 71
Plymouth Notch, Vermont, XIII 117, 117, 118
Pneumatic tires, XI 18
Poage, Bill, IX 48–49, 52
Pocahontas, see Matoaka
Podhoretz, Norman, XIX 65
Poe, Edgar Allan, IV 131, 135, 137, 138
Poetry, V 109; XIII 97–98, 97
Poetry, XI 109; XIII 97
Pogue, Calvin A., IX 80
Point Four program, XVIII 36
Point Isabel, Texas, V 72
Point of No Return, XVII 103

Poland, XII 136; XV 101, 103; XVI 138, 139, 140; XVIII 15, 21, 75
Police, X 113–114, 113; XIX 72, 128
"Police Power," XI 74, 82
Polish-Americans, X 63, 70; see also Immigration
Polish National Alliance, X 71
Political equality, see Equal opportunity
Political machines, X 43, 71; XI 51; XIII 60; XIV 52
Political Man, XVII 107
Political parties, see Party system
Polk, James K. (president), V 49, 50, 50, 65, 66, 69, 70, 70, 71, 72, 77, 86, 87, 90, 91–93, 116, 123; VI 87, 87, 88
Polk, Leonidas, VII 10
Pollard, A. F., V 63
Pollard, Edward, A., VIII 140
Pollock, Jackson, XVII 91–92, 92, 94, 94, 96, 97
Poll taxes, VIII 83, 135
Polygamy, V 109, 111, 111; IX 116
Ponce de Léon, Juan, I 13, 14, 44
Pontiac (Chief), I 54, 99, 105, 129
Pony Express, IX 26, 27, 27
Pony War Dance, IX 20
Poor Author and the Rich Book Seller, The, IV 130
"Poor People's March on Washington," XIX 55
Poor Richard's Almanack, I 136, 136
Pop art, XVII 97; see also Art
Pope, John, VII 24, 25, 28–29, 28, 63, 72; VIII 32; IX 85
Popular Front, XVIII 12
"Popular Sovereignty," VI 88, 100, 108, 116, 117, 118
Population, growth, I 62, 138; in 1815, IV 39, 41, 48; V 48; 1860, VII 10; 1865–1900, X 10; XI 10; in 1920s, XIII 35, 128; 1945–60, XVII 110
Populist party, VIII 128, 134, 135; IX 83, 97; X 21, 54, 132–134, 133, 136–141; XI 10, 48, 84; XII 56
Porgy and Bess, XIV 100
Port Arthur (Lü-shun), China, XI 74, 77
Port Arthur, siege of (1904), XI 77
Porter, David D., VII 35, 36, 125
Porter, Edwin S., XI 132
Porter, Peter B., III 121
Port Hudson, Louisiana, VII 36
Port Hudson, Battle of (1863), VII 96
Portman, H., IV 59
Port Moresby, Papua New Guinea, XVI 25, 26, 27, 32
Portrait of a Lady, X 101
Port Republic, Battle of (1862), VII 26
Port Royal, see Annapolis Royal
Portsmouth, New Hampshire, I 61
Portsmouth (New Hampshire) Conference (1905), XI 77; XII 22
Portugal, I 10, 11, 21, 22, 23, 33, 42; XVI 10
Post, Emily, XIII 77
Post, Louis F., XIII 14–15
Post-Impressionism, XI 111; see also Art
Potato famine (Ireland, 1845–49), IV 73
Potlatch, I 39–40
Potomac River, III 41; VII 19, 39
Potsdam Agreement (1945), XVI 126; XVIII 19, 21
Potsdam Conference (1945), XVIII 19, 21, 21
Pottawotomie Massacre, VI 107, 122
Potter, David, VI 59
Pound, Ezra, XI 109; XIII 18, 67, 97; XVII 101
Pousette-Dart, Richard, XVII 96
Poverty, IV 112–114; X 118–119; XI 30; Henry George, X 136–137; progressive views on, XI 86–87; in 1920s, XIII 130, 141; in Eisenhower era, XVII 81, 82, 116, 121; Johnson's war on, XIX 36–38, 37; see also Great Depression
Poverty, XI 86–87
Powderly, Terence V., X 77, 77, 78, 80, 82
Powder River, Wyoming, IX 106
Powell, John Wesley, IX 132
Powell, Lewis, XIX 107
Powell Expedition, IX 17, 132, 132
Power Elite, The, XVII 107, 108
Power industry, XIII 44, 46; see also Electricity industry; Public utilities
Power of Congress over the District of Columbia, The, VI 72
Power of Positive Thinking, The, XVII 119
Powers, Daniel, X 110, 124
Powers, Francis Gary, XVIII 80–81, 81
Powers, Hiram, IV 132, 132
Powhatan, see Wahunsonacock

Pownall, Thomas, I 129
Pragmatism, XI 114–116
Prague, Czechoslovakia, XVI 104
Prairie, The, IV 137, 137
Prairie Cattle Company, IX 57
"Praise the Lord and Pass the Ammunition," XVI 62
Precision bombing, XVI 74, 134
Pre-Emption Act (1841), IV 70, 71; IX 86, 94
Preface to Politics, A, XI 116
Prendergast, Maurice, XI 111
Preparatory Commission for Disarmament Conference, XV 17
Preparedness controversy, XII 23–24, 47, 48
Prescott, Samuel, II 22
Presbyterians, I 101, 128; IV 86, 95, 99, 100, 102; V 91; VI 74; IX 99; see also Religion
Prescott, William H., IV 138
Presidency, election, III 26, 62; powers of, III 33–34, 69; VII 20, 44, 51; VIII 18; X 46, 48; XI 63, 68; terms, III 54; IV 17; XVII 18, 80, 85; transfer of power, III 64–65; early years, III 135; character of to 1820, IV 28–29; Jacksonian change, IV 29; and Lincoln, VII 46; in Gilded Age, X 46; and Theodore Roosevelt, XI 57–59; Wilson extends powers of, XI 68; and F. D. Roosevelt, XIV 140; and Truman, XVII 25–26; Eisenhower's conception of, XVII 58, 78; Kennedy's conception of, XVII 60; XIX 10; right to send troops, XVIII 53, 58; Nixon's influence, XIX 100, 119, 135, 136; public trust in, XIX 126; reaction against untrammeled power, XIX 133
President, III 120
President Roosevelt and the Coming of the War, XV 122
President's Daughter, The, XIII 30
President's Emergency Committee for Employment, XIV 12
Presidio, I 45; V 27, 28, 29, 30, 31, 35
Presley, Elvis, XVII 121, 137, 141, 141
Press, see Newspapers
Pressed Steel Car Company, XI 98
Preston, Thomas, I 130
Prevention of Pauperism, Society for the, IV 80
Prevost, Sir George, II 120; III 126
Price, Sterling, V 83; VII 34
Price controls, in First World War, XII 103, 115; and Truman, XVII 15, 17, 18; and Korean War, XVII 29, 30; Nixon's attitude, XIX 105
Prince Hall Masons, VIII 108
Prince of Wales (ship), XVI 23, 26
Princeton, Battle of (1776), II 41, 41, 43, 98
Princeton University, I 113, 135; IV 90; X 92; XI 120, 137; XIII 66; see also Universities and colleges
Princip, Gavrilo, XII 17
Principles of Scientific Management, XIII 32
Prisons, IV 113–114, 113, 114
Privy Council, I 119, 124, 126
Processional, XIII 98
Proclamation Line, I 99, 106, 129
Proclamation of Civil Supremacy (1867), VIII 32
Proclamation of Neutrality (1939), XV 100
Proclamation of Unlimited National Emergency (1941), XV 120
Procter, Henry, III 124
Procter and Gamble Soap Company, XVI 54
Production Board Directive No. 1, XVI 66
Profiles in Courage, XIX 13
Profiteering, VII 82, 85; XII 115, 116
Profit motive, XI 25
Progress and Poverty, X 137
Progressive party (Theodore Roosevelt), XI 50, 66, 66
Progressive party (Henry Wallace), XVII 21, 24
Progressivism, origins, XI 10, 13, 31, 50–51; reform movements, XI 30–31; civic reform, XI 52–53; state reform, XI 53–56; women's rights, XI 57; foreign relations, XI 71, 82; political ideology, XI 84; social reform, XI 84–91 passim; public interest in, XI 86; elitism, XI 86; on poverty, XI 86–87; reform legislation, XI 87, 89, 91, 92; and prohibition, XI 92, 94; goals, XI 94; art XI 111; philosophy, XI 114–116; city planning, XI 118; failures of, XI 119; AEF, XII 76; First World War, XII 101; decline of, XII 127; XIII 18
Prohibition, IX 55; X 47, 53; XI 30, 92, 92, 94, 128–129; XII 118, 119–120, 120; XIII 16, 52–54, 52, 53, 55, 56–62, 60, 64–65, 64, 65; XIV 77

Prohibition Bureau, XIII 53, 57
Project Headstart, XIX 37, *37*
Projector, X 30
Promise of American Life, The, XI 84, 116
Promontory Point, Utah, IX 32, *35*
Propaganda, First World War, XII 58, 60, 110, *110*;
    Second World War, XVI 43, 60, 62, *62*
Propagation of the Gospel, Society for the, I 77
Prophet, the (Battle of Tippecanoe), III 120
Proprietory Colonies, I 65, 67, 72, 73, *102*, 103, 123
Prosser, Gabriel, VI 38
Protection (economy), X 39, 47–48, 52; see also Tariff
Protestantism, as unifier, I 128; IV 81, 99, 108; and
    nativism, X 72; XI 30; see also Religion
Protocol of Rio de Janeiro (1942), XV 43
Providence, Rhode Island, I 61; X 112
Provincetown Players, XIII 98
Provincias Internas, I 45
Provoost, Samuel, IV 99
Provost marshall general, office created, VII 51
Prudential Life Insurance Company, VIII 96
Pryor, Ike T., IX 48
Pryor, Mrs Roger, VII 78
PT-109, XIX 10
P-38, XVI 36, *37*
Public, The, XII 111

Public debt, III 40–41, 60; VIII 132, 134; XIV 140
Public Enemy, XIV, 91, *94*
Public Health Service, XI 89; XVI 58
Public income guarantees, XI 92
"Public Interest," XI 86, 118
Public Land policy, IV 70; IX 86, 87, 118–120,
    118–119, 132
Public opinion, IV 12–13; XV 94, 97, 100
Public Opinion, XIII 114
Public parks, XI 118; XIV 73; see also National parks
Public relief, XIV 12, 19–20, 30, 31–32, 47; see also
    Welfare state
Public school, IV 92, *92,* 93, 94; see also Education
Public School (English), IV 89
Public utilities, X 116; XI 51, 53; XIII 44, 46
Public Utility Holding Act (1936), XIV 128
Public Works, III 137; V 106–107; VI 91, 121, 128;
    XIV 19, 20, 32, 34
Public Works Administration, XIV 32, 34
Puccini, Giacomo, V 138
Pudd'nhead Wilson, see *Tragedy of Pudd'nhead
    Wilson*
Pueblo, I 17, *38,* 40, 41, *44,* 46; IX 15, 16–17; see
    also Indians, American
Pueblo, V 27, *29,* 30, 31, 83
Pueblo, Colorado, IX 38

Pueblo Revolt (1680), I 46
Puerto Ricans, XIX 62–63
Puerto Rico, I 13, 14; VI 10; XI 42, 78
Puget Sound, V 51, 53
Pugh, George, VI 125
Pulaski, Casimir, II 45
Pulitzer, Joseph, X 124, *124*; XI 35, 124
Pullman, George M., X 28, *28,* 29, 139
Pullman Palace Car Company, VIII 108; X 28
Punitive Expedition (1916), XII 25, 30, *30,* 53
Purchase, Storage and Traffic Division, General Staff
    (First World War), XII 108, 109
Pure Food and Drug Act (1907), XI 61, 68
Puritan ethic, IV 113
Puritanism, I 58, *58,* 59–66, 69, 77, 108, 113–114,
    128–129; II 18; IV 118, 125, 140; XIII 66; see also
    Religion
Purple Gang, XIII 60
Purple Heart, XVI *79*
"Purple Machine," XV 131
*Pursuit of Loneliness: American Culture at the
    Breaking Point,* XIX 123
Purvis, Arthur, XV 115
Putnam, Israel, II 26, 32, 34
Puzzled America, XIV 56
Pyle, Ernie, XVI 60

Quadrant conference (1943), XVI 17
Quadruplex machine, X 26, 30
Quaker Oats Company, XVI 54
Quakers, see Society of Friends
Quantrill, William Clark, VII 79, *79*
Quantrill's Raiders, VII 79, *79*; IX 67
Quarantine, IX 44
"Quarantine speech," XV 91
Quartering Act (1774), II 14
Quartermaster Bureau, XII 66, 102, 107
Quebec, I 83; II 33, *33,* 34
Quebec Act (1774), I 120, 133; II 14, 20
Quebec City, I 22, *26,* 28, 79, 88, 97, 98, *98*
Quebec conference (1943), XVI 39, 41
Quebec conference (1944), XVI 116, 138
Queen Anne's War, I 88
Queen Kelly, XIII 83
Queen's, New York City, XIII 33
Queen's County, New York, II 98
Queen's Rangers (War of Independence), II 31
Quemoy, XVIII 77
Quilombo, VI 38
Quincy, Massachusetts, II *53*
Quiroga, Santiago, XV 86
Quiz shows, XVII 120, *120*
Quota laws, X 74; see also Immigration

RA, see Resettlement Administration
Rabual, XVI 25, 29, 35, 36, 37, 39, 41
Race riots, VIII 24, 25, 84, 85, 114–115, *114*; XII
    122; XIV 68; XIX 42
"Race War in the North, The," XI 100
Racial competition, XI 43
Racial solidarity, VIII 92, 96, 106
Racism, toward blacks, V 140; VI 34, 56, 57, 65, 68,
    71, 78, 83, 90, 118; VII 57, 90, 94–95, 98; VIII 40,
    79, 88; X 47, 53, 82; XIV 66, 67, 68; XVII 50, 58;
    Chinese, VIII 96; X 82; during First World War,
    XII 122, Immigration acts, XIII 16; XV 54;
    Japanese, XV 54; XVII 51
"Racket" (crime), XIII 61
Racketeering, XIII 58, 60–64, *61–64*
Radar, XVI 36, 84
Radical Republicans, Freedmen's Bureau, VIII 25;
    Fourteenth Amendment, VIII 25, 27; 1866 mid-
    term election, VIII 26; Reconstruction, VIII 16,

27, 28, 33; Military Reconstruction Act, VIII 30;
    1868 presidential nomination, VIII 35; Johnson's
    impeachment, VIII 36, 37
Radio, XII 30, 44, *46,* 126; and F. D. Roosevelt, XIV
    24; in the 1930s, XIV 71, *71,* 100, 102, *103,* 104,
    104, 105
Radioactive energy, XI 104
Radio Corporation of America (RCA), XIII 44; XIV 10
Radio proximity fuse, XVI 57
Radisson, Pierre, I 80, 81
Raeder, Admiral Erich, XVIII 22, *22*
"Ragged Dick," X 97, *97*
Ragtime, XI 126
Railroad Administration, XII 106
Railroad Age, XI, 14, 21, 23, 25
Railroads, IV 51, *51,* 54–57, *54–56*; V 138; VI 14, 48;
    VII 84, 85, *138,* 139; VIII 12; X 10; XI 10;
    southern reconstruction, VIII 42–43, *42*;
    government aid to, VIII 81–82; in New South, VIII
    125; segregation on, VIII 138; road west, IX 13,
    24, *24,* 28–40, *28, 30, 32, 35, 36–38*; agrarian
    hostility, IX *38,* 40–41; X 22, 51, 126, 127; impact
    on West, IX 41; cattle industry, IX 44, 56;
    immigration, IX 89–90, *89*; warfare, IX 104–105;
    big business, X 161; improvements in, X 26, 28;
    Interstate Commerce Act, X 52; "Granger" laws,
    X 127, 131; Populist party, X 132; decline of, XI
    12; political power, XI 53; Hepburn Act, XI 61;
    interests in China, XI 80; First World War, XII 106,
    107; Esch-Cummins Act, XII 113; investment
    needs, XIII 130, 137
Railroad War Board, XII 106
Railway Labor Act (1926), XIV 109
Rainbow Division, 42nd Division, AEF (First World
    War), XII 80, 91, 96
"Rain Follows the Plough," IX 13, 86
Rain-in-the-Face (Chief), IX *108*
Raleigh, Sir Walter, I 48, 72
Raleigh *State Chronicle,* VIII 119
Rall, Johann, II 40–41
"Rally Round the Flag," VII 82
Ralston, William, IX 83
RAM, see Revolutionary Action Movement
Ramsay, David, III 13
Ramsay, Doctor, III 97
Ramsey, Sir Bertram, XVI *90*

Rand, Ayn, XVII 103
Rand, Sally, XIV 78
R & D, see Research and development
Randolph, Edmund, III 22, 30, 39, 45, 46
Randolph, John, III 78–79, 78
Randolph, Peyton, VI 86
Ranger, II 112
Rangoon, XVI 23
Rankin, Jeanette, XII 118, 118
Rankin, John, VI 66
Rankin, John E., XVII 38
Ransom, John Crowe, XIII 71; XVII 100
Rapidan River, VII 110, 116
Rappahannock River, VII 32, 36, 74
Rappites religious colony, IV 119
Raritan River, I 65
Rationing, XVI 60, 63, 66
Raton Pass, IX 36
Rauschenbusch, Walter, X 119
"Raven, The," IV 138
Rawdon, Lord, II 29
Rayburn, Sam, on Truman, XVII 14; on New
    Frontier experts, XVIII 88; and Kennedy, XIX 19,
    25
Rayon, XIII 130
RCA Victor, XVII 137
Read, Mary, I 87
Reader's Digest, XIII 73; XIV 105
Reading, New York, VI 98, 104
Reading Railroad, XI 97
Readjuster movement, VIII 134
Ready, Willing and Able, XIV 92
Reagan, John H., VII 59
Reagan, Ronald (president), XVII 38; XIX 46, 119; XX
    10, 18–22, 35, 68–69, 71
Real estate business, XIII 33, 35, 36–37, 38, 128,
    128, 137
Realism, X 100–101, 102, 103; XI 106–107
Reaugh, Frank, IX 43
Rebel without a Cause, XVII 134, 134
Recall, XI 56
Reclamation, IX 132
Reclamation Act (1902), IX 132
Reconstruction, X 36, 141; XI 10; Freedmen's
    Bureau, VII 51; VIII 25; 1863 formula, VII 51;
    VIII 18; Republican concern, VIII 16; Lincoln
    versus Congress, VIII 18; Andrew Johnson, VIII
    18–19; Congress, VIII 24, 27–28, 33; 1866
    elections, VIII 26; Military Reconstruction Act,
    VIII 30; Johnson's obstructions, VIII 32–33;
    Fifteenth amendment, VIII 33; impeachment of
    Johnson, VIII 35–37; reconstruction assemblies,
    VIII 44; end of radical reconstruction, VIII
    82–87; compromise of 1877, VIII 89
Reconstruction Finance Corporation (1932), XIV 16,
    19, 34; XV 43, 74
"Reconversion," XVII 14, 15
Records of the Federal Convention, III 22
Red Badge of Courage, The, X 102, 103
Redburn, IV 82
Red Cloud, (Chief), IX 106, 106
Red Cloud, Nebraska, X 92
Redcoats, II 18, 18, 23, 29, 36
Red Cross, XIV 12
Redeemers, VIII 129, 139
Redemption, VIII 66, 82–89, 129, 134
Redfield, William C., XI 80
Red Guards, XVIII 132; see also China
Red Hot Peppers, XIII 90, 90
"Red machine," XV 131
Red Man, see Indians, American
"Red Power," XIX 62
Red River, VII 115; IX 11, 53
Red River Station, IX 45
Red River Valley, IX 91, 95
"Red Scare," XIII 11, 12, 13, 15, 16, 17, 22, 111;
    see also Anti-Communist hysteria
Red shirt campaign, VIII 85
Redstone rocket, XIX 84, 86; see also Ballistic
    missiles
Red Studio, The, XI 113
Redwoods, IX 122, 123
Reed, George, II 13
Reed, Ishmael, XIX 58
Reed, Joseph, II 40
Reed, Thomas Brackett, X 53, 54
Reedy, George, XIX 133

Reeve, Tapping, IV 96
Referendum, XI 56
"Reform Darwinists," X 98
Reformed Government of the Republic of China, XV
    65
"Refractory" ores, IX 78
Refrigeration, X 32
Refuge, Houses of, IV 114
Regensburg raid (Second World War), XVI 85
Regulation, War of (1766–1771), I 106
Regulator associations, I 106
Reich, Charles A., XIX 123
Reid (ship), XVI 119
Reinhardt, Ad, XVII 96
Reinsurance Treaty (1887), XII 13
Relief agencies, X 118; XI 92; XIV 59
Religion, and the New World, I 33; Puritans, I 57,
    61; witch hunts, I 64; Society of Friends, I 66, 67,
    68; Great Awakening, I 108; pietism and
    moralism, I 109; influence on colonial culture, I
    113; anti-catholicism, IV 81; education, IV 86, 94;
    number of clergy (1840), IV 87; seminaries, IV 95;
    religious life mid-nineteenth century, IV 97–99,
    97, 98, 99; state support for, IV 99–100; sects, IV
    100; 104–105, 104; camp meeting, IV 101–103,
    101; slave, VI 34; unifier, VI 43; and reform
    movements, VI 68; Indian, I 40; IX 20, 22,
    111–112, 111; charity, X 119; during Great
    Depression, XIV 76–77; federal aid for education,
    XVII 26; boom in 1950s, XVII 119; see also
    Missionaries and names of sects
Remagen, XVI 103
Remarque, Erich Maria, XIII 67
Remington, Frederic, V 15; IX 20, 27, 49, 105, 117,
    137–138, 138, 139; XI 35
Remington & Sons, X 25, 26
Remington Arms Company, XVI 47
Remus mob, XIII 60
"Rendezvous," V 16, 17
Rendova Island, XVI 36, 39
Reno, Marcus, IX 108
Reno gang, IX 67
Rensselaer Polytechnic, IV 96
Rent Strike movement, XIX 63
Reparations (First World War), XV 24–27, 26
Repartimiento, I 42
*Report on the lands of the Arid Regions of the United
    States*, IX 132
Representatives, House of, representation, III 25;
    election, III 26; antifederalists III 46; Federalist
    victories, III 48; Jay Treaty, III 51–52; 1800
    election, III 62; Henry Clay, IV 23; 1874 elections,
    X 42; Gilded age, X 46
Republicanism, II 47–48, 51; III 18, 20; IV 21, 23,
    27, 29, 35, 36
Republican party, John Frémont, V 91, 118; founding
    of, VI 102–104, 102, 107, 108; 1856 election, VI
    110–112; Illinois elections 1858, VI 117–118, 118;
    Lincoln, VI 117–118; policy, VI 120; 1860
    convention, VI 125–126, 128; 1860 election, VI
    129, 131–132; Crittenden proposals, VI 135;
    Civil War, VII 45–46; on recession, VIII 16;
    Southern readmission to union, VIII 16, 27;
    reconstruction, VIII 18, 27, 28, 33; 1866 elections,
    VII 26; suffrage, VIII 28, 30; Southern
    Republican party, VIII 33, 42; Fifteenth
    amendment, VIII 33; Johnson impeachment, VIII
    35–37; Radical rule in South, VIII 39; Union
    league, VIII 39; power in South, VIII 42, 45;
    decline in South, VIII 46, 82–87 *passim*; on tariff,
    VIII 46; 1874 elections, VIII 84; 1876 elections,
    VIII 87, 88; collaboration with Independents,
    VIII 134; railroad, IX 28; post-Civil War policy,
    IX 36; "Stalwarts," X 36; Liberal Republican, X
    39–40; 1872 elections, X 40; elections 1872–96,
    X 45; Gilded age, X 47–48; Hayes years, X 48;
    Garfield, X 49, 49; Arthur, X 50; B. Harrison,
    X 52–54; 1890 election, X 53; 1894 election, X
    141; 1906 elections, XI 61; Taft, XI 63–64; 1912
    convention, XI 65, 66; 1916 convention, XII 46;
    1918 elections, XII 126–127; 1920 convention,
    XIII 20; 1920 elections, XIII 18, 23; 1932
    convention, XIII 64; 1932 elections, XIV 28;
    1936 elections, XIV 50–52; fate of in 1930s, XIV
    52, 137; 1946 elections, XVII 18; anti-Liberal
    programs, XVII 18; 1948 elections, XVII 22; 1952
    convention, XVII 73; McCarthyism, XVII 77;

Eisenhower, XVII 77, 78; 1954 elections, XVII 79;
    1956 elections, XVII 79, 80; changing nature of,
    XVII 80; Nixon, XIX 103–104; 1974 elections, XIX
    118; in 1980s, XX 10; see also Radical Republicans
Republican River, IX 11
Repulse, (ship), XVI 23, 26
Resaca, Battle of (1864), VII 120
Resaca de la Palma, Battle of (1846), V 74
Research and Development (R & D), XIII 32
Reservation (Indian), IX 111, 115, 116, 117, 118,
    119, 120
Reservationists, XII 140
Resettlement Administration, XIV 120
Residence of David Twining, The, II 54
Resolution 242 (United Nations), XVIII 138.
Resonator, X 30
Resumption Act (1875), X 38
Resurrection City, XIX 55, 56
Reuben James, (ship), XV 122; XVI 71
Reuterdahl, Henry, XI 78
Revels, Hiram, VIII 45
Revenue Act (1921), XIII 24
Revenue Act (1932), XIV 19
Revere, Paul, I 116, 116, 130, 133; II 22, 22, 23
Revision, Council of, II 56
Revivalism, IV 100, 102–104, 106–107, 106, 107,
    108; see also Religion
Revolutionary Action movement, XIX 53
Revolutions, America's response to, II 83–84; III 38;
    XVIII 39, 58
Rhapsody in Blue, XIII 92
Rhee, Syngman, XVIII 50, 50, 64
Rhett, R. Barnwell, VI 129, 134, 134
Rhine River, XVI 98, 99, 100, 102, 103, 104
Rhineland, XII 136; XV 84
Rhoads, Charles J., XIV 68
Rhode Island, origins of, I 51, 61; colonial
    government, I 123; state constitution, II 51;
    boundaries, II 60; against taxation, III 12; against
    revision of articles, III 22; population, III 24; on
    new constitution, III 31; not in Union, III 38;
    industry, IV 61; abolition of slavery, VI 64
Ribak, Louis, XIV 59
Ribaut, Jean, I 23, 26
Ribbentrop, Joachim von, XV 94, 101; XVIII 22, 22
Ribicoff, Abraham, XIX 19, 21
Rice, Alice Hegan, XI 124
Rice David, VI 63, 65
Rice, Elmer, XIII 98
Rice, VI 11, 12, 21–22, 42, 44, 45, 53; VIII 58, 59,
    126
Richards, Willard, V 99
Richardson, Elliot, XIX 113, 114, 118
Richardson, Henry Hobson, X 93; XI 116
Richardson, James O., XV 129
Richelieu, Cardinal Armand Jean du Plessis, I 79
Richelieu River, I 28
Richmond, Virginia, III 136; VI 13, 13; VII 19, 24,
    26, 32, 60, 77, 117, 126, 128, 128, 139; VIII 10,
    175; X 32, 109
Richmond and Danville Railroad, VII 128; see also
    Railroads
Richmond *Enquirer*, VIII 27
Richmond *Times*, VIII 138
Rickenbacker, Eddie, XII 72, 87, 87
Ride for Liberty, A, VI 67
Riders of the Purple Sage, XIII 72
Riedesel, Baroness von, II 44
Riesman, David, XVII 107, 117
Rifling, II 31
Rigden gang, I 106
Riis, Jacob, X 66, 68, 68, 118; XI 86, 89
Riley, Bennett, V 139
"Ring Shout," VI 34
Rio Abajo, V 31
Rio Arriba, V 31
Rio Grande, I 17, 41, 46; V 31, 69, 72, 93; IX 85
Rio Grande Pueblo, IX 17
Ripley, George, IV 119
"Rip Van Winkle," III 95; IV 135–136, 136
Rise of David Levinsky, The, X 69
Rise of Silas Lapham, The, X 101
"Rising of the Usurpers, The," X 19
Riskin, Robert, XIV 95
Rittenhouse, David, III 109
Ritty, James S., X 26
Ritty, John, X 26

"Rival Buses, The," XVIII 23
River, The, XIV 91
Riverside suburb, X 118; see also Suburbs
"River War" (Civil War), VII 22, *22,* 24
Roads, III 85, 137; IV 24, 50, 67–68, *68*; XIII 38, *40*
Road to War, 1914–1917, The, XII 58; XV 78
Roanoke Island, North Carolina, I *40,* 48; VII 22
Robe, The, XVII 119
Roberta, XIV 95
Roberts, Bartholomew, I 87
Roberts, Owen J., XIV 46, 54
Robertson, James, I 106; II 120
Roberval, Jean François de la Roque, Sieur de, I 22, 23
Robeson, Paul, XIII 92
Robin Hood, XIII 82
Robin Moor (ship), XV 119; XVI 71
Robins, Raymond, XV 16
Robinson, Alfred, V 21
Robinson, Edward G., XIV 91, *94*
Robinson, Edwin Arlington, XI 109, *111*
Robinson, Jackie, XVII *51*
Robinson, James Harvey, XI 115
Robinson, Sugar Ray, XVII *130*
Rochambeau, Jean Baptiste, Comte de, II *70,* 75, 79, 122, *122,* 123, 129
Rochester, New York, IV *53*; X 106, 110, 118
"Rock Around the Clock," XVII 137, *138*
Rock culture, XIX 65, 69, *69,* 75, 76, *77, 78,* 80, 121
Rockefeller, John D., IV 39; VIII 101; X 14, 21, *21, 92,* 138; XI 60
Rockefeller, John D., Jr, XIV 59
Rockefeller, Nelson, XVII 86; XIX 15, 38, 46, 118
Rockefeller Center, New York, XIV 105, *107*
Rocker, V 127; see also Mining
Rocketry, XVI 57, 124; XIX 84, 86; see also Ballistic missiles; Space program
Rockingham, Charles Watson-Wentworth, 2nd Marquess of, I 132
Rock Island Bridge, IX 28
Rock music, XIX 65, 66–67, 75, 76, *77,* 78
Rock 'n' Roll, XVII 119, 137, *138,* 141, *141*; see also Rock music
Rockwell, Norman, XII *127*; XIV *139*; XVI 62, *64, 140*; XVII *95*
Rocky Mount, Battle of (1780), II 121
Rocky Mountain Fur Company, V 20, 53
Rocky Mountain News, IX 92
Rocky Mountains, V 10, 21, 55, *59*; IX 10, 13, 15, 16, 17, 71, *72*
Rocky Mountain sheep, IX *14*
Rodgers, Richard, XIV *100*
Rodney, Admiral George, II *72,* 74, 75, *75,* 77, 79, 81
Roebling, John, X 30
Roebling, Washington, X 30
Roer River, XVI 100, 103
Roethke, Theodore, XVII 101
Rogers, Ginger, XIV *94,* 95
Rogers, Robert, I *97,* 98; II 31
Rogers, Will, XIII 65, 72; XIV 72
Rogers, William, XVIII 137, 139
Rogers, Woodes, I 87
Rogers' Rangers, I *97,* 98; II 92
Rolfe, Edwin, XV 86
Rolfe, John, I 49, *49*
Roller skating, X *106*
Rolling Stone, XIX 78
Rolling Stones, The, XIX 76, *77*
Rolvaag, Ole E., X 69
Roman Catholic Church, I 73, 80, 83, 133; IV 78, 81, 86, 94, 96, 108, *108*; VI 110; IX 99, 114; X 72; Knights of Labor, X 77; labor, X 83, *83*; parishes, X 119; Irish immigrants, XI 29, 30; First World War, XII 33; Al Smith, XIII 126; see also Religion
Roman Cup, I 137
Romanesque style, X 93
Rommel, Erwin, XVI 16, 76, *78,* 80, 86
Roosevelt, Anna Eleanor, XIV 26, *26,* 62, 102, 132; XV *49*; XVI *65*; XIX 13
Roosevelt, Franklin Delano (president), vice-presidential candidate, XIII *22*; repeal of prohibition, XIII 65; Bonus Army, XIV 20; president, XIV 24, *24*; first inaugural speech, XIV 24, *24*; early career, XIV 24, 26, 27–30; "New Deal" speech, XIV 30; "fireside chats," XIV 30; bank policy, XIV 30; cabinet, XIV 31, *31*; public relief, XIV 31–32, 65, 66; New Deal, XIV 37, 47,

50; fiscal policy, XIV, 50; 1936 elections, XIV 50–52, 53; Supreme Court, XIV 53–54, 128; wealthy's hatred of, XIV 59; and blacks, XIV 67; strikes, XIV III; resistance to New Deal, XIV 128, 132–133; cartoon caricature, XIV *134*; decline in reputation, XIV 136; assessment of New Deal policy, XIV 137, *137,* 139–140, *139, 141*; Good Neighbor policy, XV 38, *38,* 44, 47; Ogdensburg meeting, XV 49, *49*; Far Eastern policy, XV 62, 69; Geneva Disarmament conference, XV 71–72; London Economic conference, XV 73; Litvinov agreement, XV 73–74; Isolationism XV 79; Ethiopian crisis, XV 80; Rhineland incident, XV 84; Spanish Civil War, XV 90; "Quarantine speech," XV 91; Ludlow proposal, XV 94; Czech crisis; XV 95–98; Proclamation of Neutrality, XV 100; on Italian declaration of war, XV 107; on European war, XV 109; on aid to allies, XV 114; Lend-lease, XV 116, 118–119; XVI 11; Atlantic charter, XV 121–122, *121*; XVI 12; embargo on strategic materials, XV 127; "ABC-1" plan, XV 129; response to Japanese invasion of Indochina, XV 132, 134; commitment to armed support for Far East, XV 138; third term, XVI 10, 11; war, XVI 13, *14*; Allied relations 1942, XVI 15; Torch, XVI 16, 74; Casablanca conference, XVI 16–17, *16*; Teheran conference, XVI 18, *18*; Yalta, XVI 19; XVIII 10; "Great Commitment," XVI 43–44; industrial war effort, XVI 59; evacuation of Japanese, XVI 59; convoys, XVI 70–71; China policy, XVI 120; atomic bomb, XVI 128; death, XVI 133, *133, 134*; XVII 10; war leader, XVI 134–140, *139*; policy toward Soviet Union, XVIII 12, 15, 16; United Nations, XVIII 17–18; Indochina, XVIII 98
Roosevelt, Idaho, IX *70*
"Roosevelt Corollary," XI 74; XV 31
Roosevelt Recession, XIV 133
Root, Elihu, XI 74; XII 23; XV 14, 16–17, *16,* 23
Root, Erastus, III 91
Root, Robert Marshall, VI *118*
Rose, Billy, XVII 137
Rose, Carl, XIII 96
Rose, Louis, V 42
Rose (ship), II 37
Rose Bowl, Pasadena, California, XIV 75
Rosecrans, William S., VII 33, 34–35, 110–111
Rosenberg, Alfred, XVIII 22, *22*
Rosenberg, Ethel, see Rosenberg case
Rosenberg, Harold, XVII 94
Rosenberg, Julius, see Rosenberg case
Rosenberg case, XVII 25, 40, 43, *43*
Rosenman, Sammy, XIV 31
Rosenwald, Julius, VIII 100
Rose's Bar, California, V 139
Rose Tattoo, The, XVII 106
"Rosie the Riveter," XVI 62
Ross, Edward A., X 71–72; XI 86
Ross, Edmund G., VIII 36
Ross, Harold, XIII 96
Ross, Robert, III 126
Rossiter, Thomas, III *28*
Rost, Pierre, VII 100
Roszak, Theodore, XVII 97; XIX 75
Rotary Clubs, XI 126
"Rotation," IV 17
Rothko, Mark, XVII 94, *94,* 96
Rothstein, Arnold, XIII 61
Rothstein, Arthur, XIV *123*
Rough Riders (Spanish-American War), XI *40*
Roundheads (English Civil War), I 62
Rourke, Constance, XIV 88
Rousseau, Jean Jacques, IV 88
Rowing Clubs, X 119
Royal Air Force, XVI 15, 70, 74

Royal American Regiment, I 97
Royal Gorge, Arkansas, IX 36
Royal Navy, I 91; II 67–68, 73, *75,* 77; 81; XI 78, 82
Royal Society, I 114
Royalists, see Cavaliers
Royce, Josiah, X 92; XI 114
R. P. Resor (ship), XVI *70*
Rubber industry, IV 64, *64*; X 24
Rubin, Jerry, XIX 78
Ruby, Jack, XIX 29
Ruckelshaus, William, XIX 113
Ruckle, Thomas C., IV *68*
Rudd, Caroline, IV *90*
Rudolph, B. F., VIII 42
Ruef, Abe, XI 53
Ruffin, Edmund, VI 125; VII *15*
Ruhlin, Gus, XI 136
Ruhr Pocket, XVI 104
Rukeyser, Muriel, XIV 56
Rumania, XII 21; XVI 140; XVII 15, 23
Rum Row, XIII 56
"Run-away officials," V 109
Rundstedt, Karl Rudolf Gerd von, XVI 96
Runes, I 20
Rural Electrification Administration, XIV 49, 124, 128
Rural Post Roads Act (1916), XIII 38
Rush, Benjamin, II *13,* 60, 84, *84,* 104, 109, 126; IV 85, 114
Rush, Richard, III 131; IV 29; V 65, *65*
Rush-Bagot Agreement (1817), III 130
Rusk, Dean, on Korean War, XVIII 55; on China, XVIII 58; secretary of state, XVIII 85, *85*; XIX 19, *21*; Bay of Pigs, XVIII 86; Cuban Missile Crisis, XVIII 90
Russel, Bill, XVII *130*
Russell, Charles Edward, XII 57
Russell, Charles M., IX *47, 52, 61, 63,* 137
Russell, John Russell, 1st Earl of, VII 100, *103,* 107
Russell, Ken, XIV 95
Russell, Lillian, XI 137
Russell, Louis, XVII 58
Russell, Richard, XVII 60
Russell, William Howard, VII 69; IX 26, 27
Russell, Majors & Waddell, IX 27
Russell Islands, XVI 36
Russia, territory in North America, III 131; V 21; cession of claims in Oregon, V 51; and US Civil War, VII 104, 105, 107, *108*; emancipation of serfs, X 58; designs on China, XI 43, 46, 74; war with Japan, XI 48, 74, *75,* 77, *77*; XII 22; alliance system, XII 13–14, *14*; declaration of war, XII 18; Tannenberg, XII 20; Brusilov, XII 21; Brest-Litovsk, XII 53; Russian Revolution (1917), XII 53, *53,* 120, 123, 131, 136–137, *137*; XIII *12,* 13; XVIII 10; see also Union of Soviet Socialist Republics
Russian Revolution (1917), XII 53, *53,* 120, 123, 131, 136–137, *137*; XIII *12,* 13; XVIII 10; see also Union of Soviet Socialist Republics
Russo-Japanese War (1904–05), XI 48, 74, *75,* 77, *77*; XII 22
Rustin, Bayard, XIX 58
Ruth, George Herman ("Babe"), XIII 77, *78*; XIV 15, 75
Rutledge, Edward, II *13*
Rutledge, John, III 22; 25
Ryan, Joseph P., XIV 111
Ryder, Albert Pinkham, X 87
Rynning, Ole, IV 74
Ryswick, Peace of (1697), I 87, 88
Ryujo (carrier), XVI 30
Ryukyu Islands, XVI 119, 122, 124

Saarinen, Eero, XVII 99
Sabatini, Rafael, XIII 72
Sabbatarian campaign, X 47, 115, 119; XI 18
Sabotage Act (1918), XII 110
Sac, IX 15
Sacajewea, III 75–77
Sacasa, Juan, XV 31, 36, 40
Sacco, Nicola, see Sacco-Vanzetti case
Sacco-Vanzetti case, XIII 17, 18, 111
Sacramento, California, V 138; IX 27, 28, 31
Sacramento, Battle of (1846), V 83
Sacramento Valley, V 63
Sadat, Anwar, XVIII 139–140; XX 31; see also
    Egypt
Safford, Lawrence F., XV 131
Saguenay River, I 22, 23
Saigon, Vietnam, XVIII 99, 105, 105, 115
Saint Augustine, Florida, I 47, 74, 85, 90
St Brendan, I 18, 19
Saint Cecilia society, I 114
St Clair, General Arthur, III 44–45
St Eustatius, III 78, 79
Saint-Gaudens, Augustus, X 93; XI 104
St John, Vincent, XI 97
St John's Fort, II 33
St John's River, I 23
St John's University, Annapolis, XIV 65
St Joseph, Missouri, IX 27, 28, 32
St Laisson, I 81
St Lawrence, Gulf of, I 22
St Lawrence River, I 22, 23, 28, 79, 80, 85, 89, 90;
    III 122
St Lejer, Barry, II 43
St Louis, Missouri, VI 51, 51; IX 26, 28, 44, 58, 59;
    X 29, 110, 113; XI 27, 57, 128; XIII 60
St Louis blues, XIII 87
St Louis Cardinals, XIV 76; see also Baseball
St Louis University, IV 86
St Lucia, II 69, 69, 72, 73
St Marks, Florida, III 130
St Mary's Maryland, I 73
St Patrick's Day, XI 126
St Paul, Minnesota, IX 85; X 110
St Paul & Pacific Railroad, IX 35; see also Railroads
St Pierre, I 98
"Saints," I 57, 59; see also Pilgrim Fathers
Saints, Battle of the (1782), II 77, 81
St Simon, I 81
St Thomas Island, XI 78
St Thomas's Church, New York City, IV 97
St Valentines Day massacre, XIII 63, 63
Saipan Island, XVI 110, 111, 111, 112, 113
Saito, Makoto, XV 64
Saito, Lieutenant-General Yoshitsugu, XVI 112
Sakhalin Island, XV 23, 51; XVIII 39
Salamaua, New Guinea, XVI 35
"Salary Grab," X 42
Salazar, Antonio de Oliveira, XVI 10
Salem, Massachusetts, I 59–61, 64; II 93
Salem witch trials, I 64, 64; IV 138–139
Sales tax, XIV 19
Salinger, J. D., XVII 103, 104, 127
Salisbury cotton mills, VIII 121
Saloon, XI 30–31, 120; XII 119
Saltillo, Battle of (1846), V 77
"Salting," IX 80; see also Mining
Salt Lake City, Utah, V 103, 106; IX 16, 27
Salt Lake City (ship), XVI 35
Salt Lake High Council, V 101
Salt Lake Valley, V 99, 101, 105, 106–107
SALT, see Strategic Arms Limitation Talks
Salvation Army, X 119; XI 109; XIV 12
Samoa, XI 44, 74; XVI 25
Samoset, I 50
Sample, Paul, XIII 110
Sampson, William, XI 39, 40
Samuelson, Paul, XIX 23
San Andreas fault, XI 90
San Antonio, Texas, I 46, 47; V 39, 40, 41, 49
San Augustin, see Saint Augustine, Florida
San Bernardino, California, V 106
San Carlos Borromeo, V 28
San Carlos reservation, Arizona, IX 111, 115, 116
Sánchez Cerro, Luis M., XV 43
Sandal missile, XIX 83, 86; see also Ballistic
    missiles

Sandburg, Carl, XI 109, 111; XIII 98; XIV 89; XVII
    100
Sand Creek, Colorado, IX 102
Sand Creek Massacre, IX 102, 102
San Diego, California, V 30
Sandino, César Augusto, XV 35, 36
Sandwich, Edward Montagu, 1st Earl of, II 67, 68,
    73, 74
Sandy Hook, New Jersey, II 68
Sandys, Sir Edwin, I 58
"Sanford and Son," XIX 58
San Francisco, California, V 30, 118, 134, 137, 138;
    IX 26, 28, 32, 80, 82, 83; X 106, 108–109, 113,
    114; XI 30, 51, 53, 77; earthquake (1906), XI 90,
    90; fair (1915), XI 128; general strike (1934), XIV
    111, 111; art center, XVII 101
San Francisco Bay, V 63
San Francisco conference (1945), XVIII 17, 18
San Francisco de la Espade (San Antonio, Texas), I
    47; V 29
San Francisco Examiner, X 124
San Francisco State College, XIX 57
Sanitation services, X 115–116, 115, 116
San Jacinto (ship), VII 102, 103
San Jacinto, Battle of (1836), V 41, 42, 44, 44
San Joaquin Valley, California, V 21, 63
San Jose, California, V 30, 138, 139
San Juan Bautista, California, V 30
San Juan Capistrano, California, V 30
San Juan Hill, Battle of (1898), XI 40
Sankey, Ira D., X 119
Sanlúcar, Spain, I 15
San Luis Obispo, California, V 30
San Luis Rey de Francia, California, V 29
San Patricio, Texas, V 40
Sanpoil, I 40; see also Indians, American
Santa Anna, Antonia López de, V 41, 42, 44, 68, 80,
    80, 87, 91, 93; see also Mexican War
Santa Barbara, California, V 30
Santa Cruz, Battle of (1942), XVI 31
Santa Fe, New Mexico, V 12, 31, 31, 33, 33, 81, 82;
    IX 45
Santa Fe Railroad, see Atchison, Topeka & Santa Fe
    railroad
Santa Fe Trail, V 13, 13, 33, 33, 55, 125; IX 26, 101
Santa Maria (ship), I 11, 12
Santa Rita del Cobre, V 33
Santayana, George, X 92; XIII 67
Santa Ysabel massacre, XII 30
Santee Sioux, IX 101; see also Sioux
Santo Domingo, III 41, 70; X 44; XI 78
Sapwood missile, XIX 86; see also Intercontinental
    ballistic missile
Sarajevo, Yugoslavia, XII 17
Saratoga, convention of (1777), II 38, 44, 44, 66, 68,
    106, 136, 137
Saratoga (carrier), XVI 110
Sargent, Henry, IV 11
Sargent, John Singer, X 98
Sarogan, William XIV 89
Sarro, Rodney, XIV 134
Sasaki, Major-General Noboru, XVI 36
Sassacus, I 51
Saturday Evening Post, XI 124; XIII 68, 71, 74; XIV
    105; XVI 62
"Saturday Night Massacre," XIX 113
Saturday Review of Literature, XIII 73
Saturn V Rocket, XIX 89; see also Ballistic missiles
Sauckel, Fritz, XVIII 22, 22
Saudia Arabia, XVIII 139, 140
Sauk, I 41; see also Indians, American
Saunders, Alvin, IX 29
Saunders, Otis, XI 123
Savage station, Battle of (1862), VII 28
Savannah, Georgia, I 23; II 102; III 11; VI 42, 51;
    VII 124; VIII 52
Savannah River, I 16; VII 22
Savo Island, XVI 39
Sawyer, Philetus, XI 54
Sayers, Tom, VII 69
Sayler's Creek, Battle of (1865), VII 128
Saypol, Irving, XVII 43
Sazanami (ship), XVI 22
Scalawags, VIII 39, 39, 40, 44, 45; see also
    Reconstruction
Scapa Flow, Scotland, XII 131
Scarface, XIV 91

Scarlet Letter, The, IV 139, *139,* 140
Scattergood, J. Henry, XIV 68
Schacht, Hjalmar, XVIII 22
Scharnhorst (battle cruiser), XV *84*
Schecter brothers, XIV *46*
Schecter case (1935), XIV 47
Scheer (ship), XVI 73
Schenck, Carl Alvin, VIII 125
Schenke v the United States, XII 111
Schieffelin, Ed, IX 73
Schiff, Jacob, VIII 101, 115
Schine, David, XVII 44, 46, *46*
Schirach, Baldur von, XVIII 22, *22*
Schlesinger, Arthur, Jr, on F. D. Roosevelt, XIV 37;
    Great Depression, XIV 56; American liberal
    tradition, XVII 107; assistant to Kennedy, XIX 19;
    on American imperialism and presidency, XIX 119;
    on modern America, XIX 123; on Nixon, XIX 125,
    133; conservatism and liberalism in America, XIX
    137, 140
Schlieffen Plan, XII 18
Schmeling, Max, XIV 74, 75
Schmookler, Jacob, XIX 93
Schneiderman, Rose, XI 100
Schoeps, Johann, III 94
Schofield, John M., VII 122
Scholarie Valley, I 104
Schonchin John (Chief), IX *107*
School and Society, XI 115
Schoolhouse Blues, XIII 92
Schreyvogel, Charles, IX 137–138
Schultz, Dutch, XIII 60; XIV 114
Schulyer, Philip, II 26, 33, 34, 40, 44, 115
Schulz, George, XIX *104*
Schurz, Carl, VIII 22
Schwab, Charles M., XII 106
Schwammenuel Dam, XVI 103
Schwartz, Maud, XI 100
Schwarzschild & Sulzberger, X 19
Schweinfurt raid, XVI 85
Schwerpunkt, XVI 18
Science, in colonial America, I 113, 114, *115*; role of,
    in social reform, XI 86, 94; energy, XI 104;
    Second World War, XVI 56–57; see also
    Technology
Scientific American, X 25
SCLC, see Southern Christian League Conference
Scopes, John Thomas, XIII 112–113
Scopes trial, XIII 112–113, *112*
"Scorched-earth" policy, VIII 11
"Scorchers," X 115, 119
Scott, Adrian, XVII 38, *38*
Scott, Emmett J., VIII 113; XII 78
Scott, Frank A., XII 102
Scott, Hugh L., XII 65
Scott, Orange, VI 81, *81*
Scott, Thomas A., IX 37
Scott, Winfield, V 77, *85,* 86–87, *89,* 90, 91, 92; VI
    96, 97, 136, 137; VII 10, 18, 19, *20,* 131
Scranton, Pennsylvania, X 106
Screen Writers Guild, XVII 38
Scribner's, VIII 126, 139; X 93, 103
SDS, see Students for a Democratic Society
Seabees, XVI 41, *41,* 122
"Seadog," I 25
Sea Hawk, The, XIII 72
Sea Islands, South Carolina, VIII 51
Sealark Channel, XVI 29
Seale, Bobby, XIX 57
Sea otter, V 21
Sears, Roebuck & Co., VIII 100; XI 21, 128
SEATO, see South East Asia Treaty Organization
Seattle, Washington, XI 128
Sea-Wolf, The, XI 107
Secession, VI 132, *133,* 134, 135, 136, 138,
    139–140, *139, 140;* VII 12, 14, 18–19, 44, 55, 89;
    see also Civil War; South, the
Secession, XIII 70
"Second American party system," IV 27–28, 31, 36
Second Bank of the United States, III 88; VII 87
Second Division, AEF (First World War), XII 79, 89,
    91, 92
Second Marine Division (Second World War), XVI
    108, *108*
Second World War, declaration of war, XV 100;
    invasion of Poland, XV 103; "phony war," XV 101;
    "Winter War," XV 101, 103; western

blitzkrieg, XV 103, *104, 106;* Dunkirk, XV *107;* Fall
    of France, XV 103, *106;* Battle of Britain, XV 115;
    XVI 10, *10;* invasion of Russia, XV 120; XVI 10–11;
    Pearl Harbor, XVI 12, 13, 20, *20,* 22; Arcadia
    strategy, XVI 14; Allied relations 1942, XVI 15;
    Torch, XVI 15–16, 74, 76, *76,* 77, 78–81;
    Casablanca Conference, XVI 16–17; Pacific
    theater, XVI 17; Teheran Conference, XVI 17;
    Japanese advance, XVI 23, *23,* 24, 25; hump
    airlift, XVI 24; Coral Sea, XVI 26, *26,* 27; Midway,
    XVI 28, 32, *32;* Guadalcanal, XVI 29–32, *31, 32,
    34;* Papua campaign, XVI 32, 35; Aleutians
    campaign, XVI 35–36; Solomons campaign, XVI
    36–37, 39, *39;* Rabaul bombing, XVI 41; US,
    industrial war effort, XVI 44–45; finance of war,
    XVI 58; social effects of, XVI 58; home front
    during, XVI 60, *60,* 62, *62–65,* 66, 67–68; Battle
    of the Atlantic, XVI 70–71, *70–71,* 73; bomber
    command, XVI 74; New Guinea campaign, XVI
    114; Leyte Gulf, XVI 116, *116,* 118–119; Iwo
    Jima, XVI 120,122, *122;* Okinawa, XVI 122,
    124–126, *127;* atomic bomb, XVI 126, 128–130,
    130; V-J Day, XVI 131, *131;* cost of, XVI 133;
    assessment of American policy, XVI 134–140;
    Market Garden, XVI 98–99, *98;* Battle of the
    Bulge, XVI 101–102; final push, XVI 102–104,
    103, 104, V-E Day, XVI *104,* 106; Makin and
    Tarawa, XVI 108, *108;* Marianas, XVI 110–112,
    110, 111, 113; Palaus campaign, XVI 113; Sicilian
    campaign, XVI 82–84, *82, 84;* bomber
    offensive, XVI 85; Italian campaign, XVI 86, 88,
    86, 88, 89; Allied Supreme Command, XVI 90, *90;*
    Normandy invasion, XVI 92, *92,* 94–96, *94–95;*
    liberation of Paris, XVI 97, *97;* effect on race
    relations, XVII 51; Allied-Soviet relations, XVIII 14
Secretary of commerce, XI 80
Secret ballot, see Ballot, secret
Secret Correspondence, Committee of, II 133
Secret diplomacy, XII 130
Section 7(a), NRA "codes," XIV 109, 111
Securities Exchange Act (1934), XIV 34
Securities Exchange Commission, XIV 34, 128; XIX
    106
Security Council (United Nations), XVIII 17, 24
Sedalia, Missouri, IX 44
Sedgwick, John, VII 36, 37, 136
Sedgwick, Theodore, III 51
Sedition Act; see Alien and Sedition Acts
Sedition Act (1918), XII 110
Seduction of the Innocent, XVII 124
Segal, George, XIX *122*
"See It Now," XVII 48, 124
Segregation, VIII 98, 108, 115, 116, 138; XI 10, 77,
    78, *78;* XVII 21, 50, *50,* 52, 53, 53, 54, *54;* XIX
    52, 53; see also Integration; Negroes
Seigneurial system, I 80, *80,* 81, 82, 83
Seize the Day, XVII 104
Selassie, Haile; see Haile Selassie
Seldes, George, XV 78
Seldes, Gilbert, XIII 100; XIV 81
Selective Service Act (1917), XII 65–66, 77
Selective Service Act (1940), XV 118; XVI 46–47, 57
Selective Service Act (1948), XVII 115
Self-determination, XII 131, 135, 136
Self-mastery Through Conscious Auto-Suggestion,
    XIII 72
Seligman, E. R. A., X 137
Seltzer, O. C., IX 78
Seminar method, X 92
Seminole, I 54; IV 66, 67; IX 15, 93; see also Indians,
    American
Seminole War, IV 67
Semmes, Raphael, VII 125, 126
Senate, representation, III 25; election process, III
    26; treaty making, III 38–39; committee system,
    III 39; Federalists, III 46, 48; Jay treaty, III 51;
    1800 election, III 62; Oregon question, V 64, 65,
    66; response to abolition petition campaign, VI 76;
    debate on Compromise of 1850, VI 93–94; Gilded
    Age, X 46; League of Nations, XII 135, 139–141
Sendai (ship), XVI 39
Seneca, I 53, 93; see also Iroquois; Indians,
    American
Seneca chief, IV 53

Seneca Falls convention (1848), IV 123, 124, 125
Seniority system, XIX 119
Sennett, Mack, XI 132
"Separatists," I 58; see also Pilgrim Fathers;
    Puritans
Serapis (ship), II 113, *113;* III 109
Serbia, XII 16, 17
Serbs, XII 16
Serra, Juní Pero, V 29
"Sesame Street," XIX 51, *51*
Seth Jones, IX 137
Settlement houses, X 118–119; XI 56, 87
Settlers, relations with Indians, I *42,* 43, *44,* 45, *45,*
    46, *47,* 48, 49, *49,* 50–54, *54,* 55, *55,* 59, 61, 62,
    140; Massachusetts Bay colony, I 60–62; in Middle
    Colonies, I 65; Quakers, I 67, 68; in southern
    colonies, I 71–73, *73,* 74, 77, 103, 111; in
    backwoods, I 104, 105; definition of, I 134, 135;
    non-British, I 137; and British presence, III 48;
    and westward movement, IV 70–71; IX 49, 56, 66,
    85, 86, 89, 90, *90,* 92; and slavery issue, VI
    105–107, 114; life on Great Plains, IX 92,
    94–97, *95, 99;* Indian warfare, IX 101; see also
    Immigration
Seven Days' campaign (1862), VII 28
Seven Pines, Battle of (1861), VII 25, 28
Seventeenth Amendment, XI 64; see also
    Amendments, constitutional
Seventh Armored Division (Second World War), XVI
    101
Seventh Army (Second World War), XVI 90, 104
Seventh Cavalry, IX 106, 108
Seventh Corps (Second World War), XVI 90, 102
Seventy-seventh Division (First World War), XII 80
Seven Years' War (1756–1763), II 62–63; see also
    French and Indian war
Sevier, John, I 106; II 120
Sewall, Arthur, X 141
Seward, William H., VI 91, 93, 94, 96, 102, 105, 126,
    128, 129, 132, 135; VII 12, 18, 49, 100, 102, 104,
    134; XI 33, 74
Sewing machine, X 24
Seymour, Horatio, X 37, 48
Seyss-Inquart, Arthur, XVIII 22
Shafter, W. R., XI *39, 40*
Shaftesbury, Anthony Ashley Cooper, 1st Earl of, I 73,
    74, *75*
Shahn, Ben, XIII *18, 52, 60;* XIV 84, *120, 131*
Shaker Heights, Ohio, XIII 33
Shakers, I 135; IV 104, 106–107, *106–107;* X 33
"Shakespeare and Company," XIII 70
Shallow market, VI 48, 52
Shall We Dance?, XIV 94
Shamanism, I 40, 41; see also Indians, American
Shame of the Cities, The, XI 31
Shanghai, China, XV 60, *61, 65*
Shannon (ship), III 124
Shantung, China, XII 135; XV 23, 51, 54, 55
Sharecropping, VIII 59, 126, 128; XI 11; XIII 136;
    XIV 119–120; see also Agriculture
"Share our Wealth Society," XIV 41, 43
Sharkey, Tom, XI 136
Shasta (tribe), IX 16
Shaw, Artie, XIV 100
Shawnee, I 54–55, 92; III 120; see also Indians,
    American
Shawnee Creek, IX 53
Shawnee Trail, IX 44
Shays, Daniel, III 10, 13
Shays's Rebellion, III 10, *10,* 11, 13
Sheeler, Charles, XIII 101; XIV 82, 84, *87*
Sheep farming, IV 68, *69;* V 32
Sheffield, Earl of, III 90
Sheik, The, XIII 72, *73,* 84
Shelburne, William Petty Fitzmaurice, Earl of, II 140
Shenandoah (ship), VII 108, 125
Shenandoah Valley, VII 19, 26, 29, 39, 117, 119
Shepard, Alan B., XIX *84,* 86
Shepard, E. H., XVIII *23*
Shepp, Archie, XIX 58
Sheridan, Philip H., VII 116, 119, *118, 127,* 128; VIII
    11, 32
Sherman, John, VIII 27–28; XI 46
Sherman, Roger, II 12, *13;* III 22, *24,* 25, 26
Sherman, William Tecumseh, VII 35, *61,* 66, 111,
    112, 113, *113,* 115, 119–120, 122, 124, 126–127,
    127, 137, 139; VIII 11, 52; IX 30, 35, 85

Sherman Antitrust Act (1890), X 23, 52–53, 85; XI 59, 67, 96
Sherman Compromise; see Great Compromise
Sherman Silver Purchase Act (1890), X 141
Sherman (M4) tank, XVI 54, 133
Sherwin-Williams Paint Company, XVI 54
Sherwood, Robert E., XIV 26; XV 118, 120, 122
Shetland Islands, I 19
Shidehara, Kijuro, XV 51, 55, 59
Shigemitsu, Mamoru, XVI 131, *131*
Shiloh, Battle of (1862), VII *23*, 24, 113
Shils, Edward, XVII 107
Shima, Vice-Admiral K., XVI 26, 116
Shinn, Everett, XI 111
Shinny, IX 22
"Shin plasters," VII 87
Shipbuilding, I 101, 103, 106, 121, 125; II 63; III 12; IV 49, 57; XII 106, *108*; XVI 48, *49*, 52
Ship fever, IV 75
Shippherd, John, VI 75
Shipping control committee, XII 106
Shirley, Governor William, I 91, 96
Shirley plantation, Virginia, I *111*
"Shirtmen," II 32
"Shoddy," VII 85
Shoeshine, XIV *60*
Shoho (carrier), XVI 27
Shokaku (carrier), XVI 26, 27, 31
Sholes, Christopher Latham, X 25, *25*, 26
"Shoot on sight" speech, XV 122
Short Bull (Chief), IX *112*
Short land pattern musket, II *31*
"Short terms," XVI 82, 84
Shoshone, I 40; III 76; IX 16, 17; see also Indians, American
Shotwell, James T., XV 51
Show Boat, XIII 72, 92
Show Girl, XIII 92
Shriver, Sargent, XIX 37
Shultz, George, XX 35–36
Shuri line, XVI 124, 125
Sicily, invasion of, XVI 17, *80*, 81–83, *82*, *84*
Sickles, Daniel Edgar, VIII 32
Sidney, Algernon, II 48
Sierra Club, IX 128
Sierra Nevada, V 21, 22, 63, 120, 127; IX 10, 16, 32, *32*, 127, 128
Sigel, Frantz, VII 115, 117, 118
"Significance of the Frontier in American History, The," IX 140
Sigsbee, Captain, XI 35
"Silent Majority," XIX 135
Silver, IX 15, 64, 71, 73, 83; X 132, 133–134
Silver Bow, Montana, IX 73
Silver shirts, XV 110
Silver standard, X 48
Silver Star, XVI *79*
Silverton, Colorado, IX 73
Simcoe, John Graves, II 31
Simkins, Francis B., VIII 141
Simmons, Amelia, III 91
Simon and Schuster Publishing Company, XIII 72
Simons, Algie M., XII 57
Simpson, Jerry, X 127, 136
Simpson, William H., XVI 99
Sims, William S., XII *68*, 69
Since Yesterday, XIV 56
Sinclair, Harry F., XIII 29, 30
Sinclair, Upton, XIII 67; XIV 41, *41*
Singapore, XV 127, 129, 130; XVI 20, 23, *24*
Singer, Isaac, IV 64, *64*
Singer Sewing Machine Company, XVI 54
Single tax movement, X 137
Sino-Japanese War (1895), XI 43
Sino-Japanese War (1937–45), XV *61*, *62*, 64–67, *65*, *69*, 91, 125
Sino-Soviet split, XVIII 77, 79, 131
Sioux, I 41, 63; IX 16, 17, 20, 73, 101, *102*, 106–107, 108–109, 111–112, *111–112*; see also Brulé-Sioux; Oglala Sioux; Santee Sioux; Indians, American
Sirica, John, XIX 113, *116*
Sirius, IV 57
Sister Carrie, X 103; XI 107
"Sit-in," XIX 51
Sitting Bull (chief), IX 107, 108–109, *108–109*, 112

Sitzkrieg, XVI 10
Six Crises, XIX 103
Six Nations, I 54; see also Iroquois
Sixteenth Amendment, XI 64; XII 105; see also Amendments, constitutional
Sixth Marine Division (Second World War), XVI 124, 125
Sixth Panzer Army (Second World War), XVI 101
Skater, The, III *104*
Skeleton Creek, IX 53
Sketch Book of Geoffrey Crayon, The, IV 131, 135
Skip-bombing, XVI 35
Skraelings, I 20
Skybolt project, XVIII 92, *92*
Skylab, XIX 98; see also Space program
Skyscrapers, X 96, *96*, 109–110, 118; XI 116; XIII 101, *102*; see also Architecture
Slang, XI 126
Slapstick, XI 132; XIII 83, 85
Slater, Philip, XIX 123
Slater, Samuel, III *84*
Slaughter Mountain, Battle of, see Cedar Run, Battle of
Slave, I 39; see also Indians, American
"Slavebreakers," VI 25
Slave Power, VI 89, 104, 116
Slavery, I 13, 25, 42, 68, 70, 77, 102, 103, *105*; II 15, 60, 104; III 12, 25–26, 82, *83*, 85, 140; IV 10, 31, 34, 36, 82, 108; V 40, 49, 91, 109, 138, 139; origins in new world, VI 10; cotton industry, VI 10–11, 44; VIII 48; profitability, VI 12, 17–18; economic value, VI 12–13, 14; labor, VI 13–14, 21–22; rentals, VI 14; slave trade, VI *14*, 16, 18, 28, *29*, 65; VII *90*; law, VI 18–19, 21, 92, 94, 96, 118, 135; VII 91; manumission, VI 19, 21, 28; food and clothing, VI 22–23, 30; house slaves, VI *22*, 23, *24*; master-slave relations, VI 24, *24*; punishment, 24–26, *25*, *26*; master's power, VI 26; marriage, VI 26, *30*, 34, 35; sexual exploitation, VI 26, 28, 56; cultural destruction, VI 28, 30; community life, VI 31, 34, *33*; religion, VI 34; VIII 148; effects on Negro life, VI 34–35; family ties, VI 35; VIII 60; rebellions, VI 35, *35*, 36–37, *37*, 38; runaways, VI *20*, 31, 35, 38, 92, 96, *97*; effect on southern economy, VI 48, 87, 141; effect of urban life on, VI 54; and violence, VI 56; defence of, VI 57; abolition movement, VI 62–83 *passim*; VII 51–52, 89–92; Founding Fathers, VI 85; Missouri Compromise, VI 85; VII 89; Democrats and Whigs, VI 86, 88, 125; annexation of Texas, VI 87; Mexican war, VI 87–88; "squatter sovereignty," VI 88, 100; 1848 election, VI 90–91; Kansas-Nebraska Act, VI 100–102; Republicans, VI 103–104, 128; Kansas controversy, VI 105–108, 114–115; Dredd Scott, VI 112; Stephen Douglas, VI 117; Abraham Lincoln, VI 117–118, 51–52, 89–92; Crittenden compromise, VI 135; Emancipation Proclamation, VII 32, 51, 92, 94; Confederacy, VII 56–57; emancipation, VIII 48, 50; civil rights, VIII 50; see also Civil War; Negroes
Slavery Inconsistent with Justice and Good Policy, VI 63
Slaves Escaping Through a Swamp, VI 20
Slidell, John, V 69–70, 71; VII 102, 104, *103*, *105*, 108
Sloan, Alfred P., XIII 40–41
Sloan, John, XI 111, *120*
Sloat, John D., V 118
Slovaks, X 63
Slovenes, XII 16
Sluice-box, IX 77, *78*; see also Mining
Slums, X 112, 118; XI 30, *30*, 86, 87; XVII 26; see also Poverty
Smallpox, I 114; II 43
Smalls, Robert, VII 96, *97*; VIII 46
Smallwood, William, II *91*
Smart Set, XIII 96, 105, *108*, 111
Smet, Pierre-Jean de, V 54
Smibert, John, I 116
Smiley, Albert K., IX 118
Smiley, Glenn, XVII *63*
Smith, Adam, I *120*, 121; XI 48
Smith, Alfred Emanuel, XII 127; XIII 18, 125–127, *126*; XIV 26, 27, *27*, 29, 52; XVII 80

Smith, Bessie, XIII 90, *92*
Smith, Charles H., VII 80
Smith, Clarence, XIII 90
Smith, David, XIV 84
Smith David, XVII 96–97
Smith, Edmund Kirby, VII 128; VIII 20
Smith, Hoke, XI 55
Smith, Jedediah Strong, V 15–16, *15*, 19, 21, 22
Smith, Jesse W., XIII 29
Smith, John (colonist), I 49, *49*, 59, 71; III 109
Smith, John (Mormon), V 99
Smith, Joseph, IV 105; V 95, *95*, 97, 106, 111
Smith, Kate, XIV 71, *71*
Smith, Moe, XIII *59*
Smith, Samuel, III 61
Smith, Sydney, IV 127, 128
Smith, Tom, IX 63
Smith, Tommy, XIX *58*
Smith, Walter Bedell, XVI 90
Smith, Wilford H., VIII 108, 110
Smith, William, I 113
Smith, William, VII 64
Smith, William Loughton, III 51
Smith Brothers Cough Drops, XI 23, *23*
Smith college, X 92; see also Universities and colleges
Smithsonian Conference (1971), XIX 93
Smoot-Hawley Tariff (1930), XV 47
Smuggling, XIII 54, 56, *55*
Snake Indians, V 54; IX 16; see also Indians, American
Snake River, V 54, *54*, 55
SNCC, see Student Non-violent Coordinating Committee
Snow White and the Seven Dwarfs, XIV 99, *99*
Snyder, Gary, XVII 134
So Big, XIII 72, 74
Social changes, 1976–86, XX 56–66
Social Christianity, X 119
Social Darwinism, X 97; XI 84
Social insurance, XI 92, 96; see also Social security
Socialism, IV 119, 120; X 80, 87; XI 68, 94, 116; XIII 11; Populist party, X 132; Bellamy, X 137; "gas and water," XI 53; AFL's hostility, XI 97; Jack London, XI 107; New Deal, XIV 140; and Eisenhower, XVII 76
Socialist Labor party, XI 97
Socialist Party of America, XI 97; XII 57, 114; XIII 12, 13–15, *13*; XIV 41, 52, 80; XV 79
Socialist Trade and Labor Alliance, XI 97
Social reform legislation, X 83–85, *84*, *85*; XI 60–61, 87, 89, 91, 92; see also Fair Deal; Great Society; New Deal, New Frontier
Social Register, XI 28
Social security, XI 92; XIV 47
Social Security Act (1935), XIV 47, 54, 65, 67, 115
Social settlement, see Settlement houses
Social unrest, X 51, *138*, 139, 141, *141*; see also Class warfare
Social workers, X 119; XI 30, 56, *87*
Société Anonyme des Mines de Lexington, IX 80
Sociology, XI 30; XVII 107, 108
Soda Pop Moon, XIII 56
"Sod crop," IV 70
Sod house, IX 90, *90*, 92
"Soft money," X 36, 82
Soil Conservation Act (1935), XIV 49
Soil Conservation and Domestic Allotment Act (1936), XIV 124, 126
Soissons, Battle of (1917), XII 92
"Soldier Societies," IX 20
Soledad Brother, XIX 58
Solomon, Isaac, X 32
Solomon Islands, XVI 25, 26, 32, 36, 37, *39*, 41
Some Considerations on the Keeping of Negroes, VI 62
Somers, Sir George, I 72
Somers, Robert, VIII 12
Somme, Battle of the (1916), XII 21, *20*
Somoza, Anastasio, XV 36, 40
Song of Russia, XVII 38
Song of the Talking Wire, The, IX *105*
Sonntag, W. Louis, Jr., X *109*
Son of the Sheik, The, XIII 84
Sonora, Mexico, V 31
Sons of Liberty, I *129*, *130*, 132
"Sooner State" (Oklahoma), IX 93
Sorensen, Theodore, XVIII 84, 90; XIX 13, 18

Soryu (carrier), XVI 28
Soto, Hernando de, I 16, 17, *17*
Soule, William S., IX *16*
Soul on Ice, XIX 58
Souls of Black Folk, The, VIII 111
"Sound money," X 36, 37, 38, 82, 134, 141
Sousa, John Philip, XI 128
South, the, origins of, I 71–77; effects of colonial wars, I 101; dependence on slavery, I 106; in War of Independence, II 120–123, *122–124*; effects of War of Independence on, II 101–104; at Constitutional Convention, III 25; policy clashes with the North, III 46; Federalist opposition, III 88; secessionist feeling, III 137; character of the southerner, IV 10, 55; support of Democratic party, IV 31; plantation economy, IV 65; VI 10, 12–13, *12, 13*, 21–22, 51–59 *passim*; agricultural decline of, IV 70; education in, IV 92; VI 56; annexation of Texas, V 49; slavery, VI 10–11, 12, *12*, 18–19, 38, 43, 57–59; VII 57; distribution of wealth, VI 40; urban centres, VI 42, 51; geography, VI 42–43; cotton, VI 43–45; corn, VI 45–46; class structure of, VI 45, 54–56; economy, VI 48, 116; static rural society, VI 48, *49*, 51–55; VII 57; lack of industry, VI 48, 51–52; transportation, VI 46, 48, 52; hostility to change, VI 53–54; VII 57; violence in, VI 55–56; VIII 73–74; nationalism, VI 57–59, 120; free speech, VI 76; domination of federal government, VI 86, 91; Republican critique of, VI 103–104; Democratic party, VI 116, 120; expansionists, VI 120; against federal works, VI 91, 121; against cheap land policy in West, VI 121; rejection of tariffs, VI 121; reaction to Lincoln's election, VI 132; military strength of, VII 10–11, *12*; secession, VI 134–140 *passim*; VII 12, 55–56, 89; post Civil War economy, VII 87; cost of Civil War, VIII 11–12, 14; racial attitudes, VIII 14–16, 18, *31*, 46; Johnson's reconstruction, VIII 22–24; race riots, VIII 24; 14th Amendment, VIII 25, 27; Military Reconstruction Act, VIII 30, 33; 15th Amendment, VIII 33; radical rule, VIII 39, 82; new constitutions for states, VIII 40–42; state schooling, VIII 40, 64, 129, 132; collapse of land values, VIII 42, 43; radical administrations, VIII 42–46; General Amnesty Act, VIII 46; land redistribution, VIII 51–52; reconstruction of agriculture, VIII 55, 57–59; Ku Klux Klan, VIII 74, 76, 78–79; end of reconstruction, VIII 82–87; 1876 elections, VIII 87, 89; compromise of 1877, VIII 89; New South, VIII, 118–119, 121, 124, 138–141; tobacco, VIII 122–124, *122*; coal, VIII 124; lumbering, VIII 125; industrialization, VIII *124*, 125; petroleum, VIII 125, *125*; hydroelectric power, VIII 125; agriculture, VIII 126–128, *126, 128*; post Civil War politics, VIII 129; Bourbons, VIII 129, 132, 134, 135; convict leasing, VIII 132; state constitutions, VIII 134; Negro disfranchisement, VIII 135; Democratic primaries, VIII 138; segration, VIII 138; XVII 52; post Civil War industry, IX 14; Democratic loyalty, X 45; Populists, X 132; rural region, XI 11; literary renaissance, XIII 71–72; Massive Resistance, XVII 54; integration, XVII 60; Nixon, XIX 104, 107; see also Civil War; Confederate States of America; Negroes; Slavery; names of individual states.
South America, I 12, 13; X 58; XV 40; see also Latin America; names of individual countries
South Carolina, origins of, I 54, 73–74, *74*, 75; in colonial wars, I 88; colonial economic life, I 103; backwoods, I 104–106; II 86; colonial culture, I 112; first state government, II 51; in War of Independence, II 103; III 12; party politics, III 54; constitution, III 136; state's rights, IV 34; slavery, VI 18, 21, 30; cotton, VI 43; rice, VI 44; reaction to Lincoln's election, VI 132, *133*; secession ordinance, VI 134; VII 12; demand for Fort Sumter, VI 134, 136; Black Codes, VIII 15; law against racial discrimination, VIII 40, 42, 66; reconstruction constitution, VIII 42; cotton revival, VIII 43; reconstruction education, VIII 43, 65, 66; militia costs, VIII 46; reconstruction politics, VIII 85–86; tobacco, VIII 126; redemption, VIII 129; Negro politicians, VIII 134; Negro disfranchisement, VIII 135; segregation, XVII 52; see also South, the

South Carolina Gazette, I 109
South Dakota, IX 11, *11*, 44, 86, 87, *89*, 91, 92; statehood, IX 92; agriculture, IX 94, 96, 97, 99; Indian warfare, IX 106–107; Northern Alliance, X 127
South east Asia, XVIII 40, 49, 64, 88
South East Asia Treaty Organization, XVIII 64, 65, *65*, 112
Southern Alliance, X 127, 131–132
Southern Baptist Convention, IV 108
Southern Christian Leadership Conference, XIX 53, 55
Southern Historical Society, VIII 140
"Southern Manifesto" (1956), XVII 54
Southern Pacific Railroad, IX 36–37, 127–128; XI 53
Southern Review, XIII 140
"Southern Strategy," XIX 104, 107
Southern Tenant Farmer's Union, XIV 120, 124
South Fork, Pennsylvania, X 125
South Korea, XVIII 50, 53, 64; see also Korean War
South Mountain, Battle of (1862), VII 29
South Pacific, XVII 132
South Pass, Wyoming, V 16, 22, 24, 55, 63
South Vietnam, see Vietnam
Southwestern Plateau, IX 17
Soviet Union, see Union of Soviet Socialist Republics
Spaatz, Carl, XVI *72*, 74, 88, 90
Space program, XIX 23–25, *24*; Russian lead, XIX 83–84, *83, 84*; Apollo, XIX 84, 88; US-Soviet rivalry, XIX 86–88, 89; cost, XIX 88–89; space centers, XIX 88, *88*, 89; importance to politicians, XIX 89; benefits to economy, XIX 88, 93; practical spin offs, XIX 94, *95*; criticisms of, XIX 94–95; moon landing, XIX 95; space shuttle, XIX 98, *98*; energy threats to, XIX 98; Nixon, XIX 98, 105; 1976–86, XIX 49–51
Spain, American exploration and colonies, I 10–17, 21–23, 33, 42–46, *42–45*, 47; V 27–28, *29*, 30–36; colonial rivalry, I 84–86, 88–91; II 45, 67, *72*, 73, 74, 75; gains in Treaty of Paris, I 98; negotiations with British, II 78; war with British, II 73–75, 78, 79; Treaty of Paris, II 130; aid to Americans, II 135, 136, 138–139; territorial rivalry with US, III 14, 16, 70, 130–131; loss of Latin America, III 131; loss of Mexico, V 27; slavery, VI 10; Cuba, XI 34; Spanish-American War (1898), XI 35, 42; Civil War (1936–39), XV 84, 86, 88–90; Second World War, XVI 10; Spanish-American relations, XVIII 36; see also Conquistadors; Columbus, Christopher; Colonization; Exploration; Missionaries
Spanish-American War (1898), X 124, 141; XI 10, 34, 35, *36*, 39–40, 70; XII 23, 25
Spanish Civil War (1936–39), XIV 81; XV 84, 86, *86*, 88–90, *89*
"Spanish" fever, see Splenic fever
Spanish Succession, War of the, see Queen Anne's war
Spargo, John, XII 57
Sparkman, John J., XVII 75, *76*
Spaulding, Charles C., VIII 96
Speakeasies, XIII 53, *55*, 64
Special Committee on Civil Rights, XVII *20*, 21
Special Committee on Farm Tenancy, XIV 120
Special Naval Landing Force (Japan), XVI 32
Specie Resumption Act (1875), X 134
"Speculators," II 48
Speedwell (ship), I 58
Speer, Albert, XVIII 22
Spence, James, VII 102
Spencer, Herbert, X 96, 97; XI 104
Spengler, Oswald, XIII 107
Spice Islands, I 22
Spies, August, X 78, *79*
Spillane, Mickey, XVII 127
Spindletop gusher, VIII 125, *125*
"Spirit of '96," III 54
Spirit of St. Louis, XIII 80, *80*
Splenic fever, IX 43–44, 56, 59
"Splinter Fleet," XII 69
Spock, Benjamin, XVII 118
"Spoils system," V 17, 27, 35; VIII 81; X 36, 37, 39, 46, 48, 118
Spoon River Anthology, The, XI 109
Sports, X 119, *120, 123*; XI 18, 129, 134, 136–137. *134–137*; XIII 77; XIV 73, 75; see also names of individual sports

Spotsylvania, Battle of (1864), VII 117
Sprague, XVI 116
Sprague, Frank J., X 32
Springfield, Massachusetts, VII 71, 72
Springfield riot (1908), VIII 115
Spruance, Raymond Ames, XVI 28, 110, 111, 114, 122, 124
Sputnik, XVII 82, *84*; XVIII 79; XIX 24, 83, *83*, 84
Squanto, I 50
"Squatter Sovereignty," VI 88, 92
Stadacona, see Quebec City
Stagecoach, IV *49*, 67; IX 24, 26, *24, 26*, 28
Stagecoach, XIV 99
"Stagflation," XIX 105
Stagg, Alonzo, XI 137
"Stake" (Mormons), V 99
Stalin, Joseph, XV *72*, 73, 86, 101, *101*, 103; XVI 13, 15, 16, 17, *17*, 18, 19, 135, 136, 139, *139*, 140; Yalta, XVIII 10; Popular Front, XVIII 12; postwar security policy, XVIII 14–15; Potsdam, XVIII 19, 21, *21*; Nuremberg trials, XVIII 22; cold war, XVIII 24; Sino-Soviet agreement, XVIII 42; Korean War, XVIII 49–50; death, XVIII 61, 62
Stalingrad, Battle of (1943), XVI 16, 84
Stallings, Lawrence, XIII 67
Stalwarts (Republicans), X 36, 37, 39, 40
Stamesos, Theodoros, XVII *96*
Stamp Act (1765), I 117, 120, 127, *127, 128*, 131, 132, 134, 139; II 84, 85, 87
Stampede, IX 49, 52, *49*
Stampeded by Lightning, IX *49*
Stampede Gulch, IX 52
Stamp mill, V 131; IX 77
Stanbery, Henry, VIII 33
Standard Life Insurance Company of Atlanta, VIII 96
Standard of living, XI 87, 89; XIII 49; see also Affluent society
Standard Oil, X 14, 19, 20, 21, *21*, 22, 138; XI 12, 60; XV 43, *45*; see also Corporatism; Industry
Standish, Miles, I 51, 57
Stanford, Leland, IX 31, 32, 37
Stanford, Leland, Jr, X 92
Stanford University, IX 128; X 92
Stanton, Edwin M., VI 136; VII *45*, 51, 133; VIII 32, 36, 37
Stanton, Elizabeth Cody, IV 122–123, *122*, IV 123–124, 125
Stanwyck, Barbara, XIV 95
"Star Dust," XIV 100
Stark, Harold R., XV 116, *130*, 131, 134. 141
Stark, John, II 43
Star of the West, VI 136–137, *136*
Starr, Ringo, XIX 66–67, *67*
"Stars and Bars," VII *55*
"Stars and Stripes" (flag), II *135*; III 14, 18, 108
Stars and Stripes (newspaper), XII 77, *77*
"Star-Spangled Banner, The", III 128
Star system, XIII 81; see also Movies
Stassen, Harold, XIX 103
State government, powers, III 13, 18; party politics, III 54; Constitution, III 136; capital, III 136; states' rights, III 26, 137; IV 28, 29, 31, 33; corruption and reform, XI 53–56
States' rights, III 26, 137; IV 28, 29, 31, 33; V 109; VI *85*, 121; VII 55–56, 60, 63; X 36, 47; XIX 20
States' Rights party, XVII 21, *21*
Statue of Liberty, X 60, 74, *73*; XI 116
Status Seekers, The, XVII 107, 117
Statute of Westminster (1931), XV 46
Staunton, Virginia, XI 53
Steamboats, IV 50; VIII *130*
Steam power, VI 43; X 24; XIII 44
Steam turbines, XIII 44
Stearns, Abel, V 21
Stearns, Frank W., XIII 121
Stearns, Harold, XIII 70
Stearns, J. B., X 26
Steel industry, see Iron and steel industry
Steelworkers Noontime, X 13
Steffens, Lincoln, XI 31, 84, 124; XIII 134
Steichen, Edward, XI 111
Stein, Gertrude, XIII 18, 70, 71, *71*
Stein, Herbert, XIX *104*
Steinbeck, John, XIV 56, 89, *89*; XVI 60; XVII 103
Steiner, George, XVII 107
Stella, Joseph, XIII 101, *104*
Stempel, Herbert, XVII 120

Stengel, Casey, XIII *79*; XVII *130*
Stephens, Alexander H., VI 132, 138, 140; VII 12, 57, *57*, 59, 66, 89; VIII 23, *23*
Stephens, John Lloyd, V 125
Stephens, Linton, VI 138
Stephenson, David C., XIII 17
Stereoscopes, XI 18
Sterne, Hedda, XVII *96*
Stettinius, Edward R. Jr, XVI 138, *139*; XVIII 18, *19*, 99
Steuben, Frederick William, Baron von, II 45, 109, *110*
Stevens, Elisha, V 63
Stevens, Isaac, IX 28
Stevens, Thaddeus, VIII 24, *24*, 26, 27, 28, *32*, 33
Stevens, Wallace, XIII 98; XVII 101
Stevenson, Adlai, presidential candidate, XVII 31, 75, *76*, 80, *82*; ambassador to UN, XVIII 86; XIX 18–19, *21*; and Kennedy, XIX 13, 18; liberal support, XIX 13, 14
Stevenson, Robert Louis, IX 31
Steward, Ira, X 75
Stewart, Alexander, X 109
Stewart, James, XIV 95, *96*; XVI 62
Stewart, T. McCants, VIII 92, 134
Sticks and Stones, XIII 101
Stieglitz, Alfred, XI 111
Stiles, Ezra, I 128
Still, Clyfford, XVII 94, *96*
Stillness at Appomattox, A, XVII 105
Stilwell, Joseph ("Vinegar Joe"), XVI 18, 23, *25*, 120, *121*
Stimson, Henry L., XV 34, 35, 36, 37, 38, 43, 59, 60–61, 114, 139, *114*; XVI 14, 16, 126; XVIII 17
Stinking Water River, IX 73, 74
Stock Market, X *17*, 18, 19; XIII 137–138, *137*, *138*, 140–141, *140*; XIV 10; Securities Exchange Act, XIV 34
Stockton, Richard, II *13*
Stockton, Robert F., V 118, 119, 120, *120*
Stokely, James, XVII 66
Stone, Harlan Fiske, XIII 123; XIV 46, *46*, 47
Stone, John, I 51
Stone, William J., XII 42
Stone's River, Battle of (1863), VII 34
Stop Organized Slaughter, XV 17
Storage battery, X 30
"Stormy Weather," XIV 100
Story, Joseph, III 82; IV 96
Story of Philosophy, XIII 77
Storyville, New Orleans, XIII 87
"Stourbridge Lion," IV 55
Stowe, Harriet Beecher, VI 98, *99*
Straight University, VIII 66
Strange Interlude, XIII 98
"Strangers," I 57, 59; see also Pilgrim Fathers
Strategic Arms Limitation Talks, XVIII 132, *136*, 137; XX 25–26, 29–30, 32–34, 40–41
Strategic bombing, see Bombing, strategic
Stratton-Porter, Gene, XI 126
Streetcar Named Desire, A, XVII 106
Streetcars, VIII 125; X 108, *108*
Street maintenance, X 115–116, *116*
Streets of Night, XIII 66
Strength of the Strong, The, XI 107
Strictures on a Pamphlet Entitled "Friendly Address to all Reasonable Americans," II 26
Strikes, Cœur d'Alene (1899), IX 83, 97; anthracite coal (1902), X 66; XI 60, 97; Pennsylvania miners, X 75; Great Strike (1877), X *76*; Knights of Labor,

X 77; AFL, X 81; Carnegie Homestead (1892), X 139; Pullman strike (1894), X *138*, 139; Cripple Creek (1894) XI 97; Leadville (1896), XI 97; Telluride (1901), XI 97; Cripple Creek (1903–04), XI 97; Pressed Steel Car Co. (1909), XI 98; Paterson (1913), XI 98; IWW, XIII 12; Boston Police (1919), XIII 120–121, *121*; textile industry in twenties, XIII 132, *133*; coal strikes in twenties, XIII 132–133, *133*; Great Depression, XIV 44; Minneapolis (1934), XIV 111; San Francisco General (1934), XIV *111*; "Little Steel" dispute (1937), XIV 112, *112*; Automobile (1937), XIV 112, *115*; post Second World War, XVII 15, 17, *17*; steel strike (1952), XVII 31; see also Labor unions
Stripling, Robert E., XVII 38
Stroheim, Erich von, XIII 82, *82*, 83
Strong, Josiah, XI 47
Strong, William (railroad magnate), IX 36
Strong, William (judge), XVII 52
Stuart, Charles, II 29, 30
Stuart, Gilbert, III 104, *104*, 127; IV *110*, 132
Stuart, "Jeb," VII 28, 32, *34*, 39, 40, 116–117
Stuart, John Leighton, XVIII 47
Studebaker (Motor Company), XIII 40
Student Non-violent Coordinating Committee, XIX 53, 57
Students for a Democratic Society, XIX 122
Studs Lonigan, XIV 89
Stuyvesant, Peter, I 112
Styron, William, VI 37; XVII 103
Sublette, Milton G., V 53
Sublette, William L., V 53
Subchaser, XII 69, *70*
Subcontracting, XVI 52–53
Submarine warfare; the *Turtle*, II *35*; *H. L. Hunley*, VII 125; First World War, XII 22, 37–38, *37*, *38*, *39*, 42, 43, 50, 51, 52, 53, 61, 62, 68–69, *68*, *70*; Second World War, XVI 70–71, *70*, *71*, 73
Substitute brokerage, VII 76
Suburbs, XIII 33; XVII 110–111; XIX *130*
Suez Canal, XI 71; XVIII 71, 72, *72*
Suez Canal Company, XVIII 71–72
Suez Crisis (1956), XVIII 71–73, *71*, *72*, *73*, 75
Suffolk County, New York, II 98
Suffrage, II 55–56; III 26; IV 17, 21, 25, 27; V 139; VI 43, 90; VIII 27, 28, 30, 33, 40, 70–71, *70*, *71*, *73*, 134; XI 94, *94*; XII 118–119, *118*
Sugar, VI 11, 22, 42, 44, 45, *52*; VIII 59, 126; XIII 123
Sugar Act (1764), I 130
Sugar Equalization Board, XII 103
Sugar Refining Company, X 19
Sugiyama, Hajime, XV 135
Suicide pilots, see *Kamikaze*
Sullivan, Ed, XVII 141; XIX 66, *67*
Sullivan, John, II 40, 93, 115, 116, *116*, 140
Sullivan, John L., IX 68; X *120*
Sullivan, Louis, X 93, *94*, 96, *96*, 109; XI 116
Sullivan, Mark, XIV 14; XV 22
Sullivan's Island, South Carolina, VI 134
Sumatra, XVI 20
Summary View of the Rights of British America, I 130
Summerall, Charles P., XII 92, 96, 98
Summit conferences; 1955, XVII 79; XVIII 64; 1960, XVIII 79, 81
Summit Tunnel, IX 32
Sumner, Charles, IV 87; VI 89, 91, 96, *102*, 107, *107*, 132; VIII 24, *24*, 27; X 44

Sumner, William Graham, X 97–98; XI 84; XX 73
Sumter, Thomas, II 120
Sun Also Rises, The, XIII 70
Sun dance, I 40; IX 22, *22*; see also Indians, American
Sunday, Billy, XII 116, *117*; XV 16
Sunday Morning in the Mines, V *132*
Sunday Morning in Virginia, VIII 68
Sunday school, IV 86; see also Education; Religion
Sunderland, La Roy, VI 72
Sun Records, XVII 137
Sunset on the Missouri, V *14*
Sun Yat-sen, XV 51, *53*
Superior, Lake, I 81; X 14
Supersonic Transport plane, XIX 105
Supplemental Reconstruction Act (1867), VIII 32
Supply Priorities and Allocations Board, XVI 45
Supreme Court, III 38, 78, 81–82, *82*, 133; IV 16, 50; VI 92, 112, 113, 132; Reconstruction, VIII 27, 33; "grandfather clauses," VIII 108, 115; Bailey case, VIII 108; Civil Rights cases 1883, VIII 138; *Plessy v. Ferguson* (1896), VIII 138; interstate commerce, X 22; greenbacks, X 38; eight hour day, X 85; "Granger" laws, X 127; segregation, XI 10; XVII 52–53; regulation working hours, XI 91; New Deal, XIV 38, 44, 46–47, 53, *53*; and F. D. Roosevelt, XIV 53–54, 128, 132; educational equality, XIV 67; and labor, XIV 109; 1952 steel dispute, XVII 31; racial justice, XVII 52; Texas Law School case, XVII 52; *Brown v. Board of Education* (1954), XVII 53, 54, *54*; Little Rock decision (1958), XVII 58; Montgomery bus boycott, XVII 62; L. B. Johnson's appointments to, XIX 35; and Nixon, XIX 107; see also Courts
Supreme War Council, XII 74
Surgeon General's Office, XII 102
Surratt, Mary, VII *132*, 134, *134*
Surrealism, XVII 90, 91, *91*
"Survival of the fittest," X 96, 97
Susan Constant (ship), 171
Susquehanna River, I 28
Susquehanna Valley, I 106
Sussex (ship), XII 43
Sutherland, George, XIV 46
Sutherland, William J., IX 80
Sutter, John A., V 63, 120, 122
Sutter's Fort, California, V 116, 118
Sutter's sawmill, V 120, *121*
Suzutsuki (ship), XVI 126
Svinin, Pavel, VI *64*, 69
"Swanee River," VI 47
Swanson, Gloria, XIII 83
Sweat system, X 63, *64*; XI *52*
Sweden, American colonies, I 84; emigrants to US, IV 76, *78*; X 58; agricultural depression, X 58
Sweeney, Carl, IX *22*
Sweeny, Peter Barr, X 43
Sweet Bird of Youth, XVII 106
Sweetwater River, V 55
Swift, Gustavus F., X 18, 32
Swift Meat Company, X 19
Swimming, X 119, *120*; see also Sports
Swing, Raymond Gram, XIV 102
"Swing" (music), XIV 100
Swisshelm, Jane, IV 123
Sword Beach, XVI 92
Sycamore Shoals, Treaty of (1775), I 107
Sylvis, William H., X 75
Syria, XVIII 138

T

Tabernacle (Mormon), V *107*
Tabert, Martin, VIII 132
Tabor, H. A. W., IX 83
Taft, Robert A., anti-New Deal, XIV 136; opposes
   Truman, XVII 18, *18*, 70; 1952 Republican
   convention, XVII 73; and policies, XVII 75;
   opposition to NATO, XVIII 32; foreign policy,
   XVIII 37; Korean War, XVIII 53, 58
Taft, William Howard (president), X 23, 74; XII 126;
   succeeds Theodore Roosevelt, XI 63, *63, 65*; tariff
   controversy, XI 64; legislative activity, XI 64;
   break with Roosevelt, XI 64–65; foreign relations,
   XI 71; "dollar diplomacy," XI 78, 80
Taft-Hartley Act (1947), XVII 18–19, 26, 31
Taft-Katsura agreement (1905), XI 74, 77
Tait, Arthur Fitzwilliam, IX 138
Taiwan, see Formosa
Takagi, Rear-Admiral, XVI 27
Talaud Islands, XVI 114
Talbot, I 60
Talented Tenth, VIII 109, 113, 116
Tales of a Traveller, IV 135
Talkies, XIII 85; see also Movies
Tallahassee, Tennessee, I 16
Talleyrand, Charles, III *55*, 56
Tallmadge, James, VI 85
Talmage, Dewitt, X 97
Talon, Jean, I 82
Tamanend, I 53
Tamiami Trail, XIII 38
Tammany, see Tamanend
Tammany Hall, I 53; X 43; XIII 18; see also
   Political machines
Tammany Society, III 44
Tampa Bay, Florida, I 16
Tampico, Mexico, V 86
Tanaka, Giichi, XV 55
Tanaka, Major-General N., XVI 32
Tanana, I 39; see also Indians, American
Taney, Roger Brooke, IV 16; VI 118, 132; VII 48
Tango, XI 126
Tanks, First World War, XII 74, *83*, 91; Second World
   War, XVI 54, 133
Tannenberg, Battle of (1914), XII 20
Tanner, Archibald, IV *51*
Tansill, Charles C., XV 78
Taos, New Mexico, V *29*, 34
Taos, I 40; see also Pueblo; Indians, American
Tappan, Arthur, VI 71–72, *71*, 74, 75
Tappan, Henry, IV 95
Tappan, Lewis, VI 71–72, *71*, 74
Tarawa, Battle of (1943), XVI 108, *108*
Tarbell, Idaho, XI 31
Tariff Act of 1816, III 89
Tariff duties, III 20, 49, 89; IV 16, 23, 34; VI 116,
   120, 121, 128; VIII 79–81; X 14, 39, 47, 48, 49,
   50, 52, 54, 141; XI 64; XII 130; XV 47
Tarkington, Booth, XI 124
Tarleton, Banastre, II 120–121, *121*, 122
Task Force Thirty-eight (Second World War), XVI 116
Tassafaronga, Battle of (1942), XVI 32
Tassigny, Jean de Lattre de, see Lattre de Tassigny,
   Jean de
Tate, Allen, XIII 71; XVII 100
"Tattered Tom," X 97
Taxation, of the colonies, I 129, 131–133; II 15, 16;
   in the new nation, II 60; post Civil War, X 38–39;
   First World War, XII 105, 116; Harding, XII 24;
   liquor tax, XIII 64; Coolidge, XIII 123; sales tax,
   XIV 19; Second World War, XVI 58, 66; Reagan, XX
   19–20, 53, 64
Taylor, Bayard, IV 87
Taylor, Cecil, XIX 58
Taylor, Frederick Winslow, XI 16; XIII 32
Taylor, Horace, X *21*
Taylor, Maxwell, XVI 102; XVIII 85, *85*, 90, 107,
   109, 110
Taylor, Richard, VI 139; VII 115, 128
Taylor, Robert, XVII 38
Taylor, Zachary (president), IV 36; V 71, 72–77, *72*,
   80–81, *81*, 91, *91*; VI 89, *90*, 90–91, 94; VII 131
Tea Act (1773), II 14
Teach, Edward, I 87
Teacher training college, IV 88; see also Education;
   Universities and colleges
Teamsters Union, XIX 62; see also Labor unions
Teapot Dome scandal, XIII 29–30, 124; see also
   Corruption
Technicolor, XIII 85
Technocratic ideology, XI 86
Technology, IV 41, 63–65, *63–64;* VI 43; X 12, 19,
   24–26, *25, 26,* 28–30, *28–29, 31,* 32–34, *32–34,*
   110; in Progressive era, XI 13–14; First World War,
   XII 126; 1920s, XIII 32; social effects of, XVII 117;
   space, XIX 24; ballistic missiles, XIX 84; and John
   F. Kennedy, XIX 86; impact of space technology,
   XIX 92; benefits to economy, XIX 88, 93–94
Tecumseh, III 120, 122, 124; IV 24, 67
Tecumseh (ship), VII 125
Tedder, Sir Arthur, XVI 88, *90*
Teenager, XVII 136–137, *137*
Teheran Conference (1943), XVI 18, *18*; XVIII 15
Tehuántepec, Isthmus of, V 92
Telegraph, IV 57, 61; IX 26, 27, 105, *105*; X 24, 26
Telephone, X 26, *26*, 110; XI 14, 120; XIII 44, 58
Television, and Joseph McCarthy, XVII 46, 47, *47*;
   and racism, XVII 58; numbers of sets in 1960, XVII
   117; show content, XVII 121; growth of industry,
   XVII 124; quiz show, XVII 120, *120*; fears of, XVII
   125; effect on baseball, XVII 129, *130*; effect on
   film industry, XVII 132; Kennedy-Nixon debate,
   XIX *17*, 18; protest movement, XIX 69; effect of
   rock culture on, XIX 76, 80; in 1980s, XX 52, 77, 81
"Tell Me, Pretty Maiden," XI 123
Temperance Movement, IV 115–116, *116, 117;* VI
   97; X 118
Temple, John, II 106
Temple School, IV 88–89
Tenancy, VIII 55, 57–58, 126, 128; XIV 119–120,
   124; see also Farming; Sharecropping
Ten Commandments, The, XIII 82
Tender Is The Night, XIII 71
Tenderloin, New York City, XI 25, 29
Tenement House Committee, XI 89
Tenement House Laws, X 112; XI 89, 91
Tennent, Gilbert, I 109; IV 100
Tennent, William, I 113
Tennessee, I 106, 107, *107*; III 70; population, III
   16; participation in presidential elections, III 54;
   statehood, III 133; tobacco, VI 44; secession, VII
   18; confederate state, VII 60; and Reconstruction,
   VIII 19, 73, 82; Ku Klux Klan, VIII 74, 76, 78;
   convict leasing, VIII 132; Republican governor
   1880, VIII 134; segregation, VIII 138; XVII 52;
   Scopes trial, XIII 112–113, *112*; see also South,
   the
Tennessee (ship), VII *123*, 125
Tennessee Coal and Iron Company, VIII 124, 132;
   XI 65
Tennessee River, VII 24; XIII 46
Tennessee Valley, I 16
Tennessee Valley Authority, XIV 34–35, *37*, 67
Tennis, X 119, *120*; XI 18, 137; XIII 77; XIX *130*
Tenochtitlán, I 15, 17; see also Mexico City
Tenth Army (Second World War), XVI 122, 124
"Tenting Tonight," VII 82
Tenure of Office Act (1867), VIII 32, 36, 37
Tepee, IX 15, *16, 18*; see also Indians, American
Terán, Manuel Mier Y., V 40
Terkel, Studs, XIV 105
Ternay, Admiral, II 75
Territories, Senate Committee on, VI 100, 101, 120
Terry, Alfred H., VII 125; IX 108
Tet Offensive (1968), XVIII 115, *116*; see also
   Vietnam War
Teuton Sioux, III 75; see also Sioux
Tevis, Lloyd, IX 74
Tew, Thomas, I 87
Texas, I 17, 45, 46, *47*; III 131; V 34; IX 10, 38;
   colonization of, V 39–40, 48; independence, V
   40–41, 44, *44*; Alamo, V 42, *43*; US annexes, V 44,
   48–51, *49–50*, 68, *68*, 70; VI *86*, 87, 121; Mexican
   War, V 69, 93; statehood, V 139; slavery, VI 18;
   cotton, VI 44; boundary disputes, VI 91;
   Compromise of 1850, VI 92; secession convention,
   VI 132, 139–140; secession ordinance, VI 140; and
   Civil War, VII *59*; readmission, VIII 30; and
   reconstruction, VIII 84; oil, VIII 125; Bourbon
   constitution, VIII 134; cattle drives, IX 43, 44, 45,
   45; land system, IX 56; cattle lobby, IX 56, 59;
   Panhandle, IX 92; Southern Alliance, X 127, 131;
   Texas Law School case, XVII 52; see also South,
   the
Texas Admission Act (1845), V 70

Texas and New Orleans Railroad Co. v. Brotherhood of Railway and Steamship Clerks (1930), XIV 109
Texas & Pacific Railroad, IX 37, 38; see also Railroads
"Texas" fever, see Splenic fever
Texas Live Stock Association, IX 59
Texas Rangers, V 76–77, 77, 87
Textile industry, IV 61–62; VII 85; VIII *43*; XI 98; XIII 130–132, *133*; Great Depression, XIV 11, 1934 strike, XIV 111, 112; see also Garment industry
Textile Workers Union, XIII 132
Thailand, XVI 23; and SEATO, XVIII 64, 65, 112
Thames, Battle of the (1813), III 124, *124*; IV 67
Thanksgiving Day, I 50; III 39, 109
Thatcher, Margaret, XX 36
Thatcher, Oxenbridge, I 126
Thayendenagea, see Brant, Joseph
Thayer, Scofield, XIII 101
Thayer, Webster, XIII 17
Theater, immigrant, X 70; in Gilded Age, X 119, 124; in Progressive era, XI 126; in 1920s, XIII 98; in Great Depression, XIV 91; in 1980s, XX 76; see also Literature
Theater Union, XIV 91
Theory of Business Enterprise, The, XI 106
Theory of Social Forces, The, XI 116
Theory of the Leisure Class, The, XI 106
Thermonuclear weapons, XVIII 67, *67*
Theus, Jeremiah, I 116
Thieu, Nguyen Van, XVIII 109, *109*
Third Army (Second World War), XVI 94, 96, 98, 101, 102
Third Division, AEF (First World War), XII 89, 91
Third Fleet (Second World War), XVI 114
Third Reconstruction Act (1867), VIII 32
Third World, XVIII 65, 69, 85
Thirteen Days, XVIII 91
Thirteenth Amendment, VI 113; VII 99; VIII 19, 108; XVII 52; see also Amendments, constitutional
Thirteenth Division, AEF (First World War), XII 80
Thirty-eighth Infantry, Third Division, AEF (First World War), XII 91
Thirty-fifth Division, AEF (First World War), XII 96
Thirty-second Division, AEF (First World War), XII 96
"This Is No Place for a Minister's Son," XI 126
This Side of Paradise, XIII 66, 94, 108
Thomas, Bill, XVII 132
Thomas, George H., VII 111, 122, 124
Thomas, J. Parnell, XVII 48
Thomas, Lowell, XIV 102
Thomas, Norman, critic of New Deal, XIV *40*, 41; XV 79, 81, *119*; socialist presidential candidate, XIV 52; on Joseph McCarthy, XVII 48; see also Socialist party
"Thomas Flyer," XI 140
Thompson, Ben, IX 63
Thompson, Dorothy, XIV 102
Thompson, J. Walter, XIII 49
Thompson submachine guns, XIII 58
Thomson, Charles, II 13; III 26, 35
Thoreau, Henry David, IV 16, 141, *141*; V 10; IX 124, 126
Thorn, Jonathan, V 15
Thornton, William (architect), III *42*
Thornton, William (captain), V 72
Thorvald, I 19
Thoughts on African Colonization, VI 70, 71, 72
Thoughts on Government, II 47, 48, 51, 54, 56
Three-Fifths Compromise (1787), III 25, 82
Three Lives, XIII 70
369th Infantry, AEF (First World War), XII 91
Three Soldiers, XIII 67
Through the Eye of the Needle, XI 119
Thurber, James, XIII 96
Thurman, John, XIII 44
Thurmond, Strom, States' Rights party, XVII 21–22, *21*, 24, 71
Ticonderoga (fort), I 97, 98; II 15, 24, 25, *25*, 30, 33
Tidewater rulers, II 54, 55, 86
Tiffany's, XI 27
Tijerina, Reics Lopez, XIX 62
Tilden, Bill, XIII *79*
Tilden, Samuel J., VIII 87–88, *87*; X 44, 48
Tilghman, Bill, IX 64
Tillman, Benjamin, X 136

Timber and Stone Act (1878), IX 128
Timber Culture Act (1873), IX 86, 94
Timber industry, IV 61
Time, XIII 73; XIV 105; XVII 48; XIX 66
Time-and-motion study, XIII 32, 44
"Time Prices," VIII 59
Timucua, I *26*; see also Indians, American
Tinian Island, XVI 110, 112
Tinker, Joseph, XI 134
"Tin Lizzy," XI 16; see also Model T Ford
"Tiny Tim," XVI 124
Tipitapa, Agreement of (1927), XV 34, 35, 36
Tippecanoe, Battle of (1811), III 120, *120*; IV 31, *33*
Tipton, Missouri, IX 26
Tirpitz, Admiral Alfred von, XII 14, *16*
Tirpitz (ship), XVI 73
Titan, The, XI 107
Titan missile, XIX 86, *87*; see also Ballistic missiles
Tithing Office, V *107*
Tito (Broz, Josip), XVIII 32
Tituba, I 64
Tlaxcala, I 15
Tobacco, cash crop, I 37, 41, 49, *71*, 72, 73, 77, 95, 102, 103, 104; III 17, 65; IV 70; VI 10, 11, 13, *13*, 42, 44, 45; supposed benefits, I 113, 114; enumerated commodity, I 122, 125; new varieties, VIII 122, *122*, 124, 126; American Tobacco, XI II; industry, XIII 46; Agriculture Adjustment Act, XIV 119
Tobacco Road, XIV 91
Tobin, Dan, XIV 111
Tocqueville, Alexis de, III 90, 134; IV 12–13, *13*, 67, 97, 98, 99, 109, 114; XVIII 39
Tod, David, VI 125
Togo, Shigenori, XV 136, 138
Togo, Heihachiro, XII 14
To Have and Have Not, XIV 88
Tojo Hideki, XV 126; XVI 13, 20, 112; XV *125*, 135
"Tokenism," XIX 52, 57; see also Black Power
Tokko Tai, XVI 125
Tokugawa, Prince Iyesato, XV *22*
"Tokyo Express," XVI 30, 32
Tokyo fire raids, XVI 115, *115*
Toledo, Ohio, XI 51, 53; XIV 12
Toleration Act (1649), I 77
Tolley, Howard Ross, XIV 126
Tombstone, Arizona, IX 64, 73, 84
Tomlin, Bradley, XVII *96*
Tompkins, Daniel Augustus, VIII 119
Tonkin Gulf Incident (1964), XVIII 110, *111*
Toombs, Robert, VI 135, 137; VII 59
Toomer, Jean, XIII 99
Topeka, Kansas, IX 36
Topeka Convention (1855), VI *105*, 106, *106*
Topographical Corps, US Army, V 13, 22, 116
Tordesillas, Treaty of (1494), I 21
"Tories," II 10, *16*, 19, 20, *90*, 92, 95, 97, 98, 100, 101, 102, 103; see also Loyalists
Toronto, Canada, III 124, 127
Torpedoes, VII 124–125; XV 130; XVI 36
Torrents of Spring, XIII 95
Torresola, Griselio, XVII *28*
Torrio, John, XIII 58, *61*
Tortillas, V 34
Tortoise and the Hare, The, XIV 99
Toscanelli, Paolo de, I 10
Tosei-ba, XV 126
Totanac, I 15; see also Indians, American
Totem pole, I *36*, 39; see also Indians, American
Toughest Fighting in the World, The, XVI 32
Toungoo, Battle of (1942), XVI *25*
Tourgée, Albion W., VIII 138, 140
"Town Meeting of the Air," XIV 102
Townsend, Francis E., XIV 41, 53, 66
Townshend, Charles, I 132
Townshend Acts (1767), II 16, 87
Toynbee, Arnold, XV 29
Toyoda, Soemu, XVI 111, 116, 131
Toyoda, Teijiro, XV 134
Trade and commerce, fur trade, I 81–83; III 48, 50; V 14–16, 18–19, 21; regulations of colonial, I 121–125; in the new Republic, III 12, 16, 17; Jay Treaty, III 51; effect of Madison's policies on, III 85; flood of British goods after 1815, III 88; shipping, III 112, 117, 119–120; blockade, III 116–117; with Latin America, III 131; government aid to, IV 16; China trade, III 18, *19*, 112, *112*; IV 57; XI 43–44, 46–47; openings in Japan, IV 57;

Pacific trade, V 21; in Spanish California, V 30; and New Mexico, V 33; interregional, VI 42–43; and foreign policy, XI 71, 74, 77, 80; XVIII 128; First World War, XII, 60–61, 105; first foreign trade deficit, XVIII 136; decline under Eisenhower, XIX 93; boom in aerospace and electronic industries, XIX 93; see also Economy; Industry
Trade and Navigation, Acts of, I 121, *121*, 122, 124–126, 129; II 63
Trade mark, XI 23
Trade unions, see Labor unions
Trading with the Enemy Act (1917), XII 105, 110
Traffic Safety Act (1966), XIX 137
Tragedy of Pudd'nhead Wilson, The, X 103; XI 103
Train, George Francis, IX 29
Tramways, see Trolley, electric
Transatlantic communication, IV 57, 75; X 26, 57, 58, 60
Transatlantic Review, XIII 70
Transcendentalism, IV 119, 120, 121, 140–141
Transformers, X 32
Transit systems, XI 13; XIII 46
Trans-Mississippi Exposition (1898), XI 128
Transportation, IV 49–51, *49–51*, 67–68, *68*, 96; VI 46, 48, 52; IX 24, *24*, 26–28, 96–97; X 15; XII 106, 113
"Transportation" (convicts), I 121, *124*
Transportation Building, Chicago, X 93, *94*
Transylvania Company, I 106, 107
Traveler from Altruria, A, X 102
Travis, Joseph, VI 36, *36*
Travis, William B., V 42
Treasury department, III 39; X 48; XII 116; XIII 24
Treasury Island, XVI 37, 41
Treatise of Military Discipline, I 97
Tredegar Works, VI 13
Trent, William, I 92
Trent, VII 102, *103*
Trenton, Battle of (1776), II 40–41, *40*, *41*, 98
Triangle Shirt Waist Factory, XI 91, *91*
Trident Conference (1943), XVI 17
Trieste, XII 135, 136; XVIII 23
Trilling, Lionel, XVII 107
Trincomalee, XVI 25
Trinidad, I 12
Trinity Church, Boston, X 93
Tripartite Pact (1940), XV 127, *127*, 131, 132
Triple Alliance, XII 14
Triple-A Plowed Under, XIV 91
Tripoli, III 114, *115*
Tripolitan War (1801–05), III 114, *115*
Trist, Nicholas P., V 92–93, *93*
Triumph of the Egg, XIV 84
Trolley, electric, X 32, 109
Trollope, Anthony, IV 12
Trollope, Frances, IV 53
Trotter, James Monroe, VIII 91–92
Trotter, William Monroe, VIII 109–110, 111, *111*, 113, 115
Trouble in Frisco, XIV *111*
Truckee Route, V 63
True Account of America, IV 74
True American, VI 48
True Reformers, VIII 96
True Reformers Bank, VIII 98
Truk Island, XVI 39, 41, 110
Truman, Bess, XVI 65; XVII 11
Truman, Harry S. (president), First World War, XII 96, *96*; XVII 11; in 1920s, XV 14; vice president, XVI 19; XVII 12; atomic bomb, XVI 126; Lend-Lease, XVI 135; president, XVI *139*. 140: XVII 10. *14*; early career, XVII 10–11, *10*, *11*; senator, XVII 12, *12*; and Democratic party, XVII 13; New Deal, XVII 13, 15; "common man," XVII 13, 14, *14*; "reconversion," XVII 14; reform, XVII 15; and labor unions, XVII 15, 31; OPA, XVII 17; loss of New Dealers, XVII 17; 1946 campaign, XVII 18; 80th Congress, XVII 18; Taft-Hartley Bill, XVII 18–19; housing, XVII 19, *19*; 1948 Democratic convention, XVII 22, 23–24, *23*, *24*; Fair Deal, XVII 25; foreign policy, XVII 25, 30; red scare, XVII 25; congressional difficulties, XVII 25–26; assassination attempt on, XVII *28*; and Korean War, XVII 29; XVIII 50–51, 53, 55, 58; McCarran Act, XVII 29; corruption, XVII 30, *30*; loss of popularity, XVII 29, 30, *30*, 31; steel dispute, XVII 31; retires, XVII 31, *31*, *32*; assessment,

XVII 32; relations with USSR, XVIII 16, *16*, 17; Potsdam, XVIII 19, 21, *21*; cold war, XVIII 24, *25*; containment policy, XVIII 26; Truman Doctrine, XVIII 27, *27*, 28; Economic Cooperation Act, XVIII 31; Berlin blockade, XVIII 32; Point Four plan, XVIII 36; Far Eastern policy, XVIII 39, 40, 42, 44, 45, 46, 47, 48; China lobby, XVIII 47
Truman Doctrine, XVIII 27, *27*, 28
Trumbo, Dalton, XVII 38, *38*, 39
Trumbull, John (painter), II *26*, 140; III 104
Trumbull, John (poet), II *90*; III 95
Trumbull, Jonathan, II 33
Trung sisters, XVIII 96
Truscott, Lucian, XVI 88
Trusts, X 16, 19; XI 12; "money trust," X 18; anti-trust movement, X 22–23; XI 56, 60; XIII 46; XVII 26; Motion Pictures Patents Company, XI 133; Capper-Volstead Act, XIII 26; see also Corporations
Truth, Sojourner, VI 82
Truth About the Trusts, The, X 16
Truth in Packaging Act (1966), XIX 41
"Truth in Securities" Act (1933), XIV 34
Tryon, William, I 106
Tsushima Strait, Battle of (1905), XI 74, *75*
Tubac, Arizona, V 31
Tuberculosis, XI 89
Tubman, Harriet, VI 66
Tuck, Dick, XIX 135
Tucker, George, IV 87
Tucker, Joshua, VI *49*

Tucson, Arizona, V 31; IX 26
Tugwell, Rexford, XIV 30, 31, *31*, 44, 120, 133
Tulagi, XVI 25, 26, 29, 30
Tunis, XVI 76, 79, 80
Tunisia, XVI 15, 76
Tunney, Gene, XIII 77, *79*
Tunstall, John, IX 66, 67
Turgot, Anne Robert Jacques, Baron de l'Aulne, III 90
Turkey, XII 16; First World War, XII 20, 136; Communist threat, XVIII 26–27; American aid, XVIII 28; NATO, XVIII 36; CENTO, XVIII 72
Turner, Frederick Jackson, IX 140, *140*, 141; X 92; XI 80
Turner, Nat, VI 34, 36–37, *36*, 38, 75
Turner, Vice Admiral Richmond Kelly, XV 134, *134*; XVI 36
"Turquoise Trail," V 33
Turtle (submarine), II 35, *35*
Tuscarora, I 54; see also Indians, American
Tuskegee Institute, VIII 66, 101, *101*, *102*, *104*
Tuskegee Machine, VIII 105–106, 107, 108, 110, 111, 113
Tutweiler, Julia, VIII 132
Twain, Mark (Clemens, Samuel Langhorne), IV 133, 137; VII 137; VIII 122; IX 12, 16, 77; X 24, 26, 42, 87, 100, 101–102, 103, 104, *104*; XI 102, 103–104, *103*, 105, 106; XIII 66; XVII 105
Tweed, William Marcy, X 42–44, *43*
Tweed Ring, VIII 87; X 42–44, *43*
Twelfth Army Group (Second World War), XVI 90, 94, 99

Twelve O'Clock High, XVII 132
Twentieth Amendment, XIV 24; see also Amendments, constitutional
Twenty-first Amendment, XIII 65; see also Amendments, constitutional
Twenty-fourth Amendment, XIX 41; see also Amendments, constitutional
"Twenty-One Demands," XV 51, 53
Twenty-second Amendment, XVII 18, 80, 85; see also Amendments, constitutional
Twenty-seventh Division, AEF (First World War), XII 80
Twenty-sixth Amendment, XIX 118; see also Amendments, constitutional
Twenty-sixth Division AEF (First World War), XII 79
Twilight of the Presidency, XIX 133
Twine grain binder, IX 95
'Twixt Twelve and Twenty, XVII 127
Two Guns (chief), XIV *68*
Two Moon (chief), IX 108
Two-ocean Navy Act (1940), XVI 52
Two Openings in Black over Wine, XVII *94*
"Two-power" standard, XII 14
2001, XIX 76
Two years Before the Mast, V 21
Tydings, Millard, XIV 132; XVII 29
Tyler, John (president), IV 31, 33; V 49, *49*, 51, 63, 68, 91; VI 87, 140
Typee, IV 140
Typewriter, X 25–26, *25*
Typhoon fighter-bombers, XVI *95*

U

U-boats, XII 38, 69, 70, 114; XVI 70, 73, 84, 88; see also Submarine warfare
Udall, Stewart, XIX 19, *21*
Ueda, General, XV *56*
UFWU, see United Farm Workers Union
Ugaki, Vice-Admiral Motome, XVI 36
Ulithi, Atoll, XVI 113
Ulrich, Charles, X *61*
Ulster County, New York, II 98
Umatilla River, V 59
Umezu, Yoshijiro, XVI 131, *131*
"Uncle Remus," VIII 139
"Uncle Sam," III 108; IV 10; 18; VII *17*; XII *23*
"Uncle Tom," VI 98
Uncle Tom's Cabin, VI 96, 98, *99*; X 124
Uncommercial Traveller, The, V 104
Underground Railroad, VI 66, *67*
Underwood Tariff Act (1913), XI 67, 80
Uneeda biscuit, XI 23, *24*
Unemployment, X 136; XVI 12–13; in 1890s, X 139; in 1920s, XIV 10; Great Depression, XIV 11–12, 38, *38*, 68, 114; under Eisenhower, XVII 81; and Negroes, XIX 52; 1976–86, XX 47, 54, 59, 63
Unemployment insurance, X 83; XI 92; XIV 47
Union College, New York, IV 90
"Union Forever, The," VII 82
Union league of America, VIII 39
Union of Soviet Socialist Republics, Russian Revolution, XII 53, *53*, 120, 123, 131, 136–137, *137*; XIII *12*, 13; XVIII 10; Brest-Litovsk, XII 53; end of First World War, XII 74, 106; absence at Versailles, XII 136–137, American reaction to Stalinism, XIV 81; relations with Nationalist China, XV 53; US recognition of, XV 73–74; XVIII 10, 12; Spanish Civil War, XV 86, 90; Nonaggression pact, XV 100; partition of Poland, XV 101; Winter War, XV 101, 103; XVIII 12, *12*; German invasion of, XV 120; XVI 10–11; Japanese

neutrality pact, XV 130; Atlantic Charter, XVI 12; supplies, XVI 15, 18; Moscow protocol, XVI 44, 84, 102, *103*, *106*, 137; occupation zones, XVI 104, 138, 139; war with Japan, XVI 131, 140; XVIII 39, *39*; cold war, XVIII 10, 24–25; Potsdam agreement, XVII 19, 21, *21*; and Austria, XVIII 23; control of atomic power, XVIII 23–24; and Iran, XVIII 26; in eastern Mediterranean, XVIII 26; Marshall plan, XVIII 30; West German republic, XVIII 32; Berlin blockade, XVIII 32, *33*; atomic bomb, XVIII 34; in Manchuria, XVIII 42; relations with China, XVIII 47, 48; Korean policy, XVIII 49–50; Korean War, XVIII 51, *51*; East German uprising, XVIII 62; Khrushchev, XVIII 62; nuclear weapons, XVIII 67; SALT, XVIII 132, *136*, 137; Middle East, XVIII 137, 138; technology lead, XIX 83–84, *83*, *84*; ICBMs, XIX 86; space rivalry, XIX 86–87, 88, 89; see also Russia; Stalin, Joseph; US-Soviet relations
Union Pacific Railroad, IX 28–31, *28*, *30*, *32*, 37, 39; X 40
Union Theological seminary, X 97
Unitarians, IV 95; V 91
United Automobile Workers, XIV 112; XVII 37
United Confederate Veterans, VIII 140
United Council for China, XV 65
United Farm Workers Union, XIX 62; see also Agriculture; labor unions
United Fruit Company, XVIII 70
United Hatters, XI 96
United Mine Workers of America, X 66, 81; XI 97; XIII 132, 133
United Nations, XVI 13, 15, 19, 133, 136; Secretariat building, XVII *98*; San Francisco conference, XVIII 17–18, *19*; voting in security council, XVIII 17; veto, XVIII 24; and Korean War, XVIII 51; in Suex crisis, XVIII 73, *73*; United States position in, XVIII 89; Six Day War, XVIII 138; Adlai

Stevenson, XIX 19
United Nations Atomic Energy Commission, XVIII 24
United Nations Charter, XVIII 18
United Nations Relief and Rehabilitation
    Administration, XVIII 17, 28–29
United Press, XII 58
United States (ship), III 123
United States and Foreign Securities Corporation,
    XIII 138
United States Armed Forces, in 1812, III 121,
    123–124; exploration, V 10, 13; Indian warfare,
    IX 101, 102, 104–106, *105–106*, 107–109,
    108–109, 111–112, *112*, 113; pre-1914 weakness,
    XII 23–24; training, XII 67–68, 66; social role of,
    XII 101, 102; in 1939, XVI 45–46; Selective
    Service Act (1940), XVI 46–47; growth during
    Second World War, XVI 56; peacetime growth,
    XVII 15; desegregation, XVII 58; see also United
    States Navy
United States Armored Force (Second World War),
    XVI 54
United States Army Air Corps (Second World War),
    XVI *44*
United States Army Corps of Engineers, XI 77; XVI
    129
United States Asiatic Fleet, XVI 23
United States Eighth Air Force (Second World War),
    XVI *72*, 74, 90, 103
United States Employment Service, XII 105
United States Forest Service, IX 129, 131
United States Grain Corporation, XII 103
United States Housing Administration, XIV 128
United States-Japan Security Treaty (1951), XVIII 79
United States Marine Corps, XVI 56
United States Maritime Commission, XVI 48, 52
United States Military Academy (West Point), II 116;
    IV 88, 96, *96*; VII 28, 112, 134
United States Naval Academy, IV 88
United States Navy, II 112–113, *112–113*, 114; III

114, 121; V 69, 83; Civil War, VII 21–22, 36, 96,
    115, *123*, 124–126; A. T. Mahan, XI 44;
    Theodore Roosevelt's global cruise, XI 77;
    expansion to 1914, XI 82; 1917 strength, XII
    24–25, *24*; First World War, XII 69; Washington
    Naval conference, XV 20; in 1940, XVI 52; growth
    during Second World War, XVI 56; aid to British,
    XVI 70; Battle of Atlantic, XVI 73; see also United
    States Armed Forces
United States Ninth Army (Second World War), XVI
    99
United States Pacific Fleet, XVI 20, 27
United States Pacific Squadron, V 69, 83, 118
United States Rubber, XI 12
United States Sanitary Commission, VII 51, 82, *84*
United States Shipping Board, XII 106
United States-Soviet relations, in cold war, XVIII 10,
    24–25; and Russian Revolution, XVIII 10; trade,
    XVIII 10; reaction to invasion of Finland, XVIII
    12, *12*, 13; Second World War, XVIII 13; Allied
    differences, XVIII 14; Franklin D. Roosevelt, XVIII
    12, 15–16; Harry Truman, XVIII 16–17, *16*;
    postwar treaties, XVIII 23; containment policy,
    XVIII 26; and NATO, XVIII 34–36; in Far East,
    XVIII 39–40, 42; Japan, XVIII 49; Korean War,
    XVIII 50–51, *51*; John Foster Dulles, XVIII 61, *61*;
    technological rivalry, XVIII 67; summit
    conferences, XVII 69; XVIII 64, 68, 79; U-2 affair,
    XVIII 80–81, *81*; Berlin Wall, XVIII 88, *88*; Cuban
    missile crisis, XVIII 90–91, *91*; test-ban treaty,
    XVIII 94, *94*; détente, XVIII 128, 130, 132, 134,
    137; Middle East, XVIII 138; 1976–86, XX 24–34,
    38–42; see also Union of Soviet Socialist Republics
United States Strategic Bombing Survey, XVI 25, 126
United States Steel, VIII 124; X 16, 18, 20, *20*; XI 12,
    65; XIII 141; XIV 112; XIX 23
United Steelworkers Union, XVII 31
Universities and colleges, IV 86, 89–90, *89*, *90*, 95;
    X 88, 91, 92; XI 106; XIII 94–95, *95*; XIV 65; XIX

57–58, 70–71, *71*; see also Education
University of Alabama, XVII 59, *59*, 60; XIX 21
University of California, XIX 65
University of Chicago, X 92
University of Deseret, V 113
University of Miami, XIII 38
University of Michigan, IV 95, *95*; X 88
University of Mississippi, XIX 21, 52
University of Nebraska, X 92
University of Utah, V *113*
University of Virginia, IV 89, 95
University of Wisconsin, X 92; XI 55; XII 113
UNRRA, see United Nations Relief and Rehabilitation
    Administration
Unsafe at any Speed, XVII 125; XIX 137
Up from Slavery, VIII 100
Upper classes, XI 25, 28, 120
Upper Road, IV 67
Uprooted, The, XVII 107
Upshur, Abel P., V 64; VI 87
U.P. Trail, The, XIII 72
Uranium, XVI 128, 129, *129*
Urbanization, X 63, 106; XVI 58; see also Cities
Urizza, Fernando, V 42
USA, XIV 82, 88
USHA, see United States Housing Administration
Ushijima, Lieutenant-General Mitsuru, XVI 124, 125
Ushio (ship), XVI 22
Utah, IX 15, 37; Mormon state, V 109, 111;
    political activity in 1860s, V 113; Compromise of
    1850, VI 92; mining, IX 73
Utah Beach, XVI 92
"Utah War," IV 109–110
Ute, I 40, 45; V 54; IX 15, 16, 17, 20; see also
    Indians, American
Utility franchises, X 116; XI 51
Utopianism, IV 118–120, *118*, *120*; VI 82; X 102
Utrecht, Treaty of (1713), I 89, 90, 101
U-2 affair (1960), XVIII, 79, 80–81, *81*; XIX 14

V

Vaca, Gaspar Nuñez Cabeça de, see Cabeça de Vaca
"Vacant Chair, The," VII 82
Vagrancy, XIV 65
Vail, Richard, B., XVII 38
Valentino, Rudolph, XIII 72, 82, 83, 84, *84*
Vallandingham, Clement, VII 48, *49*
Vallee, Rudy, XIII 72
Vallejo, Mariano, V 116, 118, *118*, 139
Valley, The, see Shenandoah Valley
Valley Campaign (1862), VII 26, 29, 112, 119
Valley Forge, Pennsylvania, II 90, 108–109, *108, 110*
Valley of Virginia, see Shenandoah Valley
Van Allen, William, XIII *102*
Van Buren, Martin (president), IV 22, 24, 26, 28, 34,
    35, 36; V 49; VI 86, 87, *87*, 88, 89, *90*, 104
Vance, Cyrus, XVIII 123; XX 27, 30, 32
Vance, Zebulon, VII 60, 64
Van Cleave, J. W., XI 97
Vancouver, George, V 52
Vandalia Company, I 99
Vandegrift, Alexander Archer, XVI 30
Vandenberg, Arthur, XVI 140; XVII 70; XVIII 18,
    26, 28, 36, 47
Vandenberg resolution (1948), XVIII 32
Van Depoele, Charles J., X 32
Vanderbilt, William H., IX *38*; XI 27
Vanderbilt, William K., XIII 38
Vanderbilts, the, XI 27, 28, *28*
Vanderbilt University, XIII 71
Van der Rohe, Mies, XVII 90, 98, 99
Van Devanter, Willis, XIV 46
Van Doren, Charles, XVII 120, *120*

Van Dorn, Earl, VII 34
Vanguard, XIX 83, 84
Van Horne, Harriet, XVII 125
Vanity Fair, XIII 70, 96
Van Sweringen brothers, XIII 33
Van Vechten, Carl, XIII 99
Van Wagener, Isabella, see Truth, Sojourner
Vanzetti, Bartolomeo, see Sacco-Vanzetti case
Vaqueros, V 30, *37*
Vardaman, James K., VIII 114; XI 55; XII 126
Vargas, Diego de, I 46
Varieties of Religious Experience, The, XI 114
Vassar College, X 92; see also Universities and
    colleges
Vauclain, Samuel, XII 109
Vaudeville, X 124; XI 126; XIII 85, *87*
Veblen, Thorstein, XI 10, 105–106, *107*; XIII 67
Veiller, Lawrence, XI 89
Velázquez, Diego, I 13, 15, 16
Vella, Lavella, XVI 36, 37
Venezuela, I 12; XV 44–45, *45*; XVIII 135
Veracruz, Mexico, XII 27, *27*
Veracruz, Battle of (1847), V 77, *85*, 86–87
Verdict of the People, IV 27
Verdun, Battle of (1916), XII 21, *20*
Verdun Conference (1944), XVI 101
Vergennes, Charles Gravier, Comte de, II 63, 66, 67,
    69, 79, 136, 137, 139–140
Vermont, I 106; III 14, 16, 38; population in early
    Republic, III 16; statehood, III 133; V 139;
    slavery, VI 63
Vernon, Admiral, I *89*

Verrazano, Giovanni de, I 22
Versailles, Treaty of (1919), XII 135, 136, 137, *138*, 139; XIII 21; XV 13, 25, 71, 77, 84
Versailles Peace Conference, XII 135–137
Vesey, Denmark, VI 19, 38
Vespucci, Amerigo, I 12, *13*, 33
Veteran in a new field, The, IX 85
Veterans' Bureau, XIII 28, 30
Vichy government (France), XV 103, 125, 127, 132; XVI 16, 17, 76, 79, 137
Vicksburg, Battle of (1863), VII 35–36, *35*, 64, 104
Vicksburg Daily Whig, VI 52
Victim, The, XVII 103
Victor Emmanuel III (Italy), XV 84
Victory Bonds, XV 28
Victory gardens, XVI 66
Victory ships, XVI 52
Vidal, Gore, XVII 103
Viereck, Peter, XVII 108
Viet Cong, XVIII 105, 106, 107, 110, 112
Vietinghof, Lieutenant-General Heinrich von, XVI 106
Vietminh, XVIII 96, 99, *103*
Vietnam Memorial, XX 79
Vietnam War, appeal for American aid, XVIII 40; origins of American involvement, XVIII 58, 61, 79, 99, 100, 105; Dien Bien Phu, XVIII 64, 100–101, *103*; and John F. Kennedy, XVIII 84, 106, 107; history of, XVIII 96; Vietminh, XVIII 96, 99; Communist aid to, XVIII 100; Geneva conference, XVIII 101, 104, *115*; Ngo Dinh Diem, XVIII 104–109, *104*, *105*; Buddhists, XVIII 108, *108*; American opposition to Diem, XVIII 109; fall of Diem, XVIII 109; Ky and Thieu, XVIII 109; and Lyndon Johnson, XVIII 110; Tonkin Gulf incident, XVIII 110, *111*; SEATO forces, XVIII 112, *113*; bombing campaign, XVIII 112, 114, *114*, 115, *117*; escalation, XVIII 112–114, 115, 118; opposition and protest in US, XVIII 114, *128*, 130,

131, *131*; XIX 43, 46; Johnson's search for peace, XVIII 115; Tet offensive, XVIII 115, *116*; General Westmoreland, XVIII 118, *121*; General Abrams, XVIII 121; Paris peace talks, XVIII 123; "Vietnamization," XVIII 124, *124*; prisoners of war, XVIII 125; US withdrawal, XVIII 125, *125*; Communist victory, XVIII 126, *126*; effect on US foreign policy, XVIII 131; effect on Great Society programs, XIX 43; and 1968 elections, XIX 44, 46–47; Negro leaders on, XIX 55–56; *Pax Americana,* XIX 100; and Nixon, XIX 105, 110; and Watergate, XIX 110; effect on US foreign policy, XX 24–25, 27, 37
View from the Bridge, A, XVII 106
Vigilancia (ship), XII 53
Vigilantism, V 140–141, *141*; VI 125; IX 77; X 72; XII 111, *111*, 113
Villa, Francisco "Pancho," XII 29, *29*, 30
Village (Rueil), XI *113*
Village Voice, XIX 78
Villard, Henry, IX 35
Villard, Oswald Garrison, VIII 114, 115, 116
Vincent, John Carter, XVIII 42
Vindication of the Rights of Women, IV 120–121
Vine-Glo, XIII 57
Vinland, I 19, 20
Vinland Map, I *18*, 20
Vinland sagas, I 19, 20
Vinson, Fred M., XVII 52, 53
Vinson Naval Expansion Act (1938), XV 95
Virginia, origins of, I 48, 59, 65, 72, 73, 74, 75, 77; in colonial wars, I 92–93, 95–97; slavery, I 103; backwood farms, I 104; economic life, I 106; religion, I *109*; colonial architecture, I 111, *111*; theater, I 114; political maturity, I 119; shipment of convicts, I 121; conflict between assembly and Anglican clergy, I 126; territorial claims, II 14, 85; III 18; views on independence, II 18; Constitution, II 20; defeat of British, II 24; state

constitution, II 51, 54–55; IV 25; in War of Independence, II 103; III 12; population, III 16, 24; Constitutional Convention, III 22, 24–25; on Jay Treaty, III 51; party politics, III 54; tobacco, III 65; VI 13; cotton textile industry, IV 63; education, IV 92; slavery, VI 18; secession, VII 16, 18; Confederate state, VII 60, readmission, VIII 30; defeat of disfranchisement, VIII 42; redemption, VIII 73, 82; state debt, VIII 132; readjuster movement, VIII 132; Negro disfranchisement, VIII 135; segregation, XVII 52; see also South, the
Virginia (ship), VII 24
Virginia City, Montana, IX 73
Virginia City, Nevada, IX 70–71, *71*, 77, *82*
Virginia Company, I 58, 72, 73, 121
Virginia Military Institute, IV 86; VII 112, 119
Virginian, The, IX 139; XI 124
Virginia resolution, III 58
Virgin Islands, XI 82
Vision of Columbus, III 91, 95
VISTA, see Volunteers in Service to America
Vital Center, The, XVII 107
Vitaphone, XIII 85
Viviparous Quadrupeds of North America, The, III *106*
Vladivostok, USSR, XI 74
Vlaminck, Maurice de, XI *113*
Vogelkop Island, XVI 114
Vogue, XIV *56*; XVI 62
Volstead Act (1919), XII 120; XIII 52, 53, 64
Voting rights, XVII 60, 64, *64*
Volunteers in Service to America, XIX 37, *37*
Voorhis, Jerry, XIX 101
Voskhod spacecraft, XIX 89; see also Space program
Vostok spacecraft, XIX 86; see also Space program
Voting Rights Act (1965), XIX 41, 52
Voyageurs, V 14
Vulcanization, IV 64; X 24

Wabash, III 44; see also Indians, American
Wabash and Erie Canal, IV 51
Wachusett (ship), VII 125
Waddell, James I., VII 126
Waddell, William B., IX 26, 27
Wade, Benjamin F., VI 132; VII 51; VIII 18, 35, *35*; IX 31
Wage controls, XIX 105; see also Price controls
Wage Stabilization Board, XVII 30, 31
Wagner, Robert, XIV 44, 49, 109
Wagner Labor Relations Act (1935), XIV 49–50, 54, 109; XVII 18
Wagner-Steagall Act (1937), XIV 65
Wahunsonacock, I 49, 51
Wainwright Building, St Louis, X 96
Waiting for Godot, XVII 107
Waiting for Lefty, XIV 91
"Waiting for the Robert E Lee," XI 123
Wakatsuki, Reijiro, XV 59
Wake Island, XI 44, 71; XVI 20, 22, 114
Walcheren Island, Battle of (1944), XVI 99
Wald, Lillian, D., X 118–119
Walden, IV 141
Walden Pond, Massachusetts, IV 141
Waldo, Albigence, II 109
Waldorf-Astoria Hotel, XI 28
Waldseemuller, Martin, I 13
Walker, C. J., VIII 98
Walker, Frank C., XV 131
Walker, Sir Hovenden, I 88, 89

Walker, Jacob, V 42
Walker, Joseph Reddeford, V 22, 23, 63
Walker, Leroy Pope, VII 59
Walker, Robert J., VI 112, 114, *114*
Walker, William, VI 101
"Walking Purchase" Treaty (1737), I *54*
Wallace, George, XIX 21, 46–47, *47*, 108, *109*
Wallace, Henry (agriculturalist), XIII 26, *27*, 123
Wallace, Henry (vice president), secretary of agriculture, XIV 31, 116, 117, *118*, 126, 133; resignation, XVII 17–18, 26; Progressive party, XVII 21, *21*, 24, 71; on Marshall plan, XVIII 31
Wallace, Lew, VII 119; IX 67
Wallace's Farmer, XIII, 26, *27*
Walling, William English, XI 100; XII 57
Wall Street, panic of 1857; VI *114*; X *17*; crash of 1929, XIV 10
Wall Street Journal, XI 17
Walpole, Horace, I 95
Walpole, Sir Robert, I 89
Walsh, David I., XII 127
Walsh, James E., XV 131
Walsh, Thomas J., XII 127; XIII 29–30, *30*
Walsingham, Commodore, II 75
Walthall, Edward C., VIII 129
"Waltham system," IV 62
Walton, George, II *13*
Walton, William, XIX 29
Wampanoag, I 50–52; see also Indians, American
Wampum belt, I 41

Wanamaker, John, X 109
Wanamaker's (store), XI 21
Wanderer of the Wasteland, The, XIII 72
Wang Ching-wei, XV 131
Wappinger confederacy, I 51
Warbonnet Creek, Battle of (1879), IX *117*
War College division, XII 71
War crimes' trials, Civil War, VII 83; Second World War, XVIII 22
Ward, Artemas, II 25, 26, 32
Ward, Lester, Frank, IX 129; X 98; XI 84
Ward, Mrs Humphrey, XII 58
Ward, Montgomery, X 131; XI 21, *23*
War debts, XV 25–27, 73, 103, 118
War Democrats, VII 45, 46
War department, III 39, 58; Civil War, VII 51, 70, 72; Indian affairs, IX 114; conscription, XII 65, 66; reorganization, XII 67, 107–108; industrial control, First World War, XII 101, 102, 106–107; supply control, XII 101, 102, 108
Wardner, Jim, IX 74
War Finance Corporation, XIV 16
War Food Administration, XVI 48
War Hawks, III 120, 121; IV 22, 23
War hysteria, First World War, XII 111, *111*, 113, 123, *122, 123*; XIII 15; Second World War, XVI 59
War Industries Board, XII 67, 102, 107, 108–109
Waring, George, E., X 115
War Labor policies Board, XII 105
War loans, XII 33, 36, 60
War Lords, The, XVII 105
War Manpower Commission, XVI 48
Warner, Charles Dudley, VIII 134
Warner, Jack, XVII 38
Warner, Sarah, I *115*
Warner Brothers, XIII 85
War of 1812, III 88, 108, 121–124, *122,* 126–127, 128, *125–129,* 130, *133;* causes, III 112, 114, 116–117, 119–121; American strategy, III 121–122; war at sea, III 123–124; effects of, III 133; introduces political leaders, IV 22–23; effect on Indians, IV 67
War of Independence, I 55; II *37, 38;* influence of moralism on, I 110; origins of, I 119–129, 131–133, 134–142; II 10–22, 86–87, 89; outbreak, II 22, 23, 89; British advantages at outset, II 28, 29; British disadvantages at outset, II 30; tactics, II 31–32; weapons, II 31, *31;* American army, II 32; invasion of Canada, II 33–34, *33;* British take New York, II 34, *36,* 38–39; Saratoga, II 38, 44, *44,* 66, 68, 106, 136, 137. European allies, II 45, 66; British war aims, II 63–64; British strategy, II 64–65, 77; expands to world war, II 67–69, 72–81, *69–72, 75, 77, 78, 81;* Franco-American treaty, II 67, 74; battle of Trenton, II 41; battle of Camden, II 78; Yorktown, II 81; meaning of, II 83–85; III 137–140; effects on colonies, II 92–98, 100, 101–104; III 11–12; finance of, II 100–101, *100;* III 12, *12;* Paoli Massacre, II 106, 107, *107;* battle of Germantown, II 107; Valley Forge, II 108–109, *108, 110;* conspiracy against Washington, II 110–111; sea power, II 111, 112–113, *112, 113;* French aid, II 114; spies, II 115–116; massacres, II 116, *115–116;* soldiers, II *118–119;* southern campaign, II 120–123, *122–124;* map of fighting after Saratoga, II *123;* supplier of political leaders, IV 21–22; and abolition of slavery, VI 63; see also Continental Army; Great Britain; Washington, George
War of the Pacific, XV 40
"War of the Worlds, The," XIV 104
War Powers Act (1941), XVI 48
War Production Board, XVI 48
War Propaganda Bureau, XII 58
Warre, Henry, V *60*
War Relocation Authority, XVI 59
Warren, Charles Beecher, XIII 123
Warren, Earl, XVI 59; vice-presidential candidate, XVII 22; chief justice, XVII 53; *Brown v Board of Education,* XVII 53–54, *54,* 59; report on assassination of Kennedy, XIX 29
Warren, Joseph, II *26;* III 109
Warren, Peter, I 91
Warren, Robert Penn, XIII 71; XVII 100
Warren Commission, XIX 29
War Revenue Act (1917), XII 105

War Revenue Act (1918), XII 105
Warsaw pact, XVIII 75
Warsaw uprising (1944), XVI 140
War Shipping Administration, XVI 48
War Trade Board, XII 105
Washing machine, electric, XIII 44
Washington, IX 15; statehood, IX 92; urbanization, X 106
Washington, DC, III 62, 64, 124, 126, 127, *127,* 135, *135,* 136; VII 19, 28, 29, 119, 139; X 106, 116, 118; XI 118
Washington, Booker T., VIII 66, 91, 100–101, 105–109, 91; Atlanta compromise, VIII 100, *109, 110;* black capitalism, VIII 101, *106;* Tuskegee Machine, VIII 105–108, *101, 105;* secret activities, VIII 108–109; criticisms of, VIII 109–110, 111; Boston riot, VIII 110; Committee of Twelve, VIII 111; spying on critics, VIII 113–114; NAACP, VIII 115–116
Washington, George (president), early career in colonial wars, I 93, *93,* 94, 96, 97, 99, 129, 130; literary tastes, I 136; commander-in-chief revolutionary forces, II 15, 18, 25, 26, 106–109; views on independence, II 16; criticism of, in war, II 109–111; relations with d'Estaing, II 114; Battle of Monmouth, II 114; on Benedict Arnold, II 116; victory at Yorktown, II 122–123, 126, *126;* aftermath of victory, II 126–127, 128; on War of Independence, II 28; VII 139; strategy in war, II 32, 33–34, 115, 129; creation of new army, II 32, 43, 90, 91, 93, 107–108, 114; loss of New York, II 38; retreat, II 38–40, 106–107; victories, II 41, 43; and British, II 77; leadership qualities, II 83, 129, 140, *140;* III 10; ban on Negroes, II 104; on the new republic, III 10–11, 13, 14, 18; on Constitutional Convention, III 22, 28; president III 34, *34,* 35–36, *36,* 38–39, *39;* on public debt, III 41; on site of capital, III 41; on foreign relations, III 41, 45; on Indian relations, III 44–45; on government, III 45; retirement, III 46, 54, 90; at home, III *47;* second presidential term, III 48, 49; on Jay Treaty, III *50,* 51; Federalist connection, III 53; called out of retirement, III 56; American legend, III 109, *133;* presidency, III 135; slave owner, III 140; Freemason, IV *31;* on education, IV 84, 88; Greenough sculpture, IV 131, *131;* see also Continental Army; War of Independence
Washington, Martha, III 38, *38,* 45, *47*
Washington, Treaty of (1871), X 44; see also *Alabama* arbitration
Washington and Lee College, VIII 20, *20*
Washington Crossing the Delaware, X 93
Washingtonian society, IV 116
Washington Monument, XI 116, *116*
Washington Naval conference (1921–22), XV 17, 20, 22–24, *22,* 51, 53, 61
Washington-on-the-Brazos, V 41
Washington Post, XI 13, 35; XVII 48, 73; XIX 112, 113, *113*
Washington Union, VI 101
Washita River, IX 106
Washoe, Nevada, IX 70, 77
WASP (White Anglo-Saxon Protestant), XI 106; XIII 11, 16; XIX 132; see also Nativism
Wasp, (ship), XVI 31, *31,* 124
Waste Land, The, XIII 97, *97*
Watch and Ward society, XIII 109
Watergate, XIX 110–113, *111, 112, 113, 114,* 116, *116,* 118, 119, 125; see also Nixon, Richard M.
Water management, XIX 132
Water Power Act (1920), XIII 46
Water Quality Act (1965), XIX 42
Water supplies, III 66; X 110, 112, 113
Watson, Edwin, M., XV 131
Watson, John B., XIII 49, 114
Watson, Thomas A., X 26
Watson, Tom, VIII 135; X 136, 141
Watt, James, X 24
Watts, Los Angeles, XIX 58
Waugh, Samuel, IV 72
Waxhaws, Battle of (1780), II 121
Wayne, Anthony, II 107, *107,* 114; III 45, 139, *139*
Ways and Means Committee, XII 116
Wealth Against Commonwealth, X 138
Wealth of Nations, I *120*
Weare, Walter, VIII 96

Weary Blues, XIII 99
Weaver, James B., X 82, 136
Web and the Rock, The, XIV 89
Webb. Walter, P., IX 10
Webber, Charles, T., VI *67*
Weber, Max, XI 111
Webb-Kenyon Act (1914), XII 120
Webster, Alonzo, B., IX 55
Webster, Daniel, IV *23,* 24, 28, 36, 110, 115; V 63–64, 109; VI *85,* 93, 94, 96
Webster, Noah, I 139; III 90, 94, *94,* 95, 110; IV 84–85, *84,* 129–130
Webster-Ashburton Treaty (1842), V 63, *64*
We Demand, XIV 111
Wedemeyer, Albert Coady, XVI 120; XVIII 98
Weed, Thurlow, IV 26; V 65, *65;* VI 126
Weem, Mason, II 120
Weems, Parson, III 97
Weighing the Dust, V *131*
Weimar Republic, XV 74; see also Germany
Weinberger, Caspar. XX 35, 40
Weir, John F., X *13*
Weiser, Conrad, I 104
Weiss, Carl, A., XIV 43, *42*
Weissman, Solly, XIII 60
Welch, Ashbel, X 28
Weld, Theodore Dwight, VI 26, 72
Welfare state, XI 84; XIV 47, *47,* 65, 115; XIX 106; see also Public relief
Welles, Gideon, VII 22, *45*
Welles, Orson, XIV 91, 104, *104*
Welles, Sumner, XV 31, 38, 39, 91, 107, 131
Welles Peace plan, XV 91, 94
Wellesley College, X 92
Wellman, Horace, IX 62
Wellman, William, XIII 82
Wells, David, A., X 39
Wells, Daniel, H., V 110
Wells, Fargo & Co., IX 26, 28
Welty, Eudor, XVII 103
Wentworth, Paul, II 136
Werner, Edgar V., XVII 36
Wertham, Frederic, XVII 124
Wescott, Glenway, XIII 68
Wesleyan University, X 92
West, Benjamin, I 116, *135,* 136, 138, 140–141; II *130;* III *102,* 104; IV 132
West, Julian, X 137
West, Mae, XIV 91, 96
West, Nathanael, XIV 81
West, the, II 60, 120; III 10, 18, 88, 119, 122, 134; IV 10; frontier life, IV 71–72; V 34–36; early agriculture, IV 68, 70, 76; IX 10, 11; land policy, IV 70; VI 42, 116, 121; fur trade, V 18–19, 21; mountain men, V 14, 15–16, *17–18,* 20, 21; Texas, V 39–40; Oregon, V 46–47, *47,* 53–55, *54–56,* 59–60, 63; Manifest Destiny, V 48; Mormons, V 95, 97–99, 98, 103–106, *104, 105;* Know-Nothings, VI 102; 1857 panic, VI 116; North v South, VI 103–104, 116, 120–121; far West in 1861, IX 10; geography, IX 10–13, *11, 12,* 15; wild life, IX 12, *12, 14,* 13; Indians, IX 15–17, *16, 17, 18,* 19–20, *19, 20, 21,* 22–23, *22;* railroad, IX 24, 28–40, *28, 30, 32,* 35, 36–38; stagecoach, IX 24, 26, 28, *26;* pony express, IX 27; cattle industry, IX 43–45, *43, 45,* 59; cowboys. IX 46–49, 47, *49, 50,* 52–55, *52;* cattle towns, IX 53, 54, 54–56; ranch versus farm, IX 49, 56, *57,* 66; legendary heroes, IX 61–64, *61–65,* 66–68, *66–68;* mining boom, IX 70–71, *70–72,* 73–84, 74–76, *78–82, 84;* land policy, IX 85–87, *85–87,* 89–92, 93, *89–90, 93;* later agriculture, IX 92, 94–97, *95,* 99, *99;* Indian subjugation, IX 101–109, *101–102, 104, 105, 106, 107, 108, 109, 110,* 111–120 *passim, 111–112, 115–120;* parks, IX 123–128, 128–131, *129, 130, 131;* conservation, IX 123–132, *123, 125–127, 129, 130, 131;* popular myth, IX 133–139, *133–138;* Turner hypothesis, IX 140–141, *140;* Populist party, X 132; see also Westward movements
Westchester, I 65, 10
Western Development Company, IX 36
Western European Union, XVIII 68
Western Federation of Miners, IX 83, 97
Western Kansas Cattle Growers' Association, IX 56
Western Rural, X 131
Western Trail, IX 45, 59

Western Union, X 26
West India Company (Dutch), I 51
West Indies, I 13, 106; II 64, 68–69, 72, 74, 75, 77, 78, 79, 135; III 17
Westinghouse, George, X 28, 32
Westinghouse Corporation, X 16; XIII 44, 141
West Jersey, I 66, 67, 69
Westmoreland, General William, XVIII 118, 121, 121
West New Jersey Society, I 69
Westoe, I 54; see also Indians, American
West Point, see US Military Academy
West Virginia; industry, X 19; school segregation, XVII 52
Westwall, XVI 98, 99
Westward Movements, I 99; II 99; III 16, 68, 70; IV 16, 66–68, 68, 70–71; V 10, 11, 12–14, 12–14, 22, 24, 25, 39–40, 47, 55–56, 59–60, 59–60; IX 10, 15; see also West, the
Westward the Course of Empire, V 11
Wewak, New Guinea, XVI 114
Weyl, Walter, XI 116
Whaling, I 106; V 21
Wharton, Edith, XIII 72
"What Is Man," XI 103
What Price Glory, XIII 67, 67
What Social Classes Owe to Each Other, XI 84
Wheat, IX 94, 95, 96, 97; X 58; XI 82; XIV 118–119, 122
Wheeler, Burton K., XIV 132; XV 119, 119
Wheeler, Earle G., XVIII 115
Wheeler, Edward L., IX 137
Wheeler, Joseph, VII 34, 111; VIII 40
Wheeler Act (1934), XIV 70
Wheelock, Eleazar, I 55
When Guns Speak, Death Settles Disputes, IX 63
When Knighthood Was in Flower, X 104
"When this Cruel War is Over," VII 82
Wherry, Kenneth S., XVIII 37, 53
Whig party IV 26, 31, 34, 35, 110; V 48, 49, 50, 63, 66, 77, 90, 91; VI 86, 88, 89, 90–91, 97, 101, 102, 104, 110, 128
"Whigs" (War of Independence), II 10, 16, 48, 51, 90, 98, 100, 101, 102, 103, 104; see also Patriots
Whipper, William, VI 67
Whipple, William, II 13
Whiskey, XIII 56, 57, 58
Whiskey Rebellion, III 48, 49; XIII 56
"Whiskey Ring," X 42
Whiskey Trust, see Distillers' and Cattle Feeders' Trust
Whistler, James McNeill, X 98, 98
White, Andrew D., X 92
White, E. B., XIII 66
White, Elijah, V 55, 55
White, George H., VIII 107
White, Horace, X 138
White, John, I 40, 48, 48
White, Stanford, X 93; XI 116
White, William Allen, X 126, 127, 132; XV 22, 109; XVI 19
White Buildings, XIII 98
White Fang, XI 107
Whitefield, George, I 109, 135; IV 100
White Horse Tavern, Battle of (1777), II 107
White House, the, III 127, 135, 135; IV 21, 22
White House Conservation Conference of Governors (1908), IX 131
White Jacket, IV 140
White League, VIII 20, 83
Whiteman, Marcus, V 54–55, 55
Whiteman, Paul, XIII 92
Whitesboro, New Jersey, VIII 107
White Star Line, X 57
White supremacy, VIII 73, 78, 85, 89, 91, 108, 134
"White Wings," X 115, 116
Whitlock, Brand, XI 53
Whitman, Walt, IV 128, 131, 140, 140, 141; VII 130, 131; IX 133; X 96, 102; XI 106; XIV 89
Whitney, Asa, IX 28
Whitney, Eli, III 65; IV 64, 11, 11, 43; X 24; XI 17
Whitney, Richard, XIV 140
Whittaker, James, IV 106
Whittier, John Greenleaf, IV 138; XI 106
Whittier College, XIX 100
Whoopee, XIV 91
"Who's Afraid of the Big Bad Wolf," XIV 80, 99

Why England Slept, XVIII 83; XIX 10
Whyte, William H., Jr, XVII 107
Why We Fought, XV 78
Wichita, Kansas, IX 44, 45, 55, 63
Wichita City Eagle, IX 96
Wickersham Commission, XIII 53, 57, 61
"Wide-Awakes," VI 131, 131
Widows' Pensions Programs, XI 92
Wigglesworth, Michael, I 117
Wigwam, IX 15
Wilbur, Richard, XVII 101
Wilde, Oscar, IX 77
Wilderness, Battle of the (1864), VII 116
Wilderness, the, VII 36–37, 117
Wilderness Trail, IX 133–134
Wild Horse Hunters, IX 52
Wild One, The, XVII 134, 134
Wiley, Joseph E., VIII 98
Wilhelm II (Germany), XI 77; XII 49, 49
Wilkes, Charles, V 52, 53; VII 102, 103
Wilkey, Walter, IV 71
Wilkinson, James, II 109; III 73, 80, 81; V 12
Wilkinson, Jemima, IV 104
Willamette Valley, V 57, 60
Willard, Emma, IV 91
Willard, Frances, IV 123
Willard, Jess, XI 136
William and Mary (England), I 62, 63, 69, 86
William and Mary, College of, I 77, 113, 135
William of Orange, see William and Mary
Williams, David R., III 121
Williams, John A., XIX 58
Williams, John Sharp, XI 67
Williams, Roger, I 51, 61
Williams, Tennessee, XVII 106, 106
Williams, T. Harry, VII 58
Williams, Wells, IV 59
Williams, William, II 13
Williams, William Appleman, XI 48
Williams, William Carlos, XI 109; XIII 70, 97; XVII 101
Williamsburg, Virginia, I 111, 114; III 100, 101, 136
Williamsburg, Battle of (1862), VII 25
Williams College, IV 90
"Willie and Joe," XVI 60
"Willie Gillis," XVI 62, 64
Willing, Thomas, II 13
Williwaw, XVII 103
Willkie, Wendell, XV 116, 118; XVI 12
Wills, Gary, XIX 125
Wills, Helen, XIII 79
Wills Creek, I 92, 93
Will to Believe, The, XI 114
Wilmington, North Carolina, VII 62, 125
Wilmot, David, V 91; VI 88, 88
Wilmot Proviso, V 91, 92; VI 88, 89, 91, 93, 94
Wilson, Alexander, III 92
Wilson, Charles E., XVII 76, 77
Wilson, Edmund, XIII 68, 92, 96; XIV 27, 56
Wilson, James, II 13, 100; III 22
Wilson, Henry (vice president), VI 100
Wilson, Sir Henry, XII 49
Wilson, Milburn L., XIV 44, 116
Wilson, Thomas Woodrow (president), X 23, 46, 74, 92; segregation, VIII 115; progressivist, XI 57; presidential candidate, XI 66–67; legislative activity, XI 67–68; foreign relations, XI 71, 80; preparedness, XII 23, 24; Latin-American policy, XII 26; Punitive Expedition, XII 27, 27, 29–30, 29; neutrality, XII 32, 34–37; advisers, XII 33–34; German U-boat campaign, XII 38, 42–43; Lusitania crisis, XII 40–41, 41; Gore & McLemore resolutions, XII 42–43; mediation plans, XII 44, 46, 48–50; 1916 convention, XII 46; 1916 election, XII 47; break with Germany, XII 50–51; declaration of war, XII 54–55, 54; First World War, XII 101–103, 105; industrial war effort, XII 105; war revenue program, XII 105; railroad and shipping, XII 106; War Industries Board, XII 108; war propaganda, XII 110; labor legislation, XII 116; politics, XII 126–127; League of Nations, XII 129, 130, 139–141, 141; XV 11, 11; fourteen points, XII 130–131; peace conference, XII 132, 133, 134, 134, 135–136; XIII 10, 10; automobile industry, XIII 38; Japanese, XV 54; troops to Russia, XVIII 10; idealism, XVIII 133–134, 136
Wilson-Gorman Tariff Act (1893), X 141

Winchell, Walter, XIV 102
Winchester, James, III 124
Winchester, Battle of (1862), VII 26
Wind River, V 17
Wine, XIII 57
Winesburg, Ohio, XIII 66
Wings, XIII 83
Winnebago, I 41; see also Indians, American
Winning of the West, The, IX 139
Winslow, Alan, XII 84, 85
Winslow, Edward, I 50, 116
Winsor, Kathleen, XVII 103
Winter Line, XVI 86
Winter Olympics, see Olympic games
Winter Quarters, Nebraska, V 97–98, 98, 99
Winterset, XIV 91
Winterthur Museum, III 97
Winter War (1939–40), XV 103; XVIII 12, 12, 13
Winthrop, John, I 60, 60; XIII 105
Winthrop, John Jr, I 114
Winthrop, Robert, V 65–66
Wirtz, Henry, VII 83; VIII 16, 16
Wirtz, Willard, XIX 19
Wisconsin, Scandinavian settlements, IV 76; education, IV 92–93, 95; railroad, IX 28; X 22, 131; Bennett Law, X 53; La Follette, XI 54–55
"Wisconsin Idea," X 92
Wise, Henry A., VII 134
Wister, Owen, IX 82, 139; XI 124
Witchcraft, I 64
Witherspoon, John, I 136; II 13, 53
Without Knocking, IX 61
"Wobblies," see Industrial Workers of the World
Wohaw, IX 119
Wolcott, Josiah, IV 120
Wolcott, Oliver, II 13
Wolf, IX 12
Wolfe, James, I 98, 99, 134, 138; capture of Quebec, I 98, 98, 99
Wolfe, Thomas, XIII 98; XIV 89
Wolfe, Tom, XIX 78
Wolf-pack tactic (U-boats), XVI 70
Woll, Matthew, XIII 61
Wollstonecraft, Mary, IV 120–121
Woman's Christian Temperance Union, XI 30; XIII 52, 52
Woman suffrage, XII 118–119, 118; XIII 10; see also Suffrage; Women's rights
Women in the Nineteenth Century, IV 121
Women's Army Auxiliary Corps, XVI 56
Women's International League for Peace and Freedom, XV 17, 79
Women's Liberation, XIX 63–64, 64
Women's National Indian Association, IX 118
Women's rights, III 67, 138–140; IV 104, 109, 109, 120–125, 121, 122, 124; VI 81, 82; VIII 40; XI 56–57, 94; XIX 63–64; see also Women's Liberation
Women's status, XI 122, 123; XX 59–63; see also women's rights
Women's Trade Union League, XI 100, 100
"Wonder-drugs," XVI 57
Wood, Grant, XIII 106; XIV 82, 82
Wood Leonard, XII 126; XIII 20, 121
Wood, Sam, XVII 38
Woodbridge, New Jersey, I 66
Woodbury Soap, XI 23, 24
Woodin, William, XIV 31
Woodmason, Charles, I 106
Woodrow Wilson Foundation, XV 17
Woods, Robert A., X 119
Woods Hole Oceanographic Institute, XVI 56
Woodstock festival, XIX 80, 80, 122; see also Rock culture
Woodstock Nation, XIX 122
Woodward, Bob, XIX 112, 113
Woodward, C. Vann, VIII 129, 138–139
Woodworking industry, VIII 125
Woolen industry, IV 61–62; VII 85
Woolens Act (1699), I 122, 125
Woollcott, Alexander, XIII 96
Woolman, John, VI 62–63
Woolsey, King S., IX 101
Worcester v Georgia, IV 67
Work, Henry Clay, VII 82
Work, Hubert, XIV 68

Work, mechanization, X 34; immigrants, X 63; poor, XI 120; see also Industry; Labor force; Labor unions
Workingmen's parties, see Labor unions
Workingmen's party, X 82
"Workmanship," XI 106
Works Progress Administration, XIV 47, 73, 81, *81, 132,* 139
World Anti-Slavery convention, IV 122
World Bank, XVIII 17
World Council of Churches, XV 17
World Court, XV 14, 16–17, 79–80
World Disarmament conference, XV 17
World Peace Foundation, XV 17
World Peaceways, XV *19*
World's Columbian Exposition (Chicago 1893), X 93, *94,* 118; XI *105,* 109, 118, 128
World Series, XI 18, 134, *134;* XIII 77; see also baseball
World Series USA, XVII *124*
World War I, see First World War
World War II, see Second World War
Wouk, Herman, XVII 103
Wounded Knee, Battle of (1890), IX 112, *112*
Wounded Knee, South Dakota, Indian armed siege (1973), XIX 62; see also Indians, American
Wovoka, IX 111
WPA, see Works Progress Administration
Wren, Christopher, III 100
Wren, P. C., XIII 72
Wright, Benjamin, IV 52
Wright, Frank Lloyd, X 96; XIII 101; XIV 105, *107;* XVII 99, *99*
Wright, Henry C., IV 119
Wright, Martha C., IV 123
Wright, Orville, see Wright brothers
Wright, Richard, XVII 103
Wright, Wilbur, see Wright brothers
Wright brothers, XI 129, *130–131*
WSB, see Wage Stabilization Board
Wyeth, Justice, III 95
Wyeth, N. C., XI *104*
Wyeth, Nathaniel J., V 53–54, *54*
Wyoming, IX 37, 44, 56; Indian warfare, IX 106, 107; Yosemite National Park, IX 128; Populists, X 133
Wyoming Valley massacre, II 116, *115*
Wythe, George, II *13;* III 22

XYZ

X-ray, XI 104
XYZ affair (1797–98), III 55–56, *56*

Yachting, X 119; XI 137
Yack Yack Bourbon, XIII 56
Yadkin-Pee Dee valley, VIII 125
Yahagi (ship), XVI 126
Yale, Frankie, XIII 60
Yale Club, XIII 54
Yale University, I 135; III 95; IV 89, *89,* 95; X 92; XI 120, 137; see also Universities and colleges
Yalta Conference (1945), XVI 19, 102, 136, 137; XVIII 10, 15
Yamaguchi, Admiral, XVI 28
Yamamoto, Admiral Isoroku, XV 130, 136; XVI 20, 25, 27, 28, 30, *32,* 35, 36
Yamashita, Tomoyuki, XVI 23, *24,* 120
Yamato (carrier), XVI 27, 110, 125, 126
Yamazaki, Colonel, XVI 35
Yancey, William Lowndes, VI 25, 129; VII 59, 100
Yangtze River, China, XV 66
"Yankee Division," see Twenty-Sixth Division
Yankee Doodle, II *89;* III 97
"Yankee Peddler, The," IV *65*
Yap Island, XVI 113, 114, 116
Yardbirds, XIX 76
Yates, Robert, III 22, 30
Yazoo land scandal, III 78, 82
Year's Residence in America, IV 48
Yeats, William Butler, XI 109
Yellow fever, X 110; XI 77
Yellow journalism, X 124; XI 124; see also Muckrakers
Yellowknife, I 39; see also Indians, American
Yellowstone National Park, IX 124–126, *125, 126*
Yellowstone River, III 77; IX 106
Yerba Buena, V 30, 118
Yerkes, Charles T., X 118
YMCA, see Young Men's Christian Association
Yokut, I 40; see also Indians, American
Yom Kippur War (1973), XVIII 137, 140, *140*
Yonai, Mitsumasa, XV 125
York, Alvin C., XII 95, 97, *97*
York, James, Duke of, see James II
York, Toronto, III 124, 127
Yorktown, surrender at, II 81, 122–123, *121–122, 124,* 126, *126, 127,* 129, 132, 139, 140
Yorktown (carrier), XVI 26, 27, 28, *50, 51*
Yosemite National Park, IX 128; XI *62*
Yosemite Valley, IX 124, 127
Yoshida, Shigeru, XVIII 49
Yoshikawa, Takeo, XV 139
Yost, Fielding Harris, XI 137
You Can't Go Home Again, XIV 89
You Can't Take It With You, XIV 95
"You'd Be So Nice To Come Home To," XVI 62
Young, Rev. Andrew, XX 27, 29, 33
Young, Bennett, IX 67
Young, Brigham, V 81, 95, 97, *98,* 99, *100,* 105, 106, *108,* 109, 110, 111, 112, 113, 114, *114,* 122; see also Latter-day Saints
Young, Hugh, XII 78
Young, Owen D., XV 27
Younger, Bob, IX 67, *68*
Younger, Cole, VII 79; IX 67, *68*
Younger, James, VII 79; IX 67
Young Lords Organization, XIX 63
Young Men's Christian Association, XI 18; XII *76,* 77; Great Depression, XIV 12
Young Mr. Lincoln, XIV 95
Young Plan, XV 27
Young Women's Christian Association, XI 18; XV 19
"Your Show of Shows," XVII 125
Youth Culture, XIX 65, 69; Paul Goodman, XIX 70; criticisms of universities, XIX 70; hippies, XIX 73, *74;* the bomb, XIX 75; rock music, XIX 75, 76, *77,* literature, XIX 78; *Woodstock Nation*, XIX 121, anti-Vietnam War, XIX *127*
Ypiranga (ship), XII 27
Ypres, Battle of (1914), XII 19, *19*
Yuba River, V 127
Yucatán, V 90–91
Yuchi, I 54; see also Indians, American
Yugoslavia, XII 16, 136; XVII 23, 32, 36
Yukon, IX 77
Yuma, Arizona, IX 37
Yuma Indian reservation, IX 37
Yurok, I 40; see also Indians, American
YWCA, see Young Women's Christian Association

Zangwill, Israel, XIX 50
Zapata, Emiliano, XII *29*
Zec, Donald, XV *125*
"Zenith," XIII 66, 95
Zeno brothers, I 19
"Zero growth," XIX 137
Zeppelin, Ferdinand von, VII *108*
Zeppelins, XII *21;* XV 93
Zeppelin Airline Company, XV 93
Zero (aircraft), XV *139*
Ziegfeld Follies, XIII *73,* 83
Ziegier, Ron, XIX 110
Zimmerman, Fred, XVII 132
Zimmermann, Alfred, XII 52
Zimmermann Telegram, XII 52–53, *52,* 114
Zion's Herald, IV 115
Zion's Watchmen, VI 72
Zuiho (ship), XVI 31
Zuikaku (carrier), XVI 26, 27
Zuñi, I 17, 40; IX 16